Accounting for Cambridge IGCSE®

David Austen
Christine Gilchrist
John Underhill

Nelson Thornes

Published in 2012 by:
Nelson Thornes Ltd
Delta Place
27 Bath Road
CHELTENHAM
GL53 7TH
United Kingdom

12 13 14 15 16 / 10 9 8 7 6 5 4 3 2 1

A catalogue record for this book is available from the British Library.

ISBN 978 1 4085 1517 4

Cover photograph by Aliaksei Sabelnikau/Shutterstock

Artwork drawn by Flash Harold Ltd.

Page make-up by Fakenham Prepress Solutions, Fakenham, Norfolk NR21 8NN

Printed in China by 1010 Printing International Ltd.

Contents

Introduction

The most important aim of this Introduction is to welcome you to your study of principles of accounts.

At this stage it is likely that you are not really sure what accounting is about. So this introductory section sets out to give you an overview of the subject you are about to study.

What is accounting?

There is nothing new about keeping careful records of financial information. Even thousands of years ago individuals wanted to be well informed about what they received and spent, so that they could have some idea about whether they were well off or not. Nowadays these same questions apply to individuals and organisations. In the case of businesses, the owners need to know:

- whether they are making a profit, because this is the main reason for engaging in business activity
- that they have enough money to pay all of their commitments on time
- that they are making the best use of the funds they have invested in the business.

In the modern world, business activity can be on a very large scale and be very complex. Even a really simple form of business organisation (e.g. a market stall) can involve a great deal of financial activity, including handling money, buying goods to sell, paying assistants, and so on. Accounting is about providing accurate and comprehensive financial information to those involved in making decisions, so that businesses can survive, be successful and be run efficiently.

In order to provide this comprehensive financial information, it is necessary for the following things to happen:

- All financial transactions need to be recorded in a systematic way so that the owner of the business, and other users, can be provided with the information they need to make the right decisions. This record keeping aspect of accounting is often called **bookkeeping**.
- From the bookkeeping records, which often contain vast amounts of detail, it is important to select, classify and summarise information so that owners and other users can be given the appropriate information in the form of financial statements to help them manage the business effectively. The preparation of financial statements and providing some interpretation of what the statements reveal is often called **accounting**.

KEY TERM

Bookkeeping: the recording of financial information, particularly transactions, in a systematic way.

Accounting: the selecting, classifying and summarising of financial data in a way that provides the owners of businesses (and others) with useful information to help them assess performance and plan future activities.

Interested parties: individuals and organisations who are affected by or concerned about how a business performs.

Who uses accounting information?

> **KEY TERM**
>
> **Interested parties:** individuals and organisations who are affected by or concerned about how a business performs.

It is surprising just how many individuals, groups and organisations are affected by even the most basic form of business, and are, therefore, concerned about the business's financial situation. For example, just thinking about your local store, the following **interested parties** can be identified:

- The owner: who has invested personal savings in setting up the business and who is dependent on the business's success for their livelihood.
- The customers: who depend on the business being successful in order that they have a reliable source of goods to buy when they need them.
- Suppliers: who provide goods for the business to sell. They are concerned that they are paid on time and that the business will be successful so that repeat orders, and perhaps increasingly large orders, are likely.
- The bank: may have lent the business funds to get started or develop. Any organisation lending money will be concerned about the success of the business because this affects whether repayments with interest will be made in accordance with the loan agreement.
- Employees: are dependent on the success of the business for their wages or salaries and for continued employment.
- Government: checks the amounts due to be paid in taxation.

Types of business organisation

What is a business? Businesses are organisations that provide goods and/or services in order to make a profit. There are a number of ways of classifying businesses.

It is possible to think about businesses by what they do, for example by:

- providing raw materials by way of mining, farming, fishing, etc.
- manufacturing goods, turning raw materials into finished products (Unit 28 is concerned with the accounts of manufacturing organisations)
- selling goods to the general public (retailers) or to other businesses (wholesalers)
- providing services for businesses and the general public (Unit 18 covers service businesses).

It is also possible to think about businesses in terms of who owns them, for example:

- Sole trader: where one individual owns the business. The individual controls the business. If successful, the profits made by the business belong to this individual; if unsuccessful, the individual can lose whatever has been invested and private resources too.

- Partnerships: where more than one individual owns the business. Partners jointly control the business and they share profits between them. They are also jointly responsible for the debts of the business, and can lose their private resources if the partnership is unsuccessful. (Unit 25 covers accounting for partnerships.)
- Limited liability companies: these are owned by shareholders who each contribute to the funds needed to establish and run the company. Most shareholders do not take part in the day-to-day management and control of the company, they elect directors to undertake these responsibilities on their behalf. Shareholders are rewarded by receiving some of the profits made by the company if it is successful. Shareholders' responsibility for the debts of the company is limited to the amount they invest. Unlike sole traders and partners, shareholders are not at risk of losing their private funds if things go wrong. (Unit 26 covers accounting for limited liability companies.)
- Clubs and societies: these are formed by their members so that they can meet for particular activities (e.g. social or sporting activities). These organisations do not aim to make a profit, but they have to be financially viable in order to survive. (Unit 27 covers accounting for clubs and societies.)

What are the main financial statements?

Owners, managers and other interested parties will inspect the following financial statements.

For information about profit or loss

- The income statement is the chief source of information about profits or losses for sole traders, partnerships and limited companies.
- In the case of non-trading organisations, information about surpluses or deficits (these words are used instead of 'profit' and 'loss') is provided by an income and expenditure account.

For information about ability to meet commitments on time

The balance sheet provides details of the resources owned by the business that can be used to meet commitments (cash and bank balances, money to be received in the near future, etc.) and some of the commitments (e.g. amounts due to suppliers).

Balance sheets are prepared by all of the organisations listed above.

For information about the efficient use of resources

The balance sheet provides detailed information about all of the resources owned by a business and, in conjunction with information about profits, it can be used to reveal how successful, or otherwise, the owners and managers have been in using these resources well.

What are accounting principles?

Accounting involves the processing and summarising of considerable volumes of information by many individuals working for a variety of organisations, each with their own special needs and interests. As a result, there could be scope for financial records to be distorted or even manipulated. To ensure that whatever the situation, accounting statements are prepared in the same way, there are a set of rules, often referred to as accounting principles, which ensure that users can be confident in the information with which they are provided. These principles guide the owners and managers of businesses when deciding on the particular accounting policies that they will use. Some of the most important accounting principles will be introduced to you as you work your way through this book. They are summarised and explained further in Unit 19.

What part does technology play in accounting?

At one time all bookkeeping and accounting systems were kept by hand (manually). These days, computer technology has provided electronic systems for keeping financial records, and these are now used by the majority of business organisations. However, whether manual or computerised systems are used, it is important to realise that the records are based on the accounting cycle described earlier, and exactly the same principles are applied.

Questions and answers in this book

A wide range of practice material has been provided at the end of each unit.

Under the heading 'Developing your skills' there are questions which give users the opportunity to try out the techniques explained in each unit. Questions are in pairs, so that teachers have the opportunity to demonstrate a new technique using the first question in the pair and students have the opportunity to try out the technique for themselves using a second, similar question.

At the end of Units 7, 12, 17, 19 and all units thereafter, users also have the chance to apply their learning to multiple choice questions and 'other questions'. Taking them one step further towards being prepared for the examination.

Fully worked answers to every question are provided at www.nelsonthornes.com/igcse

1 The balance sheet

Introduction

In this unit you are going to learn how to prepare a simple version of a very important accounting statement called a balance sheet. Balance sheets are important because they provide the owners and managers of businesses with a useful summary of some key facts which can help with the effective running of their businesses.

First, you are going to learn about three accounting terms: **assets**, **liabilities** and **capital**. You are also going to learn that these three terms are connected to each other by a very simple formula or equation.

Finally, you will learn how to prepare a balance sheet in a horizontal style following some precise rules about how to record information and how to show figures and totals.

LEARNING OUTCOMES

When you have reached the end of this unit you will be able to:

- explain the terms 'assets', 'liabilities' and 'capital'
- explain and use the accounting equation
- prepare a simple balance sheet
- prepare a classified balance sheet.

KEY TERM

Assets: resources with a monetary value that are owned by a business.

Liabilities: amounts owed by a business to other businesses, organisations or individuals.

Capital: the investment made by the owner(s) of a business.

1.1 Assets, liabilities and capital

STUDY TIP

You will notice that assets do not include employees. Assets have to be owned by the business.

LINKS...

In Unit 19 you will learn more about the fundamental rules that all accountants use and why assets should have a monetary value and be valued at cost.

DID YOU KNOW?

The terms 'receivables' and 'trade receivables' are relatively new. A few years ago the alternative terms 'debtors', 'trade debtors' and 'accounts receivable' were more commonly used.

KEY TERM

Trade receivables: are amounts owed to the business by customers.

Trade payables: are amounts owed by a business to suppliers.

DID YOU KNOW?

The terms 'payables' and 'trade payables' are also relatively new. A few years ago the alternative terms 'creditors', 'trade creditors' and 'accounts payable' were more commonly used.

You can now try questions 1–2 on page 7.

What are assets?

All businesses own resources such as cash, vehicles, furniture and premises. These resources are known as assets. The owner of a business will have provided or purchased each asset to ensure that the enterprise can trade or provide a service effectively.

Assets have a monetary value and provide a benefit to the business.

Examples of business assets

- Land
- Buildings
- Machinery
- Equipment
- Fittings
- Inventories (stocks)

The rule in accounting is that assets should always be valued at their cost (i.e. whatever was paid for the asset).

Cash is an important asset for all businesses. Usually this asset is separated into two categories as follows:

- Cash in hand: money in the form of notes, coins, cheques, and so on, which is at the business premises (probably locked in a safe or till).
- Cash at bank: all money that has been transferred by the owner of the business to the business's bank account.

Some businesses provide goods or services to their customers on credit. This means that the customer agrees to pay for the goods or services some time after they have been sold to the customer. The amount due from credit customers is referred to as receivables or **trade receivables**.

What are liabilities?

Businesses often owe money to other businesses or organisations. Amounts owing to other businesses or organisations are called liabilities. For example, many businesses buy goods on credit from their suppliers. In other words, the goods are purchased, but payment for them is made at some later date. The suppliers to whom the business owes money are referred to as payables or **trade payables**.

Examples of liabilities

- Loans from banks and from other providers
- Bank overdrafts

What is capital?

Businesses only exist because their owners have invested private funds in the business. As a result, businesses then acquire the kinds of asset described earlier. Maybe other businesses and organisations also provide some finance – the liabilities described before. The finance or investment provided by the owner is called capital.

1.2 The accounting equation and simple balance sheets

Starting up a business – owning your own premises is an asset

KEY TERM

Accounting equation: this links the three elements that are a feature of all businesses, i.e. assets, liabilities and capital. The equation is: Assets = Capital + Liabilities

You can now try questions 3–4 on page 7.

What is the accounting equation?

There is a simple link between the three elements: assets, liabilities and capital. This link, called the **accounting equation**, is based on the following idea:

- Each business has a number of assets. These assets have either been provided by the owner of the business (capital) or by using funds provided by other businesses or organisations (liabilities).
- It follows that whatever the scale of the business:
  Assets = Capital + Liabilities

Illustration 1 The accounting equation

John is the owner of a general store. The business has assets with a total value of $75 000. John provided $60 000 from his private resources to buy these assets; the remaining $15 000 of assets was purchased by asking for a loan from the bank.

Summary: Assets $75 000 = Capital $60 000 + Liabilities $15 000

The accounting equation can be useful for calculating otherwise unknown facts about businesses. So, if you know that business has assets of $40 000 and liabilities of $5000, it is possible to work out that the owner's capital must be $35 000. In other words:

Assets = Capital + Liabilities
$40 000 = ? + $5000
So, $40 000 = $35 000 + $5000

KEY TERM

Balance sheet: a statement that shows an organisation's assets, liabilities and capital at a particular date, which is prepared at the end of a financial period.

You can now try questions 5–6 on page 7.

How to prepare a simple balance sheet

A **balance sheet** is a statement detailing a business's assets, liabilities and capital at a particular date.

There are precise rules about how a balance sheet should be prepared. The following example illustrates how these rules are applied.

Illustration 2 Preparing a simple balance sheet

The following information is available about John's General Store on 1 August 2012.

	$
Shop premises	240 000
Fixtures and fittings	30 000
Delivery vehicle	24 000
Inventory	18 000
Trade receivables	4 000
Cash at bank	10 000
Cash in hand	2 000
Bank loan	40 000
Trade payables	8 000

Step 1: Calculate the total value of assets: \$328 000.

Step 2: Calculate the total value of liabilities: \$48 000.

Step 3: Use the accounting equation to find the missing capital figure: \$328 000 − \$48 000 = \$280 000

Step 4: Proceed to produce a balance sheet, starting with a title. The title for a balance sheet should include the name of the business (or the name of the owner of the business). The correct wording for the title of a balance sheet is always: Balance Sheet [at a particular date]. For example: Balance Sheet at 1 August 2012. It is best to show the date in full, avoiding any abbreviations.

Step 5: Write a subheading 'Assets' and list all of the assets and their values in two columns on the left-hand side of the balance sheet. The money column should be headed '$'.

Step 6: On the right-hand side of the balance sheet, record the business's capital and liabilities. Start by writing 'Capital' as a subheading and recording the value of capital (\$280 000); head the money column '$'. Now write the subheading 'Liabilities' and list the liabilities and their values.

Step 7: Record a total at the foot of each money column. The totals should appear on the same level; they should, of course, be for the same amount.

John's General Store
Balance Sheet at 1 August 2012

	$		$
ASSETS		CAPITAL	280 000
Shop premises	240 000		
Fixtures and fittings	30 000	LIABILITIES	
Delivery vehicle	24 000	Bank loan	40 000
Inventory	18 000	Trade payables	8 000
Trade receivables	4 000		
Cash at bank	10 000		
Cash in hand	2 000		
	328 000		328 000

1.3 Preparing a classified balance sheet

> **KEY TERM**
>
> **Non-current assets:** assets that should be of benefit to the business for a long time (more than one year).
>
> **Current assets:** assets that are quickly turned into cash and are of benefit to the business for a short time (less than one year).
>
> **Order of permanence**: the sequence used to list items on a balance sheet. It begins with items that are likely to be longest lasting and ends with items that are likely to be shortest lasting.
>
> **Non-current liabilities**: liabilities that will be settled in the longer term (longer than one year).
>
> **Current liabilities:** liabilities that will be settled in the near future (in less than one year).

The presentation of a balance sheet can be improved by dividing assets into two categories:

- **Non-current assets:** these are assets that the business intends to keep and make use of for a long time (more than one year). Non-current assets include: premises, machinery, equipment, vehicles, furniture, fittings, and so on.
- **Current assets:** these are assets that are frequently changing in value such as inventory, trade receivables, bank and cash. So, any one item of inventory, or an amount owing from a particular customer, will only be an asset for the business for a short time (less than one year).

Assets are shown on balance sheets in a particular order. The order corresponds to how long the asset will belong to the business. So premises would be shown first, and cash in hand (which is, of course, constantly changing in value) will be shown last. This way of ordering assets is sometimes referred to as the **order of permanence**. The following guidance should help you to place assets in the right order:

- Non-current assets: place land first, followed by premises; thereafter, place other non-current assets in order of their value (unless you happen to know a little more about how long the non-current assets will belong to the business).
- Current assets: place current assets in the following order: inventory, trade receivables, bank, and cash.

Similarly, liabilities can be subdivided into two categories:

- **Non-current liabilities**: amounts due that are likely to be repaid in a future financial period (after more than one year). Non-current liabilities would normally include bank loans.
- **Current liabilities**: amounts due that will be repaid within the financial period (less than one year). Examples of current liabilities are trade payables and bank overdrafts.

It is also useful to the owner of a business if the balance sheet shows separate subtotals for non-current assets, current assets and, if appropriate, for non-current liabilities and current liabilities.

LINKS...
In Chapter 18 you will be introduced to an alternative layout for a balance sheet – the vertical form of presentation – which is now in common use.

DID YOU KNOW?

You may come across some older terms for the following during your studies:

- Inventory is sometimes referred to as stock.
- Non-current assets are sometimes referred to as fixed assets.
- Non-current liabilities are sometimes referred to as long-term liabilities.

You can now answer questions 7–8 on page 8.

Illustration 3 Preparing a classified balance sheet in order of permanence

Here is the balance sheet for John's General Store rewritten to follow the rules about classified balance sheets.

John's General Store

Balance Sheet at 1 August 2012

	$	$		$
NON-CURRENT ASSETS			CAPITAL	280 000
Shop premises	240 000			
Fixtures and fittings	30 000		NON-CURRENT LIABILITIES	
Delivery vehicle	24 000			
		294 000	Bank loan	40 000
CURRENT ASSETS			CURRENT LIABILITIES	
Inventory	18 000		Trade payables	8 000
Trade receivables	4 000			
Cash at bank	10 000			
Cash in hand	2 000			
		34 000		
		328 000		328 000

Note: in this version of the balance sheet each side has two money columns. The first column is used to record the detail about individual items (in this case about non-current assets and current assets). The second column is used to show the subtotal for each category.

Unit 1 Practice questions

DEVELOPING YOUR SKILLS

1 Identifying assets, liabilities and capital

Here is a list of assets and liabilities and references to capital. Read through the list, and then identify whether the items are assets, liabilities or capital.

- **A** Vehicle
- **B** Shop fittings
- **C** Cash at bank
- **D** Bank loan
- **E** Owner's investment in the business
- **F** Inventory
- **G** Trade receivables
- **H** Bank overdraft
- **I** Trade payables
- **J** Machinery

2 Identifying assets, liabilities and capital

Here is a list of assets and liabilities and references to capital. Read through the list, and then identify whether the items are assets, liabilities or capital.

- **A** Cash in hand
- **B** Equipment
- **C** Amounts owing to suppliers
- **D** Furniture
- **E** Land
- **F** Loan from a friend
- **G** Value of owner's stake in the business
- **H** Amounts owed by customers
- **I** Cash at bank
- **J** Fittings

3 Using the accounting equation

The following table shows details about some businesses' total assets, total liabilities and capital. For each business calculate the missing figure, making use of the accounting equation.

	Total assets	Total liabilities	Capital
	Assets =	Liabilities +	Capital
	$	$	$
Business A	80 000	20 000	
Business B	42 000	11 000	
Business C	57 000		24 000
Business D	650 000		490 000
Business E		20 000	170 000
Business F		82 000	558 000

4 Using the accounting equation

The following table shows details about some businesses' total assets, total liabilities and capital. For each business calculate the missing figure, making use of the accounting equation.

	Total assets	Total liabilities	Capital
	Assets =	Liabilities +	Capital
	$	$	$
Business A	220 000	30 000	
Business B	912 000	86 000	
Business C	325 000		273 000
Business D	560 000		483 000
Business E		52 000	865 000
Business F		42 000	220 000

5 Preparing simple balance sheets

Donnie owns a business making computer software programs. The following information is available about her business's assets and liabilities on 31 October 2012.

	$
Equipment	90 000
Cash in hand	4 000
Premises	300 000
Bank loan (repayable 2014)	60 000
Inventory	16 000
Delivery vehicle	32 000
Trade receivables	14 000
Bank overdraft	8 000
Trade payables	22 000

- **A** Calculate the total value of assets.
- **B** Calculate the total value of liabilities.
- **C** Use the accounting equation to calculate the business's capital.
- **D** Prepare a simple balance sheet at 31 October 2012.

6 Preparing simple balance sheets

Kisha owns a restaurant. The following information is available about her business's assets and liabilities on 31 January 2012.

	$
Restaurant premises	570 000
Bank loan (repayable 2015)	120 000
Furniture and fittings	45 000
Cash in hand	6 000
Equipment	51 000
Inventory (food, etc.)	24 000
Trade payables	18 000
Trade receivables	3 000
Loan from friend (repayable March 2012)	9 000
Cash at bank	12 000

A Calculate the total value of assets.

B Calculate the total value of liabilities.

C Use the accounting equation to calculate the business's capital.

D Prepare a simple balance sheet at 31 January 2012.

7 Preparing classified balance sheets

Refer to the information in question 5 and prepare a classified balance sheet at 31 October 2012.

8 Preparing classified balance sheets

Refer to the information in question 6 and prepare a classified balance sheet at 31 January 2012.

2 The effect of transactions on a balance sheet

Introduction

In this unit you are going to learn how the value of individual items shown in balance sheets change as a business continues its operations.

First of all it is necessary to understand the term **transaction**. A transaction is a financial event. All businesses operate by buying, selling, spending money, receiving money, and so on. Each purchase, sale, payment and receipt is a transaction.

Many transactions involve the receipt or payment of money. These transactions are often referred to as **cash transactions**. Money transactions can involve notes and coins, cheques, credit cards, debit cards, online payments, and so on. They are all referred to as cash transactions whatever method has been used. Therefore, cash transactions include transactions involving the business's bank account.

Credit transactions are those where the payment or receipt of money does not occur at the time of the purchase or sale, but at some later date.

For example, many businesses use credit to buy goods from suppliers for resale (a credit transaction) but pay their supplier later (a cash transaction). As you read in Unit 1, amounts owing to suppliers are recorded as 'trade payables' on the balance sheet.

Here is another example of a credit transaction. Some retailers sell their goods on credit to customers (a credit transaction) and receive payment from the customer some time later (a cash transaction). As you read in Unit 1, amounts owed by customers are recorded as 'trade receivables' on the balance sheet.

LEARNING OUTCOMES

When you have reached the end of this unit you will be able to:

- identify how a range of transactions – both cash and credit – affect balance sheet items
- record a set of transactions by preparing a sequence of balance sheets.

KEY TERM

Transaction: a financial activity or financial event.

Cash transactions: financial activities involving the immediate use of money.

Credit transactions: financial activities when the payment or receipt of money is delayed.

2.1 The effect of transactions on balance sheet items

Every time a transaction occurs items on a balance sheet will change. Of course, whatever the transaction, the accounting equation (see Unit 1) will always apply.

In the illustrations that follow you can see how a variety of transactions affect the balance sheet of one business over a period of a few days. The illustrations include both cash and credit transactions. They show transactions that affect:

- assets only
- assets and liabilities
- assets and capital.

KEY TERM

Drawings: the withdrawal of money by the owner of a business for private use.

Illustration 1 Buying a vehicle and paying by cheque

The summarised balance sheet of a business on 1 December 2012 is shown below.

Balance sheet at 1 December 2012

	$		$
ASSETS		CAPITAL	70 000
Equipment	25 000		
Bank	45 000		
	70 000		70 000

On 2 December 2012 the owner of the business purchased a vehicle for use by the business and paid by cheque $15 000.

Step 1: Work out how the transaction affects items on the balance sheet:

- A new asset will appear on the balance sheet: Vehicle +$15 000.
- The asset bank will have to be reduced because a payment has been made: Bank −$15 000.

You will notice that the capital figure of $70 000 is not affected by this transaction. This is because the value of the owner's investment in this business has not changed. All that has happened is that one asset has been exchanged for another asset.

Step 2: The redrafted balance sheet is as follows:

Balance sheet at 2 December 2012

	$		$
ASSETS		CAPITAL	70 000
Equipment	25 000		
Vehicle	**15 000**		
Bank	**30 000**		
	70 000		70 000

Did you notice that two items on the balance sheet were affected by the transaction?

Illustration 2 Buying furniture on credit

On 3 December 2012 the business purchased some furniture, costing $10 000, on credit.

Step 1: Work out how the transaction affects items on the balance sheet:

- A new asset will appear on the balance sheet: Furniture + $10 000.
- A liability will appear on the balance sheet: Trade payables + $10 000.

In this transaction, the business has acquired one more asset, but rather than paying for it immediately it has purchased the asset on credit (i.e. it has delayed paying until some future date). So the business now has a liability (i.e. a trade payable). Once again, you will notice there is no change to the figure for capital. This is because the business has acquired an extra asset and a liability, so the net value of the business has not changed.

Step 2: The redrafted balance sheet is as shown:

Balance sheet at 3 December 2012

	$		$
ASSETS		CAPITAL	70 000
Equipment	25 000		
Vehicle	15 000		
Furniture	**10 000**	LIABILITY	
Bank	30 000	**Trade payables**	**10 000**
	80 000		80 000

Once again, did you notice that two items on the balance sheet were affected by the transaction?

Illustration 3 The owner takes $1 000 from the bank account for private use

On 4 December 2012 the owner of the business withdrew $1 000 from the business's bank account for private use. The withdrawal of money from the business by the owner for private use is called **drawings**.

Step 1: Work out how the transaction affects items on the balance sheet:

- The asset bank will be reduced by $1000: Bank – $1000.
- The owner's investment in the business will be reduced by $1000: Capital – $1000.

In this transaction, the value of one of the business's assets has been reduced. At the same time the owner has deliberately reduced the amount invested in the business, so capital has been reduced.

Step 2: The redrafted balance sheet is as follows:

Balance sheet at 4 December 2012

	$		$
ASSETS		**CAPITAL**	**69 000**
Equipment	25 000		
Vehicle	15 000		
Furniture	10 000	LIABILITY	
Bank	**29 000**	Trade payables	10 000
	79 000		79 000

Once again, two items on the balance sheet were affected by this transaction.

You can now try questions 1–8 on pages 12–14.

Illustration 4 Some more typical transactions

		Assets	= Capital	+ Liabilities
1	An individual started a business by paying $35 000 into a bank account	Bank + $35 000	Capital + $35 000	
2	Machinery worth $12 000 was purchased on credit	Machinery + $12 000		Trade payables + $12 000
3	Purchased equipment for $5000 and paid by cheque	Equipment + $5000 Bank – $5000		
4	Borrowed $20 000 from the bank as a long-term loan	Bank + $20 000		Bank loan + $20 000
5	Owner withdrew a cheque for $4000 for private use	Bank – $4000	Capital – $4000	
6	Paid the trade payables $2000 by cheque	Bank – $2000		Trade payables – $2000

Practice questions

NOTE: It is suggested that simple balance sheets are used when answering questions 1–6 in this unit, in order to reduce the otherwise heavy workload involved in preparing a succession of classified balance sheets. It is, however, recommended that the final balance sheet required in questions 7 and 8 should be in classified form to provide further practice in this important technique.

DEVELOPING YOUR SKILLS

1 Recording transactions using balance sheets

Adam opened his business on 1 March 2012. His business's first balance sheet is shown below.

Adam
Balance sheet at 1 March 2012

	$		$
ASSETS		CAPITAL	40 000
Vehicle	12 000		
Bank	28 000		
	40 000		40 000

In the first few days that the business was in operation the following transactions occurred.

March 2 Purchased equipment for $15 000 and paid by cheque
3 Purchased furniture for $8000 on credit
4 Borrowed $15 000 from the bank (i.e. a bank loan). These funds were paid into the business's bank account
5 Adam withdrew a cheque for $3000 for private use (i.e. drawings)
6 Paid the trade payables $6000 by cheque

Prepare an updated balance sheet after each transaction.

2 Recording transactions using balance sheets

Tiffany opened a business on 1 January 2012. Her business's first balance sheet was as follows:

Tiffany
Balance sheet at 1 January 2012

	$		$
ASSETS		CAPITAL	110 000
Premises	90 000		
Bank	20 000		
	110 000		110 000

In the first few days that the business was in operation the following transactions occurred:

Jan 2 Purchased a vehicle for $15 000 and paid by cheque
3 Borrowed $12 000 from the bank (i.e. a bank loan). The funds were paid into the business's bank account
Jan 4 Purchased equipment for $24 000 on credit
5 Tiffany made an additional investment in her business of $8000 (i.e. additional capital). The funds were paid into the business's bank account
6 Paid the trade payables $20 000 by cheque

Prepare an updated balance sheet after each transaction.

3 Identifying how transactions affect balance sheets

In the following table, recalculate the figure for total assets, capital and total liabilities after each transaction has occurred. (The effect of the first transaction has already been worked out for you.)

		Total assets	Capital	Total liabilities
		A =	C +	L
		$	$	$
	Starting figures	40 000	30 000	10 000
1	Owner withdrew cheque $4000 for private use	36 000	26 000	10 000
2	Purchased new vehicle $16000 on credit			
3	Repaid $2000 of a loan from the bank. The funds were taken from the business's bank account			
4	Purchased some machinery for $7000 and paid by cheque			
5	Paid trade payables $5000 by cheque			
6	Sold some equipment worth $3000 and received a cheque for this amount			

4 Identifying how transactions affect balance sheets

In the following table, recalculate the figure for total assets, capital and total liabilities after each transaction has occurred. (The effect of the first transaction has already been worked out for you.)

		Total assets	Capital	Total liabilities
		A =	C +	L
		$	$	$
	Starting figures	90 000	75 000	15 000
1	Paid trade payable $8000 by cheque	82 000	75 000	7000
2	Purchased a new vehicle and paid $17 000 by cheque			
3	The owner withdrew a cheque for $1000 for private use			
4	Purchased some new equipment for $10 000 on credit			
5	Repaid part of a bank loan $6000. The funds were taken from the business's bank account			
6	Some old machinery worth $6000 was sold on credit for this amount			

5 Comparing balance sheets to see what transactions have occurred

Here are some balance sheets for one business. By comparing each balance sheet with the previous balance sheet, you should be able to work out what transaction has occurred.

The first answer is shown as an example.

Balance sheet at 1 February 2012

	$		$
ASSETS		CAPITAL	60 000
Bank	60 000		

Balance sheet at 2 February 2012

	$		$
ASSETS		CAPITAL	60 000
Vehicle	18 000		
Bank	42 000		
	60 000		60 000

Answer: A vehicle has been purchased for $18 000 and paid for by cheque.

Balance sheet at 3 February 2012

	$		$
ASSETS		CAPITAL	57 000
Vehicle	18 000		
Bank	39 000		
	57 000		57 000

Balance sheet at 4 February 2012

	$		$
ASSETS		CAPITAL	57 000
Vehicle	18 000		
Equipment	16 000	LIABILITY	
Bank	39 000	Trade payables	16 000
	73 000		73 000

Balance sheet at 5 February 2012

	$		$
ASSETS		CAPITAL	57 000
Vehicle	18 000		
Equipment	16 000	LIABILITY	
Bank	33 000	Trade payables	10 000
	67 000		67 000

6 Comparing balance sheets to see what transactions have occurred

Here are some balance sheets for one business. By comparing each balance sheet with the previous balance sheet, you should be able to work out what transaction has occurred.

The first answer is shown as an example.

Balance sheet at 1 December 2012

	$		$
ASSETS		CAPITAL	92 000
Bank	92 000		

Balance sheet at 2 December 2012

	$		$
ASSETS		CAPITAL	92 000
Equipment	22 000		
Bank	92 000	LIABILITY	
		Trade payables	22 000
	114 000		114 000

Answer: Some equipment has been purchased on credit for $22 000.

Balance sheet at 3 December 2012

	$		$
ASSETS		CAPITAL	92 000
Equipment	22 000		
Bank	107 000	LIABILITY	
		Bank loan	15 000
		Trade payables	22 000
	129 000		129 000

Balance sheet at 4 December 2012

	$		$
ASSETS		CAPITAL	92 000
Equipment	16 000		
Trade receivables	6 000	LIABILITY	
Bank	107 000	Bank loan	15 000
		Trade payables	22 000
	129 000		129 000

Balance sheet at 5 December 2012

	$		$
ASSETS		CAPITAL	92 000
Equipment	16 000		
Trade receivables	3 000	LIABILITY	
Bank	110 000	Bank loan	15 000
		Trade payables	22 000
	129 000		129 000

7 Further practice at recording transactions using balance sheets

Tarek opened a hardware store on 1 March 2012. The business's balance sheet on that date was as follows:

Tarek
Balance sheet at 1 March 2012

	$		$
ASSETS		CAPITAL	32 900
Equipment	14 100		
Bank	28 200	LIABILITY	
Cash	600	Bank Loan (2014)	10 000
	42 900		42 900

The following transactions occurred during the period 1–7 March 2012:

Mar	2	Purchased a delivery van on credit for $19 600
	3	Purchased shop fittings for $7200 and paid by cheque
	4	Tarek withdrew $500 cash for private use
	5	Tarek decided to sell some of the equipment, with a value of $2400, for that amount on credit
	6	Paid the trade payables $11 500 by cheque
	7	Received a cheque for $1200 from the trade receivables

Prepare an updated balance sheet after each transaction. The last balance sheet (at 7 March) should be set out as a fully classified balance sheet.

8 Further practice at recording transactions using balance sheets

Karita owns a hairdressing business which she opened on 1 April 2012. The business's balance sheet on that date was as follows:

Karita
Balance sheet at 1 April 2012

	$		$
ASSETS		CAPITAL	17 600
Equipment	11 000		
Receivables	2 900	LIABILITY	
Bank	6 300	Trade payables	3 400
Cash	800		
	21 000		21 000

The following transactions occurred during the period 1–7 April 2012:

Apr	2	Purchased some additional equipment on credit for $4100
	3	Received $200 cash from the trade receivables
	3	Arranged a long-term bank loan for $9000. The funds were paid into the business's bank account
	5	Karita withdrew $400 cash for private use
	6	Sold some unwanted equipment, with a value of $1500, for that amount on credit
	7	Paid the trade payables $6200 by cheque

Prepare an updated balance sheet after each transaction. The last balance sheet (at 7 April) should be set out as a fully classified balance sheet.

3 Preparing simple ledger accounts

Introduction

In this unit you are going to start to use accounts for recording transactions.

You will know from studying Unit 2, that it is possible to record transactions by using a succession of balance sheets. However, you will also realise that this is an inefficient and rather laborious method of keeping accounting records. To make the process a great deal easier, accounts are used.

An account is a two-sided form and is referred to as a **T account** because of its shape:

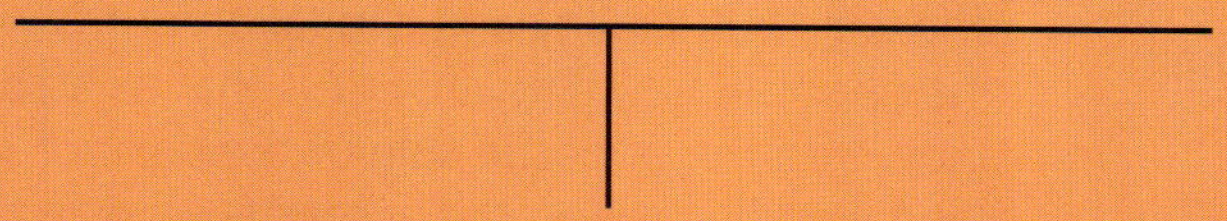

At first you will just record amounts in these T accounts, but later in this unit you will learn how to record more information in accounts so that they are even more useful to the owner or manager of a business.

LEARNING OUTCOMES

When you have reached the end of this unit you will be able to:

- record transactions using T accounts
- use the terms 'debit' and 'credit' when recording transactions
- prepare ledger accounts making detailed entries.

KEY TERM

T account: a two-sided form used to record transactions affecting a particular aspect of a business's financial activities.

3.1 Using T accounts

How to use T accounts

The following illustration shows how T accounts can be used to record the amounts involved in transactions.

Illustration 1 Using T accounts

Dale owns a village store. The business's balance sheet on 1 May 2012 was as follows:

Dale
Balance sheet at 1 May 2012

	$		$
ASSETS		CAPITAL	40 000
Equipment	37 000		
Bank	8 000	LIABILITY	
		Trade payables	5 000
	45 000		45 000

During the first few days of May several transactions occurred. Here is the first of these transactions:

- Transaction 1: some additional equipment was purchased and a payment of $6000 was made by cheque.

Step 1: Prepare T accounts for each item shown on the balance sheet.

The accounts would look like this:

Equipment account

Bank account

Capital account

Trade payables account

Step 2: Record the opening amount for each item in the appropriate T account.

It is important to note that accounts work in the following way:

Asset account

INCREASE (+) *Starting value*	DECREASE (−)

Liability account

DECREASE (−)	INCREASE (+) *Starting value*

Capital account

DECREASE (−)	INCREASE (+) *Starting value*

You may be wondering why asset accounts work in one way, but liability and capital accounts work in the opposite way. The answer is that as assets are shown on the opposite side of the balance sheet to capital and liabilities, the accounts work in opposite ways to reflect this difference.

So here are Dale's accounts with the opening figures recorded correctly:

Equipment account

37 000	

Bank account

8 000	

Capital account

	40 000

Trade payables account

	5 000

You will notice that the opening amounts are recorded on the 'increase' (positive) side of the relevant account.

Step 3: Record each transaction in these accounts. You already know that whatever the transaction, two accounts will be affected, so it will be necessary to make two entries.

First work out which two accounts will be affected by the transaction and how each account will be affected.

Here is a summary for the first transactions (i.e. some additional equipment was purchased and a payment of $6000 was made by cheque):

- Equipment +$6000
- Bank −$6000

and the updated accounts are shown on the following page:

Equipment account

37 000	
6 000	

Bank account

8 000	**6 000**

Capital account

	40 000

Trade payables account

	5 000

You will see that:

- In the Equipment account an entry has been made on the left-hand, positive, side of the account because there has been an increase in equipment.
- In the Bank account an entry has been made on the right-hand, negative, side of the account because there has been a decrease in bank.

Illustration 2 Recording Dale's second transaction

Here is a summary of the decisions to be made for the second transaction:

- Transaction 2: Dale pays the trade payables $1000 by cheque.

Decision	Answer
Which two accounts are affected by the transaction?	Bank Trade payables
How is each account affected by the transaction (**increase or decrease**)?	Bank: decrease Trade payables: decrease
On **which side** of each account should an entry be made?	Bank: right-hand (decrease) side Trade payables: left-hand (decrease) side

Here are the updated accounts:

Equipment account

37 000	
6 000	

Bank account

8 000	6 000
	1 000

Capital account

	40 000

Trade payables account

1 000	5 000

Illustration 3 Recording Dale's third transaction

Here are the decisions for the third transaction:

- Transaction 3: Dale withdraws a cheque for $200 for his private use (i.e. drawings).

Decision	Answer
Which two accounts are affected by the transaction?	Bank Capital
How is each account affected by the transaction (**increase or decrease**)?	Bank: decrease Capital: decrease
On **which side** of each account should an entry be made?	Bank: right-hand (decrease) side Capital: left-hand (decrease) side

Here are the updated accounts:

Equipment account

37 000	
6 000	

Bank account

8 000	6 000
	1 000
	200

Capital account

200	40 000

Trade payables account

1 000	5 000

Notes:

1. The illustrations show the very simplest way of recording transactions in T accounts.
2. As necessary, additional T accounts can be added to the list as new transactions occur.

You can now answer questions 1–4 on page 20.

3.2 Preparing ledger accounts

KEY TERM

Debit: the left-hand side of an account.

Credit: the right-hand side of an account.

Ledger: the book in which all financial accounts are kept.

Using the terms 'debit' and 'credit'

You may have noticed that in working through the illustrations on the previous pages, there was always a left-hand entry and a right-hand entry in the T accounts. This is the most important consequence of arranging asset accounts to work in the opposite way to liability and capital accounts. You will find that whatever transaction you record in an accounting system, it always results in a left-hand and a right-hand entry. This is a very useful outcome. It means that even if you are trying to work out how to record an unfamiliar or complex transaction, you will know that you must have a left-hand and right-hand entry.

The term **debit** is used for entries on the left-hand side of any account, and **credit** is used for entries on the right-hand side of any account.

LINKS...
In Unit 4.1 you will be shown how to record drawings in a separate account

How do accounts work?

Here is a summary of how accounts work:

Any account

Debit (left-hand) side	***Credit (right-hand) side***

Asset account

INCREASE (+) ***Debit (left-hand) side***	DECREASE (−) ***Credit (right-hand) side***

Liability account

DECREASE (−) ***Debit (left-hand) side***	INCREASE (+) ***Credit (right-hand) side***

Capital account

DECREASE (−) ***Debit (left-hand) side***	INCREASE (+) ***Credit (right-hand) side***

Or:

Debit Entries	Credit Entries
Debit an increase in an ASSET	Credit a decrease in an ASSET
Debit a decrease in a LIABILITY	Credit an increase in a LIABILITY
Debit a decrease in CAPITAL	Credit an increase in CAPITAL

LINKS...
For convenience, one account is used in Units 3–7 for all trade payables and one account for all trade receivables. In Unit 8 you will be shown how to use separate accounts for each trade payable and each trade receivable.

Ledger accounts

When recording transactions in accounts it is helpful to record not just the amounts, but also the date of the transaction and a narrative. In order to do this, simple T accounts become a little more advanced.

At one time all accounts were kept in a single book, called the **ledger**, hence the expression 'ledger accounts'. Nowadays most accounting records are electronic and make use of accounting software programs.

Illustration 4 Using ledger accounts

Here is a new version of the T accounts as shown in Illustration 3. This time they are set out as proper ledger accounts. This means the accounts now show:

- a date for each entry (using the columns for month and day)
- a narrative about each entry written in the details column:
  - for the opening entry the word 'balance' is used
  - the rule for other entries is to name the other account involved in the transaction.

You will also notice that each account now shows the abbreviation Dr (for debit) on the left-hand side of each account and the abbreviation Cr (for credit) on the right-hand side of each account.

Equipment account

Dr				Cr			
May	1	Balance	37 000				
	2	Bank	6 000				

Bank account

Dr				Cr			
May	1	Balance	8 000	May	2	Equipment	6 000
					3	Trade payable	1 000
					4	Capital	200

Capital account

Dr				Cr			
May	4	Bank	200	May	1	Balance	40 000

Trade payables account

Dr				Cr			
May	3	Bank	1 000	May	1	Balance	5 000

Note: once the name of the month is recorded on the debit and/or credit side of an account, there is no need to repeat this detail on succeeding lines.

What about balance sheets?

You can now answer questions 5–8 on page 21.

It is possible to prepare a balance sheet at any time based on all of the detailed information recorded in ledger accounts.

In Illustration 4, for example, it is relatively easy to work out an updated figure for each of the four ledger accounts:

Equipment	$43 000	(the total of the two entries on the debit side)
Bank	$800	(the difference between the debit total $8000 and the credit total $7200)
Capital	$39 800	(the difference between the debit total of $200 and the credit total of $40 000)
Trade payables	$4 000	(the difference between the debit total of $1000 and the credit total of $5000)

So, the (simple) balance sheet on 4 May after the transactions had been recorded would look like this:

Dale

Balance sheet at 4 May 2012

	$		$
ASSETS		CAPITAL	39 800
Equipment	43 000		
Bank	800	LIABILITY	
		Trade payables	4 000
	43 800		43 800

STUDY TIP

It is easy to overlook some point of detail when you are preparing a set of accounts. When you think you have completed a task, do have a look through to see if you have missed out a date or some narrative.

Balance sheets are a very important financial statement. They are prepared whenever required, but most businesses prepare them at the end of every financial year.

You can now answer questions 9 and 10 on page 22.

Practice questions

DEVELOPING YOUR SKILLS

1 Recording transactions using simple T accounts

Padma owns a business which provides a delivery service. On 1 January 2012 the business's balance sheet was as follows:

Padma
Balance sheet at 1 January 2012

	$		$
ASSETS		CAPITAL	47 000
Vehicles	40 000		
Bank	19 000	LIABILITY	
		Bank loan	12 000
	59 000		59 000

The following transactions occurred during the following few days:

Jan 2 Purchased an additional vehicle for $14 000 and paid by cheque
3 Borrowed an additional $4000 from the bank. The funds were paid directly into the business's bank account
4 Padma withdrew a cheque for $2000 for private use

Record these details in simple T accounts. Record amounts only.

2 Recording transactions using simple T accounts

John owns a café. His business's balance sheet on 1 June 2012 was as follows:

John
Balance sheet at 1 January 2012

	$		$
ASSETS		CAPITAL	29 000
Equipment	27 000		
Bank	8 000	LIABILITY	
		Trade payables	6 000
	35 000		35 000

The following transactions occurred during the next few days:

June 2 Purchased some additional equipment and paid $4000 by cheque
3 Paid the trade payables $2000 by cheque
4 John withdrew a cheque for $700 for private use

Record these details in simple T accounts. Record amounts only.

3 Deciding how accounts are affected by transactions

Complete the table shown below for each of the transactions.

Transaction	First account affected		Second account affected	
	Account	Increase/ decrease	Account	Increase/ decrease
Owner started business by investing money in a business bank account				
Purchased a vehicle and paid by cheque				
Purchased some equipment on credit				
The owner withdrew a cheque for private use				
Paid the payables by cheque				

4 Deciding how accounts are affected by transactions

Complete the table shown below for each of the transactions.

Transaction	First account affected		Second account affected	
	Account	Increase/ decrease	Account	Increase/ decrease
Some furniture was purchased by cheque				
A bank loan was arranged. The funds were paid into the business bank account				
Purchased a vehicle on credit				
Sold some unwanted furniture on credit				
Repaid part of the bank loan by a withdrawal of funds from the business bank account				

5 Using the terms 'debit' and 'credit'

Will owns a business selling fruit and vegetables. On 1 July 2012 the business's balance sheet was as follows:

Will
Balance sheet at 1 July 2012

	$		$
ASSETS		CAPITAL	17 000
Vehicle	14 000		
Bank	7 000	LIABILITY	
		Trade payables	4 000
	21 000		21 000

The following transactions occurred during the next few days:

July 2 Purchased some equipment on credit for $9000
3 Will withdrew a cheque for $300 for private use
4 Arranged a bank loan for $6000. The funds were paid directly into the business's bank account
5 Purchased some additional equipment and paid by cheque $9200
6 Paid the trade payables $2500

Record these details in simple T accounts. Record amounts only. Open additional accounts as necessary. Include the abbreviations 'Dr' and 'Cr' in the account titles.

6 Using the terms 'debit' and 'credit'

Sachin owns a plumbing business. On 1 May 2012 the business's balance sheet was as follows:

Sachin
Balance sheet at 1 May 2012

	$		$
ASSETS		CAPITAL	24 200
Vehicle	13 000		
Equipment	8 000		
Bank	4 000	LIABILITY	
Cash	400	Trade payables	1 200
	25 400		25 400

The following transactions occurred during the following few days:

May 2 Sachin withdrew $200 cash for private use
3 The trade payables was paid $1000 by cheque
4 Sold some unwanted equipment with a value of $800 on credit for that amount
5 Purchased some new equipment on credit for $5000
6 Received $100 cash from the trade receivables

Record these details in simple T accounts. Record amounts only. Open additional accounts as necessary. Include the abbreviations 'Dr' and 'Cr' in the account titles.

7 Using the terms 'debit' and 'credit'

Here is a list of transactions. In each case decide which two accounts are affected by the transaction and whether each account will increase or decrease in value. State whether you would debit or credit each of the accounts concerned. The first transaction has been completed for you.

Transaction	Accounts affected	Increase/ decrease	Debit/ credit
Purchased some furniture by cheque	Furniture	Increase	Debit
	Bank	Decrease	Credit
Paid a trade payable by cheque			
Owner withdrew cash for private use			
Purchased a vehicle on credit			

8 Using the terms 'debit' and 'credit'

Here is a list of transactions. In each case decide which two accounts are affected by the transaction and whether each account will increase or decrease in value. State whether you would debit or credit each of the accounts concerned. The first transaction has been completed for you.

Transaction	Accounts affected	Increase/ decrease	Debit/ credit
Owner withdrew a cheque for private use	Capital	Decrease	Debit
	Bank	Decrease	Credit
Purchased equipment on credit			
Paid the trade payables in cash			

Transaction	Accounts affected	Increase/ decrease	Debit/ credit
Sold some unwanted furniture on credit			
Received cash from the trade receivables			

9 Preparing detailed ledger accounts

Ross owns a music business. His business's balance sheet at 1 January 2012 was as follows:

Ross
Balance sheet at 1 January 2012

	$		$
ASSETS		CAPITAL	100 000
Premises	90 000		
Equipment	12 000	LIABILITY	
Vehicle	9 000	Bank loan	15 000
Bank	3 300		
Cash	700		
	115 000		115 000

The following transactions occurred during the next few days:

Jan 2 Repaid $1000 of the bank loan transferring funds from the business's bank account
3 Purchased some additional equipment on credit for $4100
4 Ross withdrew $300 cash for private use
5 Sold some unwanted equipment with a value of $500 on credit for that amount
6 Ross introduced some additional capital by paying in a cheque for $4000 from his private funds
7 Transferred $200 cash to the bank account

Prepare detailed ledger accounts to record this information. Record dates, narratives and amounts. Open additional accounts as necessary. Include the abbreviations 'Dr' and 'Cr' in the account titles.

Prepare a new (classified) balance sheet dated 7 January 2012 when all of the transactions have been recorded. Assume the bank loan is a long-term liability.

10 Preparing detailed ledger accounts

Becky owns an interior design business. Her business's balance sheet at 1 April 2012 was as follows:

Becky
Balance sheet at 1 April 2012

	$		$
ASSETS		CAPITAL	32 900
Vehicle	16 000		
Furniture	11 000	LIABILITY	
Trade receivables	4 400	Trade payables	2 200
Bank	2 800		
Cash	900		
	35 100		35 100

The following transactions occurred during the next few days:

April 2 Purchased some additional furniture for $2400 and paid by cheque
3 Becky withdrew a cheque for $200 for her private use
4 Received a cheque from the trade receivables for $2900
5 Arranged a long-term loan with the bank for $7200. The funds were paid into the business's bank account
6 Paid the trade payables $400 in cash
7 Transferred $100 cash to the bank account

Prepare detailed ledger accounts to record this information. Record dates, narratives and amounts. Open additional accounts as necessary. Include the abbreviations 'Dr' and 'Cr' in the account titles.

Prepare a new balance sheet dated 8 April 2012 when all of the transactions have been recorded.

4 Using expense, purchases, sales and drawings accounts

Introduction

In this unit you are going to develop yours skills in recording transactions. So far you have concentrated on recording transactions affecting just assets, liabilities and capital. You have learned that whatever the transaction, there are always two entries to be made in the accounting records: one of these is a debit entry and the other is always a credit entry. You are now going to apply the rules of **double entry** to a further important group of transactions: the payment of expenses, the purchase of goods for resale, the sale of goods, and owner's drawings.

LEARNING OUTCOMES

When you have reached the end of this unit you will be able to:

- record some new transactions involving expense payments
- record purchases and sales of goods in ledger accounts
- make entries for drawings in ledger accounts.

What are expenses?

Expenses are the everyday running costs of a business, such as electricity, wages, rent, telephone charges, and so on. All businesses make regular payments for items like these. The important feature of an expense is that the benefit received from the payment is very short-lived. After just a few days or weeks, the business will be making another payment for the same thing. Contrast this with, say, a business buying some equipment (an asset). In this situation the benefit to the business lasts over several years. On the other hand, if a business pays the shop rent (an expense) the benefit lasts just a few weeks, and then the next rent payment has to be made. This distinction is important in accounting and the terms 'revenue expenditure' (for expenses) and 'capital expenditure' (for non-current assets) are often used.

KEY TERM

Double entry: the process of making two entries for every transaction.

Expenses: payments made to purchase goods or services to run the business on a day-to-day basis.

These are some typical expenses for a small business:

- Administration expenses (e.g. postage, stationery)
- Advertising
- Carriage (delivery charges)
- Electricity
- General expenses (covering a wide range of running costs)
- Insurance
- Interest charges
- Maintenance costs
- Motor expenses (e.g. fuel charges, servicing and maintenance of vehicles)
- Operating expenses
- Repairs
- Salaries
- Selling expenses
- Telephone charges
- Wages
- Water charges

LINKS...

There is more about the terms 'revenue expenditure' and 'capital expenditure' in Unit 17.

4.1 Recording expenses, purchases, sales and drawings

STUDY TIP

The purchases account is only used when goods for resale are purchased. This account is not used for the purchase of an asset. As you know, when an asset is purchased (e.g. a new vehicle) the asset account is debited.

Recording expenses

When payment is made for an expense a record must be kept in the accounting system. As you read in Unit 3, any payment by cheque or in cash is bound to result in the following:

Asset	Bank	decreases	so credit bank account
Asset	Cash	decreases	so credit cash account

You can probably work out from the rules of double entry that the other entry for the transaction must be:

Debit   Expense account

So, expense accounts are debited when payments are made.

Illustration 1 Recording the payment of wages

On 31 May 2012 the owner of a business paid $210 wages in cash.
The two accounts involved are: Cash and Wages.

Dr Cash account Cr

				May	31	Wages	210

Dr Wages account Cr

May	31	Cash	210				

Buying goods for resale

The main activity of many businesses is buying goods from suppliers in order to sell them to customers at a profit. When goods for resale are purchased by cheque the entries required will be:

- Debit Purchases account
- Credit Bank account

If the goods for resale were purchased on credit the entries would be:

- Debit Purchases account
- Credit Trade payable account

Illustration 2 Recording the purchases of goods for resale

On 4 May a business purchased some goods for resale, value $420, and paid by cheque. On 5 May the business purchased some goods on credit, value $1700. The accounts should show the following entries:

Dr Purchases account Cr

May	4	Bank	420				
	5	Trade payables	1 700				

Dr Bank account Cr

				May	4	Purchases	420

Dr Trade payables account Cr

				May	5	Purchases	1 700

LINKS...
See Unit 6 for information about how businesses calculate profits and losses.

Selling goods

Every time goods are sold, the owner of the business will be pleased, not only because the business will receive money (or the promise of money to be received in the future), but also because the business will make a profit on the sale.

If goods are sold for cash the entries required will be:

- Debit Cash account
- Credit Sales account

Of course, the money from the customer might be banked immediately, in which case the debit entry would be in the bank account.

If goods are sold on credit the entries required will be:

- Debit Trade receivables account
- Credit Sales account

LINKS...
See Units 13 and 19 for more information about inventories.

LINKS...
There is more about the business entity principle in Unit 19 on page 180.

Illustration 3 Recording the sale of goods

On 8 May 2012 a business sold goods for $920 and received payment by cheque. On 9 May the business sold some goods on credit for $380. The accounts should show the following entries:

Sales account

Dr				Cr
	May 8	Bank	920	
	9	Trade receivables	380	

Bank account

Dr				Cr
May 8	Sales	920		

Trade receivables account

Dr				Cr
May 9	Sales	380		

What about inventories?

Of course, throughout a period of trading the owner of a business will be holding inventories (unsold goods). Information about how inventories are recorded in the accounting records is covered in Units 13 and 19.

The drawings account

So far, any drawings have been debited immediately to the capital account. It is usually considered a better idea, however, to keep a separate record of drawings throughout a financial year.

So the entries for recording drawings now become:

- Debit Drawings account
- Credit Bank or cash account

It is important to remember that drawings are a reduction in the investment of the owner in the business. Drawings are not an expense of the business. Drawings result from decisions made by the owners of a business about their personal affairs and are not directly related to the needs of the business. On the other hand, expenses result from the business's everyday trading activities. The idea of separating out from the business's affairs any transactions that relate to the owner's private affairs is often referred to as the 'business entity principle'.

STUDY TIP

The sales account is only used to record the sale of goods. It is not used to record the sale of a non-current asset. If an asset is sold (e.g. some unwanted equipment), it is the asset account that is credited.

You can now answer questions 1 and 2 on page 28.

You can now answer questions 3 and 4 on page 28.

Illustration 4 Using a drawings account

The owner of a business has invested capital of $80 000. The owner withdrew a cheque for $200 for private use on 1 August 2012. The accounting records will be as follows:

Capital account

Dr				Cr
	Aug 1	Balance	80 000	

Bank account

Dr				Cr
	Aug 1	Drawings	200	

Drawings account

Dr				Cr
Aug 1	Bank	200		

4.2 Getting used to the new accounts

How to think about these new accounts and the rules of double entry

It is possible to identify expense, purchase, sales and drawings accounts as part of the information about the capital of the business.

This means that these new accounts work in the same way as a capital account. A debit entry in an expense or drawings account indicates a decrease in capital, i.e. the value of the business has decreased. The purchases account can be regarded as a temporary expense account. Capital is increased by the difference between the value of sales and purchases (i.e. the profit made on selling goods).

Update: Summary of the rules for double entry

Asset accounts		Liability accounts		Capital accounts (and subdivisions)			
Dr	Cr	Dr	Cr	Dr	Cr	Dr	Cr
Increase +	Decrease −	Decrease −	Increase +	Decrease −	Increase +	Decrease −	Increase +
				Dr Expenses	Cr	Dr Sales	Cr
				Entries decrease capital			Entries increase capital
				Dr Drawings	Cr	Dr Purchases	Cr
				Entries decrease capital		Entries decrease capital	

Illustration 5 Applying the rules of double entry

In this short illustration there is an example of all of the transactions covered so far. The illustration includes a brief review of what entries to make and why these are the right entries.

Vladim is the owner of '4u', a shop that sells some of the latest technology. The business's balance sheet on 1 October 2012 was as follows:

4u

Balance sheet at 1 October 2012

	$		$
ASSETS		CAPITAL	57 100
Furniture and fittings	27 000		
Vehicle	25 000	LIABILITIES	
Trade receivables	2 800	Trade payables	3 800
Bank	5 900		
Cash	200		
	60 900		60 900

Here is a table showing the transactions that occurred in October and how the correct entries have been worked out.

Transactions		Which accounts are affected	Accounts by classification			Entries required	
			Asset	Liability	Capital and its subdivisions	Debit	Credit
Oct 3	Paid trade payables $2100 by cheque	Bank Trade payables	Bank	Trade payables		Trade payables (decrease in liability)	Bank (decrease in asset)
6	Paid general expenses $100 in cash	Cash General expenses	Cash		General expenses	General expenses (decrease in capital)	Cash (decrease in asset)
8	Cash sales totalled $1430	Cash Sales	Cash		Sales	Cash (increase in asset)	Sales (increase in capital)
11	Vladim withdrew cash $240 for private use	Cash Drawings	Cash		Drawings	Drawings (decrease in capital)	Cash (decrease in asset)
14	Purchased some new shop fittings; paid $850 by cheque	Bank furniture and fittings	Bank Furniture and fittings			Furniture and fittings (increase in asset)	Bank (decrease in asset)
19	Received a cheque for $2400 from a receivable	Bank Trade receivables	Bank Trade receivables			Bank (increase in asset	Trade receivables (decrease in asset)
23	Paid rent by cheque $920	Bank Rent	Bank		Rent	Rent (decrease in capital)	Bank (decrease in asset)
26	Sold goods on credit for $3100	Trade receivables Sales	Trade receivables		Sales	Trade receivables (increase in asset)	Sales (increase in capital)
30	Purchased goods for resale and paid $480 in cash	Cash Purchases	Cash		Purchases	Purchases (decrease in capital)	Cash (decrease in asset)

Here are the accounts recording all of this information.

Dr Bank account Cr

Oct	1	Balance	5 900	Oct	3	Payables	2 100
	19	Trade receivables	2 400		14	Furniture and fittings	850
					19	Rent	920

Dr Capital account Cr

				Oct	1	Balance	57 100

Dr Cash account Cr

Oct	1	Balance	200	Oct	6	General expenses	100
	8	Sales	1 430		11	Drawings	240
					30	Purchases	480

Dr Drawings account Cr

Oct	11	Cash	240				

Dr Furniture and fittings account Cr

Oct	1	Balance	27 000				
	14	Bank	850				

Dr General expenses account Cr

Oct	6	Cash	100				

Dr Trade payables account Cr

Oct	3	Bank	2 100	Oct	1	Balance	3 800

Dr Purchases Cr

Oct	30	Payables	480				

Dr Trade receivables account Cr

Oct	1	Balance	2 800	Oct	19	Bank	2 400
	26	Sales	3 100				

Dr Rent account Cr

Oct	23	Bank	920				

Dr Sales account Cr

				Oct	8	Cash	1 430
					26	Trade receivables	3 100

Dr Vehicle account Cr

Oct	1	Balance	25 000				

You can now answer questions 5–8 on pages 29–30.

Unit 4 Practice questions

DEVELOPING YOUR SKILLS

1 Recording expenses, purchases and sales

Warren opened a business selling electrical goods on 1 February 2012. The business's first balance sheet on that date was as follows:

Warren
Balance sheet at 1 February 2012

	$		$
ASSETS		CAPITAL	12 400
Bank	12 000		
Cash	400		
	12 400		12 400

The following transactions occurred during February 2012:

Feb
- 2 Purchased goods for resale and paid by cheque, $1200
- 4 Paid two weeks' rent by cheque, $420
- 5 Cash sales totalled $330
- 8 Paid insurance by cheque, $180
- 11 Purchased goods for resale on credit, $840
- 14 Sales on credit totalled $910
- 18 Paid two weeks' rent by cheque, $420
- 19 Paid insurance, $40 in cash
- 21 Received cheques totalling $520 for the sale of goods which were paid into the bank
- 24 Purchased goods for resale and paid in cash, $60

Record this information in suitable ledger accounts.

2 Recording expenses, purchases and sales

Jenny opened a business selling shoes on 1 June 2012. The business's first balance sheet on that date was as follows:

Jenny
Balance sheet at 1 June 2012

	$		$
ASSETS		CAPITAL	15 100
Bank	14 400		
Cash	700		
	15 100		15 100

The following transactions occurred during June 2012:

June
- 2 Purchased goods for resale and paid by cheque, $4700
- 3 Paid one month's rent by cheque, $740
- 6 Cash sales totalled $490
- 7 Paid wages in cash, $580
- 11 Purchased goods for resale on credit, $1 470
- 13 Sales on credit totalled $1 420
- 14 Paid wages in cash, $490
- 19 Paid electricity charges by cheque, $210
- 21 Received cheques totalling $810 for the sale of goods which were paid into the bank
- 24 Purchased goods for resale and paid in cash, $110

Record this information in suitable ledger accounts.

3 Using expense, purchases, sales and drawings accounts

Alex owns a business selling footwear. The business's opening balance sheet on 1 April 2012 was as follows:

Alex
Balance sheet at 1 April 2012

	$		$
ASSETS		CAPITAL	14 900
Equipment	6 200		
Bank	8 400		
Cash	300		
	14 900		14 900

The following transactions occurred during April:

April
- 4 Purchased goods for resale on credit, $3600
- 5 Cash sales totalled $1230
- 8 Alex withdrew a cheque for private use, $240
- 9 Sold goods on credit, $470
- 11 Purchased goods for resale and paid by cheque, $510
- 13 Paid wages in cash, $620
- 18 Purchased some additional equipment and paid by cheque, $1020
- 19 Alex withdrew cash $90 for private use
- 21 Sales of $720 were paid into the bank
- 27 Paid wages in cash, $580

Record this information in suitable ledger accounts, including a separate account for drawings.

4 Using expense, purchases, sales and drawings accounts

Paloma owns a grocery store. The business's opening balance sheet on 1 October 2011 was as shown on the following page:

Paloma
Balance sheet at 1 October 2011

	$		$
ASSETS		CAPITAL	17 100
Fittings	8 600		
Bank	7 800		
Cash	700		
	17 100		17 100

The following transactions occurred during October:

Oct 4 Purchased goods for resale and paid in cash, $500
6 Purchased goods for resale on credit, $4240
7 Cash sales totalled $990
11 Paid rent for the month by cheque, $770
12 Paloma withdrew cash $110 for private use
15 Sales on credit totalled $440
18 Sold some unwanted fittings with a value of $300 and received cash for this amount
22 Paid the trade payables $3000 by cheque
25 Received cash $210 from the trade receivables
29 Paloma withdrew a cheque for $390 for private use

Record this information in suitable ledger accounts, including a separate account for drawings.

5 Identifying transactions

The following accounts show a record of transactions over a period of five days. There is one transaction per day.

Dr Purchases account Cr

Jan	1	Bank	6 000				
	5	Trade payables	2 290				

Dr Sales account Cr

				Jan	2	Cash	3 200
					4	Trade receivables	1 730

Dr General expenses account Cr

Jan	3	Bank	320				

Dr Bank account Cr

				Jan	1	Purchases	6 000
				Jan	3	General exp	320

Dr Cash account Cr

Jan	2	Sales	3 200				

Dr Trade receivables account Cr

Jan	4	Sales	1 730				

Dr Trade payables account Cr

				Jan	5	Purchases	2 290

Identify the transactions that occurred on 1, 2, 3, 4 and 5 January.

6 Identifying transactions

The following accounts show a record of transactions over a period of five days. There is one transaction per day.

Dr Bank account Cr

May	5	Trade receivables	2 000				

Dr Cash account Cr

				May	2	Wages	280
					3	Purchases	170

Dr Trade receivables account Cr

May	1	Sales	3 790	May	5	Bank	2 000

Dr Trade payables account Cr

				May	4	Purchases	1 200

Dr Wages account Cr

May	2	Cash	280				

Dr Sales account Cr

				May	1	Trade receivables	3 790

Dr Purchases account Cr

May	3	Cash	170				
	4	Trade payables	1 200				

Identify the transactions that occurred on 1, 2, 3, 4 and 5 May.

7 Recording a variety of transactions

Salman owns a small retail store. His business's balance on 1 March 2012 was as follows:

Salman
Balance sheet at 1 March 2012

	$		$
ASSETS		CAPITAL	116 000
Premises	120 000		
Vehicle	11 500	LIABILITIES	
Equipment	8 900	Bank loan	30 000
Trade receivables	7 300	Trade payables	8 900
Bank	6 400		
Cash	800		
	154 900		154 900

The following transactions occurred during March:

March
- 3 Paid a trade payable $1700 by cheque
- 4 Cash sales totalled $1470
- 5 Paid cash $800 into the bank account
- 8 Purchased goods for resale on credit, $3200
- 10 Paid insurance by cheque, $420
- 12 Paid wages of shop assistants in cash, $580
- 15 Received cheque from a trade receivable for $2800
- 17 Sold some unwanted equipment valued at $400 and received a cheque for that amount
- 18 Paid loan interest of $120. This amount was transferred from the business bank account
- 19 Salman withdrew cash $250 for private use
- 22 Cash sales totalled $1280
- 24 Purchased some new equipment and paid by cheque, $2800
- 26 Paid wages of shop assistants in cash, $630
- 29 Paid insurance in cash, $180
- 30 Paid vehicle expenses by cheque, $230

Record this information in suitable ledger accounts.

8 Recording a variety of transactions

Nicolette owns a bookshop. Her balance sheet on 1 November 2012 was as follows:

Nicolette
Balance sheet at 1 November 2012

	$		$
ASSETS		CAPITAL	17590
Equipment	9400		
Fittings	8700	LIABILITIES	
Trade receivables	1210	Bank loan	5000
Bank	3760	Trade payables	970
Cash	490		
	23560		23560

The following transactions occurred during November:

Nov
- 1 Cash sales totalled $910
- 2 Paid rent by cheque for the month, $750
- 4 Purchased goods for resale and paid by cheque, $1440
- 5 Paid assistant's wages, $520 in cash
- 8 Purchased some new fittings worth $1300 and paid by cheque
- 11 Made a repayment of the bank loan, $500. The funds were transferred from the business bank account
- 12 Received a cheque from a trade receivable, $480
- 15 Sales totalled $1280 and this was paid into the bank account
- 17 Paid advertising charges, $130 by cheque
- 18 Paid a trade payable, $640 by cheque
- 22 Sales on credit totalled $390
- 23 Paid assistant's wages, $820 in cash
- 24 Sold some unwanted equipment valued at $250 and received a cheque for that amount
- 26 Nicolette withdrew a cheque for $610 for her private use
- 30 Purchased goods for resale on credit, $2080

Record this information in suitable ledger accounts.

5 The trial balance

Introduction

Now that you are used to recording a variety of transactions in ledger accounts, it is time to think about how you can make a quick check to ensure that you have not made a mistake and broken any of the rules of double entry. This quick check is called a trial balance.

As you know, double entry means that for any transaction there has to be a debit entry and a matching credit entry. The trial balance is based on this rule and, in effect, it checks whether the total of debit entries in a set of accounts equals the total of credit entries. So, it is often said that a trial balance checks the arithmetical accuracy of the double entry.

LEARNING OUTCOMES

When you have reached the end of this unit you will be able to:

- prepare a trial balance to check the accuracy of the double-entry records
- explain the uses of a trial balance
- explain some limitations of a trial balance.

KEY TERM

Trial balance: a summary of all the accounts in a business's books of account which provides a check on the accuracy of the double entry.

5.1 How to prepare a trial balance

Illustration 1 The idea behind a trial balance

Here is a very simple set of accounts that have been correctly maintained using the rules of double entry.

Dr — Bank account — Cr

Jan	1	Balance	13 000	Jan	4	Trade payables	2 000
	10	Sales	4 000				

Dr — Capital account — Cr

				Jan	1	Balance	11 000

Dr — Trade payables account — Cr

Jan	3	Bank	2 000	Jan	1	Balance	2 000
					7	Purchases	3 000

Dr — Purchases account — Cr

Jan	7	Purchases	3 000				

Dr — Sales account — Cr

				Jan	10	Sales	4 000

There are very few entries, so it is fairly easy to see that total debit entries are $22 000 and total credit entries are also $22 000. So, because total debit entries equal total credit entries, it appears that the rules of double entry have been followed. You can check the detail in the following table:

Account	Total of debit entries $	Total of credit entries $
Bank	17 000	2 000
Capital	–	11 000
Trade payables	2 000	5 000
Purchases	3 000	–
Sales	–	4 000
Totals	22 000	22 000

A trial balance also provides a quick check on double entry, but it also provides some useful information for those using the accounts. Here is a trial balance based on these accounts:

Trial balance at 10 January 2012

	Dr $	Cr $
Bank	15 000	
Capital		11 000
Trade payables		3 000
Purchases	3 000	
Sales		4 000
	18 000	18 000

Instead of showing total debit entries and total credit entries for each account, a trial balance shows the *net amount* in each account (the net amount is called the balance). So a trial balance can provide users with a quick update of the balance on each account in the system, which is required, for example, when preparing a balance sheet. These benefits are in addition to providing a check on whether the double-entry procedures have been followed correctly.

When is the correct procedure for preparing a trial balance?

A trial balance can be prepared at any time, but usually it is prepared at regular intervals, perhaps monthly. It is always produced at the end of a business's accounting year.

What would happen if there were errors in the double entry?

The totals of a trial balance will only agree if the double entry is correct. In other words, trial balance totals only agree if for each debit entry there has been a matching credit entry.

Illustration 2 How to prepare a trial balance

Step 1: List all of the accounts in the accounting system.

Step 2: Calculate the net value of each account. Do this by adding up and totalling all debit entries and adding up and totalling all credit entries in the account and then find the difference between the two. Here is an example:

Dr			Any account				Cr
May	4	Entry	3 000	May	6	Entry	2 000
	7	Entry	6 000		18	Entry	4 000
	26	Entry	1 000				

In this account:

- total debit entries are $10 000
- total credit entries are $6000.

So, the difference between the two sides is $4000.

Step 3: Record the net amount (the balance) in the trial balance. The amount should be recorded on the debit side in the trial balance if the debit total exceeds the credit total. Alternatively, the amount should be recorded on the credit side of the trial balance if the credit total exceeds the debit total.

In the example, the net amount of $4000 should be recorded in the debit column in the trial balance, because the debit total of $10 000 exceeds the credit total of $6000.

Trial balance at 31 May 2012

	Dr	Cr
	$	$
Any account	4 000	

Step 4: Continue to calculate the balance (net amount) on each account and record the figure as either a debit or a credit in the trial balance. When all of the account details are entered, total the trial balance. If the totals agree, it is assumed that the double entry has been completed correctly.

When trial balance totals do not agree this should instantly alert you to the fact that there is a mistake (or several mistakes) in the double-entry records. Here are some examples of typical errors which will result in a trial balance where the totals do not agree:

- Partial omission: only one part of the double entry has been made.
- Entries do not match: the amount of the debit entry is not the same as the amount of the credit entry.
- Arithmetical error: a mistake is made in calculating the balance of an account and so the wrong amount is entered in the trial balance.

Is the trial balance process reliable?

Unfortunately trial balances do have limitations. It is possible to prepare a trial balance where the totals agree, but with errors in the accounting records. To take a simple example, suppose there was a transaction for the amount of $4500, but in error the amount was misread and a debit entry was made for $5400 and a matching credit entry was made for $5400. The trial balance totals would still agree, although there is a $900 error in two accounts. This is just one of six types of error that are not revealed by a trial balance.

LINKS...
See Unit 22 for more information about errors in accounts and how to correct them.

Summary: where accounts appear in a trial balance

Here is a table that shows where various types of accounts should appear in a trial balance.

Trial balance	
Debit column	**Credit column**
Assets	Capital
Expenses	Liabilities
Purchases	Sales
Drawings	

You can now answer questions 1–8 on pages 34–36.

Unit 5 Practice questions

DEVELOPING YOUR SKILLS

1 Preparing a trial balance from a set of accounts

Here is a completed set of accounts. Prepare a trial balance to check the accuracy of the double entry. Follow the procedure:

- List all of the accounts in a trial balance headed 'At 31 December 2011'.
- Calculate the balance of each account.
- Enter the balance in the appropriate column in the trial balance.

Dr		Furniture account					Cr
Dec	1	Balance	14 500				
	22	Bank	700				

Dr		Trade receivables account					Cr
Dec	1	Balance	3 200	Dec	13	Bank	2 500
	20	Sales	1 900				

Dr		Bank account					Cr
Dec	1	Balance	2 400	Dec	5	Purchases	2 300
	13	Trade receivables	2 500		14	Trade payables	1 200
					22	Furniture	700

Dr		Cash account					Cr
Dec	1	Balance	500	Dec	6	Drawings	300
	8	Sales	1 200		15	Wages	600
					29	Wages	500

Dr		Capital account					Cr
				Dec	1	Balance	17 900

Dr		Trade payables account					Cr
Dec	14	Bank	1 200	Dec	1	Balance	2 700
					11	Purchases	1 800

Dr		Purchases account					Cr
Dec	5	Bank	2 300				
	11	Trade payables	1 800				

Dr		Sales account					Cr
				Dec	8	Cash	1 200
					20	Trade receivables	1 900

Dr		Wages account					Cr
Dec	15	Cash	600				
	29	Cash	500				

Dr		Drawings account					Cr
Dec	6	Cash	300				

2 Preparing a trial balance from a set of accounts

Here is a completed set of accounts. Prepare a trial balance to check the accuracy of the double entry. Follow the procedure:

- List all of the accounts in a trial balance headed 'At 31 January 2012'.
- Calculate the balance of each account.
- Enter the balance in the appropriate column in the trial balance.

Dr		Vehicle account					Cr
Jan	1	Balance	11 400				
	25	Bank	7 500				

Dr		Trade receivables account					Cr
Jan	1	Balance	6 200	Jan	3	Bank	2 900

Dr		Bank account					Cr
Jan	1	Balance	3 700	Jan	8	Bank loan	2 000
	3	Trade receivables	2 900		11	Drawings	800
	20	Sales	5 100		25	Vehicle	7 500
					31	Cash	300

Dr		Cash account					Cr
Jan	1	Balance	400	Jan	18	Rent	900
	7	Sales	1 400		30	Trade payables	700
	31	Bank	300				

Dr		Capital account					Cr
				Jan	1	Balance	10 200

Dr		Trade payables account					Cr
Jan	30	Cash	700	Jan	1	Balance	3 500
					14	Purchases	5 600

Dr		Bank loan account					Cr
Jan	8	Bank	2 000	Jan	1	Balance	8 000

Dr		Purchases account					Cr
Jan	14	Trade payables	5 600				

Dr		Sales account					Cr
				Jan	7	Cash	1 400
					20	Bank	5 100

Dr		Rent account					Cr
Jan	18	Cash	900				

Dr		Drawings account					Cr
Jan	11	Bank	800				

3 Preparing a trial balance from a list of accounts

On 31 December 2012 the owner of a business extracted the following list of balances from the accounting system:

	$
Advertising	600
Bank loan	7 000
Capital	10 500
Cash at bank	1 200
Drawings	2 300
General expenses	700
Purchases	6 100
Sales	8 800
Trade payables	400
Trade receivables	900
Vehicle	14 900

Prepare a trial balance dated 31 December 2012.

4 Preparing a trial balance from a list of accounts

On 31 March 2012 the owner of a business extracted the following list of balances from the accounting system:

	$
Capital	13 700
Cash at bank	600
Cash in hand	100
Drawings	2 200
Electricity	300
Furniture	14 900
Loan interest	500
Purchases	7 700
Salaries	11 200
Sales	22 700
Trade payables	2 500
Trade receivables	1 400

Prepare a trial balance dated 31 March 2012.

5 Redrafting an incorrect trial balance

The following draft trial balance was prepared by an accounts clerk with limited experience. All of the figures are correctly shown, but some of the items have been recorded in the wrong columns and, as a result, the trial balance totals did not agree.

Draft trial balance at 31 May 2012

	Dr $	Cr $
Administration expenses	4 480	
Bank overdraft	660	
Capital		85 770
Cash in hand	140	
Drawings	17 910	
Furniture and equipment		19 300
Premises	80 000	
Purchases		73 820
Sales	136 170	
Trade payables	5 100	
Trade receivables		7 260
Wages and salaries	24 790	
	269 250	186 150

Prepare a new trial balance at 31 May 2012 correcting all of the errors made by the accounts clerk.

6 Redrafting an incorrect trial balance

Kirk prepared the following draft trial balance on 31 August 2012. However, he was not sure in which column to enter some of the account balances and as a result the totals did not agree.

	Dr $	Cr $
Capital	31 300	
Cash at bank	4 950	
Delivery vehicle	22 900	
Drawings	27 480	
Furniture and fittings		14 500
General expenses		16 430
Loan interest		970
Loan (repayable 2014)	17 500	
Purchases	127 810	
Rent	14 460	
Sales		184 360
Trade payables		11 120
Trade receivables	14 780	
	261 180	186 150

Prepare a new trial balance at 31 August 2012 correcting all the errors made by Kirk.

7 Recording transactions and checking the double entry with a trial balance

Wei Xuan owns a business selling fishing equipment. The business's balance sheet on 1 April 2012 was as follows:

Wei Xuan
Balance sheet at 1 April 2012

	$		$
ASSETS		CAPITAL	30 700
Vehicle	14 800		
Equipment	11 200	LIABILITIES	
Trade receivables	4 700	Trade payables	3 600
Bank	3 100		
Cash	500		
	34 300		34 300

During April the following transactions occurred:

April
- 1 Purchased goods for resale on credit, $1100
- 4 Cash sales totalled $1000
- 7 Wei Xuan withdrew cash $200 for private use
- 9 Paid rent by cheque, $700
- 11 Purchased some additional equipment and paid by cheque, $800
- 12 Paid cash into the bank account, $600
- 15 Paid wages in cash, $500
- 18 Received a cheque from a trade receivable for $2700
- 19 Wei Xuan withdrew a cheque for $600 for private use
- 20 Paid trade payables, $2000 by cheque
- 22 Sales on credit totalled $1600
- 25 Cash sales totalled $800
- 28 Paid wages in cash, $900

Record this information in suitable ledger accounts. Prepare a trial balance dated 30 April 2012.

8 Recording transactions and checking the double entry with a trial balance

Aziza owns a health food store. The business's balance sheet on 1 May 2012 was as follows:

Aziza
Balance sheet at 1 May 2012

	$		$
ASSETS		CAPITAL	14 600
Equipment	8 500		
Fittings	7 900	LIABILITIES	
Trade receivables	900	Bank loan	4 000
Bank	2 200	Trade payables	1 700
Cash	800		
	20 300		20 300

During May the following transactions occurred:

May
- 2 Paid wages in cash, $400
- 4 Purchased goods for resale and paid by cheque, $600
- 6 Repaid part of the bank loan $700. Funds were transferred from the business bank account
- 9 Cash sales totalled $1300
- 10 Cash $900 was transferred to the bank account
- 12 Paid loan interest, $300. Funds were transferred from the business bank account
- 13 Trade receivables paid, $700 in cash
- 16 Aziza withdrew cash $500 for her private use
- 19 Paid wages in cash, $600
- 20 Some unwanted equipment worth $1000 was sold for this amount. The cheque was paid into the business's bank account
- 23 Some new fittings were purchased by cheque, $1300
- 29 Sales on credit totalled $1700

Record this information in suitable ledger accounts. Prepare a trial balance dated 31 May 2012.

6 Preparing simple income statements

Introduction

A high priority for the owner of any business will be to make a profit. Making a profit is a mark of success for any business, for not only can the owner feel justified in withdrawing cash from the business for private use, they can also feel that there is the possibility of building up the business over a period of time. In this unit you will learn how to calculate the profit (or loss) made by a business and the accounting records that are required to record this.

What is profit?

A profit occurs when a business makes a net gain in its value over a period of time due to successful trading.

To take a simple example, suppose a business started with just one asset: a bank balance of $10 000. The value of the business at this point would also be $10 000.

If the owner of the business spent $6000 on some goods for resale, and was able to sell all of these goods for $11 000, the business's value would increase by $5000. The business's bank balance would now be $15 000. The business's capital would keep in step with the value of the business and would now also be $15 000. The increase in capital is called **profit** and the profit is reflected in the increase in the value of the business's resources (i.e. its assets).

Of course, business activity is more complicated than in this simple example. For example, no business can operate without payments being made for running costs (expenses).

So, profit is the increase in value of a business caused by trading activity, and it is calculated as follows:

Profit = Sales − (Purchases + Expenses)

LEARNING OUTCOMES

When you have reached the end of this unit you will be able to:

- calculate a business's gross profit and profit
- make entries in the accounts to show a business's gross profit and profit
- make entries in the accounts to show a loss
- prepare simple income statements.

KEY TERM

Profit: the difference between a business's income (sales) and expenditure (purchases and expenses). At one time this final profit figure was called 'net profit'.

LINKS...

In Unit 13 you will find that carrying inventories (i.e. holding quantities of unsold goods) also affects the profit calculation.

6.1 Calculating and recording profits and losses

KEY TERM

Gross profit: the difference between the income from sales and the expenditure on goods sold.

Calculating profits and losses

Here is an illustration showing how profits (or losses) can be calculated. The process involves two stages:

Stage 1: calculating a **gross profit** – the profit made by buying and selling goods.

Stage 2: calculating a profit – the profit made having taken into account the running costs of the business.

Illustration 1 Calculating profits from a simple list of transactions

Andy owns a market stall. His balance sheet on 1 May 2012 was as follows:

Andy
Balance sheet at 1 May 2012

	$		$
ASSETS		CAPITAL	15 000
Vehicle	12 000		
Market stall	5 200	LIABILITIES	
Bank	1 800	Bank loan	4 000
	19 000		19 000

During May the following transactions occurred (all transactions affected the business's bank account):

	$
Purchased goods for resale	4 000
Sales of goods	12 000
Vehicle running costs	500
Wages of assistant	100
Loan interest	200

Step 1: Calculate the difference between sales and purchases to give what is called the 'gross profit'.

	$
Sales	12 000
Less purchases	4 000
Gross profit	8 000

Step 2: Calculate what is called the 'profit' by deducting all of the expenses from the gross profit.

	$
Gross profit	8 000
Less total expenses	800
Profit	7 200

Finally, we will prepare a new balance sheet for Andy's business for the end of May. During May the bank account has changed because of the transactions listed above, and the business has made a profit of $7200. The other asset and liability accounts in this simple example have not changed during May.

The business's bank account for May would be as follows:

Dr		**Bank account**			**Cr**
May	Balance	1800	May	Purchases	4000
	Sales	12000		Vehicle running costs	500
				Wages	100
				Loan interest	200

The updated balance on the bank account is $9000.

Here is the updated balance sheet:

Balance sheet at 31 May 2012

	$		$
ASSETS		CAPITAL	22200
Vehicle	12000		
Market stall	5200	LIABILITIES	
Bank	9000	Bank loan	4000
	26200		26200

Looking at the updated balance sheet confirms:

- the value of the business has increased through successful trading; the assets of the business are now worth more (+$7200)
- the increase in the net value of the business is shown by an increase in the capital of the business (+$7200).

When a profit is made (because the net value of a business increases) the extra value belongs to the owner of the business.

You can now answer questions 1 and 2 on page 45.

How do accounting records show a business's profit (or loss)?

In order to show information about a business's profit (or loss) in the accounting records, it is necessary to prepare an **income statement**. This statement is only prepared at the end of the accounting period, it is not required in the books of account at other times.

KEY TERM

Income statement: an end-of-financial-period statement that shows a business's gross profit and profit for that period (usually a year). (At one time this was known as the trading and profit and loss account.)

6.2 Preparing the first part of the income statement

Here is the story of Andy's business for May 2012 again. This time, however, the transactions are recorded in the ledger accounts.

Here are the ledger accounts for May 2012.

Illustration 2

Dr — Vehicle account — Cr

May	1	Balance	12 000				

Dr — Market stall account — Cr

May	1	Balance	5 200				

Dr — Bank account — Cr

May	1	Balance	1 800	May		Purchases	4 000
		Sales	12 000			Vehicle running costs	500
						Wages	100
						Loan interest	200

Dr — Capital account — Cr

				May	1	Balance	15 000

Dr — Bank loan account — Cr

				May	1	Balance	4 000

Dr — Sales account — Cr

			May	Bank	12 000

Dr — Purchases account — Cr

May	Bank	4 000			

Dr — Vehicle running costs account — Cr

May	Bank	500			

Dr — Wages account — Cr

May	Bank	100			

Dr — Loan interest account — Cr

May	Bank	200			

The business's trial balance at the end of May would be as follows:

Trial balance at 31 May 2012

	Dr $	Cr $
Vehicle	12 000	
Market stall	5 200	
Bank	9 000	
Capital		15 000
Bank loan		4 000
Sales		12 000
Purchases	4 000	
Vehicle running costs	500	
Wages	100	
Loan interest	200	
	31 000	31 000

At the end of the month the first part of the income statement should be prepared to reveal the gross profit.

The income statement would appear as shown. Notice the formal title which includes a clear reference to the time period covered by the income statement.

Dr	Income statement (part 1) for the month ended 31 May 2012		Cr

In order for this account to show the gross profit, it is necessary to transfer information about sales and purchases into the account.

How is total sales transferred to the income statement?

Illustration 3

As you know, there always has to be a debit entry and a credit entry when making entries in accounts. To transfer information about sales, the following entries are necessary:

Debit Sales

Credit Income statement

The accounts will then show the following:

Dr		Sales account					Cr
May	31	Income statement	12 000	May		Bank	12 000

Dr	Income statement for the month ended 31 May 2012		Cr
		Sales	**12 000**

How is total purchases transferred to the income statement?

Using the same process, the entries necessary to transfer information about purchases to the income statement are:

Debit Income statement

Credit Purchases

The accounts will then show the following:

Dr		Purchases account					Cr
May	Bank	4 000	**May**	**31**		**Income statement**	**4 000**

Dr	Income statement for the month ended 31 May 2012		Cr
Purchases	**4 000**	Sales	12 000

Notes:

1 There is no need to use the date columns in the income statement as the date for the entries (31 May) already appears in the title of the account.

2 It is important to notice that the sales account is now empty. There is no balance on the account because the total sales for the month have now been transferred to the income statement.

3 The purchases account is now empty. The purchases account does not have a balance because total purchases have now been transferred to the income statement.

How is gross profit recorded?

If you look at the income statement you will see that the difference between the two sides is the gross profit of $8000. This amount is recorded as a debit entry in the income statement.

Dr	Income statement for the month ended 31 May 2012		Cr
Purchases	4 000	Sales	12 000
Gross profit	**8 000**		
	12 000		12 000

The first section of the income statement is completed by recording a total on both sides of the account. Of course, there has to be a credit entry for this debit of $8000. As you will see in Unit 6.3, this credit entry is made in the second part of the income statement.

6.3

Preparing the second part of the income statement

Where is the credit entry for gross profit?

You will know that having made a debit entry for gross profit, there must be a matching entry in the accounts. The credit entry is made in the second part of the business's income statement as follows:

Dr	Income statement for the month ended 31 May 2012			Cr
Purchases	4000		Sales	12000
Gross profit	8000			
	12000			12000
			Gross profit	**8000**

How are expenses recorded in the second part of the income statement?

Illustration 4

Each expense is transferred to the second part of the income statement.

Here, for example, is the transfer of the vehicle running costs to the income statement.

Dr		Vehicle running costs account				Cr
May	Bank	500	**May**	**31**	**Income statement**	**500**

Dr	Income statement for the month ended 31 May 2012			Cr
Purchases	4000		Sales	12000
Gross profit	8000			
	12000			12000
Vehicle running costs	**500**		Gross profit	8000

The other expenses will also be transferred to the income statement. The accounting records will show:

Dr		Wages account				Cr
May	Bank	100	**May**	**31**	**Income statement**	**100**

Dr		Loan interest account				Cr
May	Bank	200	**May**	**31**	**Income statement**	**200**

Dr	Income statement for the month ended 31 May 2012			Cr
Purchases	4000		Sales	12000
Gross profit	8000			
	12000			12000
Vehicle running costs	500		Gross profit	8000
Wages	**100**			
Loan interest	**200**			

Note: the vehicle running costs account is now empty. The balance of the account has been transferred to the income statement.

How is the profit recorded in the accounts?

Illustration 5

If you look at the second part of the income statement, you will see that the difference between the two sides is the profit of $7200. The profit is recorded as a debit entry in the income statement.

Dr — Income statement for the month ended 31 May 2012 — Cr

Purchases	4 000	Sales	12 000
Gross profit	8 000		
	12 000		12 000
Vehicle running expenses	500	Gross profit	8 000
Wages	100		
Loan interest	200		
Profit for month	**7 200**		

The matching credit entry for the profit is made in the capital account since it represents an increase in the value of the business.

Dr — Capital account — Cr

	May	1	Balance	15 000
		31	**Profit**	**7 200**

The balance sheet for the end of May is shown below. It is important to remember that many of the accounts used during May are empty (i.e. they have no balance), so they do not appear on the balance sheet.

The list of accounts that are now empty (have no balance), and can be ignored when preparing the balance sheet, is as follows:

- Sales
- Purchases
- Vehicle running costs
- Wages
- Loan interest
- Income statement

Here is the balance sheet:

Balance sheet at 31 May 2012

	$		$
ASSETS		CAPITAL	22 200
Vehicle	12 000		
Market stall	5 200	LIABILITIES	
Bank	9 000	Bank loan	4 000
	26 200		26 200

What happens if a business makes a loss?

A loss occurs when a business's expenses are greater than the gross profit made from selling goods. A loss means the business has lost some of its resources (net assets) and that its capital has decreased. A loss will appear as a credit entry in the income statement and will be matched by a debit entry in the capital account.

You can now answer questions 3 and 4 on pages 45–46.

You can now answer questions 5 and 6 on page 46.

Completing the capital account at the end of a financial period

At the end of a financial period – usually every year – the capital account is completed by recording the profit or loss for the year and by transferring the total drawings for the year to the debit side of the account.

Illustration 6 Completing a capital account

On 31 March 2012, the end of a business's financial year, the following information was available:

	$
Capital, 1 April 2011	82 000
Profit for the year	18 900
Total drawings for the year	17 300

The capital and drawings accounts would appear as follows:

Dr — Drawings account — Cr

		Balance	17 300				

Dr — Capital account — Cr

				April	1	Balance	82 000
				March	31	Profit	18 900

At this point the total amount shown in the drawings account would be transferred to the capital account. The double entry required is:

Debit Capital

Credit Drawings

The accounts would now appear as follows:

Dr — Drawings account — Cr

		Balance	17 300	**March**	**31**	**Capital**	**17 300**

Dr — Capital account — Cr

March	**31**	**Drawings**	**17 300**	April	1	Balance	82 000
				March	31	Profit	18 900

Note: after the transfer of the balance of the drawings account, the drawings account would be empty (i.e. it would have no balance).

You can now answer questions 7 and 8 on page 47.

Practice questions

NOTE: It is suggested that simple balance sheets are used when answering questions 1–6 in this unit, in order to reduce the workload involved. It is, however, recommended that the final balance sheet required in questions 7 and 8 should be in classified form to provide further practice in this important technique.

DEVELOPING YOUR SKILLS

1 Calculating gross profit and profit

Stella owns a retail outlet. Her business's balance sheet on 1 February 2012 was as follows:

Balance sheet at 1 February 2012

	$		$
ASSETS		CAPITAL	26 000
Fittings	19 400		
Equipment	6 200	LIABILITIES	
Bank	2 300	Trade payables	1 900
	27 900		27 900

During February the following transactions occurred (all transactions affected the business's bank account):

	$
Purchased goods for resale	7 500
Sales of goods	16 300
Rent	2 500
Wages of assistant	900
Insurance	800

a Calculate the business's gross profit.

b Calculate the business's profit.

c Prepare the business's bank account for February 2012.

d Prepare an update of the business's balance sheet at 28 February 2012.

2 Calculating gross profit and profit

Henri owns a business selling electronic gadgets. His business's balance sheet on 1 June 2012 was as follows:

Balance sheet at 1 June 2012

	$		$
ASSETS		CAPITAL	88 500
Shop premises	92 000		
Vehicle	18 000	LIABILITIES	
Bank	3 500	Bank loan	25 000
	113 500		113 500

During June the following transactions occurred (all transactions affected the business's bank account):

	$
Purchased goods for resale	11 800
Sales of goods	22 500
Wages of shop assistants	4 200
Light and heat	500
Administration expenses	900

a Calculate the business's gross profit.

b Calculate the business's profit.

c Prepare the business's bank account for June 2012.

d Prepare an update of the business's balance sheet at 30 June 2012.

3 Preparing the income statement

Amy owns a café and snack bar. The business's balance sheet on 1 August 2012 was as follows:

Balance sheet at 1 August 2012

	$		$
ASSETS		CAPITAL	23 900
Equipment	11 600		
Furniture	10 500	LIABILITIES	
Bank	2 900	Trade payables	1 100
	25 000		25 000

During August the following transactions occurred (all transactions affected the business's bank account):

	$
Purchased goods for resale	3 200
Sales of goods	9 900
Wages of assistants	800
Rent	700
Light and heat	600

a Calculate the business's gross profit.

b Calculate the business's profit.

c Record the transactions in ledger accounts.

d Prepare the first part of an income statement for the month ended 31 August 2012 by transferring sales and purchases to this account and recording the gross profit on the debit side.

e Complete the first part of the income statement by recording a total on both sides of the statement.

f Prepare the second part of the income statement for the month ended 31 August 2012 by recording gross profit as a credit entry and transferring expenses to this statement.

g Update the capital account with the profit.

h Prepare a balance sheet at 31 August 2012.

4 Preparing the income statement

Monty owns a bakery. The business's balance sheet on 1 September 2012 was as follows:

Balance sheet at 1 September 2012

	$		$
ASSETS		CAPITAL	73 600
Premises	65 000		
Equipment	12 200	LIABILITIES	
Bank	4 400	Bank loan	8 000
	81 600		81 600

During September the following transactions occurred (all transactions affected the business's bank account):

	$
Purchased goods for resale	2 100
Sales of goods	10 300
Insurance	700
Loan interest	200
Wages	1 100

a Calculate the business's gross profit.

b Calculate the business's profit.

c Record the transactions in ledger accounts.

d Prepare the first part of an income statement for the month ended 30 September 2012 by transferring sales and purchases to this account and recording the gross profit on the debit side.

e Complete the first part of the income statement by recording a total on both sides of the statement.

f Prepare the second part of the income statement for the month ended 30 September 2012 by recording gross profit as a credit entry and transferring expenses to this statement.

g Update the capital account with the profit.

h Prepare a balance sheet at 30 September 2012.

5 Preparing the income statement where there is a loss

Winston owns a gift shop. The business's balance sheet on 1 July 2012 was as follows:

Balance sheet at 1 July 2012

	$		$
ASSETS		CAPITAL	13 600
Furniture	11 200		
Equipment	3 200	LIABILITIES	
Bank	1 800	Trade payables	2 600
	16 200		16 200

During July the following transactions occurred (all transactions affected the business's bank account):

	$
Purchased goods for resale	5 300
Sales of goods	7 700
Rent	1 100
Light and heat	600
Wages	1 300

a Calculate the business's gross profit.

b Calculate the business's profit.

c Record the transactions in ledger accounts.

d Prepare the first part of an income statement for the month ended 31 July 2012 by transferring sales and purchases to this account and recording the gross profit on the debit side.

e Complete the first part of the income statement by recording a total on both sides of the statement.

f Prepare the second part of the income statement for the month ended 31 July 2012 by recording gross profit as a credit entry and transferring expenses to this statement.

g Update the capital account with the loss.

h Prepare a balance sheet at 31 July 2012.

6 Preparing the income statement where there is a loss

Cleo owns a business selling sportswear. The business's balance sheet on 1 April 2012 was as follows:

Balance sheet at 1 April 2012

	$		$
ASSETS		CAPITAL	83 700
Premises	105 000		
Equipment	16 000	LIABILITIES	
Bank	2 700	Bank loan	40 000
	123 700		123 700

During July the following transactions occurred (all transactions affected the business's bank account):

	$
Purchased goods for resale	9 200
Sales of goods	12 900
Wages	3 100
Administration expenses	1 300
Loan interest	800

a Calculate the business's gross profit.

b Calculate the business's loss.

c Record the transactions in ledger accounts.

d Prepare the first part of an income statement for the month ended 30 April 2012 by transferring sales and purchases to this account and recording the gross profit on the debit side.

e Complete the first part of the income statement by recording a total on both sides of the statement.

f Prepare the second part of the income statement for the month ended 30 April 2012 by recording gross profit as a credit entry and transferring expenses to this statement.

g Update the capital account with the loss.

h Prepare a balance sheet at 30 April 2012.

7 Preparing a full set of accounts starting from a trial balance

Asif is the owner of a general store. His business has been trading for 11 months and its trial balance at the end of this period is as follows:

Trial balance at 1 December 2012

	Dr $	Cr $
Administration expenses	8250	
Bank	3190	
Bank loan		8000
Capital		31870
Cash	340	
Drawings	21210	
Fittings	8920	
Loan interest	640	
Purchases	83470	
Rent	13230	
Sales		141300
Trade payables		3480
Trade receivables	570	
Vehicle	13500	
Wages	31330	
	184650	184650

During December the following transactions occurred:

Dec 2 Purchased goods for resale and paid by cheque, $2200
3 Cash sales totalled $5220
6 Received cash $330 from a credit customer
8 Paid rent by cheque, $1250
10 Repaid part of bank loan, $500. Funds were transferred from the bank account
13 Sales on credit totalled $210
15 Paid wages in cash, $1620
16 Asif withdrew cash $600 for private use
17 Paid administration expenses in cash, $440
20 Cash sales totalled $3130
22 Paid trade payables, $2600 by cheque
23 Purchased additional fittings and paid by cheque, $970
28 Paid wages in cash, $1880
29 Cash sales totalled $2440
30 Paid cash, $6200 into the bank account

a Prepare ledger accounts to record these transactions.

b Prepare a trial balance at 31 December 2012.

c Prepare an income statement for the year ended 31 December 2012.

d Complete the capital account by transferring the profit and total drawings for the year.

e Prepare a classified balance sheet at 31 December 2012.

8 Preparing a full set of accounts starting from a trial balance

Pat is the owner of a computer software business. Her business has been trading for 11 months and its trial balance at the end of this period is as follows:

Trial balance at 1 March 2012

	Dr $	Cr $
Bank	4530	
Bank loan		24000
Capital		94140
Cash	820	
Drawings	23880	
Equipment	18500	
Insurance	8440	
Loan interest	1850	
Premises	95000	
Purchases	120480	
Sales		216480
Trade payables		7880
Trade receivables	5290	
Vehicle	18400	
Wages	45310	
	342500	342500

During March the following transactions occurred:

March 2 Cash sales totalled $4840
4 Paid wages in cash, $2270
7 Pat withdrew cash $630 for her private use
9 Purchased goods for resale on credit, $3600
11 Repaid part of bank loan, $800. Funds were transferred from the business bank account
14 Sales on credit totalled $4300
16 Paid insurance by cheque, $470

March	17	Purchased some new equipment, $2000 and paid by cheque
	21	Paid loan interest, $140. Funds were transferred from the business bank account
	22	Paid wages in cash, $2490
	23	Cash sales totalled $3990
	24	Transferred cash, $2500 to the bank
	25	Paid trade payables, $4500 by cheque
	28	Sales totalled $3750. All money received was paid into the bank account
	30	Pat withdrew a cheque for $820 for her private use

a Prepare ledger accounts to record these transactions.

b Prepare a trial balance at 31 March 2012.

c Prepare an income statement for the year ended 31 March 2012.

d Complete the capital account by transferring the profit and total drawings for the year.

e Prepare a classified balance sheet at 31 March 2012.

7 Balancing and closing accounts

Introduction

Over a period of time many of the ledger accounts you have been preparing could grow very large. Even the smallest business will have hundreds or possibly thousands of transactions to record over a period of a few months.

In this unit you will learn about **balancing accounts** and **closing accounts**. This process is important because it can benefit by:

- breaking up each record into more manageable segments based on time periods
- bringing many accounts to a neat conclusion with a clear statement or update on the net value shown in the account (the balance)
- bringing other accounts to a neat conclusion by clearly showing that there is no balance and that the account is now closed
- providing a summary of information required for the preparation of the trial balance and other financial statements.

The owner of a business will balance and close accounts at regular intervals. This could be monthly for many accounts, possibly weekly for others. All accounts should be balanced or closed at the end of the financial year.

LEARNING OUTCOMES

When you have reached the end of this unit you will be able to:

- explain why accounts are balanced
- balance ledger accounts
- close accounts that do not have a balance
- prepare accounts that have a running balance.

KEY TERM

Balancing accounts: the process of calculating the net amount left in an account and clearly stating this as a debit or credit balance at the beginning of the next accounting period.

Closing accounts: the process of completing an account that does not have a balance.

7.1 How to balance accounts

Accounts are balanced following a clear set of rules or steps which can be applied to almost every ledger account that has some net value at a particular date.

Illustration 1 Balancing an asset account

Here is a typical set of entries in a bank account:

Dr		Bank account					Cr
Sept	1	Balance	1 800	Sept	6	Purchases	200
	14	Sales	8 000		10	Payables	3 500
	22	Trade receivables	5 300		14	Loan interest	100
					21	Drawings	800
					30	Salaries	4 200

In order to balance the account the following steps are necessary.

Step 1: Calculate the balance. Here the total debit entries are $15 100 and the total credit entries are $8800. So the balance is $6300 (i.e. $15 100 – $8800).

Step 2: Start the balancing process by recording the balance on the side of the account that has the smaller total value. As you would expect with an asset account, the side with the smaller total value in the bank account is the credit side (i.e. the credit total of $8800 is less than the debit total of $15 100).

Dr		Bank account					Cr
Sept	1	Balance	1 800	Sept	6	Purchases	200
	14	Sales	8 000		10	Payables	3 500
	22	Trade receivables	5 300		14	Loan interest	100
					21	Drawings	800
					30	Salaries	4 200
							6 300

Now label this entry with the date (30 September) and the narrative 'Balance c/d'. The abbreviation 'c/d' means 'carry down'.

Dr		Bank account					Cr
Sept	1	Balance	1 800	Sept	6	Purchases	200
	14	Sales	8 000		10	Payables	3 500
	22	Trade receivables	5 300		14	Loan interest	100
					21	Drawings	800
					30	Salaries	4 200
					30	**Balance c/d**	6 300

Step 3: By making the credit entry for $6300, the two sides of the account now total the same amount ($15 100). The next step is to record this total on each side of the account.

Dr		Bank account					Cr
Sept	1	Balance	1 800	Sept	6	Purchases	200
	14	Sales	8 000		10	Payables	3 500
	22	Trade receivables	5 300		14	Loan interest	100
					21	Drawings	800
					30	Salaries	4 200
					30	Balance c/d	6 300
			15 100				**15 100**

You will notice that the totals appear on the same line and that the next available line has been used.

Step 4: As you know, you cannot make a credit entry in the accounts without also having a matching debit entry. So to complete the balancing process, make a matching debit entry in the bank account for the balance. This time label the balance 'b/d' (brought down) and for the date use the first day of the next month (here 1 October).

Dr		Bank account					Cr
Sept	1	Balance	1 800	Sept	6	Purchases	200
	14	Sales	8 000		10	Payables	3 500
	22	Trade receivables	5 300		14	Loan interest	100
					21	Drawings	800
					30	Salaries	4 200
					30	Balance c/d	6 300
			15 100				15 100
Oct	**1**	**Balance b/d**	**6 300**				

You will see that the bank account is now ready for use during October, and that all of September's transactions have been neatly summarised by stating the net value at the end of September.

Illustration 2 Balancing a liability account

Here is a typical liability account.

Dr			Trade payables account				Cr
June	10	Bank	2 400	June	1	Balance	3 300
					22	Purchases	500

Follow the same four steps:

Step 1: The balance on the account is: $3800 – $2400 = $1400

Step 2: The balance c/d (dated 30 June) will appear on the debit side because this is the side with the smaller total value.

Step 3: Record the totals on both sides of the account.

Step 4: Make a matching entry for the balance – in this case a credit entry. The balance b/d should be dated 1 July.

Dr			Trade payables account				Cr
June	10	Bank	2 400	June	1	Balance	3 300
	30	**Balance c/d**	**1 400**		22	Purchases	500
			3 800				**3 800**
				July	**1**	**Balance b/d**	**1 400**

You can now answer questions 1 and 2 on page 55.

Illustration 3 Some more examples of balanced accounts

Balancing a capital account

Before balancing:

Dr			Capital account				Cr
Oct	31	Drawings	21 500	Oct	1	Balance	65 000
					31	Profit	11 500

After balancing:

Dr			Capital account				Cr
Oct	31	Drawings	21 500	Oct	1	Balance	65 000
	31	**Balance c/d**	**55 000**		31	Profit	11 500
			76 500				**76 500**
				Nov	**1**	**Balance b/d**	**55 000**

Balancing an account where entries are all on one side

Before balancing:

Dr			Trade receivables account				Cr
April	1	Balance	6 000				
	13	Sales	2 000				
	27	Sales	1 000				

After balancing:

Dr			Trade receivables account				Cr
April	1	Balance	6 000	April	30	Balance c/d	9 000
	13	Sales	2 000				
	27	Sales	1 000				
			9 000				**9 000**
May	**1**	**Balance b/d**	**9 000**				

Sometimes accounts have entries that are all on one side. Here the only transactions affecting trade receivables have been additional sales on credit. You notice that the step-by-step balancing technique can be followed in the same way as in all the previous examples.

Accounts where there is only one entry

Before balancing:

Dr			Vehicles account				Cr
March	1	Balance	24 500				

After balancing:

Dr			Vehicles account				Cr
March	1	Balance	24 500				

Nothing needs to be done with an account with just one entry. Some accounts rarely have entries made in them. Do not be tempted to waste time balancing an account with just one entry – you will only end up where you started.

7.2 How to close accounts

Many accounts do not have a balance at the end of an accounting period. This is often because the contents of the account have been transferred elsewhere. In Unit 6 you will remember that accounts such as those for sales, expenses and drawings were emptied at the year end by transferring their contents to the income statement or capital account.

Where accounts have no balance, all that is necessary is to record a total at the end of the accounting period. Here are some examples.

Illustration 4 Closing accounts at the end of the financial period

Closing a sales account

Before closing:

Sales account (Dr / Cr)

Dr				Cr			
Dec	31	Income statement	9 200	Dec	3	Cash	2 100
					5	Trade receivables	600
					17	Cash	3 800
					30	Cash	2 700

After closing:

Sales account (Dr / Cr)

Dr				Cr			
Dec	31	Income statement	9 200	Dec	3	Cash	2 100
					5	Trade receivables	600
					17	Cash	3 800
					30	Cash	2 700
			9 200				**9 200**

Closing a drawings account

Before closing:

Drawings account (Dr / Cr)

Dr				Cr			
Jan	1	Bank	600	Jan	31	Capital	2 000
	8	Cash	300				
	22	Bank	1 100				

After closing:

Drawings account (Dr / Cr)

Dr				Cr			
Jan	1	Bank	600	Jan	31	Capital	2 000
	8	Cash	300				
	22	Bank	1 100				
			2 000				2 000

Closing an expense account

Before closing:

Wages account (Dr / Cr)

Dr				Cr			
May	14	Cash	750	May	31	Income statement	1 500
	28	Cash	750				

After closing:

Wages account (Dr / Cr)

Dr				Cr			
May	14	Cash	750	May	31	Income statement	1 500
	28	Cash	750				
			1 500				1 500

Closing an asset account with no balance

Before closing:

Trade receivables account (Dr / Cr)

Dr				Cr			
Aug	1	Balance	2 400	Aug	21	Bank	3 600
	11	Sales	1 200				

You will notice that the trade receivables have paid all that they owed, so the account has no balance.

After closing:

Trade receivables account (Dr / Cr)

Dr				Cr			
Aug	1	Balance	2 400	Aug	21	Bank	3 600
	11	Sales	1 200				
			3 600				3 600

Closing an account with just one entry on each side

Here is an account with just one entry on each side and no balance.

Before closing:

Dr			Insurance account				Cr
Nov	12	Bank	1 600	Nov	30	Income statement	1 600

In this situation, it is unnecessary to record the total (which is, of course, the same as the amount of the entries). To show that the account is closed, just show total lines.

After closing:

Dr			Insurance account				Cr
Nov	12	Bank	1 600	Nov	30	Income statement	1 600

Preparing accounts with running balances

By now you will be very familiar with two-sided ledger accounts. However, you have probably noticed that electronic accounting software packages do not use this particular format. All accounting systems follow the rules you have been learning for double entry, but they use a layout for an account which includes a debit column, credit column and a column to record the balance which is updated after every transaction.

Here is an example showing both the familiar two-sided ledger account and the format that shows a running balance.

You can now answer questions 3 and 4 on page 55.

DID YOU KNOW?

The running balance format for ledger accounts is also used in some manual systems.

Illustration 5 Preparing an account with a running balance

The following two-sided ledger account appeared in a business's books of account:

Dr			Bank account				Cr
Feb	1	Balance	750	Feb	6	Rent	340
	12	Cash	1 060		14	Insurance	270
	26	Trade receivables	880		18	Payable	190
					24	Drawings	320
					27	Salaries	650
					28	Balance c/d	920
			2 690				2 690
Mar	1	Balance b/d	920				

Overleaf is the same account, but shown as it would appear using an electronic system.

STUDY TIP

In examination questions you will find that accounts are normally presented in the T account style.

When answering examination questions, however, examiners recognise that candidates may have become accustomed to using either version of ledger accounts (i.e. T account format or running balance format), so answers can be produced in whichever format you prefer.

You can now answer questions 5–8 on pages 55–56.

Bank account						
Date		*Details*	*Dr*	*Cr*	*Balance*	
			$	$	$	
Feb	1	Balance			750	Dr
	6	Rent		340	410	Dr
	12	Cash	1 060		1 470	Dr
	14	Insurance		270	1 200	Dr
	18	Payable		190	1 010	Dr
	24	Drawings		320	690	Dr
	26	Trade receivables	880		1 570	Dr
	27	Salaries		650	920	Dr

Notice that the transactions are recorded in date order and the entries are made as before in the debit or credit columns as appropriate. However, after each transaction the balance is updated and clearly labelled either Dr or Cr. Here the balance is labelled Dr to signify that the account has a debit balance throughout the month. The abbreviations b/d and c/d are not required with the running balance format.

An accounting software package will, of course, automatically calculate the balance after each transaction is entered. You could use this layout for your manual accounts, but this means you will have to calculate the balance after each transaction.

Summary: The rules for balancing and closing accounts

Balancing accounts		Closing accounts	
Accounts with at least two entries	**Accounts with just one entry**	**Several entries on either side**	**Just one entry on each side**
Step 1 Calculate balance	Do not balance	Record totals	Record total lines
Step 2 Record balance on side with smaller total			
Step 3 Record totals			
Step 4 Bring balance down with a matching entry			

You can now answer questions 9–28 on pages 57–60.

Unit 7 Practice questions

DEVELOPING YOUR SKILLS

1 Balancing various accounts

Make a copy of the following accounts.

Dr — Cash account — Cr

Aug	1	Balance	370	Aug	12	Purchases	120
	14	Sales	130		28	Drawings	210

Dr — Capital account — Cr

Aug	31	Drawings	11 900	Aug	1	Balance	39 400
					31	Profit	18 400

Dr — Premises account — Cr

Aug	1	Balance	74 000				

Dr — Trade payables account — Cr

				Aug	1	Balance	2 100
					11	Purchases	800
					25	Purchases	1 300

Balance each account as appropriate.

2 Balancing various accounts

Make a copy of the following accounts.

Dr — Bank account — Cr

Jan	1	Balance	3 240	Jan	8	Rent	1 050
	15	Cash	620		14	Drawings	450
	28	Cash	290		29	Salaries	2 140

Dr — Capital account — Cr

Jan	31	Drawings	3 870	Jan	1	Balance	62 100
					31	Profit	15 080

Dr — Fittings account — Cr

Jan	1	Balance	14 900				

Dr — Equipment account — Cr

Jan	1	Balance	4 980				
	18	Bank	3 070				

Balance each account as appropriate.

3 Closing accounts

Make a copy of the following accounts.

Dr — Purchases account — Cr

Oct	14	Bank	3 820	Oct	31	Income statement	5 910
	29	Trade payables	2 090				

Dr — Sales account — Cr

Oct	31	Income statement	7 070	Oct	5	Cash	1 250
					11	Bank	3 780
					25	Trade receivables	2 040

Dr — Rent account — Cr

Oct	11	Bank	3 750	Oct	31	Income statement	3 750

Dr — Drawings account — Cr

Oct	15	Bank	1 980	Oct	31	Capital	1 980

Dr — Income statement for the month ended 31 October 2012 — Cr

Purchases	5 910	Sales	7 070
Gross profit	1 160		

Close each account.

4 Closing accounts

Make a copy of the following accounts.

Dr — Sales account — Cr

April	30	Income statement	5 810	April	7	Bank	3 720
					14	Trade receivables	2 090

Dr — Wages account — Cr

April	14	Cash	2 640	April	30	Income statement	4 910
	28	Cash	2 270				

Dr — General expenses account — Cr

April	6	Bank	320	April	30	Income statement	410
	18	Cash	90				

Dr — Insurance account — Cr

April	17	Bank	560	April	30	Income statement	560

Dr — Income statement for the month ended 30 April 2012 — Cr

Wages	4 910	Gross profit	12 880
General expenses	410		
Insurance	560		
Profit	7 000		

Close each account.

5 Calculating running balances

Here is a credit customer's account taken from the books of a business. The format used has been designed to show a running balance.

Trade receivables account						
Date		*Details*	*Dr*	*Cr*	*Balance*	
			$	$	$	
June	1	Balance			4800	Dr
	11	Sales	3450			
	17	Bank		3600		
	24	Sales	1400			
	30	Bank		2900		

Complete both parts of the balance column for each of the transactions.

6 Calculating running balances

Here is a credit supplier's account taken from the books of a business. The format used has been designed to show a running balance.

Trade payables account						
Date		*Details*	*Dr*	*Cr*	*Balance*	
			$	$	$	
Aug	1	Balance			2700	Cr
	5	Purchases		7400		
	11	Purchases		1200		
	18	Bank	6300			
	24	Bank	3500			

Complete both parts of the balance column for each of the transactions.

7 Preparing accounts with running balances

Here is a cash account, a credit supplier's account and a capital account taken from the books of a business. They are shown in the familiar two-sided form.

Cash account

Dr				Cr			
May	1	Balance	630	May	8	Office expenses	170
	22	Sales	1050		17	Drawings	80
					22	Bank	1200
					31	Balance c/d	230
			1680				1680
June	1	Balance b/d	230				

Trade payables account

Dr				Cr			
May	25	Bank	2300	May	1	Balance	1820
	31	Balance c/d	960		17	Purchases	1440
			3260				3260
				June	1	Balance b/d	960

Capital account

Dr				Cr			
May	31	Drawings	22300	May	1	Balance	85400
	31	Loss for year	14800				
	31	Balance c/d	48300				
			85400				85400
				June	1	Balance b/d	48300

Prepare new versions of each of these accounts using the running balance format.

8 Preparing accounts with running balances

Following is a bank account, a customer's account and a bank loan account taken from the books of a business. They are shown in the familiar two-sided form.

Bank account

Dr				Cr			
Sept	1	Balance	1420	Sept	8	Rent	520
	11	Trade receivables	1600		10	Loan	600
	15	Loan	3000		27	Purchases	1580
					30	Balance c/d	3320
			6020				6020
Oct	1	Balance b/d	3320				

Trade receivables account

Dr				Cr			
Sept	1	Balance	1420	Sept	11	Bank	1600
	10	Sales	980		30	Balance c/d	3800
	24	Sales	3000				
			5400				5400
Oct	1	Balance b/d	3800				

Bank loan account

Dr				Cr			
Sept	10	Bank	600	Sept	1	Balance	10000
	30	Balance c/d	12400		15	Bank	3000
			13000				13000
				June	1	Balance b/d	12400

Prepare new versions of each of these accounts using the running balance format.

9 Preparing a set of accounts and balancing and closing the accounts at the end of the accounting period

Mike is the owner of a business that sells furniture. His business's trial balance on 30 November 2012 was as follows:

Trial balance at 30 November 2012

	Dr	Cr
	$	$
Bank	2 040	
Capital		124 650
Cash	310	
Drawings	17 490	
Equipment	12 200	
General expenses	2 080	
Insurance	3 650	
Premises	88 000	
Purchases	142 300	
Sales		238 560
Trade payables		5 840
Trade receivables	3 140	
Vehicle	31 000	
Wages	66 840	
	369 050	369 050

During December the following transactions occurred:

Dec 1 Sales on credit totalled $4560
5 Paid trade payables $5840 by cheque
8 Received cheques from trade receivables, $6400
14 Purchased goods for resale and paid by cheque, $1290
18 Purchased some additional equipment and paid by cheque, $860
22 Cash sales totalled $2180
23 Paid wages in cash, $1450
28 Mike withdrew cash for private use, $290

a Open accounts for each item listed in the trial balance on 30 November 2012.

b Record the transactions for December 2012.

c Prepare a trial balance at 31 December 2012.

d Prepare an income statement for the year ended 31 December 2012.

e Complete the capital account by transferring the profit and total drawings for the year.

f Complete the ledger accounts by closing or balancing accounts.

g Prepare a classified balance sheet at 31 December 2012.

10 Preparing a set of accounts and balancing and closing the accounts at the end of the accounting period.

Linda is the owner of business that sells household equipment. Her business's trial balance on 30 April 2012 was as follows:

Trial balance at 30 April 2012

	Dr	Cr
	$	$
Bank	1 720	
Bank loan		8 000
Capital		62 810
Cash	690	
Drawings	23 460	
Furniture	18 500	
Light and heat	890	
Loan interest	430	
Premises	67 500	
Purchases	102 480	
Sales		184 360
Trade payables		3 210
Trade receivables	1 490	
Wages	41 220	
	258 380	258 380

During May the following transactions occurred:

May 4 Paid loan interest, $70. Funds were transferred from the bank account
5 Received cheques from trade receivables totalling $1490
8 Purchased goods for resale on credit, $950
14 Linda withdrew a cheque, $380, for private use
18 Purchased some additional furniture and paid by cheque, $1300
22 Cash sales totalled $3130
23 Paid wages in cash, $870
28 Borrowed an additional $5 000 from the bank. Funds were transferred into the bank account

a Open accounts for each item listed in the trial balance at 30 April 2012.

b Record the transactions for May 2012.

c Prepare a trial balance at 31 May 2012.

d Prepare an income statement for the year ended 31 May 2012.

e Complete the capital account by transferring the profit and total drawings for the year.

f Complete the ledger accounts by closing or balancing accounts.

g Prepare a classified balance sheet at 31 May 2012.

(The following questions cover Units 1–7.)

MULTIPLE-CHOICE QUESTIONS

11 Which of the following would provide the owner of a business with a statement of the business's financial position?

A Balance sheet
B Bank account
C Capital account
D Income statement

12 Which of the following contains only assets?

A Bank loan, equipment, trade receivables, vehicles
B Bank overdraft, equipment, machinery, trade payables
C Cash, equipment, machinery, trade receivables
D Cash, fixtures, furniture, trade payables

13 The following balances appear in the accounts of a retailer.

	$
Bank loan	8 000
Cash at bank	3 100
Trade payables	800
Trade receivables	1 400
Vehicle	18 200

What is the owner's capital?

A $12 700
B $13 900
C $15 500
D $31 500

14 The accounts of a retailer include an amount for cash drawings.

How will drawings affect the profit, current assets and capital?

	Profit	Current assets	Capital
A	Decrease	Increase	Decrease
B	Decrease	No effect	Increase
C	Increase	Decrease	No effect
D	No effect	Decrease	Decrease

15 Kwame prepares a trial balance for his business's accounts every month. Why should he prepare a trial balance?

A To balance all the ledger accounts.
B To calculate the monthly figure for profit.
C To check if any transactions have been omitted.
D To check the arithmetical accuracy of the accounting records.

16 Martha purchased goods from Jacob. How should this transaction be recorded in Jacob's books of account?

	Account to be debited	Account to be credited
A	Purchases	Martha
B	Martha	Sales
C	Martha	Purchases
D	Sales	Martha

17 On 1 March 2012 trade receivables totalled $2700. During March credit sales totalled $1200 and $700 was paid by credit customers. What was the total of trade receivables at 31 March 2012?

A $800
B $2 200
C $3 200
D $4 600

18 Stella owns a grocery store. Recently she purchased a delivery van for use by her business and paid by cheque. How should this transaction be recorded in her business's accounts?

	Account to be debited	Account to be credited
A	Bank	Vehicles
B	Purchases	Vehicles
C	Vehicles	Bank
D	Vehicles	Purchases

19 Which of the following accounts should be entered in the debit column of a trial balance?

A Capital
B Drawings
C Sales
D Trade payables

20 Which of the following accounts should be entered in the credit column of a trial balance?

A Cash
B Purchases
C Sales
D Wages

OTHER QUESTIONS

21 Mustafa opened his hotel business on 1 March 2012 by paying $70 000 into a business bank account.

a Name the account that should be credited with this transaction.

Since 1 March, Mustafa has purchased many non-current assets for his business.

b State what is meant by the term 'non-current asset'.

c Give **three** examples of non-current assets that Mustafa is likely to have purchased for his hotel business.

Mustafa prepared a trial balance on 31 August 2012. However, the totals of this trial balance did not agree.

d Explain **one** possible reason why the totals of this trial balance did not agree.

e Mustafa was not sure of the double entry for the following transactions. Complete the table below to show the account that should be debited and the account that should be credited for each transaction.

	Transaction	Account to be debited	Account to be credited
1	Paid for some stationery for office use in cash		
2	A hotel guest paid by cheque		
3	Mustafa withdrew a cheque for private use		
4	A supplier had been overpaid and sent Mustafa a cheque as a refund		
5	Mustafa made a gift of $50 to a friend using the business's cash		

22 Cherry recently opened a business selling sports equipment. On the first day of trading, 1 September 2012, the business had the following assets and liabilities:

	$
Bank loan (repayable 2016)	30 000
Cash at bank	3 000
Equipment	8 000
Inventory	14 000
Shop fittings and fixtures	12 000
Shop premises	220 000
Trade payables	9 000

a State what is meant by the term 'non-current liability'.

b Calculate the business's capital on 1 September 2012.

c Prepare the business's classified balance sheet at 1 September 2012.

23 Farad owns a furniture store. He purchases most goods for resale on credit (i.e. he uses credit to buy the goods that he resells). The following information about trade payables is available for the months of August and September 2012.

		$
August	Opening balance	11 900
	Purchases on credit	7 300
	Payments to suppliers	15 300
September	Purchases on credit	9 300
	Payments to suppliers	13 200

a State one advantage to Farad of using credit to buy goods for resale.

b Prepare the trade payables account in Farad's books of account for each of the months of August and September 2012.

Where a traditional T account is used, it should be balanced at the end of August and again at the end of September. Where the three-column running balance method is used, the balance should be updated after each entry.

c State **one** advantage of balancing ledger accounts.

24 Kalpna owns a taxi business. She has recently prepared an income statement for the year ended 30 April 2012.

a List **four** typical expenses for a taxi business that are likely to have appeared in Kalpna's income statement.

Kalpna was not sure why drawings should not be included in the income statement.

b Explain why drawings are not included in a business's income statement.

25 Kwasi owns a convenience store. Recently he completed the business's income statement for the year ended 29 February 2012.

a Complete the following table to show the account that should be debited and the account that should be credited when preparing an income statement.

		Account to be debited	Account to be credited
1	Transferred purchases for the year to the income statement		
2	Transferred sales for the year to the income statement		
3	Transferred total wages for the year to the income statement		
4	Recorded a loss for the year		

Although Kwasi's business made a large gross profit, the income statement for the year ended 29 February 2012 showed a loss had been made.

b Explain how a business can make a large gross profit but still make a loss for the year.

26 Tony, the owner of a grocery store, is not very experienced at keeping accounting records. Recently he made the following entries in his business's accounts. Some of the entries he made were incorrect.

Check the entries made by Tony in the following table. Complete the final column, indicating for each transaction whether you think the entries were correct (✓) or incorrect (✗).

	Transaction	Account debited	Account credited	Indicate: ✓ if correct ✗ if incorrect
a	Paid wages in cash	Wages	Cash	
b	Sold some unwanted shop fittings for cash	Cash	Shop fittings	
c	Purchased goods for resale on credit	Purchases	Bank	
d	Tony withdrew cheque for own use	Bank	Drawings	
e	Sold goods for cash	Cash	Sales	
f	Paid a credit supplier by cheque	Trade payables	Bank	
g	Purchased some equipment for office use by cheque	Purchases	Bank	

27 Ahmad prepared the following trial balance. However, he made some mistakes when entering ledger account balances in the debit and credit columns. Check the trial balance and indicate whether or not you think the entries were correct (✓) or incorrect (✗).

Trial balance at 31 March 2012			
	Dr	Cr	Indicate: ✓ if correct ✗ if incorrect
	$	$	
Bank overdraft	750		
Bank loan		2 100	
Capital	18 020		
Drawings		12 960	
General expenses		6 180	
Non-current assets	22 500		
Purchases		31 640	
Sales	49 930		
Trade payables	2 480		
	93 680	52 880	

28 Salma was preparing her business's trial balance at 31 December 2012. She has almost finished this task, but still has to record the following account balances:

	$
Capital	145 000
Drawings	18 300
Purchases	92 400
Sales	161 900
Trade payables	8 100
Trade receivables	6 200

a Complete Salma's trial balance by entering the account balances in the correct column. Total the trial balance columns.

Trial balance at 31 December 2012

	Dr	Cr
	$	$
Total of entries made by Salma	236 600	44 300
Capital		
Drawings		
Purchases		
Sales		
Trade payables		
Trade receivables		

b Explain to Salma what the totals of the trial balance reveal.

c Salma finds preparing trial balances useful as a check on the arithmetical accuracy of her ledger accounts. State **one** other advantage of preparing trial balances.

8 Books of prime entry: the purchases and sales journals

Introduction

At this stage in your study of accounting, you will be familiar with:

- recording a range of transactions in ledger accounts
- producing a trial balance to check the accuracy of your recordkeeping
- preparing end-of-year income statements to show the gross profit and profit made by the business
- preparing an end-of-year balance sheet which summarises the business's assets, liabilities and capital at that date.

In this unit the accounting system is going to be extended to take account of the following developments:

- Details about accounting transactions are found on what are called 'source documents'. The first of a series of source documents will be introduced in this unit.
- Before entries are made in ledger accounts for individual transactions, there is a preliminary stage where the key facts about transactions are recorded first in what are called **books of prime entry** or sometimes books of original entry. In this unit you will be introduced to two of these books of prime entry. (There are seven books of prime entry in total.)
- Instead of having just one account to record transactions affecting trade payables, from now on each credit supplier will have a personal account. These personal accounts, one for each trade payable, will be collected together and kept in a 'purchases ledger'.
- A similar process will apply to credit customers. There will be a separate account for each trade receivable, and these individual accounts will be collected together and kept in a 'sales ledger'.
- Finally, it is possible for substantial reductions to be made in the price of products being purchased and sold by businesses where certain conditions are met. You will be shown how to calculate and record this reduction in prices, which is called a 'trade discount'.

LEARNING OUTCOMES

When you have reached the end of this unit you will be able to:

- explain what is meant by the term 'source document'
- identify the source documents used when recording credit purchases and credit sales
- prepare a purchases journal and a sales journal
- post the details recorded in the two journals to accounts in the general, purchases and sales ledgers
- explain what is meant by the term 'trade discount'
- prepare accounting records based on source documents that include a trade discount.

DID YOU KNOW?

The seven books of prime entry are as follows.

- Purchases journal
- Sales journal
- Purchases returns journal (see Unit 9)
- Sales returns journal (see Unit 9)
- Cash book (see Unit 10)
- Petty cash book (see Unit 11)
- General journal (see Unit 12)

KEY TERM

Books of prime entry: this is where transactions are listed prior to being posted to the double-entry records. Sometimes referred to as subsidiary books.

8.1 Source documents and credit purchases

KEY TERM

Source documents: written documents that provide information from which accounting records can be prepared. They provide evidence that particular transactions took place.

Purchase invoice: the source document that provides information about goods purchased on credit and the amount due.

DID YOU KNOW?

Invoices contain a considerable amount of additional information which is likely to be of value to the business, though this information will not normally be required for the accounting records. Examples include:

- the address of the supplier and/or customer
- purchase order references
- contact names.

What are source documents?

So far you have been used to preparing accounting records from a list of transactions presented in date order. However, in reality, whoever prepares the accounting records of a business relies on the information shown on documents – known as **source documents** – rather than in a neat list of transactions.

These documents are received from, or sent out to, other businesses and organisations. Each document is used as a source of information. As each document is received or issued by the business, the bookkeeper or accounts clerk extracts whatever details are needed for the accounting records.

Illustration 1 Source document for credit purchases

Whenever a business purchases goods for resale on credit, as well as taking delivery of the goods, it will receive a document from the supplier called a **purchase invoice**. Here is an example of a purchase invoice.

No. J3082

PURCHASE INVOICE

West Bay Supplies

To: Kingford Stores

Date: 14 June 2012

Quantity	*Description*	*Unit price* $	*Total* $
40 packets	Kitchen roll	1.20	48.00
15 cartons	Tastie snacks	2.80	42.00
20 tins	Supa cookies	0.90	18.00
		TOTAL AMOUNT DUE	108.00

Terms: Payment within 30 days

This document tells you that:

- Kingford Stores has purchased goods from a supplier, West Bay Supplies
- the transaction is dated 14 June 2012
- the total amount due for the goods received is $108.

These are the key facts that Kingford Stores' bookkeeper will need to know in order to update the business's accounting records.

The purchase invoice also has a number (J3082) which could be useful in identifying this particular document.

At the end of the invoice there is a reference to 'terms'. These are the conditions for payment. In other words the supplier expects Kingford Stores to pay this invoice within 30 days (i.e. before 14 July 2012). The owner of Kingford Stores will need to be aware of this information to ensure that payment is made by this date, or risk upsetting an important supplier.

KEY TERM

Purchases journal: the book of prime entry used to record purchases of goods on credit. The information required to prepare this journal is taken from purchase invoices.

Recording credit purchases in a purchases journal

As purchase invoices are received, the following important information is recorded first in what is called a **purchases journal**:

- Date
- Name of supplier
- Invoice number
- Amount due

Illustration 2 Recording purchase invoices in a purchases journal

Elizabeth owns a hardware store. During April 2012 she received the following purchase invoices from her suppliers for goods for resale.

April	7	Invoice 2845	Purchase invoice received from Bell Ltd for goods $785
	11	Invoice 3901	Purchase invoice received from R Khan for goods $1450
	22	Invoice 0783	Purchase invoice received from Aldo Ltd for goods $2440
	29	Invoice 0442	Purchase invoice received from L Samson for goods $635

As each invoice is received the following entries would be made in the purchases journal:

Purchases journal

Date		*Supplier*	*Invoice number*	*$*
April	7	Bell Ltd	2845	785
	11	R Khan	3901	1 450
	22	Aldo Ltd	0783	2 440
	29	L Sampson	0442	635
		Total purchases		5 310

Notes:

1 The purchases journal is just a listing of important information shown on individual invoices.

2 The purchases journal is *not* part of the double-entry records.

3 The purchases journal only contains information about credit purchases of goods for resale. It does not include information about cash purchases or about the purchase of non-current assets.

4 The details should be recorded in strict date order.

5 The purchases journal should be totalled at agreed intervals (e.g. monthly), but this could be more frequent if there is a large volume of transactions.

STUDY TIP

Do not forget that the purchases journal is only used to record credit purchases of goods for resale. It is easy to enter cash purchases or the purchase of a fixed asset in the purchases journal by mistake.

DID YOU KNOW?

E&OE: some invoices show this abbreviation at the end of the document. You may be wondering what it stands for. It means 'errors and omissions excepted'. In other words, if a mistake has been made in preparing the invoice, the business sending the invoice has the right to make a correction.

8.2 Posting the purchases journal

KEY TERM

Purchases ledger: a part of the double-entry system that is used to keep the personal accounts of trade payables.

General ledger: a part of the double-entry system that is used to keep all of the accounts, other than those for trade payables (kept in the purchases ledger) and trade receivables (kept in the sales ledger).

Posting credit purchases of goods for resale

The correct double entry for the purchase of goods for resale on credit is:

Debit Purchases

Credit Trade payables

This rule still applies. However, instead of having just one account for trade payables, each supplier will be given their own account. It is important that the owner of the business knows how much is owed to each trade payable, not just the total amount owing to all suppliers. The accounts of trade payables are normally maintained in a separate ledger called the **purchases ledger**.

Instead of making a separate debit entry in the purchases account for each transaction, it is usual to make use of the total shown at the end of the purchases journal and update the purchases account with credit purchases say once a month.

The purchases account (along with all the other accounts except trade receivables and trade payables accounts) will be found in what is called the **general ledger**.

The information to make these entries will be taken from the purchases journal. This process is often called 'posting the purchases journal'.

Illustration 3 Posting a purchases journal

Here is the purchases journal again, followed by the ledger accounts to which the information has now been posted.

Purchases journal

Date		*Supplier*	*Invoice number*	*$*
April	7	Bell Ltd	2845	785
	11	R Khan	3901	1450
	22	Aldo Ltd	0783	2440
	29	L Sampson	0442	635
		Total purchases		5310

Following are the double-entry records for these purchases on credit.

PURCHASES LEDGER

Dr			Bell Ltd account				Cr
				April	7	Purchases	785

Dr			R Khan account				Cr
				April	11	Purchases	1450

Dr			Aldo Ltd account				Cr
				April	22	Purchases	2440

Dr			L Sampson account				Cr
				April	29	Purchases	635

GENERAL LEDGER

Dr			Purchases account				Cr
April	30	Purchases journal	5310				

Notes:

1 The posting to each trade payable account should be made as soon as possible after the purchase invoice has been listed in the purchases journal. This will ensure that the owner has up-to-date information about how much is owed to each trade payable.

2 The single entry in the purchases account matches the four individual credit entries. The usual narrative used is 'purchases journal'.

DID YOU KNOW?

All invoices (and other source documents) must be kept carefully by a business and stored in such a way that any individual source document can be found easily. Source documents are the proof that a transaction took place, so they might be required at any time to justify an entry in the accounting system.

Now you can answer questions 1 and 2 on page 71.

8.3 Recording credit sales

KEY TERM

Sales invoice: the source document that provides information about goods sold on credit and the amount due.

Sales journal: the book of prime entry used to record sales of goods on credit. The information required to prepare this book of prime entry is taken from sales invoices.

Sales ledger: a part of the double-entry system that is used to keep the personal accounts of trade receivables.

Processing credit sales

When a business sells goods on credit it will issue an invoice to the customer. The business will keep a copy of this source document – a **sales invoice** – which can then be used to make entries in its books of account in the following sequence:

Step 1: Key details from the sales invoice will be recorded in the **sales journal**.

Step 2: An account for the trade receivable will be opened in the **sales ledger** and a debit entry made to record the amount the customer owes.

Step 3: At regular intervals (usually monthly) the total of the sales journal will be credited to the sales account which is kept in the general ledger.

You will notice that this new process still has the same basic double entry for a credit sale that you have been using in previous units:

Debit Trade receivables

Credit Sales

Illustration 4 Recording credit sales

Jamie owns a furniture store. During March 2012 he issued the following invoices to credit customers:

March 3 Invoice 377 Sales invoice sent to Batfo Ltd for $1080
14 Invoice 378 Sales invoice sent to H Denman for $740
18 Invoice 379 Sales invoice sent to Jakex Ltd for $2320
22 Invoice 380 Sales invoice sent to Quilfon Ltd for $1440

As these invoices are issued the following record should be made in the sales journal:

Sales journal

Date		*Supplier*	*Invoice number*	*$*
March	3	Batfo Ltd	377	1 080
	14	H Denman	378	740
	18	Jakex Ltd	379	2 320
	22	Quilfon Ltd	380	1 440
		Total sales		5 580

Each entry in the sales journal should be posted immediately to an individual account for each trade receivable in the sales ledger. The owner of the business will want to have up-to-date information about how much is owed by each individual customer.

By the end of March the following entries should have been made:

SALES LEDGER

Dr		**Batfo Ltd account**		Cr
March	3	Sales	1 080	

Dr		**H Denman account**		Cr
March	14	Sales	740	

Dr		**Jakex Ltd account**		Cr
March	18	Sales	2 320	

Dr		**Quilfon Ltd account**		Cr
March	22	Sales	1 440	

At the end of the month the sales account should be updated with just one total entry to match these four debit entries. This requires the posting of the total of the sales journal.

GENERAL LEDGER

Dr		Sales account			Cr
		March	3	Sales journal	5 580

Notes:

1 The sales journal is *not* part of the double-entry records.

2 The sales journal only contains information about credit sales. It does not include information about cash sales or about the sale of non-current assets.

3 The details should be recorded in strict date order.

STUDY TIP

The sales journal is only used to record sales of goods on credit. Do not be tempted to include cash sales or the sales of non-current assets in this book of prime entry.

Now you can answer questions 3 and 4 on page 71.

NUMERACY SKILLS

Working with percentages

In 8.4 below you are going to prepare accounting records when there has been a trade discount. These discounts are normally given as percentages, so you may like to remind yourself how to work with percentages.

You will probably remember that 1 per cent means one in every hundred. So fractions and decimals can also be expressed as percentages.

$1\% = \frac{1}{100} = 0.01$

Here is a quick reminder about some percentages that are often used in accounting.

$5\% = \frac{5}{100}$ (or $\frac{1}{20}$) $= 0.05$

$10\% = \frac{10}{100}$ (or $\frac{1}{10}$) $= 0.1$

$15\% = \frac{15}{100}$ (or $\frac{3}{20}$) $= 0.15$

$20\% = \frac{20}{100}$ (or $\frac{1}{5}$) $= 0.2$

$25\% = \frac{25}{100}$ (or $\frac{1}{4}$) $= 0.25$

$50\% = \frac{50}{100}$ (or $\frac{1}{2}$) $= 0.5$

$75\% = \frac{75}{100}$ (or $\frac{3}{4}$) $= 0.75$

There are two percentages that need care:

$33\frac{1}{3}\%$: this is the equivalent of $\frac{1}{3}$ (one-third) but it is sometimes written as 33.33%.

$66\frac{2}{3}\%$: this is the equivalent of $\frac{2}{3}$ (two-thirds) but it is sometimes written as 66.66% or 66.67%.

DID YOU KNOW?

33.33% is not exactly one-third (because it should be written as 33.33 recurring).

66.66% or 66.67% is not exactly two-thirds (because it should be written as 66.66 recurring).

If you are using your calculator with these percentages you are in danger of getting a slightly inaccurate result if you key in 33.33% or 66.66%.

When using a calculator always divide by 3 (one-third) for 33.33%; always multiply by 2 and divide by 3 (two-thirds) for 66.67%.

As an experiment try working out $33\frac{1}{3}\%$ (i.e. one-third) of 9. The answer is 3.

If you key 33.33% into your calculator, however, you are likely to obtain the answer: 2.9997!

8.4 Trade discount

A **trade discount** is a reduction in the price to be charged for goods. However, the following important conditions normally apply to this type of discount:

- Trade discount is only offered to other businesses engaged in the same line of activity.
- Trade discounts are often given for large orders.
- Trade discount is *not* normally available to private individuals.

KEY TERM

Trade discount: a reduction in price given as a reward for buying in large quantities.

DID YOU KNOW?

Wholesalers are businesses that purchase goods from manufacturers or producers and sell these on to retailers.

Retailers are businesses that provide goods for private individuals.

STUDY TIP

Do not be misled into thinking that the purchases account should appear in the purchases ledger, or that the sales account should be in the sales ledger.

Remember the purchases account and the sales account are both part of the general ledger.

Now you can answer questions 5 and 6 on pages 71–72.

Illustration 5 Trade discounts

GCK Wholesalers sell refrigerators. Their price list shows that the normal selling price of Model 2TB is $320.

GCK Wholesalers has just received two orders:

- A private individual wishes to purchase one refrigerator Model 2TB.
- J Hudson, a retailer of electrical goods, wishes to purchase 10 refrigerators, Model 2TB.

The private individual will be charged the normal selling price of $320.

But, J Hudson, a retailer in the same line of business, could be offered a trade discount. Trade discounts are usually expressed as percentages and can be large in amount. So, if the retailer, J Hudson, was allowed a trade discount of say 25 per cent, the amount charged for the order would be:

	$
10 refrigerators Model 2TB normal price $320 each	3 200
Less: 25% trade discount	800
AMOUNT CHARGED	2 400

The retailer pays only $240 for each refrigerator, but the private individual is charged the full price of $320.

Accounting records and trade discount

Invoices usually show detailed information about the normal price for the goods and any trade discount that is being deducted.

Illustration 6 | Purchase invoice including trade discount

PURCHASE INVOICE
Batford Wholesalers Ltd

To: Saintford Retail Stores

Date: 31 Aug 12

Quantity	*Description*	*Unit price* $	*Total* $
300 tins	Emulsion paint code 3D24	2.40	720.00
500 tins	Emulsion paint code 4X68	2.80	1 400.00
		SUBTOTAL	2 120.00
LESS	20% trade discount		424.00
		AMOUNT DUE	1 696.00

In this example, the most important fact is the amount charged: $1696. It is this fact that will be recorded in the accounting system. No record will be made of the normal price of the paint or the trade discount. What matters is always the amount actually charged.

STUDY TIP

Remember that the amount of the trade discount is not recorded in the accounting system. Only the net amount after deducting trade discount is shown in the books of prime entry and ledger accounts. There is no such thing as a trade discount account.

Illustration 7 | Accounting records and trade discount

Lendford Wholesalers received the following invoice during September 2012:

Sept 8 Purchase invoice T2734 received from JFZ Manufacturers. The normal price of the goods was $7500. However, the invoice showed the deduction of a 20% trade discount

Lendford Wholesalers issued the following invoice during September 2012:

Sept 12 Sales invoice N835 sent to Amberly Stores. The normal price of the goods was $2800. However, the invoice showed the deduction of a 10% trade discount.

Step 1: Calculate the amount actually charged for the goods on each of these invoices.

Purchase invoice:

JFZ Manufacturers (8 September)	$
Goods at normal selling price	7 500
Less: 20% trade discount	1 500
AMOUNT CHARGED	6 000

Sales invoice:

Amberly Stores (12 September)	$
Goods at normal selling price	2 800
Less: 10% trade discount	280
AMOUNT CHARGED	2 520

Step 2: Prepare the purchases and sales journals.

Purchases journal				
Date		*Supplier*	*Invoice number*	*$*
Sept	8	JFZ Manufacturers	T2734	6 000
		Total purchases		6 000

Sales journal				
Date		*Supplier*	*Invoice number*	*$*
Sept	12	Amberly Stores	N835	2 520
		Total sales		2 520

Step 3: Post the journals to the purchases, sales and general ledgers.

PURCHASES LEDGER

Dr				**JFZ Manufacturers account**			**Cr**
				Sept	8	Purchases	6 000

SALES LEDGER

Dr				**Amberly Stores account**			**Cr**
Sept	12	Sales	2 520				

GENERAL LEDGER

Dr				**Purchases account**			**Cr**
Sept	30	Purchases journal	6 000				

Dr				**Sales account**			**Cr**
				Sept	30	Sales journal	2 520

Reminder: there are now three subdivisions of the ledger. There is the purchases ledger (for the accounts of trade payables), the sales ledger (for the accounts of trade receivables), and the general ledger (for all other ledger accounts). This division of the ledger into three is often used because it makes it possible to spread the work of keeping a business's books of accounts between a number of individuals. For example, in a large business there could be sales ledger clerks whose responsibility is to keep the accounts of trade receivables up to date in the sales ledger.

Note: the amount entered in the journal is the net amount actually charged by the supplier or charged to the customer.

Now you can answer questions 7–10 on page 72.

Practice questions

DEVELOPING YOUR SKILLS

1 Recording credit purchases in a purchases journal and posting to ledger accounts

Beth owns a shoe shop. During May 2012 she received the following purchase invoices:

May	3	Invoice 2730	Purchase invoice received from Whiteford Ltd for $1230
	11	Invoice 9702	Purchase invoice received from P Sackley for $2720
	24	Invoice 1818	Purchase invoice received from A Hereton for $990
	27	Invoice 2823	Purchase invoice received from Whiteford Ltd for $2440

Prepare the accounting records necessary to record these transactions as follows:

- Purchases journal
- Trade payable accounts in the purchases ledger
- Purchases account in the general ledger

2 Recording credit purchases in a purchases journal and posting to ledger accounts

Ahmed owns a retail unit selling men's clothing. During January 2012 he received the following purchase invoices:

Jan	6	Invoice 3372	Purchase invoice received from Disley Ltd for goods, $630
	11	Invoice 4941	Purchase invoice received from P Harlew for goods, $1080
	21	Invoice 3418	Purchase invoice received from Disley Ltd for goods, $1250
	27	Invoice 5053	Purchase invoice received from P Harlew for goods, $1640

Prepare the accounting records necessary to record these transactions as follows:

- Purchases journal
- Trade payable accounts in the purchases ledger
- Purchases account in the general ledger

3 Recording credit sales in a sales journal and posting to ledger accounts

Amy owns a shop selling the latest music technology. During August 2012 she issued the following sales invoices to customers:

Aug	5	Invoice T339	Sales invoice sent to Dartford Ltd for goods, $1480
	10	Invoice T340	Sales invoice sent to J Williams for goods, $920
	23	Invoice T341	Sales invoice sent to Dartford Ltd for goods, $2840
	28	Invoice T342	Sales invoice sent to J Williams for goods, $1550

Prepare the accounting records necessary to record these transactions as follows:

- Sales journal
- Trade receivable accounts in the sales ledger
- Sales account in the general ledger

4 Recording credit sales in a sales journal and posting to ledger accounts

Salim owns a retail unit selling kitchen equipment. During June 2012 he issued the following sales invoices to customers:

June	2	Invoice W1131	Sales invoice sent to Hopford Kitchens Ltd for goods, $3740
	12	Invoice W1132	Sales invoice sent to A Bandle for goods, $2670
	15	Invoice W1133	Sales invoice sent to Hopford Kitchens Ltd for goods, $5090
	29	Invoice W1134	Sales invoice sent to A Bandle for goods, $1480

Prepare the accounting records necessary to record these transactions as follows:

- Sales journal
- Trade receivable accounts in the sales ledger
- Sales account in the general ledger

5 Calculating trade discounts

Orto Ltd is a wholesaler of kitchen equipment.

During January 2012 the company received the following invoices from credit suppliers:

Jan	12	Purchase invoice received from Polonix Ltd: 24 electric kettles at $25 each, less a trade discount of 10%
	19	Purchase invoice received from Quelta plc: 18 dishwashers at $267 each, less a trade discount of $33\frac{1}{3}$%

During January 2012 the company sent sales invoices to the following credit customers:

Jan	9	Sales invoice sent to Alto Cuisines: 16 food mixers at $140 each, less a trade discount of 15%
	18	Sales invoice sent to Prozel Restaurants: 8 ice-cream makers at $295 each, less a trade discount of 20%
	27	Sales invoice sent to Alto Cuisines: 24 coffee makers at $115 each, less a trade discount of 12.5%

Calculate the actual amount charged for each purchase and sale.

6 Calculating trade discounts

Stravage Ltd is a wholesaler of computer equipment.

During October 2012 the following invoices were received from credit suppliers:

Oct 13 Purchase invoice received from Inbell Ltd for 25 laptop computers model T5Z9 at $750 each, less a trade discount of 20%

19 Purchase invoice received from Albi Supplies Ltd for 30 printers model X400 at $120 each, less a trade discount of $33\frac{1}{3}$ %

29 Purchase invoice received from Albi Supplies Ltd for 22 computer workstations at $90 each, less a 12.5% trade discount

During October 2012 the company sent the following sales invoices to credit customers:

Oct 4 Sales invoice sent to Arbri Ltd for 18 external hard drives at $54 each, less a trade discount of 25%

19 Sales invoice sent to Telcaz Stores for 24 computer monitors at $105 each, less a trade discount of 10%

Calculate the actual amount charged for each purchase and sale.

7 Preparing books of prime entry

Referring to the information in question 5, prepare the following books of prime entry in the books of Orto Ltd:

a Purchases journal

b Sales journal

Note: It is not necessary to post the information to ledger accounts.

8 Preparing books of prime entry

Referring to the information in question 6, prepare the following books of prime entry in the books of Stravage Ltd:

a Purchases journal

b Sales journal

Note: It is not necessary to post the information to ledger accounts.

9 Calculating trade discounts and recording invoices in books of prime entry and ledger accounts

Alvo Ltd is a bicycle wholesaler.

The company buys goods from a number of bicycle manufacturers. Manufacturers offer trade discounts for large orders.

During October 2012 the following invoices were received:

Oct 12 Purchase invoice received from Melfin Ltd for 20 bicycles with a price of $160 each. The invoice showed the deduction of a trade discount of 25%

28 Purchase invoice received from Harvey Bikes for 15 bicycles with a price of $430 each. The invoice showed the deduction of a trade discount of $33\frac{1}{3}$ %

Alvo Ltd sell bicycles to many retailers.

During October 2012 the following invoices were issued:

Oct 7 Sales invoice sent to W Gifford for 6 cycles with a price of $400 each. The invoice showed the deduction of a trade discount of 20%

26 Sales invoice sent to T Perry for 8 cycles with a price of $330 each. The invoice showed the deduction of a trade discount of 15%

a Calculate the actual amount charged for each purchase and sale.

b Prepare the following accounting records in the books of Alvo Ltd:

i Purchases journal

ii Sales journal

iii Purchases ledger accounts

iv Sales ledger accounts

v Appropriate general ledger accounts

10 Calculating trade discounts

Belvo Wholesale sell fishing equipment.

The company buys goods from a number of manufacturers of fishing equipment. Manufacturers offer trade discounts for large orders.

During June 2012 the following invoices were received:

June 5 Purchase invoice received from Seaspray & Co. Ltd for fishing equipment with a price of $8400. The invoice showed the deduction of a trade discount of 25%

19 Purchase invoice received from Angling Supplies Ltd for fishing equipment with a selling price of $5800 each. The invoice showed the deduction of a trade discount of 20%

Bevo Wholesale sell fishing equipment to many retailers.

During June 2012 the following invoices were issued:

June 8 Sales invoice sent to McEwan & Sons for fishing equipment with a price of $1200. The invoice showed the deduction of a trade discount of 15%

23 Sales invoice sent to Jarel Fishing Supplies for equipment with a price of $1830. The invoice showed the deduction of a trade discount of $33\frac{1}{3}$ %

a Calculate the actual amount charged for each purchase and sale.

b Prepare the following accounting records in the books of Belvo Wholesale:

i Purchases journal

ii Sales journal

iii Purchases ledger accounts

iv Sales ledger accounts

v Appropriate general ledger accounts

11 Prepare a full accounting system including purchases and sales journals up to the trial balance

Yi Ting owns a wholesale business. Her business's trial balance on 30 April 2012 was as follows:

Trial balance at 30 April 2012

	Dr $	Cr $
Bank	12 580	
Capital		166 000
Cash	2 180	
Drawings	38 600	
Furniture and fittings	37 300	
General expenses	28 900	
Purchases	147 200	
Sales		232 440
Trade payables		
TBX Manufacturing Ltd		8 300
Universal Supplies Ltd		10 100
Trade receivables		
Shivan Retail Unit	11 300	
Williams Retail Chain	5 780	
Vehicles	44 800	
Wages	88 200	
	416 840	416 840

During May 2012 the following transactions occurred.

Invoices were received from suppliers as follows:

May 14 TBX Manufacturing Ltd (invoice 3251): for goods worth $6200, less a trade discount of 25%

26 Universal Supplies Ltd (invoice 4481): for goods worth $9600, less a trade discount of $33\frac{1}{3}$ %

Invoices were sent to customers as follows:

May 7 Shivan Retail Unit (invoice 1082): for goods worth $3600, less a trade discount of 15%

17 Williams Retail Chain (invoice 1083): for goods worth $5500, less a trade discount of 20%

Other transactions:

May 4 Cash sales totalled $2800

9 Paid general expenses by cheque, $1700

13 Received a cheque from Shivan Retail Unit for $8400

16 Paid Universal Supplies Ltd by cheque in full settlement of the amount due at this date

20 Purchased goods for resale and paid by cheque, $4900

25 Paid wages in cash, $3900

28 Yi Ting withdrew a cheque for $800 for private use

Prepare the following:

- Purchases journal
- Sales journal
- Purchases ledger accounts
- Sales ledger accounts
- General ledger accounts
- Trial balance at 31 May 2012

Note: It is not necessary to balance accounts. Financial statements are not required.

12 Prepare a full accounting system including purchases and sales journals up to the trial balance

Rakesh owns a wholesale business providing office supplies. His business's trial balance on 31 July 2012 was follows:

Trial balance at 30 July 2012

	Dr $	Cr $
Bank	14 850	
Bank loan		50 000
Bank loan interest	3 360	
Capital		426 000
Cash	4 970	
Drawings	38 450	
General expenses	31 375	
Premises	600 000	
Purchases	535 280	
Sales		847 685
Trade payables		
Kingbridge Manufacturing Co.		36 380
Leon Products Ltd		22 410
Trade receivables		
Latoya Retail Unit	12 320	
Murray Stationery	5 440	
Vehicles	68 000	
Wages	68 430	
	1 382 475	1 382 475

During August 2012 the following transactions occurred (see overleaf).

Invoices were received from suppliers as follows:

Aug 5 Kingbridge Manufacturing Co. (invoice 384): for goods worth $26 700, less a trade discount of $33\frac{1}{3}$ %

21 Leon Products Ltd (invoice 8630): for goods worth $15 600, less a trade discount of 25%

Invoices were sent to customers as follows:

Aug 9 Latoya Retail Unit (invoice 2293): for goods worth $8300, less a trade discount of 20%

23 Murray Stationery (invoice 2294): for goods worth $4400, less a trade discount of 15%

Other transactions:

Aug 6 Rakesh withdrew cash for private use, $700

8 Purchased goods for resale and paid by cheque, $5400

11 Paid loan interest, $380. Funds were transferred from the business bank account

17 Paid Leon Products Ltd by cheque in full settlement of the amount due at this date

22 Cash sales totalled $6860

24 Paid wages in cash, $5580

27 Received a cheque from Latoya Retail Unit for the amount due on this date

29 Paid general expenses by cheque, $2150

Prepare the following:

- Purchases journal
- Sales journal
- Purchases ledger accounts
- Sales ledger accounts
- General ledger accounts
- Trial balance at 31 August 2012

Note: It is not necessary to balance accounts. Financial statements are not required.

9 Books of prime entry: the returns journals

Introduction

It is not unusual for a business to return goods to suppliers that have previously been purchased on credit. This can happen when some items in a delivery are:

- damaged or broken
- not as ordered (wrong model, wrong size, wrong colour, etc.)
- received too late (sell-by date has been exceeded).

The return of goods to a supplier is often referred to as **purchases returns**. The double-entry record for purchases returns is as follows:

Debit The account of the supplier (trade payables)

Credit A purchases returns account

As shown in this example:

PURCHASES LEDGER

Dr	Trade payables		Cr
Purchases returns	xxxx		

GENERAL LEDGER

Dr	Purchases returns		Cr
		Trade payables	xxxx

At the end of a financial period the total of purchases returns is deducted from the total purchases to give a net figure for purchases for the period.

Of course, it is also possible for a customer to return goods that have previously been sold on credit. This situation would be referred to as **sales returns**.

LEARNING OUTCOMES

When you have reached the end of this unit you will be able to:

- identify the source documents used when recording sales returns and purchases returns
- prepare sales returns and purchases returns journals
- post the details recorded in the two returns journals to accounts in the general, purchases and sales ledgers.

KEY TERM

Purchases returns: goods sent back by a business to the supplier.

Sales returns: goods sent back to a business by a customer.

9.1 Recording purchases returns

KEY TERM

Credit note: the source document that records the amount to be deducted from (or allowed against) a previous invoice to avoid a business being overcharged. Usually the business has returned goods to the supplier.

Source document for purchases returns

As you know, all entries in the double-entry records should be supported by source documents. In Unit 8 you learned about the source documents for credit purchases (i.e. purchase invoices) and credit sales (i.e. sales invoices).

The usual source document for purchases returns is a **credit note**, which is sent by the supplier to the business that has received damaged or unwanted goods to notify them of the amount that can be deducted from the invoice.

Illustration 1 Credit note

No. 623

CREDIT NOTE
McKoy Wholesale Ltd

To: Highbury Retail Stores
Date: 18 Aug 11

Quantity	*Description*	*Unit price* $	*Total* $
12 boxes	Detergent	15.30	183.60
	Less 20% trade discount		36.72
		NET	146.88

Goods returned damaged in transit

Notes:

1. The customer – Highbury Retail Stores – has returned some damaged goods to the supplier, McKoy Wholesale Ltd.
2. This credit note has been prepared by the supplier and sent to the customer to confirm the amount that can be deducted ($146.88).
3. The owner of Highbury Retail Stores will use this credit note as the source document for preparing the double-entry records.

KEY TERM

Purchases returns journal: the book of prime entry used to list in date order details shown on credit notes relating to goods returned to suppliers.

Purchases returns journal

The book of prime entry used to list all credit notes received from suppliers before posting information to the ledger is called the **purchases returns journal**.

Illustration 2 Preparing and posting a purchases returns journal

Here is an example of a completed purchases returns journal which has been posted to the relevant ledger accounts:

Purchases returns journal

Date		*Supplier*	*Credit note number*	*$*
Sept	14	Bennett & Co.	347	112
	27	Mungroo Ltd	1279	273
		Total purchases returns		385

Here are the double-entry records for these purchases returns:

PURCHASES LEDGER

Dr		Bennet & Co. account		Cr			
Sept	14	Purchases returns	112				

Dr		Mungroo Ltd account		Cr			
Sept	27	Purchases returns	273				

GENERAL LEDGER

Dr		Purchases returns account		Cr			
				Sept	30	Purchases returns journal	385

Notes:

1. The process for recording purchases returns is very similar to that for credit purchases and credit sales.
2. Credit notes received from suppliers are listed in date order in the purchases returns journal. The personal accounts in the purchases ledger are updated immediately.
3. At the end of the month (or more frequently if desired) the journal is totalled and the total of purchases returns is posted to the general ledger account.

DID YOU KNOW?

If a trade discount was shown on a purchase or sales invoice it must also be deducted on returned items.

Debit notes

There is also a source document called a **debit note**. This document can arise in two situations.

Now you can answer questions 1 and 2 on page 81.

A purchaser could send a debit note to the seller of goods to notify them that some of the goods are not required or are damaged and are being returned. The debit note will state the items being returned by the purchaser and the amount the purchaser expects to be deducted from the amount due. When a debit note is used in this way, it should be regarded as a request for a deduction in an invoice. No entries should be made in the purchaser's books until a credit note is received from the supplier.

KEY TERM

Debit note: a source document used by a purchaser to notify the seller that goods are being returned and the amount that should be deducted from the amount due. Alternatively, a debit note is occasionally issued by the seller of goods to notify the purchaser of an undercharge.

A debit note could also be used to correct an undercharge on an invoice. The seller would issue a debit note if the sales invoice was sent out with an incorrect total which was less than it should have been. This use of a debit note is relatively unusual. A debit note issued by a seller should be entered in that business's sales journal (as if it were an additional sales invoice). The recipient of the debit note should enter the details in that business's purchases journal (as if it were an additional purchases invoice).

9.2 Recording sales returns

KEY TERM

Sales returns journal: the book of prime entry used to list in date order details shown on copies of credit notes relating to goods returned by customers.

Now you can answer questions 3–8 on pages 81–83.

Businesses that receive goods back from credit customers will need to make a record of these sales returns.

The accounting procedures follow a similar sequence to that described for purchases returns.

The basic double entry for sales returns is:

Debit A sales returns account

Credit The account of the trade receivable

At the end of the financial period the total of sales returns will be deducted from the total sales to give the net sales for the period.

A business receiving back goods from a dissatisfied credit customer will make out a credit note, send the original version to the customer, and keep a copy from which the accounting records can be prepared. Copies of credit notes are used to prepare the sales returns journal, which is the book of prime entry used to make the first record of sales returns.

Illustration 3 Preparing and posting a sales returns journal

Here is an example of a completed sales returns journal which has been posted to the relevant ledger accounts:

Sales returns journal

Date		*Customer*	*Credit note number*	*$*
Jan	9	Garcia Ltd	103	23
	23	Rampersad & Co.	104	119
		Total sales returns		142

Here are the double-entry records for these sales returns:

SALES LEDGER

Dr Garcia Ltd account Cr

				Jan	9	Sales journal	23

Dr Rampersad & Co. account Cr

				Jan	23	Sales returns	119

GENERAL LEDGER

Dr Sales returns account Cr

Jan	31	Sales returns journal	142				

Notes:

1 Copies of credit notes issued to customers are listed in date order in the sales returns journal. The personal accounts in the sales ledger are updated immediately.

2 At regular intervals the journal is totalled and the total of sales returns is posted to the general ledger account.

Recording returns in the end-of-year financial statements

At the end of a financial year it is important to remember to transfer the totals of the returns accounts in the general ledger to the income statement.

Illustration 4 Recording returns in the income statement

On 31 December 2012 the following accounts appeared in the books of Perrier & Sons:

	$
Purchases	430 000
Sales returns	40 000
Purchases returns	30 000
Sales	680 000

The ledger accounts should appear as shown opposite. They have been closed on transfer of the balances to the first section of the income statement.

GENERAL LEDGER

Dr Purchases account Cr

Dec 31	Balance	430 000	Dec 31	Income statement	430 000

Dr Purchases returns account Cr

Dec 31	Income statement	30 000	Dec 31	Balance	30 000

Dr Sales account Cr

Dec 31	Income statement	680 000	Dec 31	Balance	680 000

Dr Sales returns account Cr

Dec 31	Balance	40 000	Dec 31	Income statement	40 000

And here is the income statement:

Dr Income statement for the year ended 31 December 2012 Cr

	$	$		$	$
Purchases	430 000		Sales	680 000	
Less purchases returns	30 000		Less sales returns	40 000	
		400 000			640 000
Gross profit		240 000			
		640 000			640 000

Notes:

1 You will see that the idea is to show net purchases and net sales in the income statement.

2 Two columns on each side of the statement are required to show the deduction of returns.

Now you can answer questions 9–12 on pages 83–84.

STUDY TIP

A common mistake is to mix up the entries for returns in the income statement.

Remember:

- total purchases returns is deducted from purchases
- total sales returns is deducted from sales.

DID YOU KNOW?

Transferring returns accounts to the income statement

If you look at the example of the income statement you may think on first glance that the rules of double entry are not being followed in regard to the treatment of the returns accounts.

Taking purchases returns as an example, it appears that:

- a debit entry has been made in the purchases returns account to close the account
- another debit entry has been made in the income statement for purchases returns.

These entries can look confusing.

But look again. You will see that what appears to be a debit entry for purchases returns in the income statement is not really that at all. In fact returns outward is being *deducted* from the debit side, not added.

A similar point applies to sales returns.

Practice questions

DEVELOPING YOUR SKILLS

1 Recording purchases returns

Ken owns a shop supplying fishing tackle. During March 2012 he returned goods to suppliers that had previously been purchased on credit.

March	11	Credit note 242	Goods returned to Scott Ltd with a value of $275
	18	Credit note 375	Goods returned to Taylor & Sons with a value of $328
	29	Credit note 247	Goods returned to Scott Ltd. These goods had been invoiced at $550, less a trade discount of 20%

Prepare the records required in Ken's books of account to record these transactions as follows:

- Purchases returns journal
- Trade payable accounts in the purchases ledger
- Purchases returns account in the general ledger

2 Recording purchases returns

Fay owns a shop selling household goods. During July 2012 she returned goods to suppliers that had previously been purchased on credit.

July	4	Credit note 331	Goods returned to Segicore Ltd with a value of $297
	15	Credit note 829	Goods returned to J Howell with a value of $115
	26	Credit note 337	Goods returned to Segicore Ltd. These goods had been invoiced at $840 less a trade discount of 25%

Prepare the records required in Fay's books of account to record these transactions as follows:

- Purchases returns journal
- Trade payable accounts in the purchases ledger
- Purchases returns account in the general ledger

3 Recording sales returns

Mike is the owner of a business supplying car accessories to local garages and car dealers. During June 2012 credit customers returned goods that had been sold to them on credit.

June	11	Credit note 454	Goods returned by Parsed Garages Ltd with a value of $220
	13	Credit note 455	Goods returned by Beretta Car Dealers with a value of $507
	24	Credit note 456	Goods returned by Parsed Garages Ltd. These goods had been invoiced at $1500, less a trade discount of $33\frac{1}{3}$%

Prepare the records required in Mike's books of account to record these transactions as follows:

- Sales returns journal
- Trade receivable accounts in the sales ledger
- Sales returns account in the general ledger

4 Recording sales returns

Mona is the owner of a business supplying designer clothes to retailers in the region. During October 2012 credit customers returned goods that had been sold to them on credit.

Oct	9	Credit note 756	Goods returned by Castries Designwear with a value of $474
	20	Credit note 757	Goods returned by Garcia Ltd with a value of $232
	23	Credit note 758	Goods returned by Garcia Ltd. These goods had been invoiced at $1640, less a trade discount of 15%

Prepare the records required in Mona's books of account to record these transactions as follows:

- Sales returns journal
- Trade receivable accounts in the sales ledger
- Sales returns account in the general ledger

5 Preparing the four journals

Simon's Catering Supplies is a wholesale business. The following source documents were received or issued during the week beginning 20 August 2012.

Aug	20	Purchase invoice 8806	From TDH Ltd for goods, $960
	21	Sales invoice T449	To Seaview Café for goods, $480
	22	Credit note received 2721	From TDH Ltd for goods, $32
	23	Purchase invoice 33902	From Datrix Supplies for goods, $2400, less 20% trade discount
	24	Credit note issued 74	To Seaview Café for goods, $39
	24	Credit note received 884	From Datrix Supplies for goods, $420, less 20% trade discount

Prepare the following books of prime entry for the week ending 24 August 2012:

- Purchases journal
- Sales journal
- Purchases returns journal
- Sales returns journal

Note: The journals should be totalled at the end of the week. Ledger accounts are not required.

6 Preparing the four journals

Wilma owns Altitude, a wholesale business supplying equipment for mountain climbers. The following source documents were received or issued during the week beginning 16 January 2012.

Jan	16	Sales invoice 44932	Sent to Trentview Sports Ltd for goods, $1832
	17	Purchase invoice X8832	Received from Supahike & Co. for goods, $2775
	17	Credit note received 113	From Bergpeak Ltd for goods, $384
	18	Credit note issued 484	To Trentview Sports Ltd for goods, $331
	18	Sales invoice 44933	Sent to Torpoint & Sons for goods, $861, less $33\frac{1}{3}$% trade discount
	19	Credit note received T902	From Supahike for goods, $183
	20	Credit note issued 485	To Torpoint & Sons for goods, $72, less $33\frac{1}{3}$% trade discount

Prepare the following books of prime entry for the week ending 20 January 2012:

- Purchases journal
- Sales journal
- Purchases returns journal
- Sales returns journal

Note: The journals should be totalled at the end of the week. Ledger accounts are not required.

7 Preparing a full accounting system including all journals up to the trial balance

Raju owns a wholesale business supplying music technology to retailers in the region. His business's trial balance on 31 January 2012 was as follows.

Trial balance at 31 January 2012

	Dr $	Cr $
Administration expenses	36480	
Bank	3620	
Capital		381400
Cash	1850	
Drawings	27280	
Non-current assets	440000	
Purchases	348200	
Sales returns	5860	
Purchases returns		6490
Sales		585000
Selling expenses	11200	
Trade payables		
HTL Manufacturing		11450
Khan's Supplies Ltd		6380
Trade receivables		
Hunter & Sons	2690	
Quinlan Music Shop	3200	
Wages and salaries	110340	
	990720	990720

During February 2012 the following transactions occurred.

Invoices were received from suppliers as follows.

Feb 6 HTL Manufacturing (invoice 559): for goods, $7500, less a trade discount of $33\frac{1}{3}$%
19 Khan's Supplies Ltd (invoice T307): for goods, $6200, less a trade discount of 25%

Invoices were sent to customers as follows.

Feb 5 Hunter & Sons (invoice 4561): for goods $1550 less a trade discount of 20%
20 Quinlan Music Shop (invoice 4562): for goods $3300 less a trade discount of 25%

Credit notes were received from suppliers as follows.

Feb 12 HTL Manufacturing (credit note 308): for goods supplied on 6 February, $420, less a trade discount of $33\frac{1}{3}$% – not as ordered
28 Khan's Supplies Ltd (credit note R119): for goods supplied on 19 February, $880, less a trade discount of 25% – damaged in transit

Credit notes were issued to customers as follows.

Feb 8 Hunter & Sons (credit note 181): for goods supplied on 5 February, $250, less a trade discount of 20% – received in a damaged condition
27 Quinlan Music Shop (credit note 182): for goods supplied on 20 February, $260, less a trade discount of 25% – not as ordered

Other transactions:

Feb 5 Paid administration expenses in cash, $380
9 Received a cheque from Hunter & Sons for the amount due on 1 February
11 Cash sales totalled $15450
12 Cash, $15200, was paid into the business bank account
15 Paid HTL Manufacturing by cheque in full settlement of the amount due at 1 February
18 Purchased goods for resale and paid by cheque, $3200
25 Paid wages and salaries by cheque, $6120
28 Raju withdrew cash for private use, $740

Prepare the following:

- Purchases journal
- Sales journal
- Purchases returns journal
- Sales returns journal
- Purchases ledger accounts
- Sales ledger accounts
- General ledger accounts
- Trial balance dated 28 February 2012

Note: It is not necessary to balance accounts. Financial statements are not required.

8 Preparing a full accounting system including all four journals up to the trial balance

Sally is the owner of a business that supplies local retailers with kitchen equipment. Her business's trial balance on 30 September 2012 was as follows:

Trial balance at 30 September 2012

	Dr	Cr
	$	$
Bank	7310	
Capital		224900
Cash	940	
Drawings	35480	
General expenses	4600	
Non-current assets	212000	
Purchases	264270	
Rent	36350	
Sales returns	4490	
Purchases returns		7060
Sales		409510
Trade payables		
LPC Kitchen Supplies		4480
Nana's Kitchens Ltd		8460
Trade receivables		
Johnson Kitchen Shop	1070	
TK Watson	4320	
Wages	83580	
	654410	654410

During October 2012 the following transactions occurred.

Invoices were received from suppliers as follows.

Oct 3 LPC Kitchens Ltd (invoice 617): for goods, $5120, less a trade discount of 25%
11 Nana's Kitchens Ltd (invoice W311): for goods, $4800, less a trade discount of 20%

Invoices were sent to customers as follows.

Oct 14 Johnson Kitchen Shop (invoice 2121): for goods, $6240, less a trade discount of $33\frac{1}{3}$%
23 TK Watson (invoice 2122): for goods, $1600, less a trade discount of 15%

Credit notes were received from suppliers as follows.

Oct 7 LPC Kitchens Ltd (credit note 113): for goods supplied on 3 October, $320, less a trade discount of 25% – some goods received in a damaged condition
18 Nana's Kitchens Ltd (credit note D008): for goods supplied on 11 October, $680, less a trade discount of 25% – not as ordered

Credit notes were issued to customers as follows.

Oct 22 Johnson Kitchen Shop (credit note 226): for goods supplied on 14 October, $420, less a trade discount of $33\frac{1}{3}$% – not as ordered
30 TK Watson (credit note 227): for goods supplied on 23 October, $200, less a trade discount of 15% – damaged items

Other transactions:

Oct 4 Paid rent $3100 by cheque
8 Paid Nana's Kitchens Ltd the amount due on 1 October
11 Purchased goods for resale by cheque, $2700
16 Sally withdrew $400 cash for her private use
21 Paid general expenses by cheque, $680
25 Cash sales totalled $3660
28 Received a cheque from Johnson Kitchen Shop in full settlement of the amount due on this date
29 Paid cash into bank so as to leave a cash balance of $750

Prepare the following:

- Purchases journal
- Sales journal
- Purchases returns journal
- Sales returns journal
- Purchases ledger accounts
- Sales ledger accounts
- General ledger accounts
- Trial balance dated 31 October 2012

Note: It is not necessary to balance accounts. Financial statements are not required.

9 Preparing income statements including returns

Raslinda owns a retail outlet. The following balances remained in her business's general ledger at the end of the financial year, 31 August 2012.

	$
Administration expenses	5360
Bank loan	6800
Bank loan interest	720
Cash at bank	390
Capital	30000
Delivery vehicles	31500
Drawings	25200
Furniture and equipment	18850
Purchases	82370
Purchases returns	1140
Rent of shop premises	8280
Sales	161380
Sales returns	460
Wages	24990

Prepare the business's income statement for the year ended 31 August 2012, selecting the information required from the details provided.

10 Preparing income statements including returns

From the following information prepare an income statement for the year ended 31 December 2012 for the business called Bolero's Shoes owned by Miranda Blake.

	$
Bank overdraft	4980
Capital	256 085
Cash in hand	392
Drawings	17 078
Electricity charges	993
Furniture and fittings	22 400
General expenses	647
Office expenses	1 182
Purchases	111 372
Purchases returns	849
Sales	204 711
Sales returns	683
Shop premises	249 000
Trade payables	840
Trade receivables	3 812
Wages	65 338
Water charges	1 195

Select the information required from the details provided.

11 Preparing end-of-year financial statements

The following trial balance was extracted from the books of P Hosein at the end of the business's financial year.

Trial balance at 31 December 2012

	Dr $	Cr $
Bank	5 950	
Bank loan		20 000
Bank loan interest	1 540	
Capital		115 000
Cash	2 020	
Drawings	32 600	
Furniture and fittings	48 400	
General expenses	17 590	
Purchases	288 470	
Rent	33 800	
Sales returns	7 130	
Purchases returns		5 440
Sales		403 810
Trade payables		22 420
Trade receivables	16 380	
Vehicle	38 500	
Wages	74 290	
	566 670	566 670

Prepare the following:

- Income statement for the year ended 31 December 2012
- Balance sheet at 31 December 2012 (classified)

12 Preparing end-of-year financial statements

Tina owns a retail business. Her business's financial year ended on 31 August 2012 when the following trial balance was extracted from the books of account.

Trial balance at 31 August 2012

	Dr $	Cr $
Administration expenses	3 580	
Bank	8 410	
Capital		421 400
Cash	720	
Drawings	28 400	
Equipment	33 600	
Insurance	7 150	
Premises	520 000	
Purchases	407 380	
Sales returns	11 210	
Purchases returns		9 360
Salaries	105 400	
Sales		737 770
Selling expenses	5 030	
Trade payables		22 480
Trade receivables	24 730	
Vehicle	35 400	
	1 191,010	1 191,010

Prepare the following:

- Income statement for the year ended 31 August 2012
- Balance sheet at 31 August 2012 (classified)

10 Books of prime entry: the cash book

Introduction

You will now be used to the idea that a fully developed accounting system requires:

- the use of source documents
- the recording of transactions in books of prime entry
- the posting of information from the books of original entry to complete the double entry in the ledgers.

This process will now be applied to the recording of money transactions.

The book of prime entry used to record all money transactions is called a cash book. Like all of the books of prime entry, the cash book is a listing in date order of relevant transactions with information taken from source documents.

LEARNING OUTCOMES

When you have reached the end of this unit you will be able to:

- identify the source documents used when recording cash and bank transactions
- prepare a two-column cash book and post details to ledger accounts
- explain why cash discounts may be offered
- prepare a three-column cash book and post details to ledger accounts.

Source documents for money transactions

The following tables summarise some of the main means of receiving and paying money.

Cash transactions			
	Source document	***Explanation***	***Entry required***
Receipts	**Cash register tapes or till rolls**	Used as evidence of cash sales: cash registers retain a record of every individual 'cash' transaction. Cash sales would include the receipt from the customer of notes and coins, cheques, debit card payments, credit card payments	**Debit cash**
	Copy of cash receipt	Occasionally a handwritten cash receipt could be issued to those giving the business cash (notes, coins, cheques, etc.) – for example for cash sales	
Payments	**Cash receipt**	Used as evidence of payment of cash (notes, coins). The receipt could be in printed form as dispensed by a cash register, or occasionally it might be a handwritten document – for example for the purchase of stationery for office use	**Credit cash**

Bank transactions			
	Source document	***Explanation***	***Entry required***
Receipts	**Paying-in slip counterfoils**	Used as evidence that money (notes, coins, cheques) has been paid into the business's bank account	**Debit bank**
	Bank statement	Funds can be transferred directly from a customer's account to the business's bank account by using electronic facilities provided by banks	
Payments	**Cheque counterfoils**	The cheque itself will not be available as a source document, because it will have been handed over in the process of payment. The cheque stub or counterfoil should be used to record the main details about the payment	**Credit bank**
	Bank statement	The bank statement will provide evidence of charges made by the bank for providing current account facilities and for interest on any overdraft. It can also be useful as evidence (and a reminder) of payments the business has authorised using standing orders and direct debts (see Unit 23)	

10.1 The two-column cash book

KEY TERM

Cash book: a book of prime entry in which all cash and bank transactions are recorded.

The cash book

The **cash book** is the book of prime entry used to record all money transactions. There are several different forms of the cash book. The simplest version takes the cash and bank accounts out of the general ledger and puts them side by side to form a two-column cash book.

Illustration 1 Two-column cash book

On 1 September 2012 a business had $740 cash in hand and cash at bank of $7280.

The following source documents are available:

Date		Source document	Transaction
Sept	5	Cheque counterfoil	Payment of a credit supplier, G Lee, $1420
	8	Till roll	Cash sales totalling $1580
	11	Cash receipt	Payment of general expenses in cash, $110
	14	Paying-in slip counterfoil	Transfer of cash to the bank account, $1400
	21	Bank statement	Bank charges for the month totalled $180
	28	Paying-in slip counterfoil	Cheque received from a credit customer, T Evans, $3170

Following is the two-column cash book for September. The cash book has been balanced at the end of the month.

Dr **Cash book** **Cr**

			Cash	Bank				Cash	Bank
			$	$				$	$
Sept	1	Balances b/d	740	7 280	Sept	5	G Lee		1 420
	8	Sales	1 580			11	General expenses	110	
	14	Cash		1 400		14	Bank	1 400	
	28	T Evans		3 170		21	Bank charges		180
						30	Balances c/d	810	10 250
			2 320	11 850				2 320	11 850
Oct	1	Balances b/d	810	10 250					

Notes:

1 The format used always has the cash column before the bank column.

2 The cash book has a double role: it is a book of prime entry (the first record of money transactions), but it is also part of the double-entry system because it replaces the cash and bank accounts that would otherwise have been found in the general ledger.

3 When cash is transferred to the bank, or cash is withdrawn from the bank, both aspects of the double entry appear within the cash book. This transfer is referred to as a **contra entry**.

4 The usual rules for balancing accounts can be applied to the cash book.

KEY TERM

Contra entry (cash book): the transfer of cash to the bank, or the withdrawal of cash from the bank. These transactions result in both the debit entry and credit entry for the transaction being recorded in the cash book columns.

You can now answer questions 1 and 2 on page 92.

10.2 Cash discounts

KEY TERM

Cash discount: a reduction in the amount paid by credit customers, or to credit suppliers, when accounts are settled within an agreed time limit.

Cash discounts

Businesses depend on their cash resources to run the business effectively and so it is important that amounts due from trade receivables are received as soon as possible. To encourage trade receivables to pay promptly, some businesses offer their credit customers a **cash discount**.

Illustration 2 Recording discount allowed

Tricia sells goods on credit to Chadee Brothers. Each invoice sent to this customer has a footnote stating 'Terms: 5%, 30 days'.

On 1 May 2012 Tricia sold goods valued at $1200 to Chadee Brothers. On 19 May 2012 the amount due was settled, less the cash discount.

Note: The invoice footnote 'Terms: 5%, 30 days' means that the customer can reduce the amount paid by 5 per cent if payment is made within 30 days. Cash discounts are usually in the range 2–5 per cent.

Step 1: The sale on credit would be entered in the sales journal in the usual way and then posted to the customer's account in the sales ledger.

SALES LEDGER

Dr — Chadee Brothers Ltd account — Cr

May	1	Sales	1 200				

Step 2: When the customer pays on 19 May, the amount paid will be $1200 less a 5 per cent cash discount (i.e. $1140). The receipt of the cheque will be recorded in the usual way in the cash book with a debit entry in the bank account. The credit entry will be as follows:

Dr — Chadee Brothers Ltd account — Cr

May	1	Sales	1 200	May	19	Bank	1 140

Step 3: It is now necessary to make entries to record the discount that this customer deducted from the amount due. Discounts given to credit customers are called discounts allowed.

The double entry for discounts allowed is:

Dr — Chadee Brothers Ltd account — Cr

May	1	Sales	1 200	May	19	Bank	1 140
					19	Discounts allowed	60

GENERAL LEDGER

Dr — Discounts allowed account — Cr

May	19	Chadee Brothers	60				

Notes:

1. The credit entry in the customer's account cancels the remaining debt.
2. The debit entry in the discount allowed account records a loss to the business. The loss is tolerated in order to receive the cash due as soon as possible.
3. The discounts allowed account is, therefore, an expense account. At the end of the year the total of discounts allowed will be transferred to the second part of the income statement.

Cash discounts might be offered to a business by a supplier, since suppliers will also be anxious to be paid as soon as possible.

Illustration 3 Recording discounts received

Tricia's main supplier is BL Trading Ltd. This supplier always offers Tricia a cash discount of 4 per cent if debts are settled within 30 days. On 4 May 2012 Tricia purchased goods worth $2400 from BL Trading Ltd. On 24 May Tricia settled the amount due, less the 4 per cent cash discount.

The purchase will be recorded in the purchases journal in the usual way, and the payment will be recorded in the cash book.

The entries in the personal account and in the discounts account are shown on the right.

PURCHASES LEDGER

Dr **BL Trading Ltd account** **Cr**

May	24	Bank	2304	May	4	Purchases	2400
	24	Discounts received	96				

GENERAL LEDGER

Dr **Discounts received account** **Cr**

				May	24	BL Trading Ltd	96

Notes:

1 Cash discounts available from suppliers are called 'discounts received'.

2 The double entry for discounts received is:

Debit Trade payable

Credit Discounts received

3 For Tricia the discount received is a small gain – she has paid her supplier less than expected.

4 The total of a discounts received account is transferred to the second part of the income statement at the end of the year, where it will increase the profit made by the business.

Statements of account

Many businesses send out a document called a **statement of account** to each of their credit customers at monthly intervals. The statement is a summary of the customer's account and is designed to remind the customer of how much is outstanding. The customer may also use the statement to check their own accounting records. Businesses also receive statements of account from their suppliers.

KEY TERM

Statement of account: a summary of transactions that have taken place between a supplier and a credit customer. The statement provides a means of checking the accuracy of accounts and of reminding customers how much they owe.

You can now answer questions 3 and 4 on page 92.

Illustration 4 A statement of account

Here is a typical statement of account. You will see that it is set out to show a running balance.

STATEMENT OF ACCOUNT
Supa Fashion Wholesalers
Queens Road, Buryford

Dress in Style
Cambridge Street
Waterbury

Account number: 373
31 May 2012

Date		Details	Dr	Cr	Balance
			$	$	$
May	1	Balance			640
	6	Payment received		624	16
	6	Cash discount		16	0
	21	Invoice 2729	1320		1320
	27	Credit note 481		230	1090
		AMOUNT NOW DUE			1090

Terms: 2.5% cash discount for settlement within 14 days

10.3 The three-column cash book

An alternative version of the cash book is often used by businesses; it has a third column to make a note of any cash discounts arising from payments to credit suppliers or receipts from credit customers. The additional column is convenient for noting cash discounts, but it is important to realise that the discount column is not part of the double-entry records.

Illustration 5 The three-column cash book

Robin is the owner of a wholesale business. He offers his credit customers a 2 per cent cash discount for prompt payment of amounts due. Robin's suppliers also offer a cash discount of 5 per cent for prompt payment.

On 1 May 2012 Robin's cash book showed balances as follows: cash $1350, bank $7480.

The following money transactions occurred during May 2012:

Date		Source document	Transaction
May	3	Cheque counterfoil	Payment of a trade payable, Campbell Traders. The amount owed was $2600. This amount was settled, less 5% cash discount
	5	Paying-in slip counterfoil	Receipt of cheque from trade receivable, K Scott, who owed $1600. This amount was settled, less 2% cash discount
	9	Till rolls	Cash sales totalling $4540
	16	Cheque counterfoil	Payment of a trade payable, LT Wright. The amount owed was $4480. This amount was settled, less 5% cash discount
	21	Paying-in slip counterfoil	Paid cash, $4200, into the bank account
	28	Paying-in slip counterfoil	Receipt of a cheque from trade receivable, D Pitts, who owed $900. This amount was settled, less 2% cash discount

Dr **Cash book** **Cr**

			Discounts allowed	Cash	Bank				Discounts received	Cash	Bank
			$	$	$				$	$	$
May	1	Balances		1 350	7 480	May	3	Campbell Traders	130		2 470
	5	K Scott	32		1 568		16	LT Wright	224		4 256
	9	Sales		4 540			21	Bank		4 200	
	21	Cash			4 200		31	Balances c/d		1 690	7 404
	28	D Pitts	18		882						
			50	5 890	14 130				354	5 890	14 130
June	1	Balances b/d		1 690	7 404						

The discount columns are totalled and the totals posted to the discount accounts in the general ledger.

GENERAL LEDGER

Dr **Discounts allowed account** **Cr**

May	31	Cash book	50				

Dr **Discounts received account** **Cr**

				May	31	Cash book	354

Notes:

1 An entry in the discounts allowed column is a note that a discount was given to customer – it is not a debit entry for that discount.

2 An entry in the discounts received column is a note that a discount was received from a supplier – it is not a credit entry for that discount.

3 Because the discount columns are just lists of discounts allowed and discounts received, the columns are not balanced at the end of the month. Instead the columns are totalled and the totals are used to make one entry per month in the discounts allowed account and discounts received account in the general ledger. These entries for discount totals replace what would otherwise have been individual debit/credit entries every time a discount was allowed or received.

DID YOU KNOW?

The idea that part of the information shown in the double-entry system is only a note about something important – as with the discount columns in the cash book – is properly described as 'memorandum' information. The word 'memorandum' means a note of something to be remembered.

You can now answer questions 4 and 5 on page 92.

STUDY TIP

It is a common mistake to try to balance the two discounts columns in the cash book. This can happen when it is not understood that the discount columns are only notes of discounts rather than debit or credit entries.

What happens when a bank account becomes overdrawn?

When a business spends more than it has paid into its bank account, then the balance becomes overdrawn. Businesses usually arrange an overdraft facility to cover this eventuality. Banks, of course, charge interest on overdrawn balances, and they set a limit on the amount by which the business can become overdrawn. From the bookkeeping point of view, no special action is required when a payment causes the bank account to be overdrawn. When the bank account is balanced, the balance brought down is shown as a credit balance (indicating that it is a current liability) rather than a debit balance.

Illustration 6 A bank account that is overdrawn

Here is the bank account of a business that becomes overdrawn during a particular month. For convenience, just the bank columns from the cash book are shown here.

Dr **Cash book (bank columns only)** **Cr**

				Bank					Bank
				$					$
June	1	Balances		2 400	June	8	Rent		1 400
	8	Cash		3 700		15	Drawings		1 100
	18	Sales		3 400		18	Equipment		8 600
	30	Balance	c/d	2 090		28	Insurance		490
				11 590					11 590
					July	1	Balance	b/d	2 090

Notes:

1 The bank account actually becomes overdrawn on 18 June when the large payment is made for new equipment.

2 However, it is only when the account is balanced at the end of the month that the overdraft balance is formally recorded.

You can now answer questions 7–12 on pages 94–96.

Practice questions

DEVELOPING YOUR SKILLS

1 Preparing a two-column cash book

On 1 March 2012 Faizah's business had cash in hand of $1340 and a balance at bank of $6270. The following source documents are available for money transactions during March 2012.

Date		Source document	Transaction
March	4	Cash receipt	Purchase of stationery for office use, $60
	7	Cheque counterfoil	Payment of water rates, $290
	11	Till roll	Cash sales totalling $3180
	15	Paying-in slip counterfoil	Transfer of cash, $3000, to the bank account
	21	Paying-in slip counterfoil	Cheque received from trade receivable, T Ram, $2240
	23	Cheque counterfoil	Payment of trade payable, D Thomas, $2350
	27	Bank statement	Bank charges for the month totalling $130

Prepare the business's two-column cash book for March 2012. Balance the cash book on 31 March 2012. Ledger accounts are not required.

2 Preparing a two-column cash book

On 1 August 2012 Simon's business had cash in hand of $370 and a balance at bank of $4 120. The following source documents are available for money transactions during August 2012.

Date		Source document	Transaction
Aug	3	Till roll	Cash sales totalling $4820
	7	Paying-in slip counterfoil	Transfer of cash, $4600, to the bank account
	11	Cheque counterfoil	Payment of general expenses, $490
	16	Bank statement	Bank charges of $110
	20	Paying-in slip counterfoil	Cheque received from trade receivable, T Lall, $1470
	27	Cheque counterfoil	Payment of trade payable, TX Supplies Ltd, $880
	30	Cash receipt	Payment of vehicle running costs, $150

Prepare the business's two-column cash book for August 2012. Balance the cash book on 31 August 2012. Ledger accounts are not required.

3 Preparing a statement of account

Tony owns a wholesale business. At the end of each month he sends statements of account to each of his credit customers. The following information is about a trade receivable, Blackford Retail Stores, for the month of April 2012.

			$
April	1	Amount due	1 820
	4	Invoice (number 7781) sent to customer	2 300
	14	Cheque received from customer	1 729
	14	Discount allowed	91
	22	Credit note (number 277) sent to customer	80

Prepare a statement of account to remind Blackford Retail Stores of the amount due at 30 April 2012.

4 Preparing a statement of account

Carla owns a furniture store and at the end of each month she sends statements of account to each of her credit customers. The following account of a trade receivable for the month of October 2012 appeared in her business's sales ledger.

Dr — Marco Lemelin — Cr

			$				$
Oct	1	Balances	2 400	Oct	6	Bank	2 340
	16	Sale	600		6	Discount allowed	60
	28	Sale	700		21	Sales return	70
					29	Sales return	110

Prepare a statement of account to remind Marco Lemelin of the amount due at 31 October 2012.

5 Preparing a three-column cash book, personal accounts and discount accounts

The following balances were extracted from the books of Apex Universal, a wholesaler, on 1 November 2012.

	$
Cash in hand	2190
Cash at bank	7330
Trade payables:	
TM Davis	1600
Ryan & Co.	2300
Trade receivables:	
Fray Ltd	900
VK Watson	1650

Trade payables give a cash discount of 5 per cent if accounts are settled within 30 days.

Apex Universal gives a cash discount of 2 per cent to its credit customers if they settle their accounts within 30 days.

During November 2012, the following transactions occurred.

Date		Source document	Transaction
Nov	5	Cheque counterfoil	Payment of amount due to TM Davis on 1 November, less 5% cash discount
	8	Paying-in slip counterfoil	Cheque received from Fray Ltd in full settlement of their account on 1 November, less 2% cash discount
	14	Till roll	Cash sales totalling $1420
	17	Paying-in slip counterfoil	Transfer of cash to bank, $1250
	21	Cheque counterfoil	Payment of amount due to Ryan & Co. on 1 November, less 5% cash discount
	24	Paying-in slip counterfoil	Cheque received from VK Watson in full settlement of their account on 1 November, less 2% cash discount

Prepare the business's three-column cash book for November 2012. Balance the cash book on 30 November 2012 and total the discount columns on that date.

Post entries to the personal accounts in the purchases and sales ledgers; post the totals of the discount columns to the discount accounts in the general ledger.

6 Preparing a three-column cash book, personal accounts and discount accounts

The following balances were extracted from the books of the business owned by Safina on 1 June 2012.

	$
Cash in hand	450
Cash at bank	2720
Trade payables:	
N Singh	3200
Zamran Stores	1500
Trade receivables:	
K Gobin	600
QR Pulchan Ltd	2080

Trade payables give a cash discount of 5 per cent if accounts are settled within 30 days.

Safina gives a cash discount of 5 per cent to her credit customers if they settle their accounts within 30 days.

During June 2012, the following transactions occurred.

Date		Source document	Transaction
June	5	Cheque counterfoil	Payment of amount due to N Singh on 1 June, less 5% cash discount
	8	Paying-in slip counterfoil	Cheque received from K Gobin in full settlement of their account on 1 June, less 5% cash discount
	14	Till roll	Cash sales totalling $3920
	17	Paying-in slip counterfoil	Transfer of cash to bank, $3800
	21	Cheque counterfoil	Payment of amount due to Zamran Stores on 1 June, less 5% cash discount
	24	Paying-in slip counterfoil	Cheque received from QR Pulchan Ltd in full settlement of their account on 1 June, less 5% cash discount

Prepare the business's three-column cash book for June 2012. Balance the cash book on 30 June 2012 and total the discount columns on that date.

Post entries to the personal accounts in the purchases and sales ledgers; post the totals of the discount columns to the discount accounts in the general ledger.

7 Preparing a three-column cash book with an overdrawn bank balance

Ombeya owns a retail business. On 1 April 2012, his business's cash in hand was $580 and cash at bank was $2260. During April the following transactions occurred.

Date		Source document	Transaction
April	4	Cheque counterfoil	Paid trade payable, B Elias, in full settlement of their account, $1800, less 5% cash discount
	7	Till roll	Cash sales totalling $830
	13	Paying-in slip counterfoil	Transferred cash to bank, $750
	14	Paying-in slip counterfoil	Cheque received from trade receivable, H Carr, in full settlement of their account, $480, less 2.5% cash discount
	21	Cheque counterfoil	Purchase of new office furniture, $2950
	22	Cash receipt	Payment of general expenses, $240
	26	Cheque counterfoil	Paid trade payable, T Ellis, in full settlement of their account, $2700, less 5% cash discount
	28	Bank statement	Bank charges for the month totalled $220

Prepare the business's three-column cash book for April 2012. Balance the cash book on 30 April 2012 and total the discount columns. Ledger accounts are not required.

8 Preparing a three-column cash book with an overdrawn bank balance

Carla owns a beachwear business. On 1 May 2012, her business's cash in hand was $1 270 and cash at bank was $1 480. During May the following transactions occurred.

Date		Source document	Transaction
May	5	Till roll	Cash sales totalling $930
	8	Cheque counterfoil	Paid trade payable, Nico Ltd, in full settlement of their account, $2600, less 5% cash discount
	11	Paying-in slip counterfoil	Transferred cash to bank, $740
	19	Cash receipt	Payment of travelling expenses, $140
	22	Paying-in slip counterfoil	Cheque received from trade receivable, Amin Supplies Ltd, in full settlement of their account, $1200, less 4% cash discount
May	24	Cheque counterfoil	Carla withdrew a cheque for her private use, $450
	30	Cheque counterfoil	Paid trade payable, BL Stores, in full settlement of their account, $3400, less 5% cash discount

Prepare the business's three-column cash book for May 2012. Balance the cash book on 31 May 2012 and total the discount columns. Ledger accounts are not required.

9 Preparing a full accounting system including a three-column cash book up to the trial balance

Janet Watson opened a business on 1 September 2012. On that date her business's assets and liabilities were as follows.

	$
Cash in hand	1 380
Cash at bank	1 750
Non-current assets	86 500
Bank loan	15 000

During September the following transactions occurred.

Date		Source document	Transaction
Sept	4	Purchase invoice (2361)	From TM Bennett Ltd for goods, $2800, less 25% trade discount
	6	Cash receipt	Paid general expenses in cash, $180
	7	Credit note received (G09)	From TM Bennett Ltd for goods not as ordered, $240, less 25% trade discount
	12	Till roll	Cash sales totalling $1090
	14	Cheque counterfoil	Paid TM Bennett Ltd in full settlement of their account at this date, less 5% cash discount
	15	Sales invoice (0001)	To KS Maharaj for goods, $2000, less 20% trade discount
	19	Cheque counterfoil	Rent for three months, $2480
	21	Paying-in slip counterfoil	Transfer of cash to bank, $730
	23	Cash receipt	Janet withdrew cash, $280, for her private use
	26	Credit note issued (01)	To KS Maharaj for damaged items sold on 15 September, $125, less 20% trade discount
	28	Paying-in slip counterfoil	Cheque received from KS Maharaj in full settlement of their account at this date, less 2% cash discount
	30	Bank statement	Bank charges for the month totalled $70

Prepare the following books of prime entry for September 2012:

- Three-column cash book
- Purchases journal
- Sales journal
- Purchases returns
- Sales returns

Post the entries in the books of prime entry to the purchases, sales and general ledgers.

The cash book should be balanced at 30 September 2012 and the discount columns totalled and posted to the general ledger. It is not necessary to balance or close any other accounts.

Prepare a trial balance at 30 September 2012.

10 Preparing a full accounting system including a three-column cash book up to the trial balance

MJ Hall Wholesale's trial balance on 1 December 2012 was as follows.

Trial balance at 1 December 2012

	Dr	Cr
	$	$
Bank	1 650	
Bank charges	480	
Capital		613 640
Cash	820	
Discounts allowed	690	
Discounts received		770
Drawings	34 580	
Insurance	8 240	
Non-current assets	725 000	
Purchases	505 300	
Rent	44 680	
Sales returns	3 130	
Purchases returns		4 290
Salaries	151 400	
Sales		852 370
Trade payable: Carter & Sons		13 400
Trade receivable: JM McNee Ltd	8 500	
	1 484 470	1 484 470

During December the following transactions occurred.

Date		Source document	Transaction
Dec	3	Sales invoice (339)	To JM McNee Ltd for goods, $9 600, less $33\frac{1}{3}$% trade discount
	4	Cheque counterfoil	Paid insurance, $1050
	7	Credit note issued (074)	To JM McNee Ltd for goods, $450, less $33\frac{1}{3}$% trade discount, returned as unsatisfactory
	9	Purchase invoice (D487)	From Carter & Sons for goods, $8840, less 25% trade discount
	12	Cheque counterfoil	Paid Carter & Sons in full settlement of their account at 1 December, less 5% cash discount
	15	Credit note received (449)	From Carter & Sons for goods, $620, less 25% trade discount, that were damaged in transit
	17	Cheque counterfoil	Rent, $3850
	18	Till roll	Cash sales totalling $13 250
	19	Paying-in slip counterfoil	Transfer of cash to bank, $13 800
	23	Cheque counterfoil	Paid salaries, $11 620
	27	Cheque counterfoil	MJ Hall withdrew a cheque, $800, for private use
	29	Paying-in slip counterfoil	Cheque received from JM McNee Ltd in full settlement of their account at this date, less 5% cash discount
	30	Bank statement	Bank charges for the month totalled $240

Prepare the following books of prime entry for December 2012:

- Three-column cash book
- Purchases journal
- Sales journal
- Purchases returns
- Sales returns

Post the entries in the books of prime entry to the purchases, sales and general ledgers.

The cash book should be balanced at 31 December 2012 and the discount columns totalled and posted to the general ledger. It is not necessary to balance or close any other accounts.

Prepare a trial balance at 31 December 2012.

11 Preparing end-of-year financial statements including discounts

On 31 March 2012 the following trial balance was extracted from the books of Khalid Supplies.

Trial balance at 31 March 2012

	Dr	Cr
	$	$
Bank overdraft		5 870
Capital		109 320
Cash	440	
Discounts allowed	1 220	
Discounts received		1 590
Drawings	22 480	
Equipment and furniture	185 000	
Office expenses	31 480	
Purchases	212 400	
Rent	18 500	
Sales returns	840	
Purchases returns		1 120
Sales		386 990
Trade payables		14 730
Trade receivables	8 360	
Wages and salaries	38 900	
	519 620	519 620

Prepare the following:

- Income statement for the year ended 31 March 2012
- Balance sheet at 31 March 2012 (classified)

12 Preparing end-of-year financial statements including discounts

On 30 September 2012 the following trial balance was extracted from the books of Pinebeach Books, owned by Ruth Williams.

Trial balance at 30 September 2012

	Dr	Cr
	$	$
Administration expenses	5 530	
Bank overdraft		720
Capital		374 140
Cash	320	
Discounts allowed	190	
Discounts received		510
Drawings	28 800	
Furniture and fittings	15 500	
Insurance	3 260	
Premises	390 000	
Purchases	98 360	
Sales returns	430	
Purchases returns		970
Sales		205 350
Trade payables		6 280
Trade receivables	920	
Wages	44 660	
	587 970	587 970

Prepare the following:

- Income statement for the year ended 30 September 2012
- Balance sheet at 30 September 2012 (classified)

11 Books of prime entry: the petty cash book

Introduction

In some businesses where there are a large number of transactions in cash, the decision is sometimes made to operate a second cash book which is used to record minor cash transactions, known as **petty cash** transactions.

Often the task of preparing the petty cash book is given to a more junior member of the accounts team, who is called the petty cashier. Responsibility for handling the business's cash has to be tightly controlled.

- The petty cashier is only allowed to handle a maximum amount of petty cash at any one time. This maximum amount is called the float or **imprest**. The size of the float or imprest is decided by the owner or manager of the business and is fixed at a specific amount (e.g. $100).
- The amount of the float or imprest is calculated to be sufficient to cover payments for a set period of time, for example, a week or a month.
- The petty cashier is only allowed to give cash to employees to reimburse them for payments they have made on behalf of the business when evidence is produced (e.g. a receipt).
- For each payment made, the petty cashier is required to complete a **petty cash voucher**. The voucher has to be signed by the person receiving the cash as well as by the petty cashier. Other evidence of the transaction (e.g. the receipt) is attached to the voucher.
- Occasionally a small cash receipt is also recorded in a **petty cash book**.
- For security, petty cash is kept under lock and key.
- The petty cash book is another example of a book of prime entry.

LEARNING OUTCOMES

When you have reached the end of this unit you will be able to:

- identify the source documents used when recording petty cash transactions
- prepare a petty cash book with analysis columns using the imprest system
- post the details recorded in the petty cash book to general ledger and purchases ledger accounts.

KEY TERM

Petty cash: small cash payments.

Imprest: a system for maintaining a petty cash book which gives the petty cashier responsibility for a fixed petty cash float.

Petty cash voucher: the source document for each petty cash payment.

Petty cash book: the book of prime entry used to make the first record of petty cash payments.

11.1 Recording petty cash payments

Source documents

The source document for petty cash transactions is a petty cash voucher.

Illustration 1 A petty cash voucher

Number **302**

PETTY CASH VOUCHER

Item	*Amount*
	$
Interviewee's travel expenses	33.74

Authorised by Lewis Pitts

Received by Irene Johnson

Notes:

1 An individual (Irene Johnson) has been given $33.74 for travel expenses for attending an interview.

2 The interviewee, Irene Johnson, has signed the petty voucher to confirm that she received the amount stated.

3 The petty cashier, Lewis Pitts, has signed the voucher to indicate that he was responsible for making this payment.

4 Lewis will attach a receipt or receipts for the travelling expenses to the voucher. These could be for a taxi, bus, train ticket, and so on.

5 You will notice that the voucher has a number – 302. This number will be used in preparing the accounting records. There will be a pad of petty cash vouchers and they will be numbered consecutively.

How petty cash transactions are recorded

An illustration of a completed petty cash book is shown above. The steps to be followed in completing a petty cash book can be summarised as follows.

A petty cashier at work

Receiving the float

Step 1: The petty cashier will receive the fixed float/imprest in the form of cash or a cheque that needs to be cashed. The double entry required will be:

Debit Petty cash

Credit Cash or bank column in main cash book

Recording each petty cash payment

Step 2: Using information shown on each petty cash voucher the petty cashier will make the following record in the petty cash book:

Credit Petty cash

Then they will make a second entry in the appropriate **analysis column**.

If you were wondering about the debit entry to go with this credit entry, see Step 4 below.

Balancing the petty cash book

Step 3: The petty cash account is balanced in the usual way and the balance is brought down to start the week or month. At this point the petty cashier will need more cash to cover the next week's or month's petty cash payments. The petty cashier will be reimbursed for the previous period's payments and will debit the petty cash account with the amount received. By receiving back exactly what was spent in the previous period the float/imprest is restored to the original amount.

Totalling and posting the analysis columns

Step 4: Finally, the analysis columns are totalled and each total is posted to the relevant ledger accounts. Usually these postings are to expense accounts, but in some cases it is possible that a trade payable is paid in petty cash because only a very small amount is due. These debit entries complete the double-entry process.

KEY TERM

Analysis column: in a petty cash book this is a means of classifying each payment to provide *totals* to be posted to general ledger accounts.

STUDY TIP

An exam question may ask you to state how much should be given to a petty cashier to 'restore the imprest' every week or month (i.e. how much should be given to top up the petty cash float). The answer is always the same as the total of petty cash payments made during that week or month.

Preparing a petty cash book

Illustration 2 An analysed petty cash book

The owner of a business decided to maintain a petty cash book. It was agreed that the imprest would be $150. The following transactions occurred:

		Voucher number	
May	1		Petty cashier received a cheque for $150
	2	1	Stationery, $32.62
	8	2	Postage, $26.29
	11	3	Travel expenses, $18.40
	15	4	Postage, $11.83
	20	5	Purchases ledger account of D Morris, $20.70
	23	6	Stationery, $11.37
	27	7	Travel expenses, $19.11
June	1		The imprest was restored with the receipt of a cheque

Here is the petty cash book based on this information:

Petty cash book

Receipts $	*Date*		*Details*	*Voucher no.*	*Payments $*	*Stationery $*	*Postage $*	*Travel $*	*Purchases ledger $*
150.00	May	1	Bank						
		2	Stationery	1	32.62	32.62			
		8	Postage	2	26.29		26.29		
		11	Travel	3	18.40			18.40	
		15	Postage	4	11.83		11.83		
		20	D Morris	5	20.70				20.70
		23	Stationery	6	11.37	11.37			
		27	Travel	7	19.11			19.11	
					140.32	43.99	38.12	37.51	20.70
		31	Balance	c/d	9.68				
150.00					150.00				
9.68	June	1	Balance	b/d					
140.32		1	Bank						

Dr **Cash book** **Cr**

	Cash $	Bank $				Cash $	Bank $
			May	1	Petty cash		150

Here are examples of the posting of analysis column totals and the payment to the credit supplier:

GENERAL LEDGER

Dr **Stationery account** **Cr**

May	31	Petty cash	43.99	

Dr		Postage		Cr
May	31	Petty cash	38.12	

Dr		Travel		Cr
May	31	Petty cash	37.51	

PURCHASES LEDGER

Dr		D Morris		Cr
May	20	Petty cash	20.70	

Notes:

1 The cheque received by the petty cashier on 1 May and 1 June would be cashed to provide notes and coins to make petty cash payments.

2 The matching entry in the cash book for 1 May would appear as shown:

- In the petty cash book the receipts column is the equivalent of the debit side of the petty cash account; the payments column is the equivalent of the credit side.
- Each payment must be cross-referenced to the relevant voucher.
- Each payment is analysed under appropriate headings for the most regularly occurring expenses. These would be decided in advance by the owner or manager of the business. Theoretically there can be as many analysis columns as are required.
- The balancing process is almost exactly the same as usual, but the payments column is first subtotalled before balancing.
- The analysis columns are totalled at agreed intervals – weekly or monthly – and the totals are posted to the relevant ledger accounts. This process saves much time as otherwise separate entries would have to be made in the ledger accounts of every petty cash payment, however small the amount involved.
- The one exception to this procedure is that each individual entry in the purchases ledger analysis column is debited to the account of credit supplier on the date of the payment, and the analysis column total is not used for this purpose. This exception is made necessary by the fact that there are many individual accounts of trade payables rather than just one account for all trade payables.

What you should do with the balance of the petty cash book

You can now answer questions 1–6 on pages 102–104.

The balance of the petty cash book is one of the business's assets. Like any cash balance it should be recorded as a debit entry in the trial balance and as the most liquid of the business's current assets on the balance sheet.

STUDY TIP

To help avoid arithmetical errors with the balancing process and totalling of analysis columns, it is a good idea to cross-check that the subtotal for payments actually agrees with the total of the analysis columns.

STUDY TIP

When you see the item 'petty cash (in hand)' in a trial balance remember this is a reference to the petty cash balance. This item should be recorded as a current asset in the balance sheet. It is a common mistake to think that this item is a reference to petty cash expenses and record the amount in the income statement by mistake.

Unit 11 Practice questions

DEVELOPING YOUR SKILLS

1 Preparing a petty cash book and posting to ledger accounts

Janet has decided that her business should use a petty cash book starting in October 2012 and that the imprest should be $200. She also decided that the petty cash book should have analysis columns as follows:

- Postage
- Stationery
- Travel
- Cleaning
- General expenses
- Purchase ledger accounts

During the first month of operation the following petty cash transactions occurred.

		Voucher number	
Oct	1		Petty cashier received a cheque for $200
	3	1	Postage, $24.52
	5	2	Office cleaning, $35.00
	8	3	Travel expenses, $11.80
	12	4	Trade payable, D Chadee, $14.48
	16	5	General expenses, $10.60
	17	6	Office cleaning, $35.00
	20	7	Travel expenses, $7.38
	22	8	Stationery, $14.23
	24	9	Cleaning materials, $12.22
	30	10	Trade payable, M Carr, $21.37
	31		The petty cash book was balanced and the analysis columns totalled
Nov	1		The imprest was restored with the receipt of a cheque

Prepare the petty cash book for October 2012. Balance the petty cash book and restore the imprest on 1 November. Post the details of the analysis columns to the accounts in the general and purchases ledgers.

2 Preparing a petty cash book and posting to ledger accounts

Jamal's business makes use of a petty cash book. On 1 February 2012 the balance of petty cash in hand was $14.55. The petty cash book operates with an imprest of $220 and with the following analysis columns:

- Postage
- Stationery
- Vehicle expenses
- Casual labour
- Office expenses
- Purchase ledger accounts

During February 2012 the following petty cash transactions occurred:

		Voucher number	
Feb	1		Petty cashier received a cheque to restore the imprest
	2	141	Stationery, $9.70
	8	142	Vehicle fuel, $35.50
	10	143	Postage, $11.10
	13	144	Casual labour, $38.25
	15	145	Office expenses, $8.42
	18	146	Trade payable, Ryan & Co. Ltd, $17.11
	21	147	Vehicle fuel, $34.22
	23	148	Trade payable, BY Scott, $9.28
	25	149	Postage, $8.56
	26	150	Casual labour, $21.80
	28		The petty cash book was balanced and the analysis columns totalled
Mar	1		The imprest was restored with the receipt of a cheque

Prepare the petty cash book for February 2012. Balance the petty cash book and restore the imprest on 1 March. Post the details of the analysis columns to the accounts in the general and purchases ledgers.

3 Preparing cash books

Melanie owns a small department store. Her accounting system includes the following.

a Petty cash book: this operates with a monthly imprest of $200. Petty cash is used to make all payments of less than $40. The petty cash book has the following analysis columns:

i Vehicle expenses

ii Postage

iii Office expenses

iv Cleaning

b Two-column cash book: this has columns for bank and discounts. All payments of more than $40 are made by cheque.

The following information is available for June 2012.

June 1 Petty cash in hand, $19; cash at bank, $3880
2 Petty cashier received cheque to restore the imprest
3 Banked cash sales of $832
7 Paid office expenses, $8.82
8 Paid for vehicle fuel, $32.30
10 Received a cheque from trade receivable, Y Khan, in full settlement of the amount due, $640, less a 2.5% cash discount
11 Paid for office expenses, $1.28
15 Paid cleaner's wages, $37.32
16 Paid trade payable, A Mohammed, in full settlement of the amount due, $1400, less a 5% cash discount
18 Purchased postage stamps, $14
21 Paid for office expenses, $7.11
22 Received a cheque from trade receivable, B Taylor, in full settlement of the amount due, $880, less 2.5% cash discount
23 Banked cash sales of $902
24 Paid for vehicle fuel, $25
25 Paid trade payable, J Ram, in full settlement of the amount due, $1860, less a 5% cash discount
26 Paid office expenses, $45
27 Purchases postage stamps, $17.14
28 Paid cleaner's wages, $31.26
29 Paid for vehicle fuel, $48
30 Paid wages, $1580
30 The petty cash book and cash book were balanced. Analysis columns and discount columns were totalled

Prepare the business's petty cash book and cash book for the month of June 2012. Invent suitable voucher numbers for petty cash transactions. Entries do not have to be posted to ledger accounts.

4 Preparing cash books

Marcus owns a wholesale business providing building materials. His business makes use of two cash books:

Petty cash book: this operates with a monthly imprest of $300. Petty cash is used to make all payments of less than $60. The petty cash book has the following analysis columns:

- Stationery
- Travel expenses
- Vehicle running expenses
- General expenses

Two-column cash book: this has columns for bank and discounts. All payments for more than $60 are made by cheque.

The following information is available for March 2012:

Mar 1 Petty cash in hand, $34; cash at bank, $1724
2 Petty cashier received cheque to restore the imprest
Mar 4 Paid for general expenses, $18.49
6 Received cheque from trade receivable, Dass & Co., in full settlement of their account, $2360, less 5% cash discount
7 Banked cash sales of $1460
9 Paid employee's travel expenses, $37.33
10 Paid trade payable, P Nanan Ltd, in full settlement of the amount due, $4580, less 5% cash discount
11 Purchased stationery, $14.37
12 Paid for vehicle fuel, $45.60
14 Paid rent, $780
15 Purchased stationery, $25.31
17 Paid vehicle repairs, $56
18 Paid employee's travel expenses, $18.42
20 Paid wages, $2480
21 Received a cheque from trade receivable, MV Tammy, in full settlement of the amount due, $3300, less 5% cash discount
23 Banked cash sales of $782
24 Paid vehicle repairs, $83
25 Paid employee's travel expenses, $24.89
27 Paid for vehicle fuel, $41.45
28 Paid for general expenses, $64
31 The petty cash book and cash book were balanced. Analysis columns and discount columns were totalled

Prepare the business's petty cash book and cash book for the month of March 2012. Invent suitable voucher numbers for petty cash transactions. Entries do not have to be posted to ledger accounts.

5 Preparing end-of-year financial statements including a petty cash balance

Emily Williams owns a shoe shop. Her business's financial year ended on 31 October 2012 when the following trial balance was extracted from the business's books of account.

Trial balance at 31 October 2012

	Dr	Cr
	$	$
Bank charges	387	
Bank overdraft		1 028
Capital		26 346
Cleaning expenses	114	
Discounts allowed	559	
Discounts received		782
Drawings	30 385	
Furniture and fittings	27 500	
Insurance	2 194	
Office expenses	1 183	
Petty cash	32	
Purchases	118 548	
Purchases returns		803
Rent	18 340	
Sales		199 281
Sales returns	258	
Travel expenses	173	
Trade payables		5 523
Trade receivables	2 804	
Wages	31 286	
	233 763	233 763

Prepare the following:

- Income statement for the year ended 31 October 2012
- Balance sheet at 31 October 2012 (classified)

6 Preparing end-of-year financial statements including a petty cash balance

Omar owns a car accessories business. His business's financial year ended on 31 August 2012 when the following trial balance was extracted from the business's books of account.

Trial balance at 31 August 2012

	Dr	Cr
	$	$
Administration expenses	4 483	
Bank charges	511	
Bank	3 700	
Bank loan (repayable May 2012)		18 000
Bank loan interest	1 040	
Capital		49 910
Discounts allowed	302	
Discounts received		181
Drawings	22 119	
Equipment and fittings	45 000	
General expenses	3 906	
Petty cash	18	
Purchases	285 480	
Purchases returns		2 205
Rent	31 360	
Sales		432 276
Sales returns	1 414	
Stationery and postage	308	
Trade payables		8 470
Trade receivables	3 374	
Vehicles	53 240	
Vehicle running expenses	6 407	
Wages	48 380	
	511 042	511 042

Prepare the following:

- Income statement for the year ended 31 August 2012
- Balance sheet at 31 August 2012 (classified)

12 Books of prime entry: the journal

Introduction

The double-entry accounting system works on the basis that all transactions should first be recorded in a book of prime entry before entries are made in ledger accounts. So far, books of prime entry have been put in place for:

Money transactions	➔	Two- or three-column cash book
		Petty cash book
Credit transactions (for goods in which the business trades)	➔	Purchases journal
		Sales journal
		Purchases returns journal
		Sales returns journal

At first sight this arrangement might seem to cover every possibility. However, there is a small group of entries in the accounting system that falls outside these categories. In order to provide the first record for these entries, the **journal** is used.

The general rule for the use of the journal is that it should be used whenever the cash books or four other journals are not appropriate. The following broad categories give some idea of when these situations occur:

- Purchase and sale of non-current assets on credit
- Cancelling entries and correcting errors in accounts
- Transferring information from one account to another
- End-of-year transfers from expense accounts to the income statement
- Opening a new set of books.

The journal is sometimes referred to by the alternative name 'general journal'.

LEARNING OUTCOMES

When you have reached the end of this unit you will be able to:

- identify situations when it is appropriate to use the journal
- make entries in a journal
- post the details recorded in the journal to ledger accounts.

KEY TERM

Journal: a book of prime entry used to make the first record of transactions that it would not be appropriate to record in the other books of prime entry (cash books and other journals).

DID YOU KNOW?

The books of prime entry are an important part of a business's accounting system. They provide the only clear record of what has happened in date order, and they also provide an important connection between the evidence for each transaction (i.e. the source documents) and the entries in the accounting system.

12.1 How to make journal entries

DID YOU KNOW?

There is a large range of possible source documents for journal entries. As well as invoices for the purchase of a non-current asset, there could be letters or emails received from other businesses or organisations, and internal notes or emails written by the owner, managers or other employees.

A journal entry is a record of which account is to be debited and which account is to be credited for a particular transaction. When preparing a journal entry the following procedures should be followed:

1 A journal entry requires the following details:
   a Date of the transaction
   b Account to be debited and the amount
   c Account to be credited and the amount
   d Short description of the transaction – called the narrative
2 It is usual to slightly indent the name of the account to be credited in the detail column.
3 Each journal entry is separated from the next one by ruling off the details column.

Illustration 1 Purchase of a non-current asset on credit

On 4 July 2012 the owner of a business purchased a new vehicle, $32 000, for business use on credit from Blue River Motors Ltd.

The journal entry is shown below.

Journal

Date	*Details*	*Dr*	*Cr*
		$	$
July 4	Vehicles	32 000	
	Blue River Motors Ltd		32 000
	Purchase of vehicle on credit,		
	invoice number 4872		

GENERAL LEDGER

Dr **Vehicles account** **Cr**

July	4	Blue River Motors Ltd	32 000			

PURCHASES LEDGER

Dr **Blue River Motors Ltd account** **Cr**

			July	4	Vehicle	32 000

Note: the journal entry would be posted through to the relevant ledger accounts.

Illustration 2 Sale of a non-current asset on credit

Here is another example of a situation when a journal entry would be required.

On 22 May the owner of a business selling groceries sold some unwanted equipment on credit to Linda MacDonald for $450.

The journal entry is as follows.

Journal			
Date	*Details*	*Dr*	*Cr*
		$	$
May 22	Linda MacDonald	450	
	Equipment		450
	Sale of non-current assets on credit		

This journal entry should be posted as follows.

GENERAL LEDGER

Dr				**Equipment account**			Cr
				May	22	Linda MacDonald	450

SALES LEDGER

Dr			**Linda MacDonald account**				Cr
May	22	Equipment	450				

Illustration 3 Correcting errors

It is inevitable that errors will be made in the accounts from time to time. The rule is always that errors should be corrected by making additional entries. It would never be acceptable to cross out or try to remove the wrong entries as this could look as if the accounts had been tampered with.

On 5 August 2012 a business's bookkeeper recorded the payment of rent by cheque, $345, as $354 in both the bank account and rent account.

The journal entry to record the correction of these entries is:

Journal			
Date	*Details*	*Dr*	*Cr*
		$	$
Aug 5	Bank	9	
	Rent		9
	Correction of error in recording the amount paid for rent		

Here are the entries in the bank account and in the rent account, showing the original entries and the posting of the corrections.

Dr			**Cash book (bank columns)**				Cr
			Bank				Bank
			$				$
Aug	5	Rent	9	Aug	5	Rent	354

GENERAL LEDGER

Dr			**Rent account**				Cr
Aug	5	Bank	354	Aug	5	Bank	9

LINKS...
There is much more about the correction of errors in Unit 22.

Illustration 4 End-of-year transfers to the income statement

At the end of each accounting year many accounts are closed and their balances transferred to the income statement. These transfers from one account to another should all be journalised first.

On 31 December 2012 the end-of-year financial statements of the business owned by Laura Cousins were prepared. This included the transfer of sales, $193 400, and wages, $32 480, to the income statement.

These transfer entries should be journalised as follows.

Journal

Date	*Details*	*Dr*	*Cr*
		$	$
Dec 31	Sales	193 400	
	Income statement		193 400
	Transfer of sales to income statement		
31	Income statement	32 480	
	Wages		32 480
	Transfer of wages to income statement		

Illustration 5 Opening a new set of books

When a new business starts up and the books of account are opened for the first time, a journal entry is used to record the starting position in the asset, liability and capital accounts. This situation occurs just once in the lifetime of any business.

On 1 January 2012 Jo Anderson opened a business with the following.

	$
Bank	55 000
Vehicle	43 000
Bank loan	20 000
Capital	78 000

The journal entry to record the opening of the books of account is:

Journal

Date	*Details*	*Dr*	*Cr*
		$	$
Jan 1	Bank	55 000	
	Vehicle	43 000	
	Bank loan		20 000
	Capital		78 000
	Entries to open books of account		

You can now answer all the questions on pages 109–114.

Unit 12 Practice questions

DEVELOPING YOUR SKILLS

1 Preparing journal entries

Prepare journal entries to record the following transactions.

July 3 Purchases new equipment, $3600, for business use on credit from J Rajah Ltd – invoice number 7361

14 It was noticed that the bookkeeper had made a mistake when recording the sale of goods, $780, on credit to TM Williams. The correct entry had been made in the sales account, but the account of T Williams Ltd had been debited in error. Entries were made to correct this mistake

19 Some of the equipment purchased from J Rajah Ltd on 3 July was returned to the supplier as it was damaged in transit. The supplier sent a letter agreeing to the deduction of $520 from the amount due

31 At the end of the business's accounting year total purchases of $156 000 were transferred to the income statement

31 The balance of the discounts received account, $943, was transferred to the income statement

Show how all of the journal entries would be posted to ledger accounts.

2 Preparing journal entries

Prepare journal entries to record the following transactions:

May 1 The owner of a business opened the books of account with the following: bank $5000, fixtures and fittings $23 000, bank loan $8000 and capital $20 000

12 An error was made when the purchase of stationery, $105, was posted to the debit side of the purchases account rather than the debit side of the administration expenses account. This mistake was corrected

15 Some fixtures, $1050, were purchased for business use on credit from Albo Shelving Ltd, invoice number 3088

31 Monthly financial statements were prepared and the total of the sales account, $28 700, was transferred to the income statement.

31 The balance of the rent account, $750, was transferred to the income statement.

Show how all the journal entries would be posted to ledger accounts.

3 Selecting the correct book of prime entry

During the month of February 2012 the following transactions occurred affecting the accounts of Rishi, a trader. Rishi maintains all seven books of prime entry as part of his books of account. In the case of each transaction, decide which subsidiary book should be used to make the first entry in the accounting system.

Feb 4 Received an invoice for goods for resale

7 Paid a trade payable by cheque

11 A voucher showed the payment of travel expenses in cash

15 Received a credit note from a trade payable for goods damaged in transit

18 A cheque was drawn for the payment of wages

22 Received an invoice for a new vehicle for business use

24 Issued a credit note to a trade receivable for goods returned as unsuitable

28 Corrected a mistake in the accounts where the wrong amount had been debited and credited in the ledger accounts

4 Selecting the correct book of prime entry

Renea is the owner of a retail unit. Her business's accounting system includes all seven books of prime entry as part of her books of account. The following transactions were among those that occurred during September 2012. In each case decide which subsidiary book should be used to make the first record of the transaction.

Sept 3 Received an invoice for some new equipment for business use

6 Cheque stub showed the payment of rent for the month

11 Entries were made to correct a mistake made by the bookkeeper

14 Invoice was issued for the sale of goods on credit

15 Credit note was issued for the return of goods by a customer

20 A voucher showed the purchase of postage stamps

23 Invoice was received for goods for resale

25 Some of the new equipment was found to be faulty and was returned to the supplier

30 Expense accounts were closed and their balances transferred to the income statement for the year ended on this date

5 Preparing a full accounting system including journal entries up to the trial balance

On 1 January 2012 Carmen opened a new business with the following:

	$
Cash at bank	3 500
Vehicle	36 000
Equipment	19 000
Capital	58 500

Carmen has decided to maintain the following books of prime entry:

- Journal
- Three-column cash book
- Purchases journal
- Sales journal
- Purchases returns journal
- Sales returns journal

During January the following transactions occurred.

Jan	4	Received an invoice (number 302) from MJT Ltd for goods for resale, $6400, less 25% trade discount
	7	Till rolls showed cash sales totalling $1240
	10	Paid operating expenses in cash, $280
	11	Banked cash, $800
	14	Received a credit note (number 073) from MJT Ltd for goods returned as damaged, $200, less 25% trade discount
	15	Received an invoice (number 478) for some additional equipment for business use from Bridge Products, $880
	16	Issued an invoice (number 001) to Geeta Stores for goods, $1200, less 15% trade discount
	19	Returned some of the additional equipment, $90, purchased on 15 January from Bridge Products
	22	Issued a credit note (number 001) to Geeta Stores for goods, $100, less 15% trade discount
	24	Paid MJT Ltd in settlement of their account at this date, less 2% cash discount
	29	Received a cheque from Geeta Stores in full settlement of their account at this date, less a cash discount of $24

Record these transactions in the books of prime entry and post to the ledger accounts. Balance the cash book and total the discount columns. Prepare a trial balance at 31 January 2012. There is no need to balance or close any other accounts.

6 Preparing a full accounting system including journal entries up to the trial balance

Omar owns a wholesale business supplying computer accessories to retailers in the region. His business's trial balance on 1 November was as follows.

Trial balance at 1 November 2012

	Dr $	Cr $
Bank overdraft		1 480
Capital		103 560
Cash	440	
Discounts allowed	1 320	
Discounts received		1 890
Drawings	37 320	
Furniture and equipment	180 000	
Operating expenses	45 360	
Purchases	578 270	
Purchases returns		5 130
Sales		732 340
Sales returns	4 890	
Trade payables		
LDZ Ltd		4 500
M Chin Ltd		3 200
Trade receivables		
Oldbridge Retail Unit	2 800	
Peterson Stores	1 700	
	852 100	852 100

During November 2012 the following transactions occurred.

Date		Source document	Details
Nov	1	Cash receipt	For operating expenses, $380
	3	Invoice	From LDZ Ltd (number 891) for goods for resale, $4500, less $33\frac{1}{3}$% trade discount
	7	Paying-in slip counterfoil	Cheque received from Oldbridge Retail Unit in settlement of their account at this date, less 5% cash discount
	8	Credit note	Received from LDZ Ltd (number 223) for goods purchased on 3 November, not as ordered, $330, less $33\frac{1}{3}$% trade discount
	12	Till roll	Cash sales totalling $2460
	13	Cheque counterfoil	Omar withdrew $720 for private use
	17	Invoice	Sent to Peterson Stores (number 407) for goods, $2450, less 20% trade discount
	18	Paying-in slip counterfoil	Banked cash, $1800
Nov	20	Invoice	For additional equipment for business use, $1460, received from Deva Office Supplies (invoice number 2789)
	22	Credit note	Sent to Peterson Stores (number 082) for goods damaged in transit, $150, less 20% trade discount
	25	Cheque counterfoil	Paid M Chin Ltd the amount due at this date, less 5% cash discount
	29	Paying-in slip counterfoil	Cheque received from Peterson Stores in settlement of their account at this date, less a cash discount of $110

Prepare the following:

- Journal
- Three-column cash book
- Purchases journal
- Sales journal
- Purchases returns journal
- Sales returns journal
- Purchases ledger accounts
- Sales ledger accounts
- General ledger accounts
- Trial balance dated 30 November 2012

Balance the cash book on 30 November 2012 and total the discount columns. End of your finacial statements are *not* required.

(The following questions cover Units 8–12)

MULTIPLE-CHOICE QUESTIONS

7 Entries in the purchases journal are taken from which of the following documents?

A Credit notes
B Delivery notes
C Invoices
D Receipts

8 To check the accuracy of the purchases returns journal, which of the following should be examined, referring to copies if necessary?

A Credit notes issued
B Credit notes received
C Invoices issued
D Invoices received

9 Which of the following source documents should be used to make entries in the sales journal?

A A credit note received from a supplier
B A debit note sent to a supplier
C An invoice sent to a customer
D A petty cash voucher for travelling expenses

10 A paying-in slip counterfoil is used to make entries in the:

A Cash book
B Petty cash book
C Purchases journal
D Sales returns journal

11 Which of these transactions should be entered in the journal?

A Correction of error in recording purchases returns
B Owner's cash drawings
C Purchase of new equipment by cheque
D Returns of goods to a supplier

12 The owner of a business purchased a new delivery vehicle for business use. A cash deposit of 10 per cent was paid at the time of purchase; the balance is to be paid in four months' time. Which subsidiary book(s) should be used to record this information?

A Journal
B Journal and cash book
C Purchases journal
D Purchases journal and cash book

13 The following totals were shown in the discount columns of a business's cash book.

Dr **Cash book** **Cr**

Discounts	Cash	Bank	Discounts	Cash	Bank
610			450		

What entries should be made in the general ledger?

A Debit discounts allowed $450
Credit discounts received $610
B Debit discounts allowed $610
Credit discounts received $450
C Debit discounts received $450
Credit discounts allowed $610
D Debit discounts received $610
Credit discounts allowed $450

14 On 1 August Salma sold goods to Riaz. Riaz returned some of these goods a week later. In which order will Salma issue documents to Riaz during April?

A Credit note, invoice, statement of account
B Invoice, credit note, statement of account
C Invoice, statement of account, credit note
D Statement of account, invoice, credit note

15 Adam is responsible for keeping a petty cash book for his employer. The monthly imprest is $200. During January the following petty cash payments were made: travel expenses $82; postage $45; office cleaning $39.

How much should Adam receive at the end of January to restore the imprest?

A $34
B $166
C $200
D $366

16 A retailer purchased $2 000 of goods from a supplier on the following terms: 25 per cent trade discount, 10 per cent cash discount if the invoice is paid within 30 days.

The retailer paid the invoice 20 days after receipt. How much should the retailer pay?

A $1300
B $1350
C $1500
D $1800

17 The purchases journal in the accounts of a food retailer is the book of prime entry for which of the following transations?

A Fittings purchased on credit
B Goods for resale purchased for cash
C Goods for resale purchased on credit
D The purchase of stationery

18 Which of the following should **not** be entered in the journal?

A Correction of an error
B Entries to open new books of account
C The purchase of a non-current asset for cash
D Transfer of wages to the income statement

OTHER QUESTIONS

19 Yeung prepared the following cash book for his business.

Cash book

Dr			Cash	Bank				Cash	Bank **Cr**
			$	$				$	$
Oct	1	Balances	370	320	Oct	5	Rent		1 450
	8	Sales	940			11	Stationery	45	
	14	Cash		1 100		14	Bank	1 100	
	31	Balance c/d		140		21	Bank charges		110
						31	Balance c/d	165	
			1 310	1 560				1 310	1 560
Nov	1	Balance b/d	165		Nov	1	Balance b/d		140

a Name the source document that would have provided the information required for the entries on:

i 5 October
ii 8 October
iii 11 October
iv 14 October
v 21 October

b What do the balances of the cash book on 1 November mean?

20 Vivian sells two types of surfboard: Excel and Supa. Recently she sold some surfboards to one of her regular customers, Peter Green.

a Complete the missing items (i to vii) (words or figures) in the following extract from the invoice that Vivian sent to Peter Green.

No. K488

INVOICE

Quantity	Description			Unit price $	Total $
6	Excel surfboards			320	**(i)**
(ii)	Supa surfboards			380	1 900
	TOTAL				**(iii)**
	Less 20%	**(iv)**	discount		**(v)**
			NET AMOUNT DUE		**(vi)**

Terms: Payment within 30 days

5% **(vii)** discount for settlement within 20 days

b Which book of prime entry will Vivian use to record this information?

c If Peter Green returns some of these surfboards, which document will Vivian need to send to Peter to show the amount to be deducted from the total due?

21 Tony runs a general store. Complete the table below to show how the transactions listed should be recorded in this business's books of account.

	Transaction	Book of prime entry	Account to be debited	Account to be credited
i	A cheque counterfoil showed the payment of rent			
ii	Bank statement showed the deduction of bank charges			
iii	A paying-in slip counterfoil showed a that cheque from a customer, AZX & Co., was paid into the bank			
iv	A credit note was received from a supplier, BTX Ltd			
v	A petty cash voucher showed a payment for stationery			
vi	An invoice showed the purchase of a new till for shop use			

22 Robbie is a trainee accounts clerk at Preston Supplies Ltd. He has been asked to file a collection of source documents.

a Explain why source documents are important when preparing accounting records.

b Complete the following table to identify the source document that is appropriate for each transaction.

	Transaction	Source document
i	Some new office furniture was purchased on credit	
ii	Some goods were returned to a supplier	
iii	Cash sales were paid into the bank	
iv	An employee was repaid the amount he had spent on travel on behalf of the business	
v	Goods were sold on credit	

23 Candy keeps a petty cash book for her employer. The monthly float is $180. During July 2012 she recorded petty cash vouchers for expense payments totalling $140 and the payment of the accounts of two trade payables totalling $30.

a What is the name of the system for keeping petty cash that makes use of a float?

b How much should Candy receive to restore the float at the end of July 2012?

c Candy's employer will prepare an income statement for the month of July 2012. How will the information given about petty cash transactions affect the income statement?

d Candy's employer will also prepare a balance sheet at 31 July 2012. What entry, if any, will result from the information about petty cash?

24 Abdul is a wholesaler of electrical goods. Recently the following transactions occurred, all of which required entries in his business's journal.

- The sale of some office furniture on credit to Tom Cheung for $230
- The purchase of a new delivery vehicle on credit from Bestride Motors Ltd for $15 400
- The transfer of general expenses for the year, $3910, to the income statement

a Describe the purpose of the journal in an accounting system.

b Prepare journal entries to record each of the transactions.

25 Paloma's accounting system includes a three-column cash book. On 30 June 2012 the cash book showed that she had cash in hand of $124; a bank overdraft of $4156; the discounts allowed column totalled $339, and the discounts received column totalled $271.

a How will this information be recorded in Paloma's balance sheet at 30 June 2012?

b Explain why discount columns were totalled rather than balanced in a three-column cash book.

c Explain one reason why Paloma allows her credit customers a cash discount.

d What entries will be made in Paloma's general ledger for the information about discounts?

13 The income statement and inventories

Introduction

Recording inventories

Until now it has been assumed that a business will sell everything it buys during a financial year. Of course, this is very unlikely – it would be a rare event to see a shop, for example, with every shelf empty on the last day of the financial year. Unsold goods are referred to as **inventory**. So the question arises as to how inventory is recorded in the accounting system. In this unit you will learn how to record the value of inventories in the income statement, including the correct treatment of a transaction where the owner of a business takes goods for own use.

Using a vertical form of presentation

In previous units you have been used to preparing simple income statements in the form of a two-sided ledger account (i.e. a horizontal format). These days most accountants have switched to using what is called a 'vertical' format for all the end-of-year financial statements.

As you will see in this unit, the vertical format gives the opportunity to improve the presentation of financial statements because, theoretically, there is the possibility of using as many columns as are necessary to set out the information clearly and systematically. The other great benefit is that the vertical format is much more accessible to non-accountants. This means that those individuals who are not familiar with the rules of debit, credit and so on, are not as likely to be confused by what they see in the end-of-year financial statements.

Carriage inwards and outwards

You will also learn about the correct accounting treatment for two similar expenses: carriage inwards and carriage outwards. Both of these expenses relate to the cost of transporting goods. Carriage inwards is a buying expense and is recorded in the first part of the income statement and carriage outwards is a selling expense and is recorded in the second part of the income statement.

Using the term 'revenue'

Finally, it has now become normal to use the word 'revenue' to describe a business's sales when preparing income statements. You will see that 'revenue' is used in the illustrations in this, and later, units.

LEARNING OUTCOMES

When you have reached the end of this unit you will be able to:

- record opening and closing inventories in the general ledger and income statements
- record carriage inwards in an income statement
- record goods taken for own use by the owner of a business
- prepare the first section of an income statement in vertical format.

KEY TERM

Inventory: goods owned by a business that have not yet been sold.

LINKS...

To make the change to the vertical form of presentation of financial statements more manageable, the subject will be covered over three units: the current unit (for the first section of the income statement), Unit 14 (for the second part of the income statement) and Unit 18 (for the balance sheet).

13.1 The effect of inventory on gross profit

KEY TERM

Closing inventory: goods unsold at the end of a trading year.

Cost of sales: the value at cost price of goods sold during a trading year. It is found as follows: Opening inventory + Purchases − Closing inventory. It is sometimes called the cost of goods sold.

LINKS...

There is more about inventories, in particular how to value inventories correctly, in Unit 19.

So far, gross profit has been calculated by deducting net purchases from net revenue for a year. However, if a business did not sell everything it purchased (i.e. it had an inventory at the end of the trading year) then this would affect the calculation.

Illustration 1 Closing inventory

During a financial year a retailer purchased goods for $150 000; revenue totalled $220 000.

At this stage it looks as if this business has a gross profit of $70 000 (revenue $220 000, less purchases $150 000).

Now, suppose the business did not sell everything it purchased and had a **closing inventory** valued at $30 000.

It is necessary to deduct the value of a closing inventory from the figure for purchases to find the **cost of sales**.

Here is a revised calculation of the gross profit.

	$	$
Revenue		220 000
Less value of goods actually sold		
Purchases	150 000	
Less closing inventory	(30 000)	
		(120 000)
Gross profit		100 000

Notes:

1 The idea here is to find the value of the goods that the business actually sold.

2 In accounting statements the value at cost price of goods actually sold is called cost of sales.

The closing inventory is entered in the income statement as a deduction from purchases. An inventory of unsold goods is a business asset, so the other entry in the double-entry system is to record this asset in the general ledger.

Illustration 2 Recording a closing inventory in the general ledger

Here is the inventory account recording the closing inventory of $30 000. Assume the accounting year end is 31 December.

GENERAL LEDGER
Inventory account

Dr				Cr
Dec	31	Income statement	30 000	

Notes:

1 The entry in the inventory account for the closing inventory is on the debit side of the account because this is the record of an asset.

2 This asset will appear on the balance sheet at this date. It is listed as the first of the current assets.

KEY TERM

Opening inventory: goods unsold at the beginning of a trading year. The amount will be the same as the closing inventory from the previous year.

The next thing to consider is the effect of this closing inventory when looking at the next trading year. The answer is that one year's closing inventory becomes the **opening inventory** for the next year.

Illustration 3 Opening inventory

The business starts the next financial year with an opening inventory of $30 000.

Purchases total $200 000 and revenue is $300 000 during this financial year. At end of the year there is a closing inventory of $40 000.

As you know, the important question to ask is: What goods were actually sold during the financial year?

Here is the calculation required to establish this figure based on the details above.

Calculating the value of goods actually sold

	$
Inventory at the beginning of the year	30 000
Add purchases	200 000
Total of goods that COULD be sold	230 000
Less inventory of unsold goods at end of year	(40 000)
Value of goods ACTUALLY sold (cost of sales)	190 000

Notes:

1 The opening inventory plus purchases gives a figure for what could be sold . . .

2 . . . and, what could be sold minus closing inventory gives the value of goods actually sold (cost of sales).

The calculation of gross profit will be as follows:

	$	$
Revenue		300 000
Less value of goods actually sold		
Opening inventory	30 000	
Purchases	200 000	
	230 000	
less closing inventory	(40 000)	
		(190 000)
Gross profit		110 000

The inventory account

At the beginning of the year the inventory account will show a debit balance (i.e. the figure for closing inventory for the previous year), which is $30 000. During the course of the year the inventory account is entirely ignored. This may seem a little strange as you may think that the level of inventory in the business will be changing all the time. The inventory account is just used to record the opening inventory and closing inventory and nothing else. All other changes in inventory levels are recorded in the accounting system as follows:

- Increases in inventory are shown in the purchases account (an 'inventory in' account).
- Decreases of inventory are shown in the sales account (an 'inventory out' account).

Here is the inventory account based on the information in Illustration 3:

Dr		Inventory account					Cr
Yr 1				Yr 2			
Dec	31	Income statement	30 000	Dec	31	Income statement	30 000
Yr 2							
Dec	31	Income statement	40 000				

This is Years 2's closing inventory

This is last year's closing inventory – the opening inventory for Year 2

This entry is to transfer Year 2's opening inventory to the trading account

STUDY TIP

Do not be tempted to make any entries in the inventory account during the course of a trading year. The inventory account is only used at the end of a year to transfer the opening inventory to the income statement, and to record the closing inventory for the year. All movements in inventory during the year are recorded in the purchases, sales and returns accounts.

You can now answer questions 1 and 2 on page 120.

You can now answer questions 3 and 4 on page 120.

13.2 Using the vertical format

The vertical form of presentation for end-of-year financial statements is now widely used. It is a more flexible form of presentation than the two-sided horizontal style of layout because you can use as many columns as you like. It is often recommended because non-specialists find the presentation easier to follow.

LINKS...
There is more about vertical presentation in Units 14 and 18.

Here is an example of how to prepare the first part of an income statement using a vertical rather than horizontal format.

Illustration 4 Preparing the first section of an income statement using a vertical format

Miguel owns a retail business. On 31 December 2012 the following information was taken from his books of account.

	$
Purchases	75 000
Purchases returns	2 000
Revenue	145 000
Sales returns	3 000
Inventories	
1 January 2012 (opening inventory)	10 000
31 December 2012 (closing inventory)	15 000

The first part of the income statement will be as shown opposite.

Miguel
Income statement for the year ended
31 December 2012

	$	$	$
Revenue		145 000	
less sales returns		(3 000)	
			142 000
Opening inventory		10 000	
Add purchases	75 000		
less purchases returns	(2 000)		
		73 000	
		83 000	
Less closing inventory		(15 000)	
Cost of sales			(68 000)
Gross profit			74 000

Notes:

1 In the vertical format always start with revenue (less sales returns).

2 Now work your way through the calculation of the cost of sales, remembering to deduct any purchases returns from purchases.

3 The figure for cost of sales, $68 000, should be clearly labelled.

4 Finally, record the gross profit ($74 000) – do not forget to label this figure.

You can now answer questions 5 and 6 on page 120.

In the illustration the vertical columns have been used as follows:

- The column *furthest on the right*: is used to record the significant figures: net revenue, cost of sales and gross profit.
- The *middle money column*: is used to show how these key figures were arrived at.
- The *first money column*: is used where there is yet more detailed working out to do (here, to show purchases less purchases returns).

KEY TERM

Goods for own use: a transaction where the owner of a business keeps goods for private use which would otherwise have been available for sale. This transaction is sometimes referred to as inventory drawings.

Goods taken for own use

The owner of a business may take **goods for own use**. For example, the owner of a grocery store might take goods from the shelves for private use at home as part of the week's food shopping. The correct double entry for this transaction is:

Debit   Drawings account

Credit   Purchases account

This transaction should first be recorded in the general journal. The debit entry probably seems obvious. However, the credit entry in the purchases account is perhaps a little more puzzling. The effect of the credit entry is to reduce the balance of the purchases account. The idea is that if the owner has taken the goods for their own use, those goods would not be available for sale and so should not be included in the total figure for purchases.

You can now answer questions 7 and 8 on page 121.

Carriage inwards and carriage outwards

Many businesses have to pay for the delivery of the goods they purchase. This expense is called **carriage inwards**. When preparing an income statement, carriage inwards should be added to the figure for purchases to show the true cost of buying goods. To achieve this, the balance of the carriage inwards account is transferred to the first part of the income statement when preparing the end-of-year financial statements.

KEY TERM

Carriage inwards: the cost of transporting goods, paid by a business on its own purchases. This expense is added to purchases in the first account section of the income statement.

Illustration 5 Vertical income statement including goods taken for own use and carriage inwards

Here is Miguel's income statement from Illustration 4. However, this time it is assumed that Miguel took home goods valued at $7000 for his own use during the year and that he has to pay carriage inwards of $4000.

Miguel
Income statement for the year ended 31 December 2012

	$	$	$
Revenue		145 000	
Less sales returns		(3 000)	
			142 000
Opening inventory		10 000	
Purchases ($75 000 less goods taken for own use $7 000)	68 000		
Carriage inwards	4 000		
	72 000		
Less purchases returns	(2 000)		
		70 000	
		80 000	
Less closing inventory		(15 000)	
Cost of sales			(65 000)
Gross profit			77 000

Notes:

1 The figure for purchases has been reduced by the amount of goods taken for own use.

2 Carriage inwards is transferred from the carriage inwards account in the general ledger.

3 It is preferable to add carriage inwards to purchases before deducting returns outwards.

4 Carriage inwards has the effect of increasing the cost of sales and, therefore, reducing the gross profit.

KEY TERM

Carriage outwards: the cost of transporting goods, paid by a business on its sales to customers. This expense is recorded in the second part of the income statement.

There is also an expense called **carriage outwards**. This is the cost of delivering goods to customers. The correct treatment for carriage outwards is to include it in the second part of the income statement along with all of the other business running costs.

You can now answer questions 9 and 10 on pages 121–122.

Practice questions

DEVELOPING YOUR SKILLS

1 Calculating gross profit when there is a closing inventory

During a financial year a retailer purchased goods for $200 000; revenue totalled $340 000. However, the retailer was not able to sell all of the goods that had been purchased and was left with an unsold inventory at the year end valued at $20 000.

Calculate the gross profit made by the retailer during the year.

2 Calculating gross profit when there is a closing inventory

During a financial year a retailer purchased goods for $450 000; revenue totalled $660 000.

At the end of the year the retailer had a closing inventory, value $40 000.

Calculate the gross profit made by the retailer during the year.

3 Calculating gross profit when there are opening and closing inventories

A retailer provided the following information for the year ended 31 December 2012.

	$
Inventory at 1 January 2012	20 000
Purchases	480 000
Revenue	710 000
Inventory at 31 December 2012	60 000

Calculate the following:

a The value of goods actually sold during the year

b The gross profit for the year

4 Calculating gross profit when there are opening and closing inventories

A wholesaler provided the following information for the year ended 31 December 2012.

	$
Inventory at 1 January 2012	80 000
Purchases	880 000
Revenue	1 200 000
Inventory at 31 December 2012	50 000

Calculate the following:

a The value of goods actually sold during the year

b The gross profit for the year

5 Preparing a vertical income statement

Billal owns a retail business. His business's financial year ended on 30 November 2012. The following information is available.

	$
Purchases	365 800
Purchases returns	4 100
Revenue	551 000
Sales returns	3 700
Inventories	
At 1 December 2011	45 200
At 30 November 2012	56 900

Prepare the first section of the business's income statement for the year ended 30 November 2012 using a vertical style of presentation. Complete the inventory account in the general ledger.

6 Preparing a vertical income statement

Raslinda is a wholesaler. Her business's financial year ended on 31 December 2012. The following information is available:

	$
Purchases	568 300
Purchases returns	9 500
Revenue	945 600
Sales returns	7 200
Inventories	
At 1 January 2012	48 000
At 31 December 2012	39 000

Prepare the first part of the business's income statement for the year ended 31 December 2012 using a vertical style of presentation. Complete the inventory account in the general ledger.

7 Preparing a vertical income statement including goods for own use

Wilma owns a shoe shop. Her business's financial year ended on 31 October 2012. The following information is available:

	$
Purchases	176 000
Purchases returns	1 900
Revenue	351 000
Sales returns	2 400
Inventories	
At 1 November 2011	11 300
At 31 October 2012	13 500

No record has yet been made of goods taken for own use by Wilma during the year ended 31 October 2012. The value of shoes taken for own use was $600.

Prepare the following:

a Journal entry to record the goods taken for own use

b The first part of the income statement for the year ended 31 October 2012, showing clearly an amended figure for purchases

8 Preparing a vertical income statement including goods for own use

Ralph owns a shop selling sports equipment. His business's financial year ended on 31 August 2012. The following information is available.

	$
Purchases	365 800
Purchases returns	5 900
Revenue	777 400
Sales returns	4 700
Inventories	
At 1 September 2011	29 300
At 31 August 2012	28 200

No record has yet been made of goods taken for own use by Ralph during the year ended 31 August 2012. The value of sports equipment taken for own use was $3700.

Prepare the following:

a Journal entry to record the goods taken for own use

b The first section of the income statement for the year ended 31 August 2012, showing clearly an amended figure for purchases

9 Preparing a vertical income statement including carriage inwards

Kavita owns a wholesale business providing bathroom fittings. Her business's financial year ended on 30 June 2012. The following information is available.

	$
Carriage inwards	8 000
Purchases	105 000
Purchases returns	4 000
Revenue	200 000
Sales returns	3 000
Inventories	
At 1 July 2011	7 000
At 30 June 2012	6 000

Prepare the first part of the business's income statement for the year ended 30 June 2012 using a vertical style of presentation. Complete the inventory account in the general ledger.

10 Preparing a vertical income statement including carriage inwards

Henry owns a retail unit selling men's clothing. His business's financial year ended on 31 July 2012. The following information is available.

	$
Carriage inwards	3 000
Purchases	98 000
Purchases returns	5 000
Revenue	184 000
Sales returns	2 000
Inventories	
At 1 August 2011	10 000
At 31 July 2012	14 000

Prepare the first part of the business's income statement for the year ended 31 July 2012 using a vertical style of presentation. Complete the inventory account in the general ledger.

14 Income statements: making adjustments

Introduction

In this unit you will continue your review of the income statement. This time the second part of the income statement will be presented using the vertical format.

You will also learn some important new rules about how profits are calculated that require adjustments to the amount recorded for certain items when preparing the second section of the income statement.

LEARNING OUTCOMES

When you have reached the end of this unit you will be able to:

- prepare the second part of an income statement using a vertical format
- record ledger entries to adjust expenses for accruals and prepayments in ledger accounts
- prepare income statements taking account of adjustments for expense accruals and prepayments
- record ledger entries to adjust income accounts for income accrued and income prepaid
- prepare income statements taking account of adjustments to income accounts.

14.1 Vertical presentation; adjusting expenses

Vertical format for the second part of the income statement

Illustration 1 Preparing a vertical second section of an income statement

Dale has produced the following second section of the income statement for his business using a horizontal format.

Income statement (second part) for the year ended 31 July 2011

	$		$
Carriage outwards	4 000	Gross profit	85 000
Discounts allowed	1 000	Discounts received	3 000
General expenses	5 000		
Rent	7 000		
Wages	28 000		
Profit for the year	43 000		
	88 000		88 000

Here is the same section of the income statement, but in vertical form.

Income statement (second part) for the year ended 31 July 2011

	$	$
Gross profit	85 000	
Discounts received	3 000	
		88 000
Carriage outwards	4 000	
Discounts allowed	1 000	
General expenses	5 000	
Rent	7 000	
Wages	28 000	
		(45 000)
Profit for year		43 000

Notes:

1. Always start with the gross profit and add any additional income (e.g. discounts received) to achieve a subtotal.
2. List all of the expenses and subtotal these.
3. Complete the format with the profit for the year or loss for the year correctly labelled.
4. Two columns are almost always sufficient for the second section of the income statement.

You can now answer questions 1 and 2 on page 131.

KEY TERM

Expense accrual: an amount owing for expenses at the end of a financial period.

Making adjustments to expenses

The rule when preparing an annual income statement is to ensure that any expense item represents the amount of that expense for that year – whether it has been paid or not. As a result some expenses need adjusting at the year end because there is an amount due but unpaid when the financial statements are prepared. The amount due but unpaid is referred to as an **expense accrual**.

Illustration 2 Recording an accrual

Natalie is preparing her business's income statement on 31 December 2011. Her electricity account at that date is as follows.

Dr Electricity account Cr

2011		$		$
Jan to Dec	Bank	22 000		

The account shows that so far $22 000 has been paid in electricity charges and this is the figure that should appear in the end-of-year trial balance.

Natalie tells you that she has received an invoice for electricity for $1000 for the last weeks of the year.

How much is the electricity charge for the year? *Answer:* $23 000 (i.e. $22 000 + accrual of $1000).

It is $23 000 that will appear in the income statement (i.e. the full amount for the year whether it has been paid or not).

Here are the entries required in the electricity account to reflect this.

Dr — Electricity — Cr

			$					$
2011				2011				
Jan to Dec	Bank		22 000	Dec	31	Income statement		23 000
Dec	Balance	c/d	1 000					
			23 000					23 000
				2012				
				Jan	1	Balance	b/d	1 000

Notes:

1 Start by making sure you transfer the correct amount to the income statement (i.e. $23 000). You will remember from Unit 12 that this transfer will appear first as a journal entry.

2 Record the unpaid invoice of $1000 as a balance on the account.

3 The balance brought down is a credit balance, so an accrued expense is a current liability as it is an amount owed. It is shown on the balance sheet as 'other payables'.

In the case of some expenses, payments will have been made that cover the business beyond the current account year. In this situation the business will have a **prepaid expense**. The same principle applies: it is essential to charge the exact amount of this year's expense to the income statement.

KEY TERM

Prepaid expense: the payment of an expense in advance of the accounting year to which it relates.

You can now answer questions 3 and 4 on page 131.

STUDY TIP

In the exam it is important to be consistent in the style of layout you choose to use; so do not produce a vertical income statement, but a horizontal balance sheet.

You can now answer questions 5 and 6 on page 132.

Illustration 3 Recording a prepaid expense

Natalie reports that this year she has paid $38 000 for insurance. Here is the insurance account in the general ledger.

Dr — Insurance account — Cr

		$		$
2011				
Jan to Dec	Bank	38 000		

It appears that this sum includes insurance for the first two months of the next accounting year, $2000.

What is the annual charge for insurance? *Answer*: $36 000 (i.e. payment $38 000 − prepayment $2000).

It is $36 000 that will be charged to the income statement. The remaining $2000 is regarded as a current asset as it represents money spent from which the benefit is still to come.

Here are the entries required to reflect this.

Dr — Insurance account — Cr

				$					$
2011					2011				
Jan to Dec		Bank			Dec	31	Income statement		36 000
				38 000		31	Balance	c/d	2 000
				38 000					38 000
2012									
Jan	1	Balance	b/d	2 000					

Notes:

1 As before, start by making sure you transfer the correct amount to the income statement (i.e. $36 000). Again a journal entry will be made first.

2 Record the prepayment of $2000 as the balance to carry down on the account.

3 The balance brought down is a debit balance as it is a current asset. It is shown on the balance sheet as 'other receivables'.

14.2 Adjusting income

Sometimes a business will earn income in addition to sales. For example, if a business owns its own property, some unused space could be sublet and rent would then be received from the tenant – this is called 'rent received'. If the owner of a business puts surplus money into a savings or investment account it could earn interest – interest received.

It is quite likely, taking the example of rent received, that the tenant could owe money to the business at the financial year end, or the tenant could have paid ahead for part of the next financial period. Where these situations arise, it will be necessary to make adjustments in the accounts.

Income received from these sources is recorded as an addition to gross profit in the second part of the income statement.

DID YOU KNOW?

A debit balance on an income account records an amount due to a business at the end of a year. The amount due would be settled early in the next year as soon as the next amount of income is received.

Illustration 4 Adjusting income for income accrued

Omar is preparing his business's income statement at 31 December 2012. The business sublets part of its premises to another business and receives rent. Here is the rent received account on 31 December 2012.

Dr — Rent received account — Cr

			$				$
				2012			
				Jan to Dec		Bank	15 000

Notes:

1 The account shows that the tenant has paid $15 000 in rent so far.

2 As this is a gain for the business, the account has been credited and the bank account debited with the amount received.

3 Rent received will appear as an entry in the credit column of the trial balance prepared before the end-of-year financial statements are drafted.

Suppose that the tenant had failed to pay $1000 in rent for the last few weeks of the year. How much will be transferred to the second part of the income statement? *Answer*: $16 000 (i.e. $15 000 + amount due $1000).

Here is the updated rent received account showing the transfer of rent received to the income statement.

Note: the transfer of rent received to the income statement will be recorded first as an entry in the general journal.

Dr — Rent received account — Cr

			$				$
2012				2012			
Dec	31	Income statement		Jan to Dec		Bank	150000

The rent received account will then be balanced as follows:

Dr — Rent received account — Cr

				$					$
2012					2012				
Dec	31	Income statement		16 000	Jan to Dec				15 000
					Dec	31	Balance	c/d	1 000
				16 000					16 000
2013									
Jan	1	Balance	b/d	1 000					

Notes:

1 Balance the account, recording the amount due from the tenant.

2 The balance is a debit balance when brought down.

3 The balance brought down is a current asset. This is because the business is owed money by the tenant. It is shown on the balance sheet as '**other receivables**'.

Illustration 5 Adjusting for income prepaid

Here is another example where a business is receiving rent from a tenant. However, this time the tenant has paid more than is necessary for the year under review by sending money to cover the first weeks of the next accounting period.

Dr **Rent received account** **Cr**

			$				$
				2011			
				Jan to Dec		Bank	8 500

Suppose that the tenant has paid $700 for rent for the first few weeks of 2012. How much will be transferred to the income statement (second section)? *Answer*: $7800 ($8500 – amount received in advance $700).

Here is the rent received account showing the transfer of rent received to the income statement.

Dr **Rent received account** **Cr**

2011			$	2011		$
Dec	31	Income statement	7 800	Jan to Dec	Bank	8 500

The rent received account will then be balanced as follows:

Dr **Rent received account** **Cr**

2011				$	2011				$
Dec	31	Income statement		7 800	Jan to Dec		Bank		8 500
	31	Balance	c/d	700					
				8 500					8 500
					2012				
					Jan	1	Balance	b/d	700

DID YOU KNOW?

A credit balance on an expense account records an accrual at the end of a year. This amount due would be settled early in the next year when the next payment for that expense is made.

Note: the transfer of rent received to the income statement will first appear in the general journal.

Notes:

1. Balance the account with the amount received in advance from the tenant.
2. The balance will appear as a credit balance when brought down.
3. The balance brought down is a current liability. This is because the business owes the tenant this money which has been received ahead of the year to which it relates. It is shown on the balance sheet as '**other payables**'.

You can now answer questions 7 and 8 on page 132.

STUDY TIP

Sometimes a great deal of care is needed when calculating the amount of an adjustment. For example, suppose a business receives rent of $900 quarterly in advance from a tenant and the most recent quarterly payment had been received at the beginning of the quarter that commenced on 1 December 2012. If the business's financial year ended on 31 December, the tenant would have prepaid rent for two months, and the balance on the rent received account would be $600.

KEY TERM

Other receivables: term used on a balance sheet to include prepaid expenses and income accrued.

Other payables: term used on a balance sheet to include accrued expenses and income prepaid.

14.3 Preparing end-of-year financial statements with adjustments to expenses and income

Illustration 6 The second part of an income statement in vertical format including adjustments and balance sheet extracts

Yasmin is preparing her income statement for the year ended 31 December 2012. Her business has made a gross profit of $125 000. Her trial balance includes the following items.

Trial balance at 31 December 2012 (extract)

	Dr	Cr
	$	$
General expenses	26 000	
Insurance	9 000	
Interest received		7 000
Rent received		14 000
Wages	75 000	

Yasmin provides the following additional information at 31 December 2012.

- General expenses is to be accrued, $4000
- Insurance is prepaid, $1000
- Interest received is to be accrued, $2000
- Rent received has been prepaid, $3000
- Wages is to be accrued, $5000.

Work out the effect of the adjustments. Here is a table summarising the effects.

	Amount in trial balance	**Adjustment**	**Amount to be recorded in the income statement**	**Adjustment in balance sheet**
	$		$	$
General expenses	26 000	Accrual $4 000	30 000	Current liability $4 000
Insurance	9 000	Prepayment $1 000	8 000	Current asset $1 000
Interest received	7 000	Amount receivable $2 000	9 000	Current asset $2 000
Rent received	14 000	Amount received in advance $3 000	11 000	Current liability $3 000
Wages	75 000	Accrual $5 000	80 000	Current liability $5 000

Here are the journal entries that would be needed to transfer the expense and income items to the income statement.

JOURNAL

Date		*Details*	*Dr*	*Cr*
2012			$	$
Dec	31	Income statement	118 000	
		General expenses		30 000
		Insurance		8 000
		Wages		80 000
		Transfer of expenses for the year to income statement		
		Interest received	9 000	
		Rent received	11 000	
		Income statement		20 000
		Transfer of income for the year to income statement		

Here are the expense and income accounts recording these adjustments and balanced.

GENERAL LEDGER

General expenses account

Dr				$	Cr				$
2012				$	2012				$
Jan to Dec		Bank		26 000	Dec	31	Income statement		30 000
Dec	31	Balance	c/d	4 000					
				30 000					30 000
					2013				
					Jan	1	Balance	b/d	4 000

Insurance account

Dr				$	Cr				$
2012				$	2012				$
Jan to Dec		Bank		9 000	Dec	31	Income statement		8 000
						31	Balance	c/d	1 000
				9 000					9 000
2013									
Jan	1	Balance	b/d	1 000					

Wages account

Dr				$	Cr				$
2012				$	2012				$
Jan to Dec		Bank		75 000	Dec	31	Income statement		80 000
Dec	31	Balance	c/d	5 000					
				80 000					80 000
					2013				
					Jan	1	Balance b/d		5 000

Interest received account

Dr				$	Cr				$
2012				$	2012				$
Dec	31	Income statement		9 000	Jan to Dec		Bank		7 000
					Dec	31	Balance	c/d	2 000
				9 000					9 000
2013									
Jan	1	Balance	b/d	2 000					

Rent received account

Dr				$	Cr				$
2012				$	2012				$
Dec	31	Income statement		11 000	Jan to Dec		Bank		14 000
	31	Balance	c/d	3 000					
				14 000					14 000
					2013				
					Jan	1	Balance	b/d	3 000

Here is the income statement set out in vertical format.

Income statement for the year ended 31 December 2012

	$	$
Gross profit	125 000	
Add other income		
Interest received	9 000	
Rent received	11 000	
		145 000
Less expenses		
General expenses	30 000	
Insurance	8 000	
Wages	80 000	
		(118 000)
Profit for the year		27 000

Here is an extract from the balance sheet at 31 December (shown in horizontal format) showing how the five adjustments will appear.

Balance sheet at 31 December 2012 (extract)

	$	$		$	$
CURRENT ASSETS			CURRENT LIABILITIES		
Inventory	xx		Trade payables	xx	
Trade receivables	xx		Other payables		
Other receivables			Income prepaid (rent)		
Income accrued (interest)	2 000		Expenses accrued	3 000	
Expense prepaid (insurance)	1 000		(general expenses and wages)	9 000	
Cash at bank	xx				
		xx			xx

KEY TERM

Accruals principle: in order to calculate a true and fair profit, income for a financial year is matched exactly with expenses that relate to that accounting year whether paid or not. This principle is sometimes called the matching principle.

LINKS...

There is more about the accruals principle in Unit 19 on page 178.

Summary: the accruals (matching) principle

The process of making adjustments to expense and income accounts at the year end results from a rule known as the **accruals principle** (sometimes called the 'matching' principle). This rule requires profits to be calculated on the basis that the income for an accounting year (whether received or not) should be matched against expenses for that accounting year (whether paid or not).

STUDY TIP

While you are getting used to making these adjustments, it is easy to make a mistake when entering details on the balance sheet. Remember that current assets represent money owed to the business (expenses prepaid and income accrued); while current liabilities represent money owed by the business (expense accruals and income prepaid).

DEVELOPING YOUR SKILLS

1 Preparing a vertical income statement

Kalpna has produced the second part of her business's income statement in a horizontal form as follows.

Income statement (second part) for the year ended 31 May 2012

	$		$
Administration expenses	21 000	Gross profit	171 000
Electricity	27 000	Discounts received	8 000
Insurance	24 000		
Interest on bank loan	8 000		
Wages and salaries	78 000		
Profit	21 000		
	179 000		179 000

Redraft this part of the income statement in vertical format.

2 Preparing a vertical income statement

Robbie is preparing his business's end-of-year financial statements. The business has made a gross profit of $98 000. The following information has been extracted from the books of account for the year under review, ended 30 September 2012.

	$
Carriage outwards	9 200
Discounts allowed	4 700
Discounts received	5 900
Electricity charges	10 200
General expenses	11 300
Rent	27 900
Salaries	38 500
Water charges	8 400

Prepare the second part of the income statement for the year ended 30 September 2012 in vertical form.

3 Recording expense accruals

A business's trial balance includes the following information about expenses paid during the year ended 30 June 2012.

	$
Electricity	7 900
General expenses	11 800

The owner of the business provides the following additional information about expense accruals at 30 June 2012:

- An invoice for electricity, $700, is due but unpaid.
- General expenses, $300, relating to the year ended 30 June 2012, remains unpaid.

Prepare the following ledger accounts recording this information. The accounts should be balanced and the balances brought down.

- Electricity
- General expenses

4 Recording expense accruals

A business's trial balance includes the following information about expenses paid during the year ended 31 March 2012.

	$
Administration expenses	15 500
Salaries	109 600

The owner of the business provides the following additional information about expense accruals at 31 March 2012:

- Administration expenses, $900, remains unpaid.
- Salaries $3200 are due but unpaid.

Prepare the following ledger accounts recording this information. The accounts should be balanced and the balances brought down.

- Administration expenses
- Salaries

5 Recording expense prepayments

A business's trial balance includes the following information about expenses paid during the year ended 31 August 2012.

	$
Insurance	9 100
Rent	27 600

The owner of the business provides the following additional information about expense prepayments at 31 August 2012:

- The payments for insurance includes $800 relating to the following year.
- Rent, $1200, is prepaid.

Prepare the following ledger accounts recording this information. The accounts should be balanced and the balances brought down.

- Insurance
- Rent

6 Recording expense prepayments

A business's trial balance includes the following information about expenses paid during the year ended 28 February 2012.

	$
Electricity	14 400
Selling expenses	19 500

The owner of the business provides the following additional information about expense prepayments at 28 February 2012:

- The payments for electricity include $500 relating to the following year.
- Selling expenses, $700, is prepaid.

Prepare the following ledger accounts recording this information. The accounts should be balanced and the balances brought down.

- Electricity
- Selling expenses

7 Recording adjustments to income accounts

A business obtains income from subletting part of its premises and from interest on an investment.

During the year ended 30 November 2012 the business received the following amounts.

	$
Rent received	22 400
Loan interest received	7 300

At 30 November 2012, the business has received rent, $600, in advance, but is owed interest of $200.

Prepare the following ledger accounts recording this information. The accounts should be balanced and the balances brought down.

- Rent received
- Loan interest received

8 Recording adjustments to income accounts

A business sublets some unused space to two tenants.

The following information is available about the year ended 31 December 2012 concerning Tenant 1:

	$
Rent received during the year	16 200
Rent due but unpaid at 31 December	1 100

The following information is available about the year ended 31 December 2012 concerning Tenant 2:

	$
Rent received during the year	18 200
Rent received in advance at 31 December	900

Prepare two rent received accounts (one for each tenant) for the year ended 31 December 2012. Balance both accounts at the year end.

15 Depreciation and the disposal of non-current assets

Introduction

As you may recall from Unit 1, one of the basic principles of accounting is that non-current assets should be valued at cost. However, non-current assets lose value as they are used by a business. The idea of *usage* causing a loss in value is often expressed as 'wear and tear'.

A non-current asset might also lose value because of the following factors:

- *Technological change*: equipment (e.g. computers) can rapidly cease being up to date and therefore become unable to meet the needs of the business that owns them.
- Some non-current assets might become *inadequate* as a business grows and they lose their value to the business as result. For example, the office photocopier might be unable to cope with increased demand if the business rapidly grew in size.
- *Time factor*: the life of some assets has a legal limit. For example, some business premises are held on what is called a lease where there is an agreement to pay rent for a period of years. The lease is likely to have no value when the expiry date is reached.

Depreciation is an *expense* and so it needs to be taken into account when calculating profit. Depreciation is another example of the accruals (or matching) principle mentioned in Unit 14.

You may be wondering whether there are any non-current assets that are not subject to depreciation. There is just one obvious example: land (except where the land is used for mining or quarrying purposes).

In this unit you will learn how to record depreciation in a business's accounting records. You will also learn how to make entries to record the disposal of a non-current asset.

LEARNING OUTCOMES

When you have reached the end of this unit you will be able to:

- explain the term 'depreciation'
- calculate depreciation charges using three different methods
- record depreciation in the journal and ledger accounts
- prepare end-of-year financial statements taking account of depreciation
- prepare accounting records to record the disposal of a non-current asset.

DID YOU KNOW?

The basic principle that non-current assets should be valued at cost is adopted by accountants because cost is an objective means of valuation. In other words, cost will be matter of fact (i.e. it will be supported by evidence such as an invoice for the non-current asset) rather than opinion.

KEY TERM

Depreciation: the loss in value of a non-current asset over its useful life.

15.1 How to calculate depreciation

> **KEY TERM**
>
> **Residual value:** the value of a non-current asset at the end of its useful life – sometimes referred to as the scrap value.
>
> **Straight-line method:** where the annual depreciation charge is based on the cost of the non-current asset and is the same amount each year. This method is also called the equal instalment method.

Depreciation is an estimate of the loss in value over the period of time when the asset is useful to the business. There are many ways of making this estimate, but three are in common use:

- Straight-line (equal instalment) method
- Reducing (diminishing) balance method
- Revaluation method

Illustration 1 The straight-line method of depreciation

A business purchased a delivery vehicle for $50 000. The owner of the business has decided that the vehicle will be of use to the business for four years.

The **straight-line method** always charges depreciation evenly over the lifetime of the asset. In this case the annual charge would be:

$$\frac{\$50\,000}{4}$$

i.e. $12 500 per year.

So, the depreciation charge is 25 per cent of the cost per year.

Sometimes, the owner of the business might take account of the fact that the vehicle will have some value when it is disposed of – this is called the **residual value**. So, in this example, if the owner estimated that the vehicle would have a residual value of $6000, the annual depreciation charge would have been calculated as follows:

Total loss in value over four years is $50 000 − $6000 residual value = $44 000

Therefore the annual depreciation charge is $\frac{\$44\,000}{4}$

i.e. $11 000 per year.

Illustration 2 The reducing balance method

This method of calculating depreciation takes into consideration the fact that non-current assets do not necessarily lose the same amount of value each year. It recognises that some non-current assets lose more value in the first years and less in the final years of their useful life. The method is referred to as the **reducing balance method**.

Take the example of the owner of a business who bought some equipment for $20 000. The owner would need to decide on an annual rate of depreciation – say 20 per cent.

Here is how the annual depreciation charge would be calculated:

Year	Calculation	Depreciation charge)	Value at end of year
1	20% × cost $20 000	$4 000	$16 000
2	20% × $16 000	$3 200	$12 800
3	20% × $12 800	$2 560	$10 240
	and so on		

Note: in this method the annual depreciation charge is based on the value of the asset at the beginning of the year in which the charge is to be made. This value is usually referred to as the **net book value**.

Illustration 3 The revaluation method

In some situations the owner of a business may find it too time consuming to keep detailed records of some groups of non-current assets that individually are of rather limited value. For example, in a vehicle repair workshop it might be difficult to keep detailed records of all of the tens or even hundreds of tools used by the mechanics. Or in a large office there may be numerous items of low-value equipment. In these situations the **revaluation method** of depreciation is used. The depreciation charge is based on an estimate of the fall in the value of the group of non-current assets during a financial year The method requires the non-current assets to be revalued at the end of each financial year.

Here are some details about the crockery owned by the Regent Restaurant.

	$
Value of crockery on 1 January 2012	4 800
New crockery purchased during 2012	1 400
Value of crockery on 31 December 2012	5 300

The depreciation charge using the revaluation method based on these figures is $900. Here are the calculation details:

	$
Value of crockery at 1 January 2012	4 800
Add new crockery	1 400
	6 200
Less value of crockery at 31 December 2012	5 300
Depreciation charge for 2012	900

This method is simple to use and avoids the practical problems of attempting to physically count and value many individual items.

KEY TERM

Reducing balance method: where the annual depreciation charge is based on the value of the non-current asset at the beginning of the year under review. This method is also referred to as the diminishing balance method.

Net book value: the value of a non-current asset that takes account of its cost less the total depreciation to date.

Revaluation method: where the annual depreciation charge is based on comparing the estimated value of a group of non-current assets at the end of a financial year with the value at the beginning of the financial year.

You can now answer questions 1 and 2 on page 142.

15.2 Recording depreciation in the accounts

Businesses normally keep separate records of the cost of each type of non-current asset and the accumulating depreciation on each type of non-current asset. So, in the general ledger you are likely to find, for example, the following two accounts:

- Vehicles (at cost) account
- Provision for depreciation of vehicles account

At the end of each financial year the provision for depreciation account is updated with the annual depreciation charge. The procedure is as follows:

Step 1 Journal: record the annual depreciation charge

↓

Step 2 Post the journal entry to the accounts:
Dr Income statement
Cr Provision for depreciation

The income statement is debited with depreciation to ensure that profits are reduced for the year under review; the credit entry in the provision account has the effect of reducing the value of the non-current asset to be shown on the balance sheet.

Illustration 4 Accounting records for depreciation

A business owns equipment that cost $50000 and was purchased at the beginning of year 1. The policy is to depreciate equipment by 20 per cent per annum using the straight-line method.

Let us look at how to depreciate this equipment at the end of year 1 and year 2.

Year 1

Step 1: Calculate the depreciation charge: 20% × $50000, i.e. $10000.

Step 2: Make a journal entry at the end of the year to record the depreciation.

JOURNAL

Date	Details	Dr	Cr
Yr 1		$	$
Dec 31	Income statement	10000	
	Provision for depreciation (equipment)		10000
	Entries to charge depreciation of equipment at the year end		

Step 3: Post the entries in the journal to the accounts.

Dr Equipment account Cr

			$		$
Yr 1					
Jan	1	Balance	50000		

Dr Provision for depreciation of equipment account Cr

$				$
	Yr 1			
	Dec	31	Income statement	10000

Income statement for the year ended 31 December year 1

	$	$
Gross profit		xx
Expenses	xx	
Depreciation of equipment	**10000**	
		xx
Profit for year		xx

Year 2

Step 1: Calculate the depreciation charge – as the business uses the straight-line method the depreciation charge is again $10000.

Step 2: At the end of year prepare the journal entry to record depreciation for the second year.

JOURNAL

Date	Details	Dr	Cr
Yr 2		$	$
Dec 31	Income statement	10 000	
	Provision for depreciation (equipment)		10 000
	Entries to charge depreciation of equipment at the year end		

Step 3: Post the entries in the journal to the accounts.

Dr Equipment account Cr

			$		$
Year 1					
Jan	1	Balance	50 000		

Dr Provision for depreciation of equipment account Cr

	$				$
		Yr 1			
		Dec	31	Income statement	10 000
		Yr 2			
		Dec	**31**	**Income statement**	10 000

Income statement for the year ended 31 December year 2

	$	$
Gross profit		xx
Expenses	xx	
Depreciation of equipment	**10 000**	
		xx
Profit for year		xx

Notes:

1 The key feature to note is how the provision account steadily accumulates depreciation charges over the years. By the end of year 1 the balance on this account is $10 000, by the end of year 2 the balance is $20 000. At the end of year 3 the balance would become $30 000, and so on.

2 In the ledger, you will remember, the non-current asset (at cost) account does not change because depreciation is recorded separately.

Illustration 5 Accounting entries where the revaluation method is used

When the revaluation method of depreciation is used, the accounting entries are more straightforward as all of the information is recorded in just one account. In the case of the Regent Restaurant (see Illustration 3), the information about crockery should be recorded as follows:

JOURNAL

Date	*Details*	Dr	Cr
		$	$
Dec 31	Income statement	900	
	Crockery		900
	Entries to charge depreciation of crockery at the year end		

Dr Crockery account Cr

			$				$
2012				2012			
Jan	1	Balance	4800	Dec	31	Income statement	900
Jan-Dec		Bank	1400		31	Balance c/d	5300
			6200				6200
2013							
Jan	1	Balance b/d	5300				

Notes:

1 A journal entry is required to show the transfer of the annual depreciation charge. However, there is no separate account for depreciation.

2 The non-current asset account contains all of the information: opening balance, purchases of additional items, annual depreciation charge and the closing balance.

You can now answer questions 3 and 4 on page 142.

15.3 Depreciation and the balance sheet

When a balance sheet is prepared at the end of each financial year, it will need to show the net value of each non-current asset.

Taking the information about equipment in Illustration 4, here are extracts from the business's balance sheets for each of Years 1 and 2.

Illustration 6 Balance sheets and depreciation

Summary of information about equipment:

Year	Cost	Balance of provision account at end of year	Net value of equipment at end of year
	$	$	$
Year 1	50 000	10 000	40 000
Year 2		20 000	30 000

Here is an extract from the business's balance sheet at the end of year 1.

Balance sheet at 31 December year 1 (extract)

	$ Cost	$ Total depreciation	$ Net
NON-CURRENT ASSETS			
Equipment	**50 000**	**10 000**	**40 000**
CURRENT ASSETS			
Inventory		xx	
Trade receivables, etc.		xx	

And here is a similar extract but for the balance sheet at the end of year 2.

Balance sheet at 31 December year 2 (extract)

	$ Cost	$ Total depreciation	$ Net
NON-CURRENT ASSETS			
Equipment	**50 000**	**20 000**	**30 000**
CURRENT ASSETS			
Inventory		xx	
Trade receivables, etc.		xx	

In the case of the crockery, the balance sheet will show only the updated value of the non-current asset.

Regent Restaurant
Balance sheet at 31 December year 2012 (extract)

	$	$	$ Net
NON-CURRENT ASSETS			
Crockery at valuation			**5 300**
CURRENT ASSETS			
Inventory		xx	
Trade receivables, etc.		xx	

Notes:

1 As there is no separate record of cost and depreciation, just the net book value is shown on the balance sheet.

2 It is good practice to add the words 'at valuation' as shown. This makes it clear to anyone using the balance sheet that this non-current asset's value has been estimated by the owner or manager of the business.

STUDY TIP

When using the straight-line and reducing balance methods of depreciation it is important to remember that the income statement for a particular year will only show that year's depreciation. However, the balance sheet entries must take account of the original cost and the total depreciation to date.

You can now answer questions 5 and 6 on pages 142–143.

15.4 Recording the disposal of a non-current asset

When a business sells a non-current asset it will be necessary to:

- establish whether a profit or loss was made on the disposal
- remove all details of the non-current asset from the accounting records.

Illustration 7 How to record a disposal

Robbie owns a business and the end-of-year financial statements are prepared annually on 31 December. On 8 May 2012 Robbie sold his business's vehicle for $3500 and received a cheque for that amount. On that date the accounting records for the vehicle were as follows:

Dr — Vehicle account — Cr

			$		$
2012					
Jan	1	Balance	30 000		

Dr — Provision for depreciation of equipment account — Cr

	$				$
		2012			
		Jan	1	Balance	24 000

So the accounting records show that the vehicle has a net book value of $6000.

Step 1: Open a disposal account to record the transactions relating to the sale of the non-current asset.

Dr — Vehicle disposal account — Cr

	$		$

Step 2: Remove the record of the cost of the vehicle from the vehicle account by transfer to the vehicle disposal account. A journal entry is required to make this transfer.

JOURNAL

Date	Details	Dr	Cr
		$	$
May 8	Vehicle disposal	30 000	
	Vehicle		30 000
	Entries to transfer the cost of vehicle upon disposal		

The ledger records will now show:

Dr — Vehicle account — Cr

			$				$
Jan	1	Balance	30 000	**May**	**8**	**Vehicle disposal**	**30 000**

Dr — Vehicle disposal account — Cr

			$		$
May	**8**	**Vehicle**	**30 000**		

Notes:

1 The transfer entries will be made on the date of the disposal.

2 As a result of the transfer, the vehicle account shows that the business no longer owns a vehicle and so the account can be closed.

Step 3: Make a journal entry to transfer the accumulated depreciation of the vehicle to the disposal account and update the ledger accounts.

JOURNAL

Date	Details	Dr	Cr
		$	$
May 8	Provision for depreciation of vehicle	24 000	
	Vehicle disposal		24 000
	Entries to transfer the provision for depreciation upon disposal of the vehicle		

The ledger records will now show:

Vehicle account

Dr			$	Cr			$
Jan	1	Balance	30 000	May	8	Vehicle disposal	30 000

Provision for depreciation of equipment account

Dr			$	Cr			$
May	**8**	**Vehicle disposal**	**24 000**	Jan	1	Balance	24 000

Vehicle disposal account

Dr			$	Cr			$
May	8	Vehicle	30 000	**May**	**8**	**Provision for depreciation**	**24 000**

Notes:

1 As a result of the transfer, the depreciation has been removed from the accounting system and the provision account can be closed.

2 At this point the disposal account shows, on balance, the net book value of $6000.

Step 4: The amount received for the vehicle is now recorded in the disposal account.

Vehicle disposal account

Dr			$	Cr			$
May	8	Vehicle	30 000	May	8	Provision for depreciation	24 000
					8	Bank	3 500

Note: the debit entry for the cheque will have been made in the cash book.

Step 5: At 31 December, the accounting year end, the disposal account will be closed and the balance transferred to the income statement.

Vehicle disposal account

Dr			$	Cr			$
2012							
May	8	Vehicle	30 000	May	8	Provision for depreciation	24 000
					8	Bank	3 500
				Dec	**31**	**Income statement (loss on disposal)**	**2 500**
			30 000				30 000

Notes:

1 In the illustration the disposal account has a final credit balance of $2500. This amount represents a loss on the sale of the non-current asset.

2 The loss on disposal can be thought of as an under-provision for depreciation.

3 The other entry for the loss is in the second part of the income statement.

It is possible for a business to make a profit on a disposal. In this situation, there will be a debit balance on the asset disposal account. A profit on disposal can be thought of as arising from an over-provision for depreciation.

DID YOU KNOW?

In some businesses it may be the policy to depreciate a non-current asset in the year of its disposal. In the illustration above, it was assumed that this was not the business's policy.

Illustration 8 | Recording a profit on a disposal

On 11 August 2012 Salma sold some unwanted office equipment and received a cheque for $900. The equipment had cost $3800 and had been depreciated by $3450. The business's accounting year end is 31 December.

Here is the equipment disposal account showing a profit on the sale of the equipment:

Dr **Equipment disposal account** **Cr**

2012			$				$
Aug	11	Equipment	3800	May	8	Provision for depreciation	3450
Dec	**31**	**Income statement (profit on disposal)**	550		8	Bank	900
			4350				4350

You can now answer questions 7–14 on pages 143–145.

Practice questions

NOTE: As the vertical style of presentation of balance sheets is not covered until Unit 18, answers to some questions in this unit will involve the use of a mixture of formats for financial statements. It should be noted that in an examination, only one style of presentation should be used.

DEVELOPING YOUR SKILLS

1 Calculating depreciation

Amina opened a hotel. On 1 January 2011 the following non-current assets were purchased.

	Cost $
Equipment	25 000
Furniture and fittings	20 000
Crockery	5 000

Amina has made the following decisions about annual depreciation charges:

- The equipment should be depreciated using the straight-line method. It is expected to have a useful life of five years and have a residual value of $2000.
- Furniture and fittings should be depreciated using the reducing balance method. The rate of depreciation to be used is 20 per cent.
- There are many items of crockery, each of which has a relatively small value, so Amina has decided to use the revaluation method.

At 31 December 2011, crockery was revalued at $4300. During the year ended 31 December 2012, Amina purchased additional items of crockery costing $1300. At 31 December 2012 the crockery was revalued at $4700.

Complete a table to show depreciation charges on each non-current asset for each of the years ended 31 December 2011 and 31 December 2012.

2 Calculating depreciation

Edward opened his car repair business on 1 January 2011. On that date the following non-current assets were purchased.

	Cost $
Machinery	120 000
Fixtures	30 000
Tools	11 200

Edward has made the following decisions about annual depreciation charges:

- Machinery should be depreciated using the straight-line method. It has a useful life of five years.
- Fixtures should be depreciated using the reducing balance method. The rate of depreciation to be used is 30 per cent.
- There are many tools, each of which has a low value, so the revaluation method of depreciation will be used.

On 31 December 2011 tools were revalued at $9900. During the year ended 31 December 2012 Edward purchased additional tools costing $2600. On 31 December 2012 tools were revalued at $11 100.

Complete a table to show depreciation charges on each non-current asset for each of the years ended 31 December 2011 and 31 December 2012.

3 Accounting records for depreciation

Refer to your answer for question 1 and prepare the accounting records to record information about non-current assets and depreciation charges for both 2011 and 2012. Include the following:

- Journal entries
- Non-current asset accounts
- Provision for depreciation accounts (for vehicles and furniture and fittings)
- Extracts from the income statements

4 Accounting records for depreciation

Refer to your answer for question 2 and prepare the accounting records to record information about non-current assets and depreciation charges for both 2011 and 2012. Include the following:

- Journal entries
- Non-current asset accounts
- Provision for depreciation accounts (for machinery and fixtures)
- Extracts from the income statements

5 Balance sheets and depreciation

Refer to your answer for question 3 and prepare extracts from the balance sheets for the end of 2011 and 2012 to show how information about non-current assets should be recorded.

6 Balance sheets and depreciation

Refer to your answer for question 4 and prepare extracts from the balance sheets for the end of 2011 and 2012 to show how information about non-current assets should be recorded.

7 Preparing a disposal account

Sherelle owns a music store. The business's financial year ends on 31 December.

On 1 January 2012 the business's general ledger included the following accounts.

Furniture and fittings (at cost)	Balance $21 000
Provision for depreciation of furniture and fittings	Balance $16 400

On 10 August 2012 Sherelle sold all of the furniture and fittings for $2500 and received a cheque for that amount.

Prepare the following accounting records to record the disposal:

- Journal entries
- Furniture and fittings account
- Provision for depreciation of furniture and fittings account
- Furniture and fittings disposal account

Assume that it is the policy not to provide depreciation on a non-current asset in the year of disposal.

8 Preparing a disposal account

Samir recently sold one of his business's delivery vehicles. The business's accounting year ends on 31 December. The following accounts appeared in the business's books on 1 January 2012.

Delivery vehicles (at cost)	Balance $88 000
Provision for depreciation of delivery vehicles	Balance $39 000

The delivery vehicle had originally cost $22 000 and had been depreciated by $17 500. The vehicle was sold for $5800 and a cheque for that amount was received on 14 March 2012.

Prepare the following accounting records to record the disposal:

- Journal entries
- Delivery vehicles account
- Provision for depreciation of delivery vehicles account
- Delivery vehicle disposal account

Assume that it is the policy not to provide depreciation on a non-current asset in the year of disposal.

9 Preparing end-of-year financial statements including depreciation for a business, Year 1

Great Value Stores was opened on 1 January 2012. At the end of the business's first year of trading the following trial balance was extracted from the books of account after the gross profit for the year had been calculated.

Trial balance at 31 December 2012

	Dr $	Cr $
Capital		68 000
Cash at bank	6 000	
Drawings	37 000	
Furniture and fittings	41 000	
Gross profit		100 000
Inventory at 31 December 2012	12 000	
Office equipment	3 000	
Other operating expenses	24 000	
Rent	13 000	
Trade payables		18 000
Trade receivables	15 000	
Vehicles	35 000	
	186 000	186 000

Additional information:

- Rent, $1000, is prepaid at 31 December 2012.
- Other operating expenses, $3000, are due but unpaid at 31 December 2012.

The depreciation policy is as follows:

- Furniture and fittings should be depreciated over a four-year period using the straight-line method taking account of the expected residual value of $4000.
- Vehicles are to be depreciated by 25 per cent per annum using the reducing balance method.
- Office equipment is to be depreciated using the revaluation method. On 31 December 2012 office equipment was revalued at $2400.

Prepare the business's first end-of-year financial statements.

10 Preparing end-of-year financial statements including depreciation for a business, Year 1

Jody opened her coffee bar on 1 January 2012. At the end of the business's first year of trading the following trial balance was extracted from the books of account after the gross profit for the year had been calculated.

Trial balance at 31 December 2012

	Dr $	Cr $
Bank overdraft		11 300
Capital		41 300
Crockery etc.	6 400	
Drawings	42 400	
Equipment	23 000	
Fixtures and fittings	30 000	
Gross profit		145 700
Insurance	8 400	
Inventory at 31 December 2012	14 900	
Other operating expenses	75 300	
Trade payables		6 200
Trade receivables	4 100	
	204 500	204 500

Additional information:

- Insurance $700 is prepaid at 31 December 2012.
- Other operating expenses $2200 is due but unpaid at 31 December 2012.

The depreciation policy is as follows:

- Equipment should be depreciated over a five-year period using the straight-line method, taking account of the expected residual value of $2000.
- Fixtures and fittings are to be depreciated by 40 per cent per annum using the reducing balance method.
- Crockery is to be depreciated using the revaluation method. On 31 December 2012 Jody revalued the crockery at $5700.

Prepare the business's first end-of-year financial statements.

11 Preparing an income statement for an established business including a profit on disposal of a non-current asset

Esther was preparing her business's income statement for the year ended 31 May 2012. She was able to provide the following information:

- The business made a gross profit of $234 000 during the year ended 31 May 2012.
- The following amounts should be charged to the income statement for business expenses: administration expenses $4800, electricity charges $7200, general expenses $6600, wages and salaries $63 780.

- On 1 February 2012 Esther sold a delivery vehicle for $5400. The vehicle had cost $22 000 and had been depreciated by $17 500.
- Esther's policy is to depreciate her business's non-current assets by 25 per cent per annum using the reducing balance method. Depreciation should be based on a net book value of $156 000.

Prepare an income statement for the year ended 31 May 2012.

12 Preparing an income statement for an established business including a loss on disposal of a non-current asset

Ombeya was preparing his business's income statement for the year ended 30 November 2012. He was able to provide the following information:

- The business made a gross profit of $382 500 during the year ended 30 November 2012.
- The business received some additional income from renting out its premises. During the year ended 30 November 2012 the tenant had paid $8400 in rent. At 30 November 2012 the tenant owed $560 in rent for the year ended on that date.
- The following amounts should be charged to the income statement for business expenses: general expenses $10 120, electricity charges $7140, insurance $8890, repairs and maintenance $3540, wages $47 800, water charges $4810.
- On 17 October 2012 Ombeya sold some unwanted office equipment for $850. The office equipment had cost $9500 and had been depreciated by $7800.
- Ombeya depreciates some of his business's non-current assets by 20 per cent per annum using the straight-line method. These non-current assets cost $112 000. Other non-current assets are depreciated using the revaluation method. At 1 December 2011 these non-current assets were valued at $15 400; at 30 November 2012 they were revalued at $13 800.

Prepare an income statement for the year ended 30 November 2012.

13 Preparing end-of-year financial statements for an established business including a profit on disposal of a non-current asset

Kavita owns a health-food wholesale business which was opened three years ago on 1 January 2010. The following trial balance has been extracted from the business's books of account at the end of the third year of trading.

Trial balance at 31 December 2012

	Dr $	Cr $
Capital		44 850
Cash at bank	11 850	
Drawings	29 900	
Electricity	7 840	
Furniture and fittings		
Cost	32 000	
Provision for depreciation		12 800
Gross profit		137 230
Inventory at 31 December 2012	15 600	
Office equipment	3 780	
Profit on disposal of fittings		840
Rent	14 190	
Selling expenses	3 860	
Trade payables		11 210
Trade receivables	7 470	
Vehicles		
Cost	48 000	
Provision for depreciation at 1 January 2012		21 000
Wages	53 440	
	227 930	227 930

Additional information:

- The following expenses are prepaid at 31 December 2012: rent $880, selling expenses $190.
- The following expenses were accrued at 31 December 2012: electricity $330; wages $2020.

The business's depreciation policy is as follows:

- Furniture and fittings are depreciated by 20 per cent per annum using the straight-line method.
- Vehicles are depreciated by 25 per cent per annum using the reducing balance method.
- Office equipment is depreciated using the revaluation method. On 31 December 2012, Kavita revalued office equipment at $3100.

Prepare the business's income statement for the year ended 31 December 2012 and a balance sheet at that date.

14 Preparing end-of-year financial statements for an established business and including a loss on disposal of a non-current asset

'Samad Fresh Foods' is a retail unit opened three years ago by Samad Abbas. The following trial balance has been extracted from the business's books of account at the end of the third year of trading.

Trial balance at 31 December 2012

	Dr $	Cr $
Bank overdraft		2 370
Capital		24 000
Carriage outwards	470	
Drawings	33 500	
Furniture and fittings		
Cost	28 000	
Provision for depreciation at 1 January 2012		16 800
General expenses	3 340	
Insurance	7 290	
Inventory at 1 January 2012	15 510	
Loss on disposal of a vehicle	1 700	
Office equipment	2 850	
Purchases	247 610	
Returns	2 210	3 720
Revenue		382 880
Trade payables		4 830
Trade receivables	4 020	
Vehicles		
Cost	60 000	
Provision for depreciation		39 280
Wages	67 380	
	473 880	473 880

Additional information:

- The inventory on 31 December 2012 was valued at $16 530.
- The following expense was prepaid at 31 December 2012: insurance $320.
- The following expenses were accrued paid at 31 December 2012: wages $1420.

The business's depreciation policy is as follows:

- Furniture and fittings are depreciated by 20 per cent per annum using the straight-line method.
- Vehicles are depreciated by 20 per cent per annum using the reducing balance method.
- Office equipment is depreciated using the revaluation method. On 31 December 2012, Samad revalued office equipment at $2280.

Prepare the business's income statement for the year ended 31 December 2012 and a balance sheet at that date.

16 Bad debts and provisions for doubtful debts

Introduction

In this unit you are going to learn how to deal with a potentially serious problem for any business: a bad debt. You will also learn how businesses that experience bad debts try to make sure that their financial statements give a fair view of the value of trade receivables: a provision for doubtful debts.

Bad debts

Sometimes businesses have to face the serious problem that a credit customer is unable or unwilling to pay the amount due. This might arise when the customer concerned disputes the amount owed or when the customer has gone out of business. Why is this serious? The answer is that a business, faced with a **bad debt**, is going to lose not only some of the profit it had expected to make, but also the cash that the trade receivable should have been paying.

Provisions for doubtful debts

Since businesses can experience bad debts from time to time, it follows that the owners of those businesses continually face some uncertainty about whether all of their trade receivables will actually be received. The question then arises as to whether it is right to show the total of trade receivables on a balance sheet without indicating that a portion of the amount due may never be received (i.e. that some debts are doubtful).

To ignore the possibility of doubtful debts would be a breach of an important accounting principle, and that is that all accounting statements should present a **true and fair** view of the business's financial position. To overcome this problem many balance sheets show what is called a **provision for doubtful debts**.

LEARNING OUTCOMES

When you have reached the end of this unit you will be able to:

- explain the term 'bad debt'
- record bad debts in the accounts
- record bad debts recovered in the accounts
- explain why some businesses have a provision for doubtful debts
- prepare the accounting records for a provision for doubtful debts.

KEY TERM

Bad debt: a trade receivable that will not be paid.

True and fair: the principle that accounting records should be factually accurate and present a reasonable estimate of, or judgement about, the financial position.

Provision for doubtful debts: an amount set aside from profits to take account of the likelihood that some trade receivables will not pay the amount due and so will reduce the value of this asset on a balance sheet. Sometimes the alternative name 'provision for bad debts' is used.

16.1 Bad debts and bad debts recovered

When the owner of a business becomes aware that a credit customer will not pay the amount outstanding, it is important that action is taken promptly and the amount due is written off.

How to write off bad debts

Accounting records need amendment when a bad debt occurs so that the account of the credit customer is closed and profits are reduced.

KEY TERM

Prudence: an accounting principle that requires that where there is doubt, asset and profit values are understated rather than overstated, and, conversely, that losses and liabilities are overstated rather than understated.

Illustration 1 Writing off a bad debt

Kimberly owns a business that sells goods on credit to many customers, one of which is Oasis Ltd. This customer's account in Kimberly's sales ledger shows that a sale took place on 11 January 2010 and the amount due was $1800. However, by 15 May 2010 it became clear that this debt would not be paid. Kimberly decided that the debt should be written off and the account closed.

Here are the required entries in Kimberly's books of account, starting with a journal entry.

JOURNAL

Date	Details	Dr	Cr
2010		$	$
May 15	Bad debts	1800	
	Trade receivable: Oasis Ltd		1800
	Entries to write off bad debt		

SALES LEDGER

Oasis Ltd account

Dr							Cr
			$				$
Jan	11	Sales	1800	May	15	Bad debts	1800

GENERAL LEDGER

Bad debts account

Dr							Cr
			$				$
May	15	Oasis Ltd	1800				

Notes:

1 The account of Oasis Ltd is now closed.

2 The bad debts account is an expense account.

3 At the financial year end the bad debts account will be closed and the total of bad debts for the year will be transferred to the income statement.

The prudence principle

When Kimberly wrote off the bad debt she was following another important accounting rule which is called **prudence**. This rule requires all businesses to ensure that users of their accounts are not misled into thinking that assets and profits have a greater value than is realistic, or that losses and liabilities are less than is the case. So, in this case Kimberly was right to recognise the bad debt as soon as she was reasonably certain that no money would be received. To have kept the account of Oasis Ltd open in her books of account could have given others the idea that the business had a valuable asset, when, of course, this was not the case.

You can now answer questions 1 and 2 on page 156.

LINKS...
There is more about prudence and other principles in Unit 19.

Bad debts recovered

Fortunately, in a few cases, the amount lost when a bad debt is written off may be recovered at a later date. A **bad debt recovered** can occur many months, even years, after the original debt was written off. Usually the former customer is prompted to make a settlement because they are anxious to restore good relationships with the owner of the business and hopes to be given credit facilities again.

Illustration 2 Recording a bad debt recovered

On 12 February 2012, Kimberly received a cheque for $1800 from Oasis Ltd in settlement of the company's account which had been written off in 2010 (see Illustration 1).

Here are the accounting records to record this transaction:

JOURNAL

Date	Details	Dr	Cr
2012		$	$
Feb 12	Trade receivable: Oasis Ltd	1800	
	Bad debt recovered		1800
	Entries to reinstate customer's account		

Cash book (bank columns only)

Dr			Bank				Cr Bank
			$				$
Feb	12	Oasis Ltd	1800				

SALES LEDGER

Oasis Ltd account

Dr							Cr
			$				$
Feb	12	Bad debts recovered	1800	Feb	12	Bank	1800

GENERAL LEDGER

Bad debts recovered account

Dr							Cr
			$				$
Dec	31	Income statement	1800	Feb	12	Oasis Ltd	1800

Income statement for the year ended 31 December 2012

	$	$
Gross profit	xxx	
Other income		
Bad debt recovered	1800	
etc.	xxx	
		xxxx

Notes:

1 The first step is to reinstate the customer's account and that requires a journal entry. So a debit entry is made for the amount due in the customer's account in the sales ledger and a matching credit entry is made in a bad debts recovered account in the general ledger.

2 The cheque is debited to the bank account and a credit entry is made in the customer's account which is now closed.

3 The bad debts recovered account is closed at the end of the financial year and the balance is transferred to the income statement where it is shown as part of the business's 'other income'.

KEY TERM

Bad debt recovered: when a debt that has previously been written off is settled by the customer.

You can now answer questions 3 and 4 on page 156.

16.2 Provisions for doubtful debts

Many businesses ensure that their balance sheet gives a true and fair view of trade receivables not just by stating the total of all the balances in the sales ledger, but also by making a deduction for an estimate of doubtful debts, called a provision for doubtful debts.

Provisions are usually calculated at the year end using one of the following methods:

- The estimate of doubtful debts is often based on the past experience of bad debts and is usually expressed as a percentage of trade receivables. For example, the owner of a business could check what has happened in previous years and calculate that, on average, 3 per cent of trade receivables become bad debts.
- In some cases, however, the provision might be based on a detailed end-of-year review of each trade receivable. This means preparing an analysis of how long debts have been outstanding, usually referred to as an **ageing schedule of trade receivables**. The view might be taken that the longer a debt has been outstanding the more doubtful it has become. A sliding scale of percentages might be used to calculate the provision, with the oldest debts receiving the highest percentage.

KEY TERM

Ageing schedule of trade receivables: a list of all amounts due from credit customers shown in a sequence based on how long the debt has been outstanding.

Illustration 3 Using an ageing schedule of trade receivables to calculate a provision for doubtful debts

Mustafa & Sons is a wholesaler. The business's provision for doubtful debts is based on the length of time debts have been outstanding. Here is its ageing schedule of trade receivables showing the calculation of the provision for doubtful debts.

Length of time outstanding (weeks)	Amount	Estimated likely bad debts as a percentage	Provision for doubtful debts
	$		$
5–10	12 000	1	120
11–25	8 000	2	160
26–50	3 000	5	150
51+	1 000	50	500
Total provision for doubtful debts			930

A provision for doubtful debts is a further example of the principle of prudence (i.e. businesses taking care not overstate the value of assets and profits). It is also a further illustration of the accruals principle (i.e. ensuring that the profit for a year is based on matching the income for a year with the costs for that year).

Illustration 4 | Balance sheets and provisions for doubtful debts

On 31 December Year 1 Ralph's trial balance showed total trade receivables to be $40 000. However, based on past experience Ralph is doubtful that 5 per cent of this amount will be received.

Here is an extract from Ralph's balance sheet showing a true and fair view of trade receivables.

Balance sheet at 31 December year 1 (extract)

	$	$	$
CURRENT ASSETS			
Inventory		xx	
Trade receivables	40 000		
Less provision for doubtful debts	(2 000)		
		38 000	

Ledger accounts and provisions for doubtful debts

When a business creates a provision for doubtful debts, it is not enough to show this information on the balance sheet, it is important to complete a double-entry record too.

The accounting entries to create a provision for doubtful debts are:

Debit Income statement

Credit Provision for doubtful debts account

Illustration 5 | Accounting entries to create a provision for doubtful debts

Taking the information about Ralph's provision for doubtful debts in Illustration 4, here are the accounting records starting with a journal entry.

JOURNAL

Date	Details	Dr	Cr
Yr 1		$	$
Dec 31	Income statement	2 000	
	Provision for doubtful debts		2 000
	Entries to create a provision for doubtful debts		

GENERAL LEDGER

Dr **Provision for doubtful debts account** **Cr**

	$				$
		Yr 1			
		Dec	31	Income statement	2 000

Notes:

1 Creating a provision for doubtful debts reduces the profits of the year in which it is created. So the provision is debited in the income statement.

2 The provision for doubtful debt accounts is deducted from trade receivables on the balance sheet (see Illustration 4).

Income statement for the year ended 31 December year 1

	$	$
Gross profit		XX
Expenses	XX	
Provision for doubtful debts	**2 000**	
		XX
Profit		XX

Once a provision for doubtful debts account has been created it remains in the business's books of account. The credit balance on the account will appear on any trial balance that is prepared.

Avoiding bad debts, and credit control

Many businesses depend on selling their goods (or services) on credit, but naturally they want to minimise the risk of bad debts. It is important, therefore, for the owner of a business to give some attention to the idea of credit control. The following procedures could be put in place:

- Credit facilities are only made available to a potential customer whose creditworthiness has been investigated, usually by means of acquiring references from, for example, the customer's bank. Sometimes it is also possible to use a specialist agency to check an individual's credit rating.
- Once a customer has been allowed credit, it is usual to set a limit on the amount of credit available at any one time. All customer accounts should be reviewed carefully to ensure the credit limit is not exceeded.
- Payment should be encouraged in the case of outstanding debts with reminders and statements of account (see Unit 10) issued at regular intervals.

16.3 Keeping a provision for doubtful debts up to date

Once a provision for doubtful debts is created it will be reviewed annually.

When should a business increase its provision for doubtful debts?

If there is an increase in the total of trade receivables at the year end, then the provision should be increased to keep in step with this change.

The entries required to *increase* a provision for doubtful debts are:

Debit Income statement *with the amount of the increase*

Credit Provision for doubtful debts accounts *with the amount of the increase*

When should a business decrease its provision for doubtful debts?

The total of trade receivables could decrease from one year to the next. In this situation the amount of the provision for doubtful debts should be decreased to keep in step with the decrease in trade receivables.

The entries required to *decrease* a provision for doubtful debts are:

Debit Provision for doubtful debts accounts *with the amount of the decrease*

Credit Income statement *with the amount of the decrease*

DID YOU KNOW?

As well as responding to changes in the total of trade receivables at the year end, a provision for doubtful debts could be changed because the business's experience of actual bad debts has decreased or increased.

Illustration 6 | Changing the provision for doubtful debts

Returning to the case of Ralph's business, at the end of year 1 a provision for doubtful debts of $2000 was created.

- At the end of year 2 trade receivables totalled $46 000.
- At the end of year 3 trade receivables totalled $34 000.

Ralph wishes to maintain the provision for doubtful debts at 5 per cent of trade receivables.

So, the provision needs to change to $2300 at the end of year 2 (i.e. 5 per cent of $46 000). At the end of year 3 the provision needs to change to $1700 (i.e. 5 per cent of $34 000).

Setting the changes out as a calculations:

End of year 2	**$**
Provision at the end of year 2 to be 5% × $46 000	2 300
Existing provision (at end of year 1)	2 000
Increase in provision for doubtful debts	300

End of year 3	$
Provision at the end of year 3 to be 5% × $34 000	1 700
Existing provision (at end of year 2)	2 300
Decrease in provision for doubtful debts	600

Here are the entries in the accounting system for year 2 and year 3 to put into effect the changing value of the provision for doubtful debts.

Year 2 (increasing the provision)

JOURNAL

Date	Details	Dr	Cr
Yr 2		$	$
Dec 31	Income statement	300	
	Provision for doubtful debts		300
	Entries to increase the provision for doubtful debts		

Provision for doubtful debts account

Dr					Cr				
				$	Yr 1				$
Yr 2					Dec	31	Income statement		2 000
Dec	31	Balance	c/d	2 300	Yr 2				
					Dec 31		**Income statement**		**300**
				2 300					2 300
					Yr 3				
					Jan	1	Balance	b/d	2 300

Income Statement for the year ended 31 December Year 2

	$	$
Gross profit		xx
Less expenses	xx	
Increase in provision for doubtful debts	**300**	
		xx
Profit		xx

The balance sheet will show the latest position.

Balance sheet at 31 December year 2 (extract)

	$	$	$
CURRENT ASSETS			
Inventory		xx	
Trade receivables	46 000		
Less provision for doubtful debts	(2 300)		
		43 700	

STUDY TIP

When preparing the end-of-year financial statements always check to see if there is already a provision for doubtful debts. If there is, remember any change in the provision is recorded in the income statement, but the full amount is shown on the balance sheet. Also, avoid using informal abbreviations like PDD. Financial statements are very formal documents, so PDD is not correct.

You can now answer questions 5–12 on pages 156–158.

Year 3 (decreasing the provision)

JOURNAL

Date	Details	Dr	Cr
Yr 3		$	$
Dec 31	Provision for doubtful debts	600	
	Income statement		600
	Entries to decrease the provision for doubtful debts		

Provision for doubtful debts account

Dr					$					Cr $
						Yr 1				
Yr 2						Dec	31	Income statement		2 000
Dec	31	Balance	c/d		2 300	Yr 2				
						Dec	31	Income statement		300
					2 300					2 300
						Yr 3				
Yr 3						Jan	1	Balance	b/d	2 300
Dec	**31**	**Income statement**			**600**					
Dec	31	Balance	c/d		1 700					
					2 300					2 300
						Yr 4				
						Jan	1	Balance	b/d	1 700

Income statement for the year ended 31 December year 3

	$	$
Gross profit	xx	
Other income:		
Add: decrease in provision for doubtful debts	**600**	
		xx
Less expenses	xx	
Expenses	xx	
		xx
Profit		xx

The balance sheet will show the latest position.

Balance sheet at 31 December year 3 (extract)

	$	$	$
CURRENT ASSETS			
Inventory		xx	
Trade receivables	34 000		
Less provision for doubtful debts	(1 700)		
		32 300	

Unit 16 Practice questions

NOTE: As the vertical style of presentation of balance sheets is not covered until Unit 18, answers to some questions in this unit will involve the use of a mixture of formats for financial statements. It should be noted that in an examination, only one style of presentation should be used.

DEVELOPING YOUR SKILLS

1 Writing off a bad debt

The following balances appeared in the sales ledger of a business on 1 March 2010.

	$
Bestservice Ltd	3 850
Q&A Ltd	840

By 31 August 2010 it was apparent that neither of these trade receivables would be able to pay the amount due and their accounts were written off as bad debts.

Prepare the journal entries and ledger accounts to show how this information should be recorded in the books of account.

2 Writing off a bad debt

The following balances appeared in the sales ledger of a business on 1 July 2010.

	$
Murray Lee	540
Shantal Watson	1 720

By 30 September 2010 it was apparent that neither of these trade receivables would be able to pay the amount due and their accounts were written off as bad debts.

Prepare the journal entries and ledger accounts to show how this information should be recorded in the books of account.

3 Recording a bad debt recovered

Refer to the information given in question 1. On 3 September 2012 a cheque was received from Bestservice Ltd for $3850 in payment of the debt written off in 2010.

Prepare the journal entries and ledger accounts to show how the bad debt recovered should be recorded in the books of account.

4 Recording a bad debt recovered

Refer to the information given in question 2. On 9 October 2012 a cheque was received from Murray Lee for $540 in payment of the debt written off in 2010.

Prepare the journal entries and ledger accounts to show how the bad debt recovered should be recorded in the books of account.

5 Calculating provisions for doubtful debts

The owner of a business decided to create a provision for doubtful debts. It was agreed that the provision should be maintained at 5 per cent of trade receivables at each year end.

Trade receivables at 31 December:

Year 1 $36 800 Year 2 $39 200 Year 3 $35 200

Complete the following table recording information about the business's provision for doubtful debts.

Year	Provision for doubtful debts $	Amount to be entered in the income statement $	Entry in the provision for doubtful debts account: enter debit or credit
1			
2			
3			

6 Calculating provisions for doubtful debts

The owner of a business decided to create a provision for doubtful debts. It was agreed that the provision should be maintained at 2.5 per cent of trade receivables at each year end.

Trade receivables at 31 December:

Year 1 $48 000 Year 2 $36 000 Year 3 $56 000

Complete the following table recording information about the business's provision for doubtful debts.

Year	Provision for doubtful debts $	Amount to be entered in the income statement $	Entry in the provision for doubtful debts account: enter debit or credit
1			
2			
3			

7 Accounting records for provisions for doubtful debts

Using the information in question 5, prepare the following accounting records for each of the years 1, 2 and 3 relating to provisions for doubtful debts:

- Journal entries
- Extract from income statement
- Provision for doubtful debts account
- Extract from balance sheet

8 Accounting records for provisions for doubtful debts

Using the information in question 6, prepare the following accounting records for each of the years 1, 2 and 3 relating to provisions for doubtful debts:

- Journal entries
- Extract from income statement
- Provision for doubtful debts account
- Extract from balance sheet

9 Preparing end-of-year financial statements including the creation of a provision for doubtful debts

Tricia owns a retail store. Her business's financial year end is 31 December. The following trial balance was extracted from the business's books of account on 31 December 2012.

	Dr $	Cr $
Bad debts	850	
Bad debt recovered		190
Capital		62 210
Cash at bank	3 890	
Drawings	31 300	
Equipment		
Cost	35 000	
Provision for depreciation at 1 January 2012		14 000
Gross profit		151 270
Inventory at 31 December 2012	29 480	
Operating expenses	57 610	
Rent	25 400	
Trade payables		11 660
Trade receivables	27 000	
Vehicles		
Cost	45 000	
Provision for depreciation at 1 January 2012		16 200
	255 530	255 530

Additional information at 31 December 2012:

- Rent, $1320, was prepaid.
- Operating expenses, $2080, were due but unpaid.
- Tricia decided to create a provision for doubtful debts of 5 per cent of trade receivables at the year end.
- Depreciation was charged on non-current assets as follows:
  - Equipment – 20 per cent per annum using the straight-line method.
  - Vehicles – 20 per cent per annum using the reducing balance method.

Prepare end-of-year financial statements.

10 Preparing end-of-year financial statements including the creation of a provision for doubtful debts

Patrick, a wholesaler, extracted the following trial balance from his business's books of account at 31 August 2012.

	Dr $	Cr $
Bad debts	1 475	
Bad debt recovered		246
Capital		72 688
Cash at bank	9 872	
Discounts	889	2 071
Drawings	44 482	
Electricity	3 783	
Fixtures and fittings		
Cost	45 000	
Provision for depreciation at 1 Sept 2011		27 000
Gross profit		194 356
Insurance	7 794	
Inventory at 31 August 2012	58 384	
Trade payables		22 373
Trade receivables	18 360	
Vehicles		
Cost	80 000	
Provision for depreciation at 1 Sept 2011		48 250
Wages and salaries	96 945	
	366 984	366 984

Additional information at 31 August 2012:

- Prepaid expenses were: insurance $375; electricity $446.
- Expenses due but unpaid were: wages and salaries, $2970.
- Patrick decided to create a provision for doubtful debts of 5 per cent of trade receivables at the year end.
- Depreciation was charged on non-current assets as follows:
  - Fixtures and fittings – 20 per cent per annum using the straight-line method.
  - Vehicles – 25 per cent per annum using the reducing balance method.

Prepare end-of-year financial statements.

11 Preparing end-of-year financial statements including revising the provision for doubtful debts

The following trial balance was extracted from the books of Magna, a wholesale business, on 31 July 2012.

	Dr $	Cr $
Bad debts	320	
Bad debts recovered		130
Capital		476 620
Carriage inwards	4 620	
Cash at bank	3 080	
Discounts	450	1 730
Drawings	45 450	
Equipment		
Cost	58 000	
Provision for depreciation at 1 August 2011		11 600
General expenses	24 490	
Inventory at 1 August 2011	62 330	
Premises		
Cost	480 000	
Provision for depreciation at 1 August 2011		9 600
Provision for doubtful debts at 1 August 2011		820
Purchases	568 380	
Rent received		26 380
Returns	6 360	8 940
Revenue		909 490
Trade payables		33 670
Trade receivables	18 900	
Vehicles		
Cost	70 000	
Provision for depreciation at 1 August 2011		17 500
Wages	138 580	
Water charges	15 520	
	1 496,480	1 496,480

Additional information at 31 July 2012:

- Inventory was valued at $47 370.
- Prepaid expenses were: general expenses, $805
- Expenses due but unpaid were: wages $4110, water charges $660.
- Rent received, $1270, is due but unpaid.
- The policy is to maintain the provision for doubtful debts at 5 per cent of trade receivables at the year end.
- Depreciation was charged on non-current assets as follows:
  - Premises – 2 per cent per annum using the straight-line method.
  - Equipment – 20 per cent per annum using the straight-line method.
  - Vehicles – 25 per cent per annum using the reducing balance method.

Prepare the business's income statement for the year ended 31 July 2012 and a balance sheet at that date.

12 Preparing end-of-year financial statements including revising the provision for doubtful debts

Leon Fray is the owner of Palm Beach Store. The business's trial balance on 31 May 2012 was as follows.

	Dr $	Cr $
Administration expenses	8 480	
Bad debts	960	
Bad debts recovered		340
Bank overdraft		8 490
Capital		567 150
Carriage outwards	4 470	
Drawings	52 390	
Equipment and furniture		
Cost	140 000	
Provision for depreciation at 1 June 2011		61 250
Insurance	11 820	
Inventory at 1 June 2011	34 230	
Premises		
Cost	500 000	
Provision for depreciation at 1 June 2011		45 000
Provision for doubtful debts at 1 June 2011		930
Purchases	375 300	
Rent received		14 800
Revenue		502 810
Trade payables		16 660
Trade receivables	14 400	
Wages	75 380	
	1 217,430	1 217,430

Additional information at 31 May 2012:

- Inventory was valued at $36 200.
- Prepaid expenses were: administration expenses $340, insurance $770
- Expenses due but unpaid were: wages, $1190.
- The policy is to maintain the provision for doubtful debts at 5 per cent of trade receivables at the year end.
- Depreciation was charged on non-current assets as follows:
  - Premises – 3 per cent per annum using the straight-line method.
  - Equipment and furniture – 25 per cent per annum using the reducing balance method.

Prepare the business's income statement for the year ended 31 May 2012 and a balance sheet at that date.

17 Capital and revenue expenditure and receipts

Introduction

Accounting has many precise rules. All of these rules are designed to ensure that financial statements present owners, managers and any other interested parties with a true and fair view in which they can have confidence.

In this unit some new rules are introduced that help to distinguish between different types of expenditure and different types of receipt. These new rules have an impact on the calculation of profits, asset values and capital, all of which are necessary for the effective management of a business.

LEARNING OUTCOMES

When you have reached the end of this unit you will be able to:

- define the terms 'capital expenditure' and 'revenue expenditure'
- explain the importance of correctly distinguishing between capital and revenue expenditure
- define the terms 'capital receipts' and 'revenue receipts'
- explain the importance of correctly distinguishing between capital and revenue receipts
- record capital and revenue expenditure and capital and revenue receipts correctly.

17.1 Capital and revenue expenditure

KEY TERM

Capital expenditure: money spent on non-current assets that is intended to be of benefit in future financial years.

Revenue expenditure: money spent on running costs that benefits only the current financial year.

Any money spent by the owner or manager of a business for business purposes can be divided into categories:

- **Capital expenditure** is money spent on non-current assets.
- **Revenue expenditure** is money spent on everyday running costs.

Capital expenditure is shown on a balance sheet, but revenue expenditure is charged to the income statement.

Capital expenditure

A more complete definition of the term 'capital expenditure' would state that the benefit from this type of payment arises over a longer period, and to be precise, it is expected to arise in a period longer than one year. Here are situations where capital expenditure has taken place:

- All payments to purchase non-current assets are capital expenditure because businesses buy non-current assets to benefit the business for several years.
- Money spent on improving non-current assets is also regarded as capital expenditure. So if a business extended its premises, or put air conditioning into its existing buildings, the money spent in both these situations would be capital expenditure because the benefit from the expenditure is intended to last for several years and the value of the non-current asset would increase.
- Capital expenditure also includes some items that sound as if they are routine expenses, but which in fact will benefit the business for a longer period. For example, carriage charges on some new office equipment should be treated as capital expenditure and added to the cost of the office equipment. Legal charges paid in connection with the purchase of business premises should also be included as part of the value of the premises. In both these cases, the 'capitalisation' of the payments for these two expenses is correct, because the view is taken that the benefit from the payments will last as long as the business is using the office equipment and the business premises.

DID YOU KNOW?

If a business purchased a delivery vehicle but sold it only a few months later because it had not proved satisfactory, the payment would still count as capital expenditure. This is because presumably the original intention was that the delivery vehicle would benefit the business for a long time.

Revenue expenditure

A more complete definition of the term 'revenue expenditure' is that the benefit from this type of payment lasts for a short term, i.e. within a year from the date of the payment. A feature of most revenue expenditure is that it is recurring (i.e. it has to be paid for again and again). So expense payments qualify as revenue expenditure, such as rent, electricity costs, water charges, wages, salaries, and so on.

It is important to note that money spent on repairs, renewals, maintenance and servicing is also regarded as revenue expenditure. For each of these items the view is taken that there has not been any improvement to the non-current asset being repaired or serviced, the non-current asset is merely being kept in its original state. If there was any improvement then the amount spent should be regarded as capital expenditure. For example, contrast a payment made to decorate a new extension to a business's premises: this would be regarded as capital expenditure because it is an improvement to the non-current asset. On the other hand, a payment made to redecorate the existing premises would be regarded as revenue expenditure because the non-current asset is being brought back to its original state and no improvement is taking place.

Receipts can also be divided into two categories.

Illustration 1 | Separating capital and revenue expenditure

Gabrielle owns a business that delivers groceries to customers. Recently she purchased a new delivery vehicle for business use. The following information is available.

	$
New delivery van	18500
Addition of shelving in the van for improved storage	600
Fuel to fill tank	50
Insurance premium	320
Cost of painting business's name on exterior of the van	140

The capital expenditure arising from this purchase is as follows.

	$
New delivery van	18500
Addition of shelving for improved storage	600
Cost of painting business's name on exterior	140
	19240

Each of these payments will benefit the business for more than one financial year.

The revenue expenditure arising from these purchases is as follows.

	$
Fuel to fill tank	50
Insurance premium	320
	370

Each of these payments will benefit the business for less than one financial year (assuming the insurance is an annual premium or covers a period of less than one year).

In the business's accounting system $19240 should be debited to the delivery vehicle account. It is this amount which will be the basis for the annual depreciation charge.

The revenue items will be debited to the appropriate expense accounts.

You can now answer questions 1–4 on page 164.

17.2 Capital and revenue receipts

Capital receipts

Capital receipts arise from selling off non-current assets or from the owner(s) or lenders providing additional investment in the business. Capital receipts do not appear in the income statement but are shown in the balance sheet.

Revenue receipts

Illustration 2 Recording capital receipts

Marietta owns a book shop. Recently the following transactions occurred:

- Marietta increased her investment in the business by providing $3000 from her private funds which was paid into the business bank account.
- Marietta's car, value $14 000, which had previously been used only for personal use, was in future to be used exclusively for business purposes.
- A bank loan was arranged for $15 000. The funds were paid into the business's bank account.

The correct double entry for each of these transactions is as follows.

Additional money invested:	Dr Bank $3 000	Cr Capital $3 000
Car to be used by business:	Dr Vehicle $14 000	Cr Capital $14 000
Bank loan:	Dr Bank $15 000	Cr Bank loan $15 000

Notes:

1 Each of these transactions is a capital receipt.

2 All of the entries in the accounting system will directly affect balance sheet items.

3 None of the entries in the accounting system will directly affect the income statement.

Revenue receipts arise from normal business activities (i.e. the sale of goods or services). Some revenue receipts can be incidental to the main business activity: rent received from a tenant; commission received; or interest on investment accounts are all good examples. Revenue receipts are credited to the income statement and so directly affect the calculation of profit (or loss).

Why does the distinction between capital and revenue matter?

Revenue receipts and expenditure directly affect a business's income statement and so if items are wrongly classified, the business's profit or loss will be inaccurate.

On the other hand, capital receipts and expenditure directly affect a business's balance sheet. If items are wrongly classified a balance sheet could show incorrect totals for assets, liabilities and capital.

Errors in end of year financial statements can have serious consequences. Any inaccuracies in profit, capital or asset values could mislead those who depend on these figures and result in poor decision-making.

Illustration 3 The importance of correctly classifying capital and revenue items

Error in an income statement

Hasib was recently presented with a copy of his business's end-of-year financial statements. Unfortunately an error was made by the accounts clerk who incorrectly classified a capital receipt as a revenue receipt. The accounts clerk included a bank loan of $20 000 in the income statement by mistake. As a result the income statement showed a profit of $30 000 instead of just $10 000.

Hasib, who was unaware of the error and pleased with the reported profit of $30 000, decided to increase his monthly drawings from the business.

Notes:

1 The error in the accounts led to the owner making an unwise decision.

2 The increase in drawings was probably not justified and could lead to the business being short of funds during the months ahead.

Error in a balance sheet

Raslinda owns a retail business. Her accounts clerk made a mistake when valuing assets to be shown on her business's balance sheet at 31 December 2012. During the year ended 31 December 2012 $10 000 had been spent on installing air conditioning throughout the shop premises. The accounts clerk had treated this item as revenue expenditure instead of adding this amount to the value of the shop premises.

As a result of this error:

- the business's profit would be incorrect because it includes some capital expenditure of $10 000
- the shop premises will be undervalued on the business's balance sheet by $10 000
- the depreciation charge on shop premises for the year ended 31 December 2012 could be miscalculated because the calculation is likely to have been based on an incorrect value of the shop premises.

Notes:

1 Raslinda could be misled by the understated profit and make cuts in expenditure that are not justified.

2 If Raslinda were to sell her business, a potential purchaser could be undercharged because the non-current assets are incorrectly valued.

You can now answer questions 5–17 on pages 164–166.

Unit 17 Practice questions

DEVELOPING YOUR SKILLS

1 Classifying revenue and capital expenditure

Payments were made for the following by Marie, the owner of a retail business:

- Electricity charges
- Office furniture
- Interest on a loan
- Shelving for shop
- Repairs to delivery van

In each case, state whether the transactions represent revenue expenditure or capital expenditure and give reasons for your decision.

2 Classifying revenue and capital expenditure

Payments were made for the following by Josh, the owner of a wholesale business:

- Telephone charges
- Staff wages
- Delivery vehicle
- Maintenance charges on office equipment
- Computer printer

In each case, state whether the transactions represent revenue expenditure or capital expenditure and give reasons for your decision.

3 Calculating total revenue and capital expenditure

Paula is the manager of a wholesale business. Recently a new computer system was installed in her office. The amounts paid were as follows.

	$
Computer hardware	900
Printer cartridge	24
Computer software	170
Paper for printer	30
Computer printer	140

Calculate the total revenue expenditure and total capital expenditure.

4 Calculating total revenue and capital expenditure

Marco owns a successful catering business. Recently he has made the following payments.

	$
Servicing charges for existing catering equipment	340
Purchase of some additional second-hand catering equipment	1 080
Payments to upgrade second-hand catering equipment	230
Redecoration of catering facilities	440
Carriage paid to deliver second-hand catering equipment	90

Calculate the total revenue expenditure and total capital expenditure.

5 Classifying revenue and capital receipts

Philo owns a restaurant. Recently the following amounts were received:

- Rent from the tenant who lives in the flat above the restaurant
- One week's cash takings
- Additional investment by Philo from his private funds
- Loan from a friend due for repayment in 2014

In each case, state whether the transactions represent a revenue receipt or a capital receipt and give reasons for your decision.

6 Classifying revenue and capital receipts

Kalpna owns a bakery. Recently the following amounts were received:

- Kalpna received interest on one of her business's investment accounts
- Kalpna transferred furniture from her home to be used in her office at the bakery
- Cash sales
- A bank loan was arranged and the funds were paid into the business's bank account

In each case, state whether the transactions represent a revenue receipt or a capital receipt and give reasons for your decision.

7 Further practice at classifying items

The following table lists items of capital and revenue expenditure and capital and revenue receipts. Identify which type of expenditure or receipt is appropriate by placing a tick under one of the column headings.

	Expenditure		Receipt	
	Capital	Revenue	Capital	Revenue
Paid for extension to office block				
Bank loan arranged to pay for extension				
Rent received from tenant who is using part of new office block				
Paid wages of office staff				
Paid for installation of air conditioning in new office block				

8 Further practice at classifying items

Mumtaz owns a furniture store. The following table lists items of capital and revenue expenditure and capital and revenue receipts that occurred recently. Identify which type of expenditure or receipt is appropriate by placing a tick under one of the column headings.

	Expenditure		Receipt	
	Capital	Revenue	Capital	Revenue
Purchased furniture for resale				
Mumtaz made an additional investment in the business from private funds				
Purchased furniture for use in the business's accounts office				
Sold furniture in the showroom to a credit customer				
Sold some unwanted office furniture for cash				

PREPARING FOR THE EXAMINATION

(The following questions cover Unit 17)

MULTIPLE-CHOICE QUESTIONS

9 Which of the following should be treated as capital expenditure in the accounts?

- **A** Purchase of a new stapler for the office for $16
- **B** Purchase of two vehicles costing $31 000
- **C** Quarterly office rent, $14 300
- **D** Repairs to the air conditioning unit for $440

10 Which of the following should be treated as revenue expenditure in the accounts?

- **A** Building repairs
- **B** Delivery cost of new machinery
- **C** Legal costs of a new lease
- **D** Wages of employees building a new extension

11 Which one of the following items should be treated as a capital receipt in the books of a hotel?

- **A** Interest received on business savings account
- **B** Receipts from guests using the restaurant
- **C** Rent received from tenant
- **D** Sale of unwanted furniture

12 During a recent period the owner of a taxi business made the following payments from the business's bank account.

	$
Taxi driver's wages	2 200
Servicing of taxi	400
Cost of adapting seating in a new taxi	900

The business's revenue expenditure amounted to which of the following:

A $900

B $2200

C $2600

D $3500

13 Capital expenditure should include which of the following:

A An increase in non-current assets

B A payment for the hire of machinery

C A purchase of inventory for resale

D The payment for maintenance of machinery

14 Revenue receipts should be credited to which of the following:

A A customer's account

B An asset account

C The capital account

D The income statement

15 Which of the following lists contains only revenue receipts?

A Additional capital, cash takings, rent received

B Cash takings, discounts received, commission received

C Commission received, additional capital, bank loan

D Rent received, proceeds of sale of non-current asset, bank loan

16 Which one of following lists contains only revenue expenditure?

A Maintenance of machinery, machine operator's wages, replacement of worn part

B New computer system, new printer, printer cartridges

C Redecoration of staff rest room, new furniture for rest room, wages of catering staff

D Repairs to equipment, staff salaries, carriage on new non-current asset

OTHER QUESTION

17 Electra opened a business selling children's toys a few months ago.

She is not very experienced at keeping financial records and believes she made some mistakes recently. Electra recorded the cost of some new equipment, $11000, in her business's income statement for the first three months in operation. The income statement showed a loss of $5000 for this three-month period.

a State what is meant by the term 'revenue expenditure'.

b Give two examples of revenue expenditure that could apply to Electra's business.

c State the correct profit or loss made by Electra's business for the first three months that it was in operation.

d Explain why making errors in an income statement could be serious.

18 Vertical balance sheets and end-of-year financial statements of a service business

Introduction

You are now familiar with the vertical presentation of income statements. In this unit you will learn how to apply your skills to balance sheets.

You will also produce balance sheets that include intangible assets and you will identify two new terms: 'net current assets' and 'capital employed'. These new ideas mean that you will be able to make balance sheets even more useful to the people who use them.

Many businesses do not sell goods but instead provide services for their customers. Service businesses are a very important part of the economy of many countries. The accounting records of both types of business are very similar, but in this chapter you will learn about the differences in the end-of-year financial statements of a service business.

LEARNING OUTCOMES

When you have reached the end of this unit you will be able to:

- prepare a balance sheet in a vertical format
- set out a detailed capital section on a balance sheet
- prepare balance sheets including goodwill
- identify working capital and capital employed on a balance sheet
- prepare end-of-year financial statements for a service business.

18.1 The balance sheet

Detailed capital section on a balance sheet

The owners of many businesses choose to show additional information about their capital on the balance sheet. This can make the balance sheet more helpful to users.

Illustration 1 Setting out a detailed capital section on a balance sheet

The following capital account appears in a business's general ledger.

Dr			**Capital**				**Cr**
Dec	31	Drawings	30 000	Jan	1	Balance b/d	100 000
	31	Balance c/d	110 000	Dec	31	Profit	40 000
			140 000				140 000
				Jan	1	Balance b/d	110 000

On the balance sheet at 31 December, the owner has the choice of presenting this information in two ways.

Option 1: Quoting final balance only

Balance sheet at 31 December 2012 (extract)

	$	$
CAPITAL		110 000

Option 2: Providing detail about capital

Balance sheet at 31 December 2012 (extract)

	$	$
CAPITAL		
Opening balance	100 000	
Add profit	40 000	
	140 000	
Less drawings	(30 000)	
		110 000

Why is option 2 potentially more useful? At a glance the owner can see how much profit has been made in relation to their investment at the beginning of the year. The owner can also see whether profit was sufficient to cover drawings, and to lead to an increase in capital by the end of the year.

Working capital (net current assets)

A vertical balance sheet is now the most common form of presenting this financial statement. Not only does it present information in a way that is more user friendly, it also provides the flexibility to show an important subtotal which cannot be recorded in the horizontal format. This subtotal is the difference between current assets and current liabilities, which is sometimes called **working capital** and increasingly is called **net current assets** (or net current liabilities). This figure is important for the owner of the business because it can help in deciding whether the business has enough resources to keep the business running efficiently on a day-to-day basis.

Capital employed

It is also possible to identify another important figure on a vertical balance sheet, this is **capital employed**. Capital employed is the total of longer-term finance being used by a business. It is made up of the owner's capital and the non-current liabilities, in other words the finance that will be available to the business well into the future. Alternatively, capital employed can be looked at as the net value of resources being used by a business (i.e. the non-current assets plus the working capital (net current assets)). Note that the same figure is obtained whichever way you look at capital employed. It is helpful to know a business's capital employed because the figure needs to be considered when analysing how well a business has performed.

Intangible assets

There is a small but important group of assets that do not have any physical presence (i.e. they cannot be seen or touched) but do have a monetary value. These assets are called **intangible assets**. Here are some examples:

- Goodwill (see below)
- Brand names (e.g. the ownership of designer labels)
- Film rights
- Copyright on books and written articles

Goodwill

When a business is sold it can often be sold for more than the net value shown by the balance sheet. Why is this? From the purchaser's point of view there is likely to be less risk in buying an established business rather than setting one up from scratch. The purchaser of an existing business is, therefore, prepared to pay for the advantage of acquiring a well-established organisation, and that advantage is referred to as **goodwill**.

An established business will have a record of just how successful it has been. It will be clear whether or not the business has regular customers, is well located, has a good reputation, and so on. On the other hand, a completely new business can easily fail if it turns out that the location is not quite right, or the owner and staff do not have the skills and knowledge to make the business work well.

Goodwill can only be shown on a balance sheet when it has been paid for. A business could have built up goodwill over several years, but its value cannot be recognised until the business is sold. In other words, it is not possible for the owner of a business to estimate the value of the goodwill and record this figure on the balance sheet. This is because accounting information needs to be as factual as it can be in order to ensure that users have confidence in the reliability of the data shown. So matters of opinion are avoided wherever this is possible. The rules for the treatment of goodwill are also another good example of the prudence principle, which requires assets to be under- rather than overstated where there is doubt.

KEY TERM

Working capital: the difference between total current assets and current liabilities. The figure (which can be positive or negative) gives some idea of the funds available to run the business on a day-to-day basis.

Net current assets: a term often used instead of working capital and calculated in the same way: current assets less current liabilities. When the figure is negative the term should be 'net current liabilities'.

Capital employed: the total of capital and non-current liabilities, which is a key element in the analysis of how well a business has performed. Alternatively, the same figure can be found by adding non-current assets and working capital.

LINKS...

There is more about working capital/net current assets and capital employed in Units 20 and 21.

KEY TERM

Intangible assets: assets that have a monetary value but which do not have a physical presence.

Goodwill: the additional value of an established and successful business, above the value of its tangible assets. Goodwill is an intangible asset.

LINKS...

There is more about prudence and the other formal rules of accounting in Unit 19.

DID YOU KNOW?

The word 'intangible' means it is not capable of being touched.

Illustration 2 How to prepare a vertical balance sheet

Here is a business's balance sheet in horizontal format followed by the same statement but in vertical form:

Balance sheet at 31 December 2012

	$	$	$		$	$
NON-CURRENT ASSETS	Cost	Accumulated deprcn	Net	CAPITAL		
				Opening balance	400 000	
Goodwill	50 000		50 000	Add profit	60 000	
Premises	260 000	10 000	250 000		460 000	
Vehicles	120 000	30 000	90 000	Less drawings	(40 000)	
	430 000	40 000	390 00			420 000
				NON-CURRENT LIABILITY		
CURRENT ASSETS				Bank loan		20 000
Inventory		40 000				
Trade receivables	20 000			CURRENT LIABILITIES		
Less provision for doubtful debts	(1 000)			Trade payables	8 000	
		19 000		Other payables	3 000	
Other receivables		3 000		Bank overdraft	1 000	
			62 000			12 000
			452 000			452 000

Notes:

1. In a vertical form the final column is for the most important subtotals; the second-to-last column is to show how those subtotals were arrived at; the third column from the right is used to provide detail supporting information in the second column from the right, and so on.
2. Always start with the non-current assets.
3. Intangible assets are placed at the top of the list of non-current assets in the balance sheet.

Here is the balance sheet in vertical form. Note that the balance sheet includes the new ideas: goodwill, working capital (net current assets), capital employed.

Balance sheet at 31 December 2012

	$	$	$	$
NON-CURRENT ASSETS		Cost	Accumulated deprcn	Net
Goodwill		50 000		50 000
Premises		260 000	10 000	250 000
Vehicles		120 000	30 000	90 000
		430 000	40 000	390 00
CURRENT ASSETS				
Inventory		40 000		
Trade receivables	20 000			
Less provision for doubtful debts	(1 000)			
		19 000		
Other receivables		3 000		
			62 000	
Less CURRENT LIABILITIES				
Trade payables		8 000		
Other payables		3 000		
Bank overdraft		1 000		
			(12 000)	
WORKING CAPITAL/NET CURRENT ASSETS				50 000
CAPITAL EMPLOYED				440 000
Less NON-CURRENT LIABILITIES				
Bank loan				(20 000)
				420 000
CAPITAL				
Opening balance			400 000	
Add profit			60 000	
			460 000	
Less drawings			(40 000)	
				420 000

4 Goodwill appears on this balance sheet. This must mean that $50 000 was recently paid to purchase this business.

5 Current assets are shown next and follow the sequence: inventory, trade receivables, prepayments, etc.

6 Record the current liabilities. Total current liabilities is deducted from the total of current assets. Label the figure either working capital or net current assets (or net current liabilities if the subtotal of current liabilities is greater than the subtotal for current assets).

7 Add the total of non-current assets to the working capital figure.

8 Deduct any non-current liabilities to reach the first balance sheet total.

9 The second part of the balance sheet consists of the capital section only.

10 Capital employed $440 000 has been identified on the balance sheet. It is the total of non-current assets and working capital/net current assets.

11 Capital employed can also be found by taking capital ($420 000) and adding non-current liabilities ($20 000) to give the same total of $440 000.

You can now answer questions 1–4 on pages 173–174.

DID YOU KNOW?

The detailed capital section of the balance sheet can be introduced with the words 'Finance by'.

18.3 Service businesses

All of the businesses covered to date have been selling goods. However, as you are no doubt aware, many businesses provide a service rather than selling goods.

Examples of service businesses

Here are just a few examples of some businesses providing services:

- Accountant
- Beautician
- Bookkeeper
- Car repairs
- Cleaner
- Hairdresser
- Health club
- Legal services
- Plumber

Financial statements of a service business

The end-of-year financial statements for a service business are prepared in very much the same way as for all of the businesses you have studied so far. There is one important difference, however, and that is that the first part of the income statement is not required because a service business does not sell goods. Instead only the second part of the income statement is required, starting with the revenue from providing the service less all of the business's expenses, ending, of course, with a figure for profit or loss.

Illustration 3 Example of a service business's income statement

Here is a typical income statement of a service business.

Snippets Hairdressing Salon

Income statement for the year ended 31 August 2012

	$	$
Revenue (receipts from customers)		98 000
Less expenses		
Administration expenses	5 000	
Depreciation (equipment, etc.)	18 000	
Electricity	3 500	
Insurance	4 100	
Wages of assistants	39 500	
Water charges	4 200	
		(74 300)
Profit for year		23 700

You can now answer questions 5–8 on pages 175–176.

DEVELOPING YOUR SKILLS

1 Preparing a balance sheet using a vertical format

The following balance sheet was prepared on 31 December 2012.

Balance sheet at 31 December 2012

	$	$	$		$	$
NON-CURRENT ASSETS	Cost	Accumulated deprcn	Net	CAPITAL		
				Opening balance	60 000	
Equipment and furniture	60 000	30 000	30 000	Add profit	38 000	
Vehicles	50 000	28 000	22 000		98 000	
	110 000	58 000	52 000	Less drawings	(32 000)	
						66 000
CURRENT ASSETS				NON-CURRENT LIABILITY		
Inventory		25 000		Bank loan		15 000
Trade receivables	17 000					
Less provision for doubtful debts	(500)			CURRENT LIABILITIES		
		16 500		Trade payables	14 000	
Other receivables		1 500		Other payables	2 000	
Cash at bank		2 000				16 000
			45 000			
			97 000			97 000

Redraft this balance sheet using a vertical presentation. Identify the figure for working capital (net current assets) and capital employed.

2 Preparing a balance sheet using a vertical format

The following balance sheet was prepared on 31 March 2012.

Balance sheet at 31 March 2012

	$	$	$		$	$
NON-CURRENT ASSETS	Cost	Accumulated deprcn	Net	CAPITAL		
				Opening balance	321 200	
Premises	290 000	58 000	232 000	Less loss	(14 700)	
Vehicles	80 000	30 000	50 000		306 500	
	370 000	88 000	282 000	Less drawings	(34 900)	
						271 600
CURRENT ASSETS				NON-CURRENT LIABILITY		
Inventory		21 800		Bank loan		32 000
Trade receivables	22 000					
Less provision for doubtful debts	(1 100)			CURRENT LIABILITIES		
		20 900		Trade payables	17 200	
Other receivables		600		Other payables	900	
			43 300	Bank overdraft	3 600	
						21 700
			325 300			325 300

Redraft this balance sheet using a vertical presentation. Identify the figure for working capital (net current assets) and capital employed.

3 Preparing end-of-year financial statements using a vertical format

The following trial balance was extracted from the books of Aquasupreme Ltd.

Trial balance at 31 December 2012

	$	$
Administration expenses	11 470	
Capital		115 380
Cash at bank	3 720	
Discounts	280	310
Drawings	31 500	
Goodwill	40 000	
Insurance	2 740	
Inventory 1 January 2012	33 000	
Non-current assets		
Cost	84 600	
Provision for depreciation 1 January 2012		42 300
Provision for doubtful debts 1 January 2012		790
Purchases	184 400	
Rent	13 100	
Revenue		309 340
Trade payables		23 290
Trade receivables	18 800	
Wages and salaries	67 800	
	491 410	491 410

Additional information at 31 December 2012:

- Inventory was valued at $36 400
- Insurance, $170, was prepaid
- Rent, $390, was due but unpaid
- The provision for doubtful debts should be adjusted to $940
- Depreciation should be provided at the rate of 25 per cent per annum using the straight-line method

Prepare suitable end-of-year financial statements using a vertical format.

4 Preparing end-of-year financial statements using a vertical format

The following trial balance was extracted from the books of Hosein & Co.

Trial balance at 31 May 2012

	$	$
Bank loan (repayable 2017)		14 000
Bank loan interest	1 310	
Bank overdraft		320
Capital		65 220
Drawings	28 860	
Electricity	2 080	
General expenses	3 160	
Goodwill	15 000	
Inventory 1 June 2011	14 330	
Non-current assets		
Cost	75 000	
Provision for depreciation 1 June 2011		15 000
Provision for doubtful debts 1 June 2011		270
Purchases	224 360	
Returns	1 640	2 220
Revenue		341 000
Salaries	83 450	
Trade payables		18 300
Trade receivables	4 890	
Water charges	2 250	
	456 330	456 330

Additional information at 31 May 2012:

- Inventory was valued at $11 840.
- Salaries, $780, were due but unpaid; general expenses, $440, were prepaid.
- Depreciation on non-current assets for the year is $15 000.
- The provision for doubtful debts should be reduced by $50.

Prepare suitable end-of-year financial statements using a vertical format.

5 Preparing the income statement of a service business

Chen is the owner of a business called Sorted, which provides bookkeeping services for local businesses. On 30 September 2012 he was able to provide the following information for the financial year which ended on that date.

	$
Electricity charges	3 680
Equipment at net book value	21 300
Furniture and fittings at net book value	14 800
Insurance	1 880
Manager's salary	38 800
Office expenses	4 190
Rent	14 370
Revenue	249 500
Staff wages	69 840

Additional information:

- Electricity, $330, and staff wages, $720, were due but unpaid at 30 September 2012.
- Insurance, $150, and rent, $630, were prepaid at 30 September 2012.
- Chen's policy is to depreciate all non-current assets by 20 per cent per annum using the reducing balance method.

Prepare an income statement for the year ended 30 September 2012.

6 Preparing the income statement of a service business

Fay owns an interior design business. On 30 June 2012 the following information was available about her business's financial year, which ended on that date.

	$
Advertising charges	810
Bad debts	380
Insurance	1 470
Non-current assets	
Cost	36 500
Provision for depreciation at 1 July 2011	18 250
Provision for doubtful debts at 1 July 2011	680
Revenue	173 200
Travelling expenses	790
Wages	48 320

Additional information:

- Advertising charges, $80, were prepaid at 30 June 2012.
- Wages, $550, were due but unpaid at 30 June 2012.
- The provision for doubtful debts should be decreased to $450.
- Depreciation is provided at 25 per cent per annum using the straight-line method.

Prepare an income statement for the year ended 30 June 2012.

7 Preparing end-of-year financial statements for a service business

Kisha owns Venus Beauty Studios. Her business's financial year ended on 31 May 2012 when the following trial balance was extracted from her business's books of account.

Trial balance at 31 May 2012

	$	$
Capital		45 580
Cash at bank	8 580	
Drawings	31 850	
Electricity	8 810	
Equipment		
Cost	56 000	
Provision for depreciation at 1 June 2011		14 000
Furniture and fittings		
Cost	28 000	
Provision for depreciation at 1 June 2011		5 600
General expenses	9 440	
Materials (cosmetics, etc.) (expense)	25 320	
Profit from sale of old equipment		270
Rent	18 150	
Revenue (receipts from customers)		192 990
Trade payables		1 820
Wages of assistants	66 370	
Water charges	7 740	
	260 260	260 260

Additional information at 31 May 2012:

- Rent, $630, was due but unpaid; general expenses, $490, were prepaid.

- Depreciation should be provided as follows: equipment 25 per cent per annum using the straight-line method; furniture and fittings 20 per cent per annum using the reducing balance method.

Prepare an income statement for the year ended 31 May 2012 and a balance sheet at that date.

8 Preparing end-of-year financial statements for a service business

Zamran owns Zamran's Taxis. His business's financial year ended on 31 July 2012 when the following trial balance was extracted from his business's books of account.

Trial balance at 31 July 2012

	$	$
Bank loan (repayable 2015)		50 000
Bank overdraft		4 510
Capital		167 120
Cash in hand	460	
Drawings	41 580	
Drivers' wages	95 420	
Furniture and equipment		
Cost	18 500	
Provision for depreciation 1 August 2011		3 700
Goodwill	25 000	
Insurance	14 340	
Loan interest	3 320	
Loss on sale of vehicle	760	
Office expenses	5 570	
Rent	22 240	
Revenue (receipts from customers)		174 330
Trade payables		640
Trade receivables	770	
Vehicle fuel charges	22 730	
Vehicle repairs	5 610	
Vehicles		
Cost	180 000	
Provision for depreciation 1 August 2011		36 000
	411 300	411 300

Additional information at 31 July 2012:

- Drivers' wages, $1450, were due but unpaid; insurance, $860, was prepaid.
- Depreciation should be provided as follows: furniture and equipment 20 per cent per annum using the straight-line method; vehicles 20 per cent per annum using the reducing balance method.

Prepare an income statement for the year ended 31 July 2012 and a balance sheet at that date.

19 Accounting principles and policies

Introduction

Now is a good opportunity to review the **accounting principles** that have been mentioned throughout the preceding units and to introduce some additional principles. The benefits of international accounting standards will also be covered. These principles and standards have to be considered by business owners and managers when deciding the **accounting policies** that will be followed by the business (i.e. what rules and procedures will be used when producing financial statements).

Why have accounting principles?

Accounting techniques and procedures can often seem very clear cut, leaving no room for disagreement or uncertainty. However, businesses can be very complex organisations, and keeping the accounting records for even a small business can involve recording countless transactions and making many important decisions. As a result, there can be occasions when an accountant or bookkeeper is faced with making the right decision about the correct treatment of a financial matter and what procedures should be put in place when producing financial statements.

Illustration 1 Making the right decision

A business owns a delivery vehicle which cost $30 000 when it was purchased two years ago. It is expected to have a useful life of four years, so the owner of the business has provided for depreciation of $7500 at the end of year 1. At the end of year 2 it appears that the business has not performed well, so the owner has suggested to the accountant that no charge should be made for depreciation in order that the business can avoid reporting a small profit figure.

Accounting principles help in situations like these because they provide those responsible for producing financial statements with clear rules to be followed. In this case the accountant will be able to give a very definite 'No!' to the owner's suggestion. The accountant will no doubt explain that accounting is designed to give a *true and fair view* of a business's affairs, and this applies whether a business is doing well or badly. It is not the job of an accountant to manipulate information to provide a desirable outcome. In this particular case, the specific rule is that profit must be based on matching the business's income for the year with the costs for the year which were necessary to achieve that income. Depreciation of the vehicle is one of the business's costs for the year and has to be shown in the income statement and balance sheet.

LEARNING OUTCOMES

When you have reached the end of this unit you will be able to:

- identify the most important accounting principles
- explain the benefits that accounting principles and policies provide
- explain the rule covered by each principle
- apply accounting principles to a variety of situations

KEY TERM

Accounting principles: the basic rules that are to be applied by all those who prepare accounting records; these are also called accounting concepts.

Accounting policies: the rules and procedures that are adopted by a business when producing its financial statements.

19.1 The main accounting principles (part 1)

Accruals (matching) principle

This is the idea that profits or losses should be based on an accounting year and be based on taking the income for the year, whether actually received or not, and matching this with all of the costs that were necessary to achieve that income, whether paid for or not. For that reason this rule, which is usually called the **accruals principle**, is also called the 'matching principle'.

This rule means that when an annual income statement is put together, great care has to be taken to ensure that every entry relates to the year in question, not to some other accounting period, and every entry presents a full picture for that year.

KEY TERM

Accruals principle: in order to calculate a true and fair profit, income for a financial year is matched exactly with expenses that relate to that accounting year whether paid or not. This principle is also called the matching principle.

Prudence principle: where there is uncertainty, profits should be under- rather than overstated; losses and liabilities should be over- rather than understated.

Lower of cost or net realisable value: the rule that must be applied to the valuation of inventories.

Illustration 2 Applying the accruals principle

Here are two examples of the accruals principle in practice.

- *Expenses and accruals and prepayments*: each expense is reviewed to ensure that the amount recorded in the income statement is the correct amount for the current year under review, adjusting for any amount due but unpaid (accruals) or amounts paid that relate to the next accounting period (prepayments).
- *Depreciation*: non-current assets are purchased so that they can help a business to make a profit. Each non-current asset will have a number of years over which it can benefit the business by earning income. So, when calculating profit an estimate is made of the contribution made towards earning income for that particular year. In this way the cost of the asset is matched with the income it generates.

Prudence principle

Accountants have to ensure that financial statements do not mislead users into thinking that a business is doing better than is really the case. The **prudence principle** is used in situations where there is some doubt about the value of an asset or the amount of profit being made, by ensuring that in those cases the lower value for an asset or profit is reported. The principle also ensures that where there is some doubt, losses and liabilities are never understated; losses have to be written off immediately once they are recognised.

Creating a provision for doubtful debt and writing off bad debts promptly are good examples of the application of this principle.

The prudence principle and the valuation of inventories

The rule for valuing inventories is that they should be valued at the **lower of cost or net realisable value**. The following illustration demonstrates what these terms mean and how this rule is applied.

Illustration 3 | Applying the prudence principle to the valuation of inventories

Part 1

Esther is a retailer. On 30 September 2011 she was preparing her business's end-of-year financial statements. As part of this process she valued her unsold goods. She found that five items that cost \$10 each were slightly damaged. Esther estimated that she could sell each damaged item for just \$8.

She was not sure how to value these damaged items. She could value them at cost (i.e. 5 × \$10 = \$50) or she could value them the special selling price (i.e. 5 × \$8 = \$40). Normally, of course, she would use cost to value this asset. However, since their likely value to the business is actually less than cost, this *lower value* should be used. In other words, there is doubt about how to value this part of the closing inventory, and so she should be prudent and under- rather than overvalue the damaged items.

Part 2

A year later, on 30 September 2012, Esther was faced with a similar problem. This time there were six items that had cost \$15 each and had been damaged. Esther estimated that the items could be sold for \$16 each but that she would need to spend \$3 per item on repackaging before a sale could take place.

The possible valuations of these damaged items are as follows.

Cost:	6 × \$15 = \$90
Realisable value:	6 × \$16 = \$96
Net realisable value:	6 × \$13 (i.e. \$16 realisable value less repackaging \$3) = \$78

Esther should select the *lowest value* in accordance with the prudence principle (i.e. the net realisable value of \$78).

Notes:

1 The term used to describe an item's estimated selling price is **realisable value**.

2 The term used to describe an item's estimated selling price less any costs that have to be incurred before the sale can take place is **net realisable value**, which is sometimes abbreviated as 'nrv'.

3 The following rule should be used for valuing inventories: 'inventories should be valued at the lower of cost or net realisable value'. This is an excellent example of the prudence principle.

KEY TERM

Realisable value: sale value.

Net realisable value: sale value less any costs to be incurred before a sale can take place.

19.2 The main accounting principles (part 2)

KEY TERM

Consistency principle: accounting policies should be carried out in the same way year on year.

DID YOU KNOW?

If the owner of a business could make a strong case for changing a business policy, it is possible to do so. For example, perhaps the percentage used to calculate the provision for doubtful debts needs to be increased because the business experiences much higher levels of bad debts during a difficult time for the national economy. However, financial statements must indicate that there has been a change of policy, and alternative figures using the former policy should also be provided.

KEY TERM

Business entity principle: a business's transactions and the owner's private transactions are recorded separately in a business's accounting system.

You can now answer questions 1–6 on pages 184–185.

Consistency principle

The owners of businesses have choices to make when preparing financial statements. Having made a decision, the **consistency principle** requires that the business keeps to that decision from one year to another. This ensures that financial statements are prepared on the same basis each year. As a result, those comparing results can be sure that their comparisons will not be distorted in any way, and so the decisions based on these comparisons are more likely to be valid.

Illustration 4 Example of where the consistency principle should be applied

Depreciation method: Having chosen a depreciation method (e.g. straight line), the business should continue to use that method from one year to the next, otherwise depreciation charges and profits will not be comparable.

Business entity principle

The **business entity principle** ensures that transactions recorded in an organisation's accounting system clearly distinguish between those relating to the business's affairs and the owner's private affairs. The most important application of this principle is that a sole trader's accounting records focus on how that business is performing, and the owner's private affairs are not part of that story.

Illustration 5 Applying the entity principle

Farad is the owner of a retail business. Recently Farad paid for his family to fly to a nearby island to stay with some relatives. The payment came from Farad's private bank account, so this transaction was not recorded in the business's accounts because it does not affect the business.

If Farad had paid for the trip from the business's bank account, it would have been necessary to debit the drawings account and credit the business bank account – it would have been wrong to have debited the business's travel expenses account. These correct entries ensure that the business's profit was not affected in any way by the non-business cost.

Duality principle

When preparing accounting records there are always two ways of looking at a transaction. This basic rule means that for any transaction it is necessary to consider the following aspects:

1 How does the transaction affect the business's resources (i.e. its assets)?

2 How does the transaction affect the way in which those resources have been financed (i.e. the business's capital and liabilities)?

The **duality principle** leads to the idea of double-entry bookkeeping and making a debit and credit entry for each transaction in a business's accounting system (the processes you have been putting into practice since Unit 2).

KEY TERM

Duality principle: every transaction has two aspects leading to the making of two entries for each transaction in the accounting system.

Money measurement principle: in accounting, only transactions that have a definite monetary value are recorded.

Illustration 6 Applying the duality principle

Here are some transactions in which the two aspects above have been considered:

Transaction	Aspect 1	Aspect 2
Sold goods on credit	Business has an extra asset (trade receivable)	Business has gained value (increase in capital)
Paid an expense in cash	Business has a decrease in assets (cash)	Business has lost value (decrease in capital)
Business borrows money from bank	Business has an increase in assets (additional money)	Business gains an additional source of finance (non-current liability, bank loan)
Owner withdraws a cheque for private use	Business has a decrease in assets (bank)	Business has lost value (decrease in capital)

Money measurement principle

Financial statements can only record information that has a monetary value. This is known as the **money measurement principle** and means that some aspects of business activity cannot be recorded because they are too difficult to value. For example, it would not be possible to value whether or not a business:

- has a dedicated and highly skilled workforce
- has good customer relationships
- has high-quality management
- is well located.

Illustration 7 Applying the money measurement principle

Amhari owns a very successful hotel in a local resort. Her business has an exceptional reputation which is illustrated by the fact that several of the hotel's guests have been coming for many years. The hotel guests are enthusiastic about Amhari's hard work and management skills and the outstanding service provided by her skilful staff. Although important to the success of the business, management skills, effective staff and a good reputation with customers cannot be directly recorded in the accounting records because their value is only a matter of a opinion.

19.3 The main accounting principles (part 3)

Going concern principle

When preparing accounting records it is assumed that the business will continue to trade or provide a service for many years to come (i.e. that the business is a going concern). As a result of applying the **going concern principle**, the potential resale value of any of the business's assets is not considered to be relevant, and so is not recorded in the accounts. When a business is no longer a going concern – perhaps it is being shut down – assets should be recorded as their realisable values. You have probably noticed how goods and other assets are often sold off very cheaply when a business has a closing down sale.

KEY TERM

Going concern principle: while a business continues to trade, assets are valued at cost less depreciation. When a business ceases to trade, assets are valued at their realisable value.

Illustration 8 Applying the going concern principle

Robbie's business owns some furniture and fittings which were purchased some years ago for $10 000. As Robbie's business has been a going concern these assets have been shown in the financial statements at cost less a provision for depreciation. In the balance sheet at 31 March 2012, these assets were shown at cost less a provision for depreciation of $4000.

However, falling profits led Robbie to decide to close down his business on 1 July 2012 when the assets were sold off. The value of the furniture and fittings was reduced considerably in the financial statements at the time of closing the business to just $1 500 because this was considered a realistic resale value.

Notes:

1. While the business is a going concern Robbie's assets have been valued at cost less depreciation in accordance with the going concern principle.
2. When the business is closing down, the going concern principle no longer applies, and assets are shown at their estimated realisable value.

Realisation principle

When does a sale of goods or services actually take place? Is it when the customer makes an order, receives the goods, is sent an invoice, pays the supplier? This question is important because it also raises the issue of exactly when a business makes a profit from trading or providing services. The **realisation principle** gives a clear ruling on this question: a sale takes place when the customer either pays the supplier (i.e. cash sales) or when the customer agrees to pay the supplier (credit sales), which in effect means when the invoice is issued. Invoices will be issued when the goods have been delivered and accepted or when the service has actually been provided. This principle prevents a business from claiming to have made profits that are not yet definite.

KEY TERM

Realisation principle: a sale occurs when the customer pays or when an invoice is issued for the goods or services.

Illustration 9 | Applying the realisation principle

Yasmin prepares her business's end-of-year financial statements on 31 December. On 31 December 2012 Yasmin received an order from a regular customer for goods with a resale value of $2300. Yasmin thought it would be sensible to include this amount in the total sales for 2012 on the grounds that this particular customer was very reliable. However, Yasmin's accountant disagreed and said that the order could not be included, arguing that the customer could cancel the order, or Yasmin might find that she was unable to provide the goods needed in time. The accountant pointed out that only when the customer paid for the goods or when Yasmin had sent out an invoice could the sale (and therefore the profit) be said to be definite and recordable.

You can now answer questions 7–12 on pages 185–186.

International accounting standards

In recent years progress has been made to ensure that financial statements are prepared using the same rules and guidelines internationally. A team of leading accountants drawn from many countries has the task of preparing these **international accounting standards**.

The standards are designed to protect those who use accounting statements and stop them being misled. They ensure:

- comparability
- relevance
- reliability
- understandability.

Comparability means that users of financial statements can use them to make valid comparisons of the results and financial activities of businesses from a wide range of countries.

Standards ensure that financial information is of *relevance* to those making business decisions.

The international standards have done much to increase the *reliability* of accounting statements. Users will know that information provided in statements would have been much the same whoever had prepared them, so the information will be objective (factual and free from bias) rather than subjective (a matter of opinion). The basis for every standard is that accounting statements must present a true and fair view of the financial position.

Those who produce the standards are also required to ensure that accounting statements are *understandable*. In other words, the needs of users are given a high priority when standards are designed, so that decisions made on the basis of financial statements will be reliable and valid.

KEY TERM

International accounting standards: a set of rules and guidelines that businesses in many countries must follow in producing financial statements.

DID YOU KNOW?

At the time of writing there are about 40 standards and well over 100 countries have adopted them with many more countries moving to adopt them in the near future.

You can now answer questions 13–27 on pages 186–188.

Unit 19 Practice questions

DEVELOPING YOUR SKILLS

1 Identifying accounting principles

Here are some recent transactions that affected a retail business. Complete the table, identifying the name of the principle that has been applied in each case.

Transaction	Relevant principle
When preparing the income statement an adjustment was made to an expense account to record a prepayment	
Occasionally items are damaged in a business's stockroom. These items are often valued at net realisable value because it is less than cost	
A business always a makes a provision for doubtful debts based on 5% of trade receivables at the year end	
The owner purchased a birthday gift for a member of the family using the business's money. The amount spent was debited to the drawings account	

2 Identifying accounting principles

Here are some recent transactions that affected a retail business. Complete the table, identifying the name of the principle that has been applied in each case.

Transaction	Relevant principle
The business has always used the straight-line method of depreciation at 20% per annum every year	
A customer's account which has been unpaid for 12 weeks has now been written off as a bad debt	
The owner paid the business's rent from his private funds. In the business's accounts a debit entry was made in the rent account and a credit entry in the drawings account	
The business receives rent from a tenant. The amount transferred to the income statement took account of the fact that the tenant owed an amount for rent at the year end	

3 Summarising accounting principles

Complete the following table about two of the accounting principles.

Principle	One key point about this principle	Example of the principle being used
Accruals		
Prudence		

4 Summarising accounting principles

Complete the following table about two of the accounting principles.

Principle	One key point about this principle	Example of the principle being used
Consistency		
Business entity		

5 Applying the prudence principle to inventory valuation

Jason, a retailer, recently found that some items in the stockroom had been damaged. The following facts are available:

- There are eight damaged items.
- The cost of each damaged item was $20.
- The items would normally be sold for $30 each.
- Jason thinks the damaged items could now be sold for just $22 each.
- It will be necessary to spend $5 per item on minor repairs before the items can be sold at $22 each.

a Calculate the total value of the damaged items

(i) At cost

(ii) At normal selling price

(iii) At current realisable value

(iv) At net realisable value

b State which value should be used for valuing the damaged items.

c Explain why this is the correct method of valuation.

6 Applying the prudence principle to inventory valuation

Miriam is a wholesaler of kitchen appliances. Recently some microwave ovens were slightly damaged in her stockroom. The following facts are available:

- There are four damaged items.
- The cost of each damaged item was $40.
- The items would normally be sold for $60 each.
- Miriam thinks the damaged items could now be sold for just $43 each.
- It will be necessary to spend $8 per item on minor repairs and repackaging before the items can be sold at $43 each.

a Calculate the total value of the damaged items

(i) At cost

(ii) At normal selling price

(iii) At current realisable value

(iv) At net realisable value

b State which value should be used for the valuing the damaged items.

7 Identifying accounting principles

Here are some recent transactions that affected a retail business. Complete the table, identifying the name of the principle that has been applied in each case.

Transaction	Relevant principle
The owner sent some samples to a potential new customer. However, this transaction has not been entered in the sales account	
The fittings could be sold for far less than is shown on the balance sheet. However, no changes have been made to the accounting records	
When a bank loan was repaid two entries were made in the accounting records affecting an asset account and a liability account	
No record has been made in the accounting system of the fact that the workforce had a very high morale	

8 Identifying accounting principles

Here are some recent transactions that affected a retail business. Complete the table, identifying the name of the principle that has been applied in each case.

Transaction	Relevant principle
The payment of interest has resulted in making two entries in the accounting system	
The staff have been praised for their very positive customer relations. No record has been made of this in the accounting system	
The business has been very successful, but no record has been made of the value of goodwill in the accounts	
Goods have just been sent to a customer. No payment has been made by the customer and the invoice for the goods will not be sent until next week. No entries have been made for this sale so far	

9 Matching concepts and their definitions

In the table below there are definitions of some accounting principles. Identify the principle being described in each case by selecting the appropriate item from the right-hand column.

Choose from the following list:

Accruals

Duality

Business entity

Realisation

Definition	Principle
Accounting for a sole trader's business is clearly separated from accounting for the owner's private transactions	
A sale occurs when money or the promise of money is received	
Accounting systems are based on the idea that there is a two-fold aspect to every transaction	
Profits are assessed on the basis of amounts due or receivable for a period of time rather than amounts actually paid or received	

10 Matching principles and their definitions

In the table below there are definitions of some accounting principles. Identify the principle being described in each case by selecting the appropriate item from the right-hand column.

Choose from the following list:
Going concern
Prudence
Consistency
Money measurement

Definition	Principle
The assumption is made that the business will continue to trade indefinitely when valuing assets	
A business should endeavour to maintain the same accounting policies from one year to the next to aid comparability of results	
Some important aspects of a business's performance cannot be quantified in financial terms	
Where there is doubt, the lower value for an asset or profit is preferred	

11 Summarising accounting principles

Complete the following table about two of the accounting principles.

Principle	One key point about this principle	Example of the principle being used
Duality		
Realisation		

12 Summarising accounting principles

Complete the following table about two of the accounting principles.

Principle	One key point about this principle	Example of the principle being used
Money measurement		
Going concern		

13 International accounting standards

Describe two ways in which international accounting standards are likely to help the users of financial statements.

14 International accounting standards

Describe two ways (not mentioned in answer to question 13) in which international accounting standards are likely to help the users of accounting statements.

PREPARING FOR THE EXAMINATION

(The following questions cover Unit 19)

MULTIPLE-CHOICE QUESTIONS

15 The owner of a business recently introduced a policy of providing for doubtful debts.

This is an example of the application of which one of the following principles?

A Accruals
B Business entity
C Consistency
D Prudence

16 A trade receivables account was written off as a bad debt as soon as it became clear that no money would be received.

This is an example of the application of which one of the following principles?

A Business entity
B Consistency
C Money measurement
D Prudence

17 The owner of a business paid for a friend's birthday present from the business's bank account. The accounts clerk correctly recorded the amount in the drawings account in the business's general ledger.

This is an example of the application of which one of the following principles?

A Accruals
B Business entity
C Consistency
D Realisation

18 The owner of a business considered switching from using the reducing balance method of depreciation to the straight-line method. The owner has been advised to continue using the straight-line method so that one year's accounts can be compared with another year's accounts on the same basis.

This is an example of the application of which one of the following principles?

A Business entity

B Consistency

C Duality

D Prudence

19 When preparing financial statements it is important to consider not only what cash has been paid for an expense but also what should have been paid for the expense for that time period.

This is an example of the application of which one of the following principles?

A Accruals

B Business entity

C Consistency

D Realisation

20 Some damaged inventory was valued at the lower of cost and net realisable value. Which accounting principle was applied to the valuation of the damaged inventory?

A Business entity

B Duality

C Going concern

D Prudence

21 The owner of a business paid for some building work at his home from his private bank account. This transaction was recorded in the business's books of account. Which accounting principle was wrongly applied?

A Accruals

B Business entity

C Consistency

D Prudence

22 The owner of a business has decided to create a provision for doubtful debts. This is an example of applying which two accounting principles?

A Accruals and business entity

B Accruals and prudence

C Business entity and consistency

D Consistency and prudence

23 When should sale on credit be recorded in the accounts?

A When the customer pays for the goods

B When the goods are delivered to the customer

C When the invoice is sent to the customer

D When the order is received from the customer

24 A payment of wages in cash has been debited to the wages account and credited to the cash account. This is an example of which principle?

A Accruals principle

B Duality principle

C Money measurement principle

D Realisation principle

25 It is assumed that a business will continue to trade for many years to come. Which accounting principle is based on this assumption?

A Business entity principle

B Going concern principle

C Money measurement principle

D Prudence principle

OTHER QUESTIONS

26 Khalaf sells music technology. At his business's financial year end, he is unsure how to value a loudspeaker system that cost \$160. One of the speakers has been slightly dented and the packaging has been badly torn. However, this item is still in good working order. Khalaf believes he could repackage the loudspeaker system at a cost of \$5 and sell it at a reduced price of \$150. Complete the following sentences.

a Khalaf should value the loudspeaker system at \$ ...

b Khalaf should value the loudspeaker at the lower of ...... or ......

c This is an example of using the ... principle.

27 Beth sells washing machines. At the end of her business's financial year she had 23 unsold washing machines in her stockroom. Each of these machines had cost $320 when purchased. They normally sell at $400 each. Beth has noticed that four machines (machines A, B, C and D) have become damaged in the stockroom.

Machine A can be sold as shop soiled at a reduced price of $330. The other three machines (machines B, C and D) will need some relatively minor repairs, costing $40 per machine. Beth estimates that once they are repaired she can sell each of these machines for $340.

a Calculate the total value of the Beth's undamaged inventory of washing machines.

b State the correct valuation of washing machine A.

c Calculate the correct total valuation of washing machines B, C and D.

20 Accounting ratios

Introduction

You know that a lot of hard work goes into preparing accounting records! However, some of this effort may be wasted if the financial statements are not used by interested parties to discover how well or badly the business is performing. In this unit you are going to learn how to calculate the ratios that are used to analyse a business's accounts. In Unit 21 you will learn about what to look for when you have calculated a set of ratios.

LEARNING OUTCOMES

When you have reached the end of this unit you will be able to:

- identify a range of ratios that can be used to analyse the performance of a sole trader
- state the formula to be used when calculating each accounting ratio
- calculate ratios based on the end-of-year financial statements of a sole trader.

How useful are accounting ratios?

Ratios provide a very valuable means of analysing and comparing the performance of a business:

- from one year to the next
- with other similar businesses.

They enable changes in important aspects of a business's performance to be pinpointed and quantified. When ratios are calculated year after year, it is possible to see where any significant trends are becoming apparent.

However, it is not enough just to calculate ratios. Ratios have to be interpreted and this requires skill and judgement if the owner or manager of a business is to be well informed when making important decisions.

Who are the interested parties?

The following table lists most of the individuals and groups who would take an interest in a business's financial statements. The table also shows some of their key concerns.

Interested party	Main concerns
Owners	How well is the business performing? Is it profitable and can it pay it debts on time?
Managers	Do we have the information needed to make decisions that are in the best interests of the business?
Suppliers	Can the business pay the amounts due on time? Is there a chance of more orders in the future?
Investors (relevant to limited companies, see Unit 26)	How safe is the investment? Can the business afford to pay the expected return on the investment?
Banks	Can the business fulfil the terms of the loan? Will repayments of the loan and interest be made on time?
Club members (relevant to club and societies, see Unit 27)	Has the club/society sufficient funds to maintain or develop the facilities provided by the club?
Government/tax authorities	Is the business liable to pay taxes and can these taxes be paid on time?

20.1 Income statement and balance sheet ratios

KEY TERM

Percentage of gross profit to revenue (gross profit margin): gross profit in relation to revenue (measured as a percentage).

Rate of inventory turnover: cost of sales divided by average inventory (expressed as 'so many times' in a particular financial year, e.g. '12 times').

Percentage of profit to revenue (profit margin): profit in relation to revenue (measured as a percentage).

NUMERACY SKILLS

How to calculate an average inventory

To calculate the rate of inventory turnover ratio you need to work out an average figure for inventory. To do this, take the following steps:

Step 1 add together the figures for the opening inventory ($16 000) and closing inventory ($14 000) which gives $30 000.

Step 2 divide this total by the number of inventory figures you have used in your calculation, i.e. 2.

Step 3 calculate the average:

$$\frac{\$30\,000}{2} = \$15\,000$$

Now you can answer questions 1 and 2 on page 193.

There are three important ratios that can be used to analyse an income statement. They are:

Percentage of gross profit to revenue (gross profit margin) $\frac{\text{Gross profit} \times 100}{\text{Revenue}}$

Rate of inventory turnover $\frac{\text{Cost of sales}}{\text{Average inventory}}$

Percentage of profit to revenue (profit margin) $\frac{\text{Profit} \times 100}{\text{Revenue}}$

Illustration 1 Calculating income statement ratios

Here is an example of how to calculate the three income statement ratios.

Income statement for the year ended 31 December 2011

	$	$
Revenue		240 000
Opening inventory	16 000	
Add purchases	178 000	
	194 000	
Less closing inventory	(14 000)	
Cost of sales		(180 000)
Gross profit		60 000
Less expenses		
General expenses	10 000	
Depreciation	14 000	
		(24 000)
Profit		36 000

Percentage of gross profit to revenue (gross profit margin) $\frac{\text{Gross profit} \times 100}{\text{Revenue}}$ $\frac{\$60\,000 \times 100}{\$240\,000} = 25\%$

Rate of inventory turnover $\frac{\text{Cost of sales}}{\text{Average inventory}}$ $\frac{\$180\,000}{\$15\,000} = 12$ times

Percentage of profit to revenue (profit margin) $\frac{\text{Profit} \times 100}{\text{Revenue}}$ $\frac{\$36\,000}{\$240\,000} = 15\%$

Balance sheet ratios

Five important ratios are used to analyse a balance sheet. They are:

Current ratio	Current assets : current liabilities
Quick ratio (acid test ratio)	Liquid assets (i.e. current assets less inventory) : current liabilities
Return on capital employed (ROCE)	$\frac{\text{Profit} \times 100}{\text{Capital employed}}$
Trade receivables collection period	$\frac{\text{Trade receivables} \times 365}{\text{Credit sales}}$
Trade payables payment period	$\frac{\text{Trade payables} \times 365}{\text{Credit purchases}}$

Note: The trade receivables collection and trade payables payment period is expressed in days. It is usual to give the answer in whole days and to always round upwards, so a ratio of 30.21 days would become 31 days.

Illustration 2 Calculating balance sheet ratios

Balance sheet at 31 December 2012

	$	$	$	$
NON-CURRENT ASSETS		Cost	Accumulated deprcn	Net
		350 000	125 000	225 000
CURRENT ASSETS				
Inventory		15 000		
Trade receivables		30 000		
Other receivables		3 000		
Cash at bank		2 000		
			50 000	
CURRENT LIABILITIES				
Trade payables		26 000		
Other payables		4 000		
			(30 000)	
NET CURRENT ASSETS				20 000
Less Non-current liability				245 000
Bank loan				30 000
				215 000
CAPITAL				
Opening balance			195 000	
Add profit			60 000	
			255 000	
Less drawings			(40 000)	
				215 000

Note: the business had credit sales of $372 000 and credit purchases of $300 000 for the year ended 31 December 2012.

DID YOU KNOW?

It is possible to work out the rate of inventory turnover in terms of days. In the illustration, average inventory was sold 12 times during the year. This would be the equivalent of every *30* days (i.e. 365/12).

KEY TERM

Current ratio: current assets in relation to current liabilities. The ratio is sometimes called the working capital ratio. The ratio is always expressed in the form xx : 1, e.g. 1.8 : 1.

Quick ratio: liquid assets in relation to current liabilities. Liquid assets are all of a business's current assets excluding inventories. This ratio is often referred to as the 'acid test ratio' and is also expressed in the form xx : 1.

Return on capital employed (ROCE): the profit made by the business in relation to the funds invested in the business (i.e. owner's capital and non-current liabilities). The ratio is expressed as a percentage.

Trade receivables collection period: trade receivables in relation to credit sales. The ratio is usually expressed in days.

Trade payables payment period: trade payables in relation to credit purchases. The ratio is usually expressed in days.

Ratio	Formula	Calculation	Answer
Current ratio	Current assets : current liabilities	$50 000 : $30 0000	= 1.67 : 1
Quick ratio (acid test ratio)	Liquid assets (i.e. current assets less inventory) : current liabilities	$35 000 : $30 000	= 1.17 : 1
Return on capital employed (ROCE)	Either: $\frac{\text{Profit} \times 100}{\text{Capital employed (capital + non-current liabilities)}}$ or: $\frac{\text{Profit} \times 100}{\text{Capital employed (non-current + net assets)}}$	$\frac{\$60\,000 \times 100}{\$245\,000}$	= 24.49%
Trade receivables collection period	$\frac{\text{Trade receivables} \times 365}{\text{Credit sales}}$	$\frac{\$30\,000 \times 365}{\$372\,000}$	= 30 days
Trade payables payment period	$\frac{\text{Trade payables} \times 365}{\text{Credit purchases}}$	$\frac{\$26\,000 \times 365}{\$300\,000}$	= 32 days

STUDY TIP

When you are asked to calculate a ratio it is a good idea to:

- state the formula
- select the appropriate figures
- calculate the final answer.

Always check that you have given the answer in the right form (i.e. each answer should have an appropriate descriptor, e.g. xx%, xx times, xx : 1, xx days, etc.).

Unless you are told otherwise, work to two decimal places for most ratios.

You can now answer questions 3 and 4 on pages 193–194.

Unit 20 Practice questions

DEVELOPING YOUR SKILLS

1 Calculating income statement ratios

The following extract from an income statement was prepared for the business owned by David McKoy.

Look at the income statement and calculate the following ratios:

- Percentage of gross profit to revenue (gross profit margin)
- Rate of inventory turnover
- Percentage of profit to revenue (profit margin)

In each case state the formula used and if necessary work to two decimal places.

Income statement for the year ended 31 January 2012

	$	$
Revenue		800 000
Opening inventory	29 000	
Add purchases	646 000	
	675 000	
Less closing inventory	(35 000)	
Cost of sales		(640 000)
Gross profit		160 000
Less expenses		
Office expenses	14 000	
Rent	28 000	
Depreciation	18 000	
		(60 000)
Profit for the year		100 000

2 Calculating income statement ratios

The following extract from an income statement was prepared for the business owned by Deva Wray.

Look at the next income statement and calculate the following ratios:

- Percentage of gross profit to revenue (gross profit margin)
- Rate of inventory turnover
- Percentage of profit to revenue (profit margin).

In each case state the formula used and if necessary work to two decimal places.

Income statement for the year ended 31 October 2012

	$	$
Revenue		720 000
Opening inventory	32 500	
Add purchases	475 000	
	507 500	
Less closing inventory	(27 500)	
Cost of sales		(480 000)
Gross profit		240 000
Less expenses		
Administration expenses	58 900	
Carriage outwards	7 300	
Wages and salaries	71 000	
Depreciation	45 200	
		(182 400)
Profit for the year		57 600

3 Calculating balance sheet ratios

The following balance sheet (see over) was prepared for the business owned by Jackie Davis at the end of its financial year.

The business had credit sales of $224 000 and credit purchases of $154 000 for the year ended 31 December 2012.

Look at the balance sheet and calculate the following ratios:

- Current ratio
- Quick ratio (acid test ratio)
- Return on capital employed (ROCE)
- Trade receivables collection period
- Trade payables collection period

In each case state the formula used and if appropriate work to two decimal places.

Balance sheet at 31 December 2012

	$	$	$
NON-CURRENT ASSETS	Cost	Accumulated deprcn	Net
	490 000	196 000	294 000
CURRENT ASSETS			
Inventory	17 000		
Trade receivables	16 000		
Other receivables	1 000		
Cash at bank	2 000		
		36 000	
CURRENT LIABILITIES			
Bank loan	7 000		
Trade payables	14 000		
Other payables	3 000		
		(24 000)	
NET CURRENT ASSETS			12 000
			306 000
Less Non-current liabilitiy			
Bank loan			(15 000)
			291 000
CAPITAL			
Opening balance		283 000	
Add profit		45 000	
		328 000	
Less drawings		(37 000)	
			291 000

4 Calculating balance sheet ratios

The following balance sheet was prepared for the business owned by Rudy Cousins at the end of its financial year.

The business had credit sales of $72 000 and credit purchases of $429 000 for the year ended 30 June 2012.

Look at the balance sheet below and calculate the following ratios:

- Current ratio
- Quick ratio (acid test ratio)
- Return on capital employed (ROCE)
- Trade receivables collection period
- Trade payables collection period

In each case state the formula used and if appropriate work to two decimal places.

Balance Sheet at 30 June 2012

	$	$	$
NON-CURRENT ASSETS	Cost	Accumulated deprcn	Net
	860 000	215 000	645 000
CURRENT ASSETS			
Inventory	54 000		
Trade receivables	8 000		
Other receivables	2 000		
Cash at bank	8 000		
		72 000	
CURRENT LIABILITIES			
Trade payables	39 000		
Other payables	1 000		
		(40 000)	
NET CURRENT ASSETS			32 000
			677 000
Less NON-CURRENT LIABILITY			
Loan from DDKT Finance			(22 000)
			655 000
CAPITAL			
Opening balance		639 000	
Add profit		75 000	
		714 000	
Less drawings		(59 000)	
			655 000

(The following questions cover Unit 20)

MULTIPLE-CHOICE QUESTIONS

5 A sole trader is able to provide the following information about his business.

	$
Revenue	800 000
Cost of sales	600 000
Expenses	100 000

What is the business's gross profit as a percentage of revenue (gross profit margin)?

A 12.5%

B 25%

C 62.5%

D 75%

6 During a year a business sold goods that had cost $720 000. The inventory at the beginning of the year was $70 000 and at the end $90 000.

What was the annual rate of inventory turnover?

A 4.5 times

B 7.2 times

C 9 times

D 12 times

7 Which of the following is not required when calculating the quick ratio (acid test ratio)?

A Cash at bank

B Cash in hand

C Inventory

D Trade receivables

8 Martin had the following assets and liabilities.

	$
Fixtures and fittings	21 000
Delivery vehicle	16 000
Inventory	8 000
Trade receivables	9 000
Trade payables	7 500
Bank loan (2 years)	30 000
Cash	14 500

What was his quick assets ratio (acid test ratio)?

A 2.27 : 1

B 3 : 1

C 3.13 : 1

D 4.2 : 1

9 Pat had the following assets and liabilities.

	$
Premises	90 000
Equipment	40 000
Inventory	12 000
Trade receivables	8 000
Trade payables	6 000
Bank loan (6 months)	18 000
Cash at bank	4 000

What was her current ratio?

A 1 : 1

B 1 : 2

C 2 : 1

D 4 : 1

10 The following figures were taken from a business's financial statements.

	$
Revenue	700 000
Expenses	110 000
Gross profit	440 000
Capital	1 000,000
Cost of sales	260 000

What was the percentage of profit on capital employed (ROCE)?

A 23%

B 33%

C 44%

D 59%

OTHER QUESTIONS

11 Abdullah has prepared the following income statement at the end of his business's financial year, 31 December 2012. However, there are several blank spaces that need to be completed.

Abdullah

Income statement (extract)

for the year ended 31 December 2012

			$	$
Revenue				320 000
Opening inventory			17 000	
Purchases		253 000		
Add carriage	**(i)**	3 000		
			256 000	
			273 000	
Closing inventory			33 000	
Cost of sales				**(ii)**
Gross profit				80 000
Discounts	**(iii)**		2 000	
General expenses			8 000	
Wages and salaries			**(iv)**	
Depreciation			11 000	
				64 000
(v)				16 000

a Insert the missing word or figures into each of the blank spaces labelled (i)–(v).

b Calculate the following ratios:

- **i** Percentage of gross profit to revenue (gross profit margin)
- **ii** Rate of inventory turnover
- **iii** Percentage of profit to revenue (profit margin)

12 Sherelle produced the following balance sheet for her business at the end of its financial year, 30 September 2012. However, there are several blank spaces that need to be completed.

Balance sheet at 30 June 2012

	$	$	$	$
NON-CURRENT ASSETS		Cost	Accumulated deprcn	Net
		440 000	220 000	**(i)**
CURRENT ASSETS				
Inventory		14 000		
Trade receivables		13 000		
Other receivables		5 000		
Cash at bank		8 000		
			(ii)	
CURRENT LIABILITIES				
Trade payables		**(iii)**		
Other payables		3 000		
			(iv)	
(v)				20 000
				240 000
CAPITAL				
Opening balance			200 000	
Add profit			80 000	
			280 000	
Less drawings			**(vi)**	
				(vii)

Additional information:

- Total credit sales for the year ended 30 September 2012 were $155 000.
- Total credit purchases for the same period were $204 000.

a Insert the missing words or figures in each of the blank spaces (i)–(vii).

b Calculate the following ratios:

- **i** Current ratio
- **ii** Quick ratio (acid test ratio)
- **iii** Return on capital employed (ROCE)
- **iv** Trade receivables collection period
- **v** Trade payables collection period.

21 Interpreting accounting statements

Introduction

You are now able to calculate eight accounting ratios. These ratios can be used to analyse how well or badly a business has been performing and to provide a basis for helping owners, managers and other users to make improvements to their businesses. It is necessary to focus on two matters when interpreting a business's performance:

- **Profitability**: Are the owners and managers of a business successful in increasing the business's value over time through trading or providing services?
- **Liquidity**: Are the business's resources well managed so that the business can pay its short-term debts, including running costs, without difficulty from one week to the next, and also provide the owner with a reasonable income?

Businesses can fail if their owners or managers do not give these issues enough attention. There are many cases of profitable businesses that have not survived, for example, because their working capital has been inadequate.

LEARNING OUTCOMES

When you have reached the end of this unit you will be able to:

- explain what each accounting ratio can tell you about a business
- make judgements about the strengths and weaknesses of a business's performance
- prepare inter-firm comparisons
- make recommendations that will enable the business's performance to improve
- explain the limitations of inter-firm comparisons and ratio analysis.

KEY TERM

Profitability: a measure of performance highlighting profit in relation to the resources used in the business.

Liquidity: a business's ability to have available sufficient cash to pay its short-term debts.

21.1 Interpreting ratios: the income statement

What does the percentage of gross profit to revenue ratio (gross profit margin) tell you about a business's performance?

The percentage of gross profit to revenue ratio tells you:

- how much gross profit is being made in relation to revenue
- how much gross profit (in cents) is being made for every $1 of revenue.

If you have a business's results for several years you can make a comparison of the ratios, and investigate the following.

If the percentage is *increasing* from one year to the next this means one of the following:

- The business has changed its pricing policy and has put selling prices per unit up.
- The business is paying less per unit for the goods it sells.
- Some combination of both of these factors has occurred.

If the percentage is *decreasing* from one year to the next this means one of the following:

- The business has changed its pricing policy and has put prices per unit down.
- The purchase cost per unit has increased.
- Some combination of both of these factors has occurred.

There could be variety of reasons behind any changes in the percentages, for example.

- the need to face up to increasing competition, so selling prices have had to be reduced
- the desire to try to make more gross profit to help cover the business's running costs has led to an increase in selling prices
- suppliers are charging more for the goods they supply.

If you have information about the performance of similar businesses you could comment on whether:

- the selling price is out of step with these similar businesses
- the business is paying too much or too little for the goods it sells.

The idea of comparing one business with another is usually referred to as making an **inter-firm comparison**.

KEY TERM

Inter-firm comparison: analysing the performance of similar businesses and using the results to indicate success or under-achievement.

What does the percentage of profit to revenue (profit margin) tell you about a business's performance?

The profit to revenue percentage (profit margin) tells you:

- how much profit is being made in relation to revenue
- how much profit (in cents) is being made for every $1 of revenue.

Comparing one year with a previous year you may find the following.

The percentage is *increasing*, due to one of the following:

- The business is making more gross profit.
- Costs have been held at previous levels or reduced.
- Other income has increased.
- Some combination of these factors is occurring.

The percentage is *decreasing* due to one of the following:

- The business is making less gross profit.
- Costs have risen above previous levels.
- Other income has decreased.
- Some combination of these factors has occurred.

If you can make an inter-firm comparison, you can comment on whether the control of costs is more or less effective.

What does the rate of inventory turnover tell you about the business's performance?

This ratio:

- compares average inventory to the total cost of inventory sold during a period
- indicates how quickly inventory is sold.

If the rate is *increasing*:

- the business is selling more inventory, or
- the closing inventory is being reduced.

If the rate is *decreasing*:

- the business is selling less inventory, or
- the closing inventory is being increased.

It would normally be a positive sign if a business's rate of inventory turnover increases. However, it is important to find out just why it was selling more goods. If, for example, the selling price per unit has been reduced and the price cuts have been too severe, this might reduce profits.

If inventory levels have changed, it is important to investigate the reasons for the change. If inventory levels were too high, a reduction could be welcome because it would reduce wastage and storage costs. However, if levels were reduced too severely, this could mean that opportunities for a sale were lost and revenue will be less.

Knowing the average for other similar businesses can help users to interpret how well a business is doing.

How can a business improve its profitability as shown in the income statement?

Profitability could be improved by:

- *increasing revenue*: by reviewing pricing policy to make the business more competitive, or by considering the quality or range of the products sold, or by reviewing marketing strategies
- *reducing costs*: by reducing wastage, finding cheaper suppliers of goods and other services
- *improving control of inventories*: by reducing inventory levels so that there is less wastage and reduced storage costs, or by reviewing how inventories are ordered to ensure that every item is always available for sale

You can now answer questions 1 and 2 on page 206.

21.2 Interpreting ratios: the balance sheet (part 1)

What does the return on capital employed (ROCE) ratio tell you about a business's performance?

The return on capital employed ratio measures:

- profit in relation to the capital employed
- how much profit (in cents) is made for every $1 of capital employed.

Comparing one year with a previous year you may find the following.

The percentage is *increasing* because:

- the business is making more profit
- the business has less capital employed
- some combination of the above factors
- the business is using its resources more effectively.

The percentage is *decreasing* because:

- the business is making less profit
- the business has more capital employed
- some combination of the above factors
- the business is using its resources less effectively.

If you can make an inter-firm comparison, you should be able to judge which business is using its resources more effectively.

DID YOU KNOW?

It is also possible to consider how well the owner of the business might do if the capital was invested and earning interest, and if the owner was in employment earning a salary. In making such a comparison it would be important to bear in mind just how risky it is to own a business, and how relatively safe it is to invest in some form of savings account.

What do the current ratio and quick (acid test) ratios tell you about a business's ability to meet its everyday commitments?

The *current ratio* measures:

- current assets in relation to current liabilities
- the funds the business has available to pay the short-term debts of the business.

The *quick (acid test)* ratio is similar because it measures:

- liquid assets (current assets excluding inventories) compared to current liabilities
- the amount of liquid assets available to pay the short-term debts of the business.

Both of these ratios measure what is often called liquidity. The difference between these two ratios is one of timing. The current ratio looks further ahead than the quick assets ratio. The quick assets ratio is a more immediate measure of liquidity, hence the term 'acid test ratio'.

If the two ratios are *increasing*:

- this could mean that the business will find it easier to pay its debts (this is a strength)
- but it could mean that it has too many resources tied up as current or liquid assets (this is a weakness).

If the two ratios are *decreasing*:

- this could imply that the business will find it more difficult to pay its debts (this is a weakness)
- but it could mean that it has reduced the resources tied up as current or liquid assets and so it is making more effective use of these resources.

When commenting on liquidity ratios it is important to know about the typical ratios for the type of business you are looking at. Levels of liquidity vary considerably depending on the goods or services the business provides. For example, think about your local food retailer where most of the goods will be sold within a short space of time and where all sales will be for cash. This situation is very different to, say, a furniture store, where much of the inventory is slow moving and where credit sales are far more likely.

A business could improve liquidity/working capital in a number of ways:

- *Increased profit*: this will benefit liquidity, perhaps by increasing revenue but also keeping control of costs. The business will find that there is increased cash flowing into the business. This may not be immediate because the business will have to wait for trade receivables to pay.
- *Reduced drawings*: if the owner can take less cash from the business, this will have a positive impact on liquidity. However, the owner's personal commitments may not make this possible.
- *Increasing non-current liabilities*: the business may be able to arrange a long-term loan. This would instantly boost liquidity. However, loans will have to be repaid and interest charges could be high and will, of course, reduce profits.
- *Delaying expenditure on non-current assets*: the owner of the business could delay plans to replace or increase non-current assets. This would mean that cash that would otherwise have been spent is retained within the business. However, the delay could have a negative impact on the quality of the business's operations if its non-current assets are deteriorating.

DID YOU KNOW?

Short-term debts of the business include all of the transactions on which the business will need to use cash resources in the near future. In other words, all of the payments to which the business is committed for the next few weeks and months. Here is a list of possible short-term debts:

- trade payables
- most expenses
- loan repayments
- owner's drawings
- payment of taxes
- purchase of new non-current assets.

21.3 Interpreting ratios: the balance sheet (part 2)

What does the trade receivables collection period and trade payables payment period tell you about the business's performance?

Trade receivables collection period

The *trade receivables collection period* measures how many days on average a credit customer takes to pay. The normal credit period is 30 days.

If the collection period is increasing, this tells you that credit customers are taking longer to pay than previously.

An *increase* could be interpreted as being:

- a weakness, because it could imply that credit control is not being as carefully managed as previously and this could lead to an increase in bad debts
- a strength if previously credit control was too tight and that had deterred some potential customers.

A *decrease* could be interpreted as being:

- a strength because it could imply that credit control is being managed more carefully than previously with an improvement in cash flow and a reduction in the incidence of bad debts
- a weakness if previous credit control was about right, and the change has resulted in a decline in credit sales because some customers can get longer credit terms elsewhere.

Trade payables payment period

The *trade payables payment period* measures how many days on average it takes to pay a credit supplier. Again the normal credit period is 30 days.

If the payment period is increasing, this tells you that the business is taking longer to pay its suppliers.

An *increase* could be interpreted as being:

- a weakness, because the business is taking longer to pay its trade payables, and if the credit terms are being exceeded, the suppliers may cease to offer credit facilities
- a strength, because cash is being retained in the business longer.

If the payment period is decreasing, the business will have reduced the time it takes to pay its suppliers.

A *decrease* could be interpreted as being:

- a strength because it could mean that payments to suppliers are being managed more effectively and that problems with suppliers over exceeding their credit terms no longer occur
- a weakness if the business is paying suppliers earlier than necessary, resulting in a negative impact on cash flow as cash is leaving the business sooner than required.

Changes in the ratio may cause cash discounts to be gained or lost, and this, in turn, will have an effect on profits.

Ideally the trade receivable collection period should be shorter than the trade payable payment period, because this will be beneficial for the business's cash flow.

You can now answers questions 3 and 4 on pages 206–207.

Difficulties making inter-firm comparisons

The owner of a business could learn valuable lessons from comparing ratios with those of another similar business. However, it will be important to take account of the following:

- Business A and Business B have broadly similar non-current assets. However, Business A uses the straight-line method of depreciation, but Business B uses the reducing balance method. These differences in accounting policies will affect the results shown the businesses' income statements and balance sheet valuations.
- Business C owns its premises but Business D rents its premises. As a result Business C will have a larger capital employed (it owns more assets), but Business D will have more expenses to charge to its income statement. In all other respects, the businesses could appear identical, but the accounting ratios would be greatly affected by this important difference.
- Business E and Business F report quite different returns on their capital employed. It would be easy to jump to the conclusion that one business is better than the other. However, it could be that each business has used a different definition of capital employed, so that a direct comparison of the ratio cannot be used.
- Business G appears to have performed much better than Business H. However, it has now emerged that Business H was closed for six weeks because of serious flooding, so its results were not really typical.

In addition, it may be difficult to obtain all of the information required about similar businesses, particularly performance trends.

Limitations of accounting ratios

Using ratios to investigate the relative success or otherwise of businesses is a valuable procedure. However, the following should be borne in mind:

- By the time a business has been able to produce its end-of-year financial statements, important events may have occurred that are not shown in the accounts. Perhaps there has been some bad economic news which could have serious consequences for the future performance of the business, for example a recession or an oil crisis.
- Ratio analysis ignores what can be important non-financial aspects of a business. For example, the fact that the management and/or workforce in one business is highly motivated and committed to the success of a business, or the fact that a business is well located.
- The valuation of non-current assets can be quite different depending on when the asset was bought. Two businesses may occupy very similar premises, but one business could have been established many years ago when property prices were low and the other business could have been established quite recently when property prices were much higher. As a result the capital employed by each business could be significantly different.
- Inflation is generally ignored when comparing financial statements, but this can distort the analysis. For example, this year's total revenue may seem much higher than that of three years ago, but if inflation has been high during this period, the real difference in the business's revenue performance may not be that great.

21.4 Interpreting a business's results

How to comment on a business's performance

When you compare a business's results from one year to the next, the following steps are a useful guide:

Step 1: Prepare a table that summarises the ratios you have calculated. Have a column for each year in the review.

Step 2: Look to see if the trend in revenue is upward or downward. Often the trend in revenue figures is the most important key to understanding all of the other aspects of a business's performance.

Step 3: What has happened to each of the ratios? What trend emerges in each case? Is the overall picture one of improving or declining ratios – or is the picture more mixed?

Step 4: Make it clear what the strengths for the business are and what the weaknesses are, and explain why you are making this judgement. Can you suggest reasons for the changes in each ratio?

Step 5: Overall do you feel the business is improving? Make suggestions about how the business could improve its performance, recommend actions that would help to overcome any weaknesses.

Illustration 1 Commenting on performance

Here is an example of how to interpret a business's performance following the approach set out above.

Laura Edwards has calculated the following accounting ratios based on the end-of-year financial statements for each of the years ended 31 December 2011 and 2012.

	2011	**2012**
Gross profit margin	35%	37%
Profit margin	18%	16%
Return on capital employed (ROCE)	12%	15%
Current ratio	1.6 : 1	1.4 : 1
Quick (acid test) ratio	0.7 : 1	0.9 : 1
Rate of inventory turnover	13 times	11 times
Trade receivables collection period	35 days	31 days
Trade payables payment period	27 days	32 days

The following information is also available.

Total revenue in each of the years ended 31 December:

2011	$440 000
2012	$500 000

Some typical ratios for this type of business are:

Current ratio	1.7 : 1
Quick (acid test) ratio	0.9 : 1

Here are the main points to be made in a report based on this information following the step-by-step approach above.

Look at the trend in revenue.

There has been a substantial increase in revenue ($60 000) – around 14% comparing 2012 with 2011.

Look at each ratio and comment on performance.

Strengths:

- The gross profit margin has increased by 2%, meaning that the business is making more gross profit per $1 of revenue. This could be due to an increase in selling prices that has not lead to a fall in demand. This change could account for the increase in revenue.
- The return on capital employed (ROCE) has also increased by 3%, meaning that the business is making more profit per $1 of capital invested by the owner. This could result from a more effective use of the business's resources so that the business is earning more profit than before.
- The quick (acid test) ratio has increased (from 0.7 : 1 to 0.9 : 1) and is now near to the average for this type of business. This means the business will be in a better position to pay its more immediate short-term debts and that the business is managing its liquid resources effectively.
- The trade payables payment period has increased slightly (by five days) and it is now longer than the receivable collection period. This change will improve the business's cash flow, and because it is only a slight change it should not concern suppliers unduly.
- The receivables collection period has decreased slightly (by four days). This means that money is being collected more quickly from customers. This should improve cash flow and reduce the risk of bad debts through poor credit control.

Weaknesses:

- The profit margin percentage has fallen by 2%. This has happened despite an improvement in revenue and in the gross profit margin. The problem appears to be that operating expenses have not been controlled as effectively as in the past and this has had a negative effect on profit.
- The current ratio has decreased (from 1.6 : 1 to 1.4 : 1) and has moved further away from the average for this type of business. This means that the business will have more difficulty paying short-term debts and that the business is not managing its current assets effectively. Since the quick ratio has improved, it is likely that the problem lies with inventories. The business might have too much money tied up in inventory, and that means inventory levels are unnecessarily high.
- The rate of inventory turnover has declined (from 13 to 11 times). Since the figure for revenue has increased, this could be due to the business increasing its average inventory. This appears to have had a negative effect on liquidity and may increase the risk of some inventory deteriorating.

Finally, look at the overall picture.

What could the owner do to improve performance?

Overall the business's performance has improved comparing 2012 with 2011. However, profit as a percentage of revenue has fallen due to a failure to control operating expenses. There is evidence that the money tied up in inventories has not been managed effectively, leading to a decline in the rate of inventory turnover and a decline in the current ratio.

To improve the business's performance the owner should aim to:

- control operating expenses more effectively by reducing waste or finding ways of paying less for some of the costs
- reduce the amount of money tied up inventories, but without reducing choice or quality for customers, which could have a negative effect on revenue.

You can now answer questions 5–15 on pages 207–210.

Unit 21 Practice questions

DEVELOPING YOUR SKILLS

1 Commenting on income statement ratios

The following ratios have been calculated as a result of analysing the end-of-year financial statements of Horizon Stores, a business owned by Robbie Spencer.

	For year ended 31 December		
	2010	**2011**	**2012**
Percentage of gross profit to revenue (gross profit margin)	40%	38%	37%
Percentage of profit to revenue (profit margin)	14%	13%	11%
Rate of inventory turnover	9 times	10 times	12 times

Revenue figures for each of these years are as follows.

2010	$600 000
2011	$580 000
2012	$570 000

Comment on the trend in revenue and on the business's performance during the three-year period. For each ratio:

- describe the trend and state whether this is a strength or a weakness
- explain what may have caused the change.

2 Commenting on income statement ratios

The following ratios have been calculated as a result of analysing the end-of-year financial statements of the retail business owned by Wilma Morris.

	For year ended 31 December		
	2010	**2011**	**2012**
Percentage of gross profit to revenue (gross profit margin)	20%	23%	26%
Percentage of profit to revenue (profit margin)	9%	10%	12%
Rate of inventory turnover	18 times	15 times	14 times

Revenue figures for each of these years are as follows.

2010	$700 000
2011	$730 000
2012	$780 000

Comment on the trend in revenue and the business's performance during the three-year period. For each ratio:

- describe the trend and state whether this is a strength or a weakness
- explain what may have caused the change.

3 Commenting on balance sheet ratios

The following ratios have been calculated as a result of analysing the end-of-year financial statements of Horizon Stores, a business owned by Robbie Spencer (see also question 1).

	For year ended 31 December		
	2010	**2011**	**2012**
Return on capital employed (ROCE)	12%	11%	10%
Current ratio	1.7 : 1	1.6 : 1	1.5 : 1
Quick (acid test) ratio	0.9 : 1	0.8 : 1	0.7 : 1
Trade receivables collection period	26 days	30 days	35 days
Trade payables payment period	32 days	31 days	27 days

The typical ratios for this type of business are:

Current ratio	1.8 : 1
Quick (acid test) ratio	0.8 : 1
Trade receivables collection period	30 days
Trade payables payment period	30 days

Comment on the business's performance as shown by these balance sheet ratios during the three-year period. For each ratio:

- describe the trend and state whether this is a strength or a weakness
- explain what the trend means for the business.

4 Commenting on balance sheet ratios

The following ratios have been calculated as a result of analysing the end-of-year financial statements of the retail business owned by Wilma Morris (*see also question 2*).

	For year ended 31 December		
	2010	**2011**	**2012**
Return on capital employed (ROCE)	13%	15%	16%
Current ratio	1.1 : 1	1.2 : 1	1.4 : 1
Quick (acid test) ratio	0.4 : 1	0.5 : 1	0.6 : 1
Trade receivables collection period	37 days	36 days	35 days
Trade payables payment period	27 days	28 days	30 days

The typical ratios for this type of business are:

Current ratio	1.2 : 1
Quick (acid test) ratio	0.9 : 1
Trade receivables collection period	30 days
Trade payables payment period	30 days

Comment on the business's performance as shown by these balance sheet ratios during the three-year period. For each ratio:

- describe the trend and state whether this is a strength or a weakness
- explain what the trend means for the business.

5 Commenting on performance

Omar has been looking at his business's end-of-year financial statements for each of the years ended 31 December 2011 and 2012. He has worked out the following accounting ratios based on these statements.

	2011	**2012**
Percentage of gross profit to revenue (gross profit margin)	40%	43%
Percentage of profit to revenue (profit margin)	8%	7%
Rate of inventory turnover	9 times	10 times
Return on capital employed	11%	7%
Current ratio	1.2 : 1	1.3 : 1
Quick (acid test) ratio	0.8 : 1	0.6 : 1
Trade receivables collection period	29 days	35 days
Trade payables payment period	36 days	30 days

The following information is available about revenue in each of the years ended 31 December.

2011	$200 000
2012	$180 000

Typical liquidity ratios for this type of business are:

Current ratio	1:3 : 1
Quick (acid test) ratio	0.8 : 1

Comment on this business's performance.

6 Commenting on performance

Samah has been looking at her business's end-of-year financial statements for each of the years ended 31 December 2011 and 2012. She has worked out the following accounting ratios based on these statements.

	2011	**2012**
Percentage of gross profit to revenue (gross profit margin)	27%	26%
Percentage of profit to revenue (profit margin)	10%	9%
Rate of inventory turnover	11 times	10 times
Return on capital employed	11%	12%
Current ratio	1.1 : 1	1.4 : 1
Quick (acid test) ratio	0.9 : 1	0.8 : 1
Trade receivables collection period	38 days	31 days
Trade payables payment period	37days	30 days

The following information is available about revenue in each of the years ended 31 December.

2011	$320 000
2012	$360 000

Typical liquidity ratios for this type of business are:

Current ratio	1:2 : 1
Quick (acid test) ratio	0.8 : 1

Comment on this business's performance.

7 Making an inter-firm comparison

The following table has been prepared to show comparative ratios for two similar retail businesses for the year ending 30 September 2012: Garford Stores and Hobson Stores.

	Garford Stores	Hobson Stores
Percentage of gross profit to revenue (gross profit margin)	33%	31%
Rate of inventory turnover	14 days	16 days
Percentage of profit to revenue (profit margin)	9%	11%
Return on capital employed (ROCE)	14%	12%
Current ratio	1.4 : 1	1.1 : 1

Additional information: the usual current ratio for this type of retail business is 1.2 : 1.

Compare the performance of these two businesses.

a For each ratio identify which business you think is stronger and give reasons for your choice.

b In each case where a business is performing less well than the other business, make *one* suggestion that could improve that business's performance.

c State *one* reason why these ratios may not be strictly comparable.

8 Making an inter-firm comparison

The following table has been prepared to show comparative ratios for two similar wholesale businesses for the year ending 30 June 2012: Anwar & Sons and Mopsa Wholesale.

	Anwar & Sons	Mopsa Wholesale
Percentage of gross profit to revenue (gross profit margin)	38%	43%
Rate of inventory turnover	8 days	5 days
Percentage of profit to revenue (profit margin)	10%	13%
Return on capital employed (ROCE)	16%	11%
Quick (acid test) ratio	1.1 : 1	0.9 : 1
Trade receivables collection period	34 days	31 days
Trade payables payment period	38 days	36 days

Additional information for this type of wholesale business:

- The usual quick ratio (acid test ratio) is 0.9 : 1.
- The usual receivables collection period is 34 days.
- The usual payable payment period is 36 days.

Compare the performance of these two businesses.

a For each ratio identify which business you think is stronger and give reasons for your choice.

b In each case where a business is performing less well than the other business, make one suggestion that could improve that business's performance.

c State one reason why it may be difficult to make a fair comparison of these two businesses.

PREPARING FOR THE EXAMINATION

(The following questions cover Unit 21)

MULTIPLE-CHOICE QUESTIONS

9 A business's quick (acid test) ratio changed from 0.9 : 1 to 1.2 : 1 during the course of one financial period. Which one of the following statements is a correct explanation of the effect of this change?

A The business increased the value of inventories

B The business improved its gross profit

C The business improved its liquidity position

D The business reduced its profit

10 A business increased its rate of inventory turnover during a financial period. Which of the following is a correct explanation of the reason for this increase?

A The business improved its profitability

B The business improved its quick assets ratio

C The business purchased more goods for resale

D The business reduced its average inventory

11 A business wishes to improve its percentage of profit to revenue. The business could achieve this by which one of the following?

A Increasing the value of average inventories

B Offering cash discounts

C Reducing drawings

D Reducing running costs

12 The table shows a comparison of the performance of business P and business Q for the same financial period.

Business	Gross profit as a % of revenue	Profit as a % of revenue
P	28%	8%
Q	24%	11%

Which one of the following statements is a correct explanation of this information:

A Business P has a higher cost of sales than Business Q

B Business P is more effective at controlling expenses than Business Q

C Business Q has a higher cost of sales than Business P

D Business Q is more effective at controlling expenses than Business P

13 Alison's business has a larger return on capital employed (ROCE) than Beth's business. Which one of the following statements is a correct explanation of this information:

A Alison's business has more liquidity than Beth's business

B Alison's business is more effective at using its resources than Beth's business

C Beth's business achieves a lower profit than Alison's business

D Beth's business is less effective at controlling its costs than Alison's business

OTHER QUESTIONS

14 Sally is a trader. She wanted to compare her business's results for the year ended 31 December 2012 with the results for the year ended 31 December 2011.

She is able to provide the following information about the year ended 31 December 2011.

Gross profit as a percentage of revenue (gross profit margin)	35%
Profit as a percentage of revenue (profit margin)	11%
Return on capital employed (ROCE)	13%
Current ratio	1.4 : 1

She can also provide the following information about the year ended 31 December 2012.

	$
Revenue	480 000
Cost of sales	288 000
Total running costs	153 600
Current assets	66 000
Current liabilities	60 000
Capital employed	256 000

a Prepare a table to show the following ratios for the year ended 31 December 2012:

i Gross profit as a percentage of revenue (gross profit margin)

ii Profit as a percentage of revenue (profit margin)

iii Return on capital employed (ROCE)

iv Current ratio

Set out the table to show the ratios for both of the years for which there is information.

b Give **one** reason that would explain the change in the gross profit as a percentage of revenue ratio from 2011 to 2012.

c Do you think Sally will be pleased with the profit to revenue percentage for the year ended 31 December 2012? Give a reason for your answer.

d Sally is concerned about the change in the current ratio from 2011 to 2012. Describe **two** ways in which she could improve this ratio in future.

e Give **one** reason for the change in the return in capital employed ratio from 2011 to 2012.

f Sally is aware that financial statements are of limited value when looking at how well her business has performed. For example, Sally realises that the effects of price inflation have been ignored in her financial records. Explain one other way that financial statements may be of limited value when looking at how well her business has performed.

15 Samir wants to compare his business's performance with that of a similar business owned by Kim. The most recent financial year for both businesses ended on 30 September 2012.

Kim is able to provide the following information about her business.

Rate of inventory turnover	17 times
Quick ratio (acid test ratio)	0.8 : 1
Trade receivables collection period	29 days
Trade payables payment period	32 days

Samir has extracted the following information from his business's financial statements.

	$
Credit sales	384 000
Credit purchases	264 900
Inventory 1 October 2011	16 300
Inventory 30 September 2012	18 700
Trade receivables	34 718
Cash at bank	1 482
Trade payables	21 773

Samir confirms that there were no other current assets or current liabilities at 30 September 2012. Samir's accountant has said that the usual quick ratio for this type of business is 1.5 : 1.

a Prepare a table to show the following ratios for the year ended 30 September 2012:
   i Rate of inventory turnover
   ii Quick assets (acid test) ratio
   iii Trade receivables collection period
   iv Trade payables payment period

Set out the table to show the ratios for both businesses.

b Which of the business has the better rate of inventory turnover? Give **one** reason why this business may have a better ratio than the other business.

c Which business has the better quick assets (acid test) ratio? Give **one** benefit that could arise because this business has a better ratio.

d Samir feels that Kim's business has a better position in regard to its trade receivables collection period and trade payables payment period. Explain why Samir's view is correct. Describe **one** way in which Samir could improve the trade receivables collection period.

e Samir is aware that there are limitations to making inter-firm comparisons. Describe **two** of these limitations.

22 The trial balance and the correction of errors

Introduction

The purpose of the trial balance

By now you will have prepared many trial balances. You will know how useful the trial balance can be as a guide as to whether your double-entry records are correct or not. The trial balance's main function is to check the arithmetical accuracy of the double-entry records. In effect it checks that the total of debit entries matches the total of credit entries. The trial balance is a very useful summary of all the balances in the ledger accounts, from which it is possible to prepare the end-of-year financial statements.

However, the trial balance process does not detect every error that could be made in an accounting system. You could produce a trial balance where the totals agree, but where you have made some mistakes in recording transactions. In general, as long as you have made a matching debit and credit entry your trial balance totals will agree. In this unit you will learn about the six types of error that are not revealed by a trial balance and how these errors should be corrected.

We have all experienced the situation where the totals of a trial balance do *not* agree. When this happens it means that somewhere in the accounting records a debit entry has not matched a credit entry, and maybe this has happened several times.

When the totals of a trial balance *do not agree* an extra account is included in the trial balance to make it agree temporarily. This extra account is called a suspense account. You will learn how to set up a suspense account and use this account as part of the correcting procedure.

Finding errors in accounting systems can take some time, so it is possible for a business's draft financial statements to have been prepared before all of the errors have been found and corrected. As a result it may be necessary to correct a draft profit and redraft an incorrect balance sheet. In Unit 22.4 you will learn how to carry out these procedures.

LEARNING OUTCOMES

When you have reached the end of this unit you will be able to:

- identify six types of errors that are not revealed by a trial balance
- prepare journal entries to correct these errors
- explain the correct process to follow when trial balance totals do not agree
- prepare journal entries to include entries in a suspense account to correct errors
- prepare statements to correct draft profits and draft balance sheets.

22.1 Errors not revealed by the trial balance (part 1)

DID YOU KNOW?

When errors are made in a set of accounts they should never be crossed out. This is because any attempt to cross out or alter figures could look as if someone was tampering with the accounting records. Instead, additional entries have to be made which have the effect of both cancelling any mistakes and recording the correct entries.

There are six types of error that would not be revealed by a trial balance and these are described below. In each case you will see that:

- there is always a matching debit and credit entry (so the trial balance totals would agree)
- a journal entry is necessary to correct the error
- the accounts before and after the correction are shown.

Error of commission

KEY TERM

Error of commission: where a debit or credit entry is made in the wrong account.

Illustration 1 Correcting an **error of commission**

On 23 February a supplier, M Rajiv, was paid $1 100 by cheque in settlement of the amount due. The entries made were as follows.

Cash book (bank columns)

Dr							Cr
				Feb	23	M Rajiv	1 100

K Rajah account

Dr							Cr
Feb	23	Bank	1 100				

JOURNAL

			$	$
Feb	23	M Rajiv	1 100	
		K Rajah		1 100
		To correct entry for payment incorrectly credited to M Rajiv's account instead of the account of K Rajah		

K Rajah account

Dr							Cr
Feb	23	Bank	1 100	**Feb**	**23**	**M Rajiv**	**1 100**

M Rajiv account

Dr							Cr
Feb	**23**	**K Rajah**	**1 100**				

Notes:

1. A trial balance would not have detected this error because there was a matching debit and credit entry (although the debit entry was actually in the wrong account).
2. By making a credit entry in K Rajah's account the incorrect entry is cancelled. The matching debit entry in M Rajiv's account records the correct entry.

Error of omission

KEY TERM

Error of omission: where a transaction is overlooked so that no debit and credit entry is made in the accounts.

Illustration 2 Correcting an **error of omission**

On 3 June 2012 a sales invoice was received from a customer Jarel Ltd for $330. However, no entries were made for the invoice because it was misplaced. The invoice was found on 22 June.

JOURNAL

			$	$
June	22	Jarel Ltd	330	
		Sales		330
		Correction of error of omission of invoice number B372		

Dr — Jarel Ltd account — Cr

June	22	Sales	330				

Dr — Sales account — Cr

				June	22	Jarel Ltd	330

Notes:

1. You will notice that no attempt is made to correct the book of prime entry. This is because at this stage it is the accuracy of the ledger accounts that matters; the book of prime entry has served its purpose.
2. The correction puts in place the entries in the ledger accounts that should have been made when the sales invoice was originally received.

KEY TERM

Error of principle: where a debit or credit entry is made for the correct amount but in the wrong class of account.

Error of principle

Illustration 3 Correcting an **error of principle**

On 17 August 2012 a cheque for $490 was paid for repairs to machinery. The accounts clerk made the following entries for this transaction: Dr Machinery $490; Cr Bank $490.

Here are the ledger accounts showing this error.

Dr — Cash book (bank columns) — Cr

				Aug	17	Machinery	490

Dr — Machinery account — Cr

Aug	17	Bank	490				

Dr — Repairs account — Cr

Here is the journal entry to correct this error.

JOURNAL

			$	$
Aug	17	Repairs	490	
		Machinery		490
		To correct entry for machinery repairs debited in error to the machinery account		

Dr — Machinery account — Cr

Aug	17	Bank	490	**Aug**	**17**	**Repairs**	**490**

Dr — Repairs account — Cr

Aug	**17**	**Machinery**	**490**				

Notes:

1. A trial balance would not have detected this error because there was matching debit and credit entry (although the debit entry was actually in the wrong class of account).
2. The journal entry cancels the incorrect entry by crediting the machinery account, and records the correct debit entry in the repairs account.

DID YOU KNOW?

It is easy to confuse an error of commission with an error of principle. An error of commission occurs when an entry is made in the *right type* of account (e.g. a mix up with the names of trade receivables, or a mix up with two expense accounts such as carriage inwards and carriage outwards). An error of principle occurs when an entry occurs in the *wrong class* of account (e.g. mixing up an asset with an expense, mixing up an item of income with a liability, etc.).

22.2 Errors not revealed by the trial balance (part 2)

KEY TERM

Error of original entry: when a mistake is made transferring an amount from a source document to a subsidiary book so both the debit entries and credit entries are incorrect.

DID YOU KNOW?

It is worth noting that when an entry is made on the wrong side of an account, it always requires double the amount to put the error right.

Note: the correction requires entries to be made for the difference in the amount ($978 – $798, i.e. $180).

Note: a trial balance would not have detected this error because there was matching debit and credit entry (although for the wrong amount).

Error of original entry

Illustration 4 Correcting an **error of original entry**

On 27 January 2012 an invoice was sent to a customer, KT Evans, for $978. The accounts clerk misread the figure as $798. As a result the entry in the sales day book was for the wrong figure and the following double-entry was made: Dr KT Evans $798; Cr Sales $798.

Here are the ledger accounts showing the error made by the accounts clerk.

Dr — KT Evans account — Cr

Jan	27	Sales	798				

Dr — Sales account — Cr

				Jan	27	KT Evans	798

JOURNAL

			$	$
Jan	27	Trade receivable: KT Evans	180	
		Sales		180
		To correct an error recording a sales invoice for $978 as $798		

Here are the ledger accounts recording the additional entries required to correct the error.

Dr — KT Evans account — Cr

Jan	27	Sales	798				
	27	**Sales**	**180**				

Dr — Sales account — Cr

				Jan	27	KT Evans	798
					27	**KT Evans**	**180**

Compensating error

KEY TERM

Compensating error: where two or more errors of the same amount cancel each other out.

Illustration 5 Correcting a **compensating error**

An accounts clerk made the following errors during September 2012.

Sept	14	The entries made for the payment of wages in cash of $760 were: Dr Wages $670; Cr Cash $760
	30	The sales day book was incorrectly totalled. The correct total was $5 390, but the accounts clerk entered $5 300 in the sales day book and credited the sales account with $5 300 as a result

Here are the relevant ledger accounts showing the incorrect entries.

Dr		Wages account					Cr
Sept	14	Sales	670				

Dr		Sales account					Cr
				Sept	30	Sales day book	5300

The journal entry required to correct the errors is as follows.

JOURNAL

			$	$
Sept	30	Wages	90	
		Sales		90
		To correct the error made recording wages of $760 as $670 and the incorrect undercasting of the sales journal by $90		

Here are the ledger accounts showing the corrections to the errors:

Dr		Wages account					Cr
Sept	14	Sales	670				
	30	**Sales**	**90**				

Dr		Sales account					Cr
				Sept	30	Sales day book	5300
					30	**Wages**	**90**

Note: there is no connection between the two mistakes. By chance the mistake in the wages account of $90 is matched by a mistake in the sales account for the same amount.

Error of complete reversal

Illustration 6 Correcting an **error of complete reversal**

On 28 October 2012 the owner of a business withdrew a cheque for $400 for private use. The accounts clerk made the following entries: Dr Bank $400; Cr Drawings $400.

Here are the ledger accounts showing the errors made by the accounts clerk.

Dr		Cash book (bank columns)					Cr
Oct	28	Drawings	400				

Dr		Drawings account					Cr
				Oct	28	Bank	400

JOURNAL

			$	$
Oct	28	Drawings	800	
		Bank		800
		Correction of error of complete reversal		

Dr		Cash book (bank columns)					Cr
Oct	28	Drawings	400	**Oct**	**28**	**Drawings**	**800**

Dr		Drawings account					Cr
Oct	**28**	**Bank**	**800**	Oct	28	Bank	400

Notes:

1. A trial balance would not have detected this error because there was matching debit and credit entry (although both of these entries were on the wrong sides of the two accounts involved).
2. The correction is for twice the amount of the original entry. This is because $400 is required to cancel the errors, and a further $400 is required to record the correct entries.

KEY TERM

Error of complete reversal: when the account that should have been debited is credited in error, and the account that should have been credited is debited in error.

You can now answer questions 1–4 on page 221.

22.3 Errors that are revealed by the trial balance

KEY TERM

Suspense account: a temporary account used to make the totals of a trial balance agree.

What is the correct procedure when trial balance totals do not agree? The answer is to temporarily add an extra amount to either the debit or credit column, as appropriate, to make the totals agree. This extra entry is labelled **suspense account**. At the same time it will be necessary to open a suspense account in the general ledger to record this amount.

Illustration 7 Procedure where trial balance totals do not agree

An accounts clerk found that the totals of a trial balance did not agree. The trial balance was as follows.

Trial balance at 31 August 2012

	Dr	Cr
	$	$
Total of ledger account balances	38 400	38 800

Step 1: Make the trial balance totals agree by adding an extra amount – in this case this is $400 and it needs to be added to the debit column.

Trial balance at 31 August 2012

	Dr	Cr
	$	$
Total of ledger account balances	38 400	38 800
Suspense account	**400**	
	38 800	38 800

The totals now agree.

Step 2: Open a suspense account in the general ledger to record this item.

Dr **Suspense account** **Cr**

Aug	**31**	**Balance**	**400**	

Note: the entry in the suspense account is made on the same side as the entry in the trial balance – in this case on the debit side. (Like all entries in a trial balance, the column used matches where the balance appears in the ledger account.)

Once a suspense account is set up, it is necessary to check the accounts to find any situation where a debit entry has not been matched by a credit entry. As each of these errors is found a correction is made in the ledger account containing the error, and a matching entry (debit or credit as appropriate) is made in the suspense account. When all of the errors in matching the double entry have been found, the suspense account will close, because at that point a revised trial balance would show agreement of the totals. Errors not revealed in the trial balance (see 22.1 and 22.2 above) are not corrected through the suspense account as they do not cause the trial balance totals to disagree.

Illustration 8	Correcting errors where the double entry does not match

Referring to the situation in Illustration 7, the following *three* errors were discovered where the double entry did not match. In each case the illustration shows the journal entry to correct the error and the ledger accounts once the journal entries have been posted.

Error 1: The payment of water charges by cheque, $420 had been recorded as follows: Dr Water charges $240; Cr Bank $420.

The error is in the water charges account where the existing entry is for less than it should be (the bank account is correct).

JOURNAL

			$	$
		Water charges	180	
		Suspense		180
		Correction of misposting of payment for water charges		

Dr — Water charges account — Cr

		Bank	240			
		Suspense	**180**			

Dr — Suspense account — Cr

Aug	31	Balance	400		**Water charges**	**180**

Notes:

1 Correcting this error has reduced the balance on the suspense account, which now stands at $220.

2 If a revised trial balance was prepared at this stage, the gap between the totals would be $220.

Error 2: The total of the discounts allowed column in the cash book was **miscast**. The correct total should have been $70, but the total given by the accounts clerk was $90.

The error is in the discounts allowed account. The entries for discounts allowed in the trade receivables accounts are correct because the individual entries in the discounts allowed column are correct.

JOURNAL

			$	$
		Suspense	20	
		Discounts allowed		20
		Correction of posting of miscast discounts allowed column		

Dr — Discounts Allowed account — Cr

		Cash book	90		**Suspense**	**20**

Dr — Suspense account — Cr

Aug	31	Balance	400		Water charges	180
		Discounts allowed	**20**			

Notes:

1 The correction of this error has increased the balance of the suspense account to $240.

2 If a revised trial balance was prepared at this point, the gap between the totals would be $240.

KEY TERM

Miscast: incorrectly totalled. Undercast would mean that a total is too small; overcast would mean that a total is too large.

Notes:

1 The correction of this entry has left the suspense account with a nil balance.

2 When a revised trial balance is prepared after these corrections, the totals will agree.

Error 3: Cash drawings of $240 had been correctly entered in the cash book, but no entry had been made in the drawings account.

The error is in the drawings account (the cash book is correct).

JOURNAL

			$	$
		Drawings	240	
		Suspense		240
		Entries required to correct omission of entry from drawings account		

Dr		**Drawings account**			**Cr**
		Suspense	**240**		

Dr		**Suspense account**			**Cr**
Aug	31	Balance	400	Water charges	180
		Discounts allowed	20	**Drawings**	**240**
			420		**420**

DID YOU KNOW?

It is often quite difficult to work out the right journal entries when faced with the description of an error. You may find it helpful to quickly draw up the accounts involved and record the error. You should then find it easier to visualise the entries required to correct the mistakes.

You can now try questions 5–10 on pages 221–222.

22.4 Correcting profits and balance sheets

Correcting draft profit figures

Errors are not always easily found and it can take some time to trace errors and correct them. As a result it is possible that a draft end-of-year financial statement will be prepared which contains some incorrect information. When this happens, it is necessary to prepare a statement correcting the draft profit as soon as any errors are found. In these situations, care has to be taken to distinguish between errors that affect the calculation of profits and those which do not. In general, where items recorded in an income statement are incorrect the draft profit will also be incorrect, but errors in items that are not recorded in an income statement will have no effect on the draft profit.

Illustration 9 Correction of a draft profit figure

Best Grocery Store's draft income statement for the year ended 31 December 2012 showed a draft profit of $68 300. However, it was found that errors had been made in the accounts, some of which affected the calculation of the draft profit. The errors were as follows.

1 Insurance, $500, had been omitted from the income statement.

2 Sales had been overstated by $360.

3 Trade payables had been mistotalled at $14 360 instead of $15 360.

4 Rent, $440, had been prepaid at the year end, but this had been overlooked when preparing the income statement.

5 Closing inventory had been understated by $600 when preparing the income statement.

6 Discounts allowed, $450, were added to the gross profit in the income statement rather than deducted.

Here is a detailed statement showing how the draft profit figure should be corrected.

Best Grocery Store
Correction of draft profit for the year ended 31 December 2012

	Increases to draft profit	Decreases in draft profit	Profit
	$	$	$
Draft profit			**68 300**
1 Insurance		(500)	
2 Sales		(360)	
3 Trade payables	no effect	no effect	
4 Prepaid rent	440		
5 Closing inventory	600		
6 Discount allowed		(900)	
Totals	**1 040**	**(1 760)**	**(720)**
Corrected profit			**67 580**

DID YOU KNOW?

Sometimes it needs careful thought to make the right correction to a draft profit figure. Did you realise, for example, that if closing inventory is understated, profit will increase when a correction is made? How would a mistake in returns outwards affect the profit calculation? The answer is not that easy to work out! So, it is suggested where there is a problem working out the answer, an experimental income statement is drawn up, so that the effect of correcting errors can be visualised and worked out.

Remember that if an item is placed on the wrong side in the income statement, it will require a correction of double the amount to put things right.

Notes:

1 It is good practice to present the corrections in a formal statement such as in the illustration. You will notice the proper title, the clear labelling of each item, and the fact that the statement starts with the draft figure and ends with clearly labelled correct profit figure.

2 Item 5: the more closing inventory a business has, the greater the gross profit. This is because the figure for closing inventory reduces the cost of sales figure, and the smaller the cost of sales the greater the gross (and therefore final) profit figure.

3 Item 6: discount allowed was recorded on the wrong side of the income statement, so it is necessary to double the amount to correct the mistake.

You can now answer questions 11 and 12 on page 223.

Correcting a draft balance sheet

If there are undetected errors in a business's accounts they may affect not only the income statement but also the balance sheet. When the totals of a draft balance sheet do not agree it is possible to *make* the totals agree by making a temporary entry for a suspense account.

Illustration 10 Correcting a draft balance sheet

Here is a table showing how to correct some errors made by an inexperienced bookkeeper when preparing a balance sheet. Assume the bookkeeper has made a suspense account entry in the first part of the balance sheet for $120.

Error	How to correct the draft balance sheet
The annual depreciation charge had been miscalculated and should have been $2 000 greater	Reduce the value of non-current assets Reduce the value of draft profit shown in the capital section
A bad debt should have been written off at the year end	Reduce the value of trade receivables Reduce the value of draft profit shown in the capital section
The figure for closing inventory was miscalculated; it should have been $18 720 instead of $17 820	Increase inventories (current assets) by $900 Increase the draft profit shown in the capital section by $900
The bookkeeper had omitted the balance of petty cash, $120, from the balance sheet	Increase current assets by including petty cash $120 Reduce the suspense account entry by $120 (suspense account is now eliminated)

You can now answer questions 13–23 on pages 223–226.

DEVELOPING YOUR SKILLS

1 Identifying errors not revealed by a trial balance

The following errors were made by an accounts clerk during a recent financial year. In each case identify the type of error that has occurred.

	Error	Type of error
1	An invoice received from a supplier for $657 was recorded in the purchases day book as being for $567	
2	A sales returns of $89 from a trade receivable, S McNee, was credited to the account of S McKoy	
3	Cash sales of $820 were recorded in the accounts as Dr Cash $820 Cr Sales $800. The total of the travel expenses analysis column in the petty cash book was mistotalled at $30 rather than the correct figure of $50	
4	A cheque counterfoil for rent $680 was entirely overlooked	
5	The purchase of some new office equipment, $2 300, was debited to the purchases account	
6	The entries made for the payment of a trade payable, L Mohammed, by cheque $320 were: Dr Bank $320, Cr L Mohammed $320	

2 Identifying errors not revealed by a trial balance

The following errors were made by an accounts clerk during a recent financial year. In each case identify the type of error that has occurred.

	Error	Type of error
1	A till roll showed that cash sales had totalled $2 320. The entries in the accounts were Dr Cash $2 230 and Cr Sales $2 230	
2	A petty cash voucher for stationery $18 was mislaid	
3	Discounts allowed of $28 were debited to the trade receivable account and credited to the discounts allowed account	
4	The payment of interest $110 was debited to the insurance account	
5	The payment of vehicle running costs, $80, was debited to the motor vehicles account	
6	The sales returns journal was mistotalled at $170 instead of $160. Rent received from a tenant of $380 was entered in the rent received account as $390	

3 Correcting errors with journal entries

Referring to the errors listed in question 1, make journal entries to correct the errors.

4 Correcting errors with journal entries

Referring to the errors listed in question 2, make journal entries to correct the errors.

5 Correcting errors involving the suspense account

An accounts clerk was unable to get the totals of a trial balance to agree. The totals were Dr $82 500, Cr $81 100.

Subsequently, the following errors were discovered where there was a mismatch between the debit entry and credit entry.

Error 1: Cash sales of $3640 had been correctly entered in the cash book, but had been credited to the sales account as $3240.

Error 2: The total of the purchases journal, $700, had not been posted to the ledger account.

Error 3: Rent received of $1700 had been correctly entered in the cash book, but had not been posted to the rent received account.

a Prepare journal entries to correct these errors.
b Prepare the suspense account.

6 Correcting errors involving the suspense account

An accounts clerk was unable to get the totals of a trial balance to agree. The totals were Dr $38 620, Cr $39 480.

Subsequently, the following errors were discovered where there was a mismatch between the debit entry and credit entry.

Error 1: The total of the discounts received column in the cash book of $720 had not been posted to the discounts received account.

Error 2: The sales returns journal had been undercast by $90.

Error 3: The payment of wages in cash, $980, had been correctly entered in the cash book, but had been posted to the debit of the wages account as $750.

a Prepare journal entries to correct these errors.
b Prepare the suspense account.

7 Correcting errors involving the suspense account where the difference in the trial balance totals is unknown

The totals of a business's trial balance failed to agree. Subsequently the following errors were discovered.

Error 1: A cheque received from a trade receivable of $360 had been correctly entered in the cash book, but had been posted to the trade receivable account as $630.

Error 2: The total of the postage column in the petty cash book, $70, had not been posted to the ledger account.

Error 3: The purchases returns journal had been undercast by $380.

a Prepare journal entries to correct these errors.

b Prepare the suspense account and identify the original difference in the trial balance totals.

8 Correcting errors involving the suspense account where the difference in the trial balance totals is unknown

The totals of a business's trial balance failed to agree. Subsequently the following errors were discovered.

Error 1: The sales journal had been overcast by $410.

Error 2: The payment of rent by cheque, $730, had not been posted from the cash book.

Error 3: The total of the 'discounts allowed' column in the cash book of $110 had been posted to the discounts allowed account as $100.

a Prepare journal entries to correct these errors.

b Prepare the suspense account and identify the original difference in the trial balance totals.

9 Correcting errors, some of which affect the suspense account

When Janet Spencer prepared her business's trial balance on 31 October 2012 the totals failed to agree. The total of the debit column was $178 440, whereas the total of the credit column was $176 970.

The accounting records were checked and the following errors were discovered.

Error 1: Sales returns of $370 had been credited to the account of Joseph Wright instead of Joshua Wright.

Error 2: The receipt of $830 from a trade receivable, T Patel, had been correctly entered in the cash book but had not been posted to the trade receivable account.

Error 3: The total of the general expenses analysis column in the petty cash book, $40, had not been posted to the general ledger.

Error 4: A cheque for $780 in payment of the supplier, J K Samson, had been entered in the accounts as $870.

Error 5: The total of the purchases returns journal, $680, had not been posted to the purchases returns account.

Error 6: A payment by cheque for insurance, $350, had been debited in the cash book and credited to the insurance account.

a Identify whether or not each error would be revealed by the trial balance.

b Prepare journal entries to correct the errors.

c Prepare the suspense account.

10 Correcting errors, some of which affect the suspense account

The totals of a business's trial balance did not agree. The totals were: Dr $423 890, Cr $425 290. The following errors were found.

Error 1: The total of the discounts received column in the cash book had been overcast by $300.

Error 2: A sale on credit to Steven Taylor, $830, had not been posted from the sales journal to the customer's account.

Error 3: A cash receipt for stationery, $40, had been mislaid and no entries had been made in the accounts.

Error 4: The total of the sales returns journal, $470, had been posted to the sales returns account as $740.

Error 5: The payment of water charges by cheque, $340, had been correctly entered in the cash book, but had not been posted to the water charges account.

Error 6: The entries made for cash sales of $690 were Dr Sales $690, Cr Cash $690.

a Identify whether or not each error would be revealed by the trial balance.

b Prepare journal entries to correct the errors.

c Prepare the suspense account.

11 Correcting a draft profit figure

Sharon Lee recently prepared the end-of-year income statement for her business. The income statement showed a draft profit of $89 500 for the year ended 30 November 2012. However, the following errors in the accounting records were discovered.

Error 1: No entry was made for depreciation of equipment, $3000, in the income statement.

Error 2: The purchases figure was understated by $400 in the income statement.

Error 3: The loan account was incorrectly balanced. The balance brought down should have been $11 500, not $10 500.

Error 4: Wages due but unpaid, $450, was overlooked when preparing the income statement.

Error 5: Carriage outwards, $720, was recorded in the trading section of the income statement.

Error 6: The expense, rent $4700, was added to the gross profit rather than deducted.

Error 7: Sales returns $3280 was overlooked when preparing the income statement.

Prepare a statement showing the effect of correcting these errors on the draft profit for the year ended 30 November 2012.

12 Correcting a draft profit figure

The draft income statement for the year ended 30 September 2012 for Zero Stores showed a draft profit of $132 850. However, the following errors were found in the accounting records.

Error 1: General expenses totalling $2140 had been entirely omitted from the income statement.

Error 2: Depreciation had been charged on the business's motor vehicles (cost $74 000) at the rate of 20 per cent per annum. However, the correct rate should have been 25 per cent.

Error 3: Sales had been overstated by $710 when preparing the income statement.

Error 4: The balance of trade receivable account, $1240, had been brought down as $2140.

Error 5: Discounts received, $480, had been added to sales in the trading section of the income statement.

Error 6: Rent, $630, was due but unpaid at the year end. This detail had been overlooked.

Error 7: Purchases returns were overstated by $300 when preparing the income statement.

Prepare a statement showing the effect of correcting these errors on the draft profit for the year ended 30 September 2012.

13 Correcting a draft balance sheet

Monty produced the following draft balance sheet at 31 December 2012.

	$	$	$
	Cost	Accumulated depreciation	Net
Non-current assets	470 000	120 000	350 000
Current assets			
Inventories	33 000		
Trade receivables	18 000		
Cash at bank	7 000		
		58 000	
Less current liabilities			
Trade payables	16 000		
Other payables	3 000		
		(19 000)	
Net current assets			39 000
			389 000
Capital			
Opening balance		362 000	
Add profit		53 000	
		415 000	
Less drawings		(31 000)	
			384 000
Suspense account			5 000
			389 000

Monty has now made the following discoveries:

- Depreciation for the year had been incorrectly calculated, it should have been $30 000 rather than $40 000.

- Some expenses had been prepaid by $4000, but this had been entirely overlooked.
- It now appears that some items in the stockroom were damaged. These items should have been reduced in value by $2000.
- The balance of the drawings account had been incorrectly calculated, it should have been $26000.

Prepare a correct balance sheet at 31 December 2012.

14 Correcting a draft balance sheet

Amhari produced the following draft balance sheet at 31 July 2012.

	$	$	$
	Cost	Accumulated depreciation	Net
Non-current assets	145 000	28 000	117 000
Current assets			
Inventories	16 000		
Trade receivables	20 000		
Other receivables	2 000		
		38 000	
Less current liabilities			
Trade payables	11 000		
Bank overdraft	6 000		
		(17 000)	
Net current assets			21 000
Suspense account			3 000
			141 000
Capital			
Opening balance		137 000	
Add profit		24 000	
		161 000	
Less drawings		(20 000)	
			141 000
			141 000

Amhari discovered the following errors had been made in the business's accounting records:

- No depreciation on non-currents assets had been provided in the income statement for the year ended 31 July 2012. Depreciation should have been calculated as 20 per cent of cost.
- An accrual of $1000 on some expenses had been entirely overlooked.
- The balance of the bank account was incorrect, the balance had been overstated by $3000.
- A bad debt of $2000 should have been written off at 31 July 2012.

Prepare a correct balance sheet at 31 July 2012.

PREPARING FOR THE EXAMINATION

(The following questions cover Unit 22)

MULTIPLE-CHOICE QUESTIONS

15 What is the purpose of a trial balance?

A To calculate the profit or loss

B To check that all of the transactions have been included in the books of account

C To check that there are no bookkeeping errors

D To check the arithmetical accuracy of the bookkeeping

16 Griffin posted $650 to the debit of T Smith's account instead of to the debit of T Smythe's account. What is this mistake known as?

A A compensating error

B An error of commission

C An error of omission

D An error of principle

17 Chen entered the purchase of a non-current asset in the purchases account. What is this mistake known as?

A An error of commission

B An error of complete reversal

C An error of original entry

D An error of principle

18 A trial balance had the following totals: Dr $82 600, Cr $82 800. Which of the following errors could have caused this disagreement?

A A computer printer, cost $200, purchased for office use had been debited to the purchases account

B Drawings of $200 had been completely omitted from the books

C Telephone charges, $200, had been debited to the stationery account

D The sales returns journal had been overcast by $200

19 Which of the following errors would affect the agreement of the totals of a trial balance?

A A credit note received from a supplier for $300 was completely omitted from the books

B A purchase invoice for $670 was entered in the purchases journal as $760

C Owner's drawings of $300 was debited to the bank account and credited to the drawings account

D The total of the travel expenses column in the cash book was overcast by $40

20 The purchase of goods for resale had been debited to the office equipment account by mistake. How would this error affect the business's end-of-year financial statements?

	Profit		Non-current assets	
	Too high	**Too low**	**Too high**	**Too low**
A		✓		✓
B		✓	✓	
C	✓		✓	
D	✓			✓

21 An amount of $70 has been entered on the credit side of an account instead of the debit side. How will this error affect the totals of a trial balance?

A Debit total is $70 less than credit total

B Debit total is $140 less than credit total

C Debit total is $70 more than credit total

D Debit total is $140 more than credit total

22 It was discovered that a discount of $40 received had been debited to the trade payables account and debited to the discount received account. In order to correct this error which of the following entries were required?

A Debit discount received $40
Credit suspense account $40

B Debit discount received $80
Credit suspense account $80

C Debit suspense account $40
Credit discount received $40

D Debit suspense account $80
Credit discount received $80

OTHER QUESTIONS

23 On 31 October 2012, Morag prepared her business's trial balance but found that the totals did not agree. The total of debit entries was $92 340 and the total of credit entries was $93 770. She found the following errors.

Error 1: Cash drawings of $120 had been entirely omitted from the accounts.

Error 2: A payment by cheque for insurance, $830, had been correctly entered in the bank account but no entry had been made in the insurance account.

Error 3: Cash purchases of $300 had been correctly entered in the cash book but had been credited to the purchases account.

a Prepare journal entries to correct these errors.

b Prepare the suspense account.

Morag had used the trial balance as the basis for the preparing a draft income statement for the year ended 31 October 2012. The draft income statement showed a profit for the year of $16 380.

c Prepare a statement to show a correction of the draft profit of $16 380.

23 Bank reconciliation statements

Introduction

In this unit you will learn how to check that a business's record of its bank transactions as recorded in the cash book is accurate and up to date. The process involves comparing the bank columns in the business's cash book with the relevant **bank statement** issued by the business's bank.

First, it is important to understand how a bank statement works.

Banks keep computerised records of each customer's account using the running balance method which was illustrated in Unit 7.

It is very important to realise that from the bank's point of view each customer's account (assuming it has a positive balance) is a liability account. The reason for this is that any funds in an account do not belong to the bank they belong to the customer, hence the balance is a current liability. In effect the bank owes these funds to the customer; hence the balance is a liability. However, if the account becomes overdrawn, then the customer owes the bank the amount of the overdrawn balance, and at that point the account is one of the bank's assets. A bank statement is a copy of the bank's record of a customer's account which is sent to the customer at regular intervals – perhaps on a monthly basis – or on request.

Cash book bank balances and bank statement balances rarely agree

In this unit you will learn how to prepare bank statements and about some of the facilities that banks provide for their customers.

When a business receives its bank statement, it is usual practice to check the bank statements against the bank account in the cash book. It is usually the case that the two records are not identical. In this unit you will learn why this is so and you will find out about the procedure used to make sure that the two records can be made to agree.

LEARNING OUTCOMES

When you have reached the end of this unit you will be able to:

- explain some terms used in bank statements
- prepare simple bank statements
- compare the cash book (bank columns) with the bank statement to identify differences
- update a cash book using information overlooked or not available until the bank statement was available
- prepare a statement reconciling the updated cash book balance with that shown on the bank statement
- prepare bank reconciliation statements when the bank balance is overdrawn
- explain the benefits of preparing bank reconciliation statements.

KEY TERM

Bank statement: a copy of a customer's bank account, sent to the customer at regular intervals.

23.1 How to prepare a bank statement

Illustration 1	Preparing a bank statement

Here are some straightforward transactions that affect the current account of a business called Beachspray which banks with Anybank plc.

March	1	Balance at bank $800
	3	Paid insurance $360 (cheque number 303472)
	5	Paid telephone charges $230 (payment made by direct debit)
	11	Drawings by cheque $250 (cheque number 303473)
	18	Banked cash takings $890
	21	Paid rent $280 (payment made by standing order)
	24	One of business's trade receivables (M Lee) paid $480 directly into Beachspray's account (using credit transfer facility)
	27	Bank deducted charges of $80

Here is the bank statement recording these details.

ANYBANK plc

Bank statement for Beachspray

Date		Details	Dr	Cr	Balance	
			$	$	$	
March	1	Balance			800	Cr
	5	303472 General Assurance plc	360		440	Cr
	5	DD Regional Telecoms plc	230		210	Cr
	14	303473	250		40	Dr
	18	Cash and cheques		890	850	Cr
	21	SO Landward Properties plc	280		570	Cr
	24	Credit transfer – Michael Lee		480	1 050	Cr
	27	CHR	80		970	Cr

Notes:

1 A credit balance on a bank statement is a positive balance for the customer and is a liability for the bank. The balance is owed by the bank to the customer.

2 When the account has a negative balance it is described as Dr (an asset) – this is the balance owed by the customer to the bank. This is the situation on 14 March.

3 Additions to the balance are recorded in the credit column; deductions from the balance are recorded in the debit column.

4 Banks record information in the details column in a number of ways. For example:

- **a** cheque numbers are identified
- **b** 'CHR' is an abbreviation for charges.

5 DD, SO and Credit transfer are banking facilities and these are explained opposite.

6 Banks use a variety of descriptions and abbreviations. Those shown above are just a few examples of the entries that could be made.

7 The bank statement shows that on 27 March Beachspray has a positive balance of $970 at the bank.

Some specialist banking facilities explained

- **Direct debit**: a banking facility that enables the bank's customer to give the bank the authority to make payments on its behalf to particular organisations who request payment. In the illustration, the bank's customer (Beachspray) has instructed the bank to pay its telephone charges automatically whenever the telephone company (Regional Telecoms plc) requests payment. Beachspray would set an upper limit to the amount that can be paid. Because the payment is made automatically by the bank, the customer may not be aware that the payment has happened until the bank statement is received. The abbreviation 'DD' has been used by Anybank plc to indicate a direct debit payment.
- **Standing order**: a banking facility that enables the bank's customer to give the bank the authority to make regular payments of an agreed amount to named organisations. In the illustration the bank has paid Beachspray's rent of $280 to the company owning the property (Landward Properties plc). This payment will be made automatically by the bank, say every month, and the payment will always be $280, until Beachspray changes its instructions to the bank. Again, it is quite likely that the bank's customer will overlook the standing order payment (because it is automatic) and the bank statement will act as a reminder. The abbreviation SO has been used by Anybank plc to indicate a standing order payment.
- **Credit transfer**: it is possible for a business's customers to pay the amount they owe directly into that business's bank account using a facility known as a credit transfer. In the illustration, one of Beachspray's customers (Michael Lee) has paid Beachspray $480 by using this facility. Michael Lee has authorised his bank to make this payment. Michael Lee's bank has then made an automatic transfer of funds from Michael Lee's account to Beachspray's account held by Anybank plc. This automatic transfer of funds between banks is faster, more secure and generally more convenient for all concerned. The bank statement will act as a reminder that this credit transfer has occurred.
- **Bank charges**: at regular intervals banks charge their business customers for operating their current accounts (i.e. processing cheques, direct debits, standing orders, etc). Charges will include interest on any overdrawn balances. The bank's customer will not normally be aware of the amount of the charge until the bank statement is received.

DID YOU KNOW?

The key difference between a direct debit and a standing order is that the amount can vary in the case of a direct debit (up to an agreed limit), but in the case of a standing order the amount is always the same.

DID YOU KNOW?

Credit transfers are also sometimes referred to as BACS transfers. BACS stands for 'Bankers Automated Clearing Services'. It is also becoming common to use telephone and online banking to arrange payments.

KEY TERM

Direct debit: authority is given to a bank by one of its customers to make payments on its behalf to another organisation. The amount paid will be the sum requested by that organisation up to a specified limit.

Standing order: a bank's customer gives instructions for the automatic payment to another organisation of a fixed amount at regular intervals.

Credit transfer: the automatic transfer of funds into a business's bank account by one of the business's customers.

Bank charges: payments deducted automatically from a current account at regular intervals as a reward to the bank for operating the account.

You can now answer questions 1 and 2 on page 235.

23.2 Comparing a cash book (bank columns) with a bank statement

There are several reasons why a business's cash book (bank columns) will not exactly match the detail shown in a bank statement for the same period.

Timing differences affecting the bank statement

It takes time for banks to process transactions. As a result some cheques paid by the business towards the end of the period may not appear on the bank statement. It is possible, of course, that a recipient of a cheque may have taken some time to pay the cheque into their own current account, adding to the delay. Cheque payments made by a business which do not appear on a bank statement are called **unpresented cheques**. These cheques are very likely to appear on the next bank statement unless the recipient loses the cheque or fails to pay the cheque into their bank account.

> **KEY TERM**
>
> **Unpresented cheques:** cheques that have not been cleared by the bank and have not yet been recorded on a business's bank statement.
>
> **Amounts not yet credited:** amounts paid into a business's bank statement but which have not yet been recorded on the bank statement as credit entries.

In the same way, money paid into the bank by a business may not appear on the bank statement for a few days while the transaction is processed by the bank. So details on paying-in slips completed towards the end of a month may be missing from the bank statement. Money paid into a current account but which has not yet appeared on the bank statement is referred to as **amounts not yet credited**. These amounts will appear on the next month's bank statement.

Information missing from the cash book

Although the cash book will have been prepared with great care, it may be that some details will be missing because of an oversight by the business's cashier or because the information was not available until the bank statement arrived. Here are some common examples:

- *Oversights*: automatic payments made by the bank that have been overlooked (standing order and direct debit payments perhaps); receipts from customers made by credit transfer, or interest added to the account by the bank.
- *Information not available*: bank charges and/or bank interest charges will not be known to the cashier until the bank statement arrives.

Illustration 2 Comparing a cash book record with a bank statement

In Illustration 1 Beachspray's bank statement for March 2011 was prepared. Opposite is an extract from Beachspray's cash book for the same month showing the bank columns.

BOOKS OF BEACHSPRAY

Cash book (bank columns only)

Dr				Cr			
March	1	Balance	800	March	3	Insurance (chq 303472)	360
	16	Sales	890		11	Drawings (chq 303473)	250
	27	Sales	750		19	P Joseph (chq 303474)	440
					27	Water charges (chq 303475)	220
					31	Balance c/d	1 170
			2 440				2 440
April	1	Balance b/d	1 170				

Just a glance at this cash book shows that there are differences with the bank statement. The most obvious point is that the closing balances shown in the two documents are different: the cash book balance is $1 170, but the bank statement shows a balance of $970 (both positive).

It is important to use a systematic way to find all of the possible reasons for a difference, particularly as, in reality, a business's cash book and the matching bank statement may be many pages long.

The technique to use is to match every item that appears in *both* documents and place a tick (✓) beside the entry in each document. Always start by checking whether the opening balances agree and then work systematically through the documents.

Here are the two statements showing ticked entries.

BOOKS OF BEACHSPRAY

Cash book (bank columns only)

Dr				Cr			
March	1	Balance	✓800	March	3	Insurance (chq 303472)	✓360
	16	Sales	✓890		11	Drawings (chq 303473)	✓250
	27	Sales	750		19	P Joseph (chq 303474)	440
					27	Water charges (chq 303475)	220
					31	Balance c/d	1 170
			2 440				2 440
April	1	Balance b/d	1 170				

Here is a reminder of the bank statement for this month.

ANYBANK plc

Bank statement for Beachspray

Date		Details	Dr	Cr	Balance	
			$	$	$	
March	1	Balance			✓800	Cr
	5	303472 General Assurance plc	✓360		440	Cr
	5	DD Regional Telecoms plc	230		210	Cr
	14	303473	✓250		40	Dr
	18	Cash and cheques		✓890	850	Cr
	21	SO Landward Properties plc	280		570	Cr
	24	Credit transfer – Michael Lee		480	1 050	Cr
	27	CHR	80		970	Cr

Items that are not ticked will have caused the two closing balances to be different. The unticked items will have arisen for the reasons described above. Here is a summary of the unticked items.

Timing differences:

- Unpresented cheques (cheques not shown on the bank statement): P Joseph, $440; Water charges $220.
- Amount not credited (amounts paid in not shown on bank statement): $750.

Oversights by, or information not available to, Beachspray staff:

- Direct debit for $230; standing order for $280; credit transfer for $480; bank charges $80.

You can now answer questions 3 and 4 on page 236.

23.3 The reconciliation process

Updating the cash book

The next step is to correct those oversights in the cash book that have become apparent from looking at the bank statement and to use any information on the bank statement that was not previously available. So, additional entries are made in the cash book and a new, up-to-date balance is extracted.

Illustration 3 Updating the cash book

Here is an updated version of the cash book starting with the balance that had been brought down on 1 April.

BOOKS OF BEACHSPRAY

Cash book (bank columns only)

Dr							Cr
April	1	Balance b/d	1 170	**April**	**1**	**Telephone charges (DD)**	**230**
	1	**Michael Lee**	**480**				
					1	**Rent (SO)**	**280**
					1	**Bank charges**	**80**
					1	**Balance c/d**	**1 060**
			1 650				**1 650**
April	**1**	**Balance b/d**	**1 060**				

At the same time the double entry would be recorded in the ledger accounts in the usual way.

You can now answer questions 5 and 6 on page 236.

KEY TERM

Bank reconciliation statement: a document prepared by businesses at regular intervals (say monthly) to check that their bank records agree with those provided by the bank.

DID YOU KNOW?

The word 'reconcile' – as used in 'bank reconciliation statement' – means to make two apparently conflicting things (the cash book balance and the bank statement balance) consistent with each other.

Completing the process: the bank reconciliation statement

Having updated the cash book, the business's accounts team will want to know if the bank statement balance would agree with the updated cash book if the bank statement was brought up to date. To do this they will prepare a **bank reconciliation statement**. This statement makes use of the list of timing differences discovered when comparing the cash book and the bank statement. When this has been done the two balances should agree. However, if the balances do not agree it means that somewhere there is an error – or errors. (The errors could be in the business's accounting records, but they could be in the bank's recordkeeping. Banks do sometimes make mistakes!)

Illustration 4 | Preparing a bank reconciliation statement

Here is one version of the statement that begins with the bank statement balance.

BEACHSPRAY
Bank reconciliation statement at 1 April 2011

	$	$
Balance as per **bank statement**		970
Less: unpresented cheque		
P Joseph (303474)	440	
Water charges (303475)	220	
		(660)
		310
Add: amount not yet credited		750
Balance as per **cash book**		1 060

Alternatively, some individuals prefer to start the bank reconciliation statement with the updated cash book balance.

BEACHSPRAY
Bank reconciliation statement at 1 April 2011

	$	$
Balance as per **cash book**		1 060
Add: unpresented cheque		
P Joseph (303474)	440	
Water charges (303475)	220	
		660
		1 720
Less: amount not yet credited		(750)
Balance as per **bank statement**		970

Notes:

1 In this alternative approach, the reconciliation statement starts with the updated cash book balance.

2 The process is now as follows:

a Unpresented cheques: if these had not been issued, the cash book balance would have been higher – so the unpresented cheques are added back.

b Amount not yet credited: if this was removed from the cash book the balance would be lower – so the item is deducted.

Notes:

1 When the timing differences are taken into account, the reconciliation statement shows that the bank statement balance and the updated cash book balance would agree. So, all appears to be well.

2 In this version, which starts with the bank statement balance, the thinking process is:

a Unpresented cheques: when these are included in the bank statement, the balance will decrease – hence they are deducted.

b Amount not yet credited: when this item is included on the bank statement, the balance will increase – hence the amount is added.

3 It is useful to list all of the unpresented cheques with their numbers (as shown above) because this will help to trace them when the next bank statement arrives.

You can now answer questions 7–10 on pages 237–238.

What about overdrawn balances?

Sometimes the reconciliation process will take place when the cash book balance or the bank statement balance (or both) are overdrawn. Where this happens, follow the same processes as described above, but remember that an overdrawn figure should be recorded as a negative, with a reverse consequence for any arithmetical process.

You can now answer questions 11 and 12 on pages 239–240.

Advantages of the reconciliation process

The main benefits:

- The process checks that if the cash book and bank statement are different, the difference is caused by timing differences rather than errors.
- The process enables a business's cashier to make sure that the cash book is fully updated at monthly intervals by including transactions undertaken automatically by the bank.
- Because there are frequent checks on this important business financial record, it helps to reduce the risk of fraud taking place.

You can now answer questions 13–20 on pages 240–242.

Unit 23 Practice questions

DEVELOPING YOUR SKILLS

1 Preparing a bank statement

Natalie Clarke is the owner of Natalie's Jewellery Store. Her business banks with Anybank plc. The following information is available about the business's current account for the month of May 2012.

Date		Transaction details	Amount $
May	1	Balance of cash at bank (positive)	1 400
	4	Payment of general expenses by cheque (number 27204)	320
	8	Bank made direct debit payment for electricity charges to Interstate Power plc	670
	12	Payment of supplier, Latoya Fray, by cheque (number 27205)	820
	15	Cash takings were paid into the bank account	1 780
	20	Bank made standing order payment for rent to Ford Holdings plc	480
	24	Credit transfer of funds from customer, Smartjewels Ltd	950
	29	Bank charges were deducted	110

Use these details to prepare Natalie's Jewellery Store's bank statement for May 2012. Use the running balance style of presentation and use appropriate terms and abbreviations in the details column of the bank statement.

2 Preparing a bank statement

The following details are available concerning the current account of the business owned by Tahir, called Tahir's Sports Supplies. The information is for July 2012.

Date		Transaction details	Amount $
July	1	Balance of cash at bank (positive)	930
	6	Payment of supplier, TMT Ltd, by cheque (number 787891)	640
	11	Drawings made by cheque (number 787892)	310
	12	Bank made standing order payment for loan repayment to Quality Finances plc	450
	17	Cash takings were paid into the bank account	1 370
	19	Credit transfer of funds from customer, Nana Retail	590
	23	Bank made direct debit payment for telephone charges to Telecoms plc	220
	28	Bank charges were deducted	140

Use these details to prepare the Tahir's Sports Supplies bank statement for July 2012. Use the running balance style of presentation and use appropriate terms and abbreviations in the details column of the bank statement.

3 Comparing a cash book with a bank statement

Referring to the situation in question 1, here is the cash book (bank columns only) record for Natalie's Jewellery Store as maintained by Natalie's cashier for May 2012.

BOOKS OF NATALIE'S JEWELLERY STORE

Cash book (bank columns only)

Dr								Cr
May	1	Balance	1 400	May	2	General expenses	(chq 27204)	320
	13	Sales	1 780		9	Latoya Fray	(chq 27205)	820
	28	Sales	1 240		23	Supagems	(chq 27206)	740
					28	Drawings	(chq 27207)	480
					31	Balance	c/d	2 060
			4 420					4 420
June	1	Balance b/d	2 060					

Compare this cash book with the bank statement prepared in answer to question 1. Place ticks alongside entries that appear in both documents (include a check on whether the opening balances matched). Identify and list any items that are not ticked.

4 Comparing a cash book with a bank statement

Referring to the situation in question 2, here is the cash book (bank columns only) record for Tahir's Sports Supplies as maintained by Tahir's cashier for July 2012.

BOOKS OF TAHIR'S SPORT SUPPLIES

Cash book (bank columns only)

Dr								Cr
July	1	Balance	930	July	3	TMT Ltd	(chq 787891)	640
	13	Sales	1 370		8	Drawings	(chq 787892)	310
	29	Sales	990		20	Stationery	(chq 787893)	100
					29	Salary	(chq 787894)	1 700
					31	Balance	c/d	540
			3 290					3 290
Aug	1	Balance b/d	540					

Compare this cash book with the bank statement prepared in answer to question 2. Place ticks alongside entries that appear in both documents (include a check on whether the opening balances matched). Identify and list any items that are not ticked.

5 Updating a cash book

Referring to the information in questions 1 and 3, update the cash book balance of $2060 for Natalie's Jewellery Store.

6 Updating a cash book

Referring to the information in questions 2 and 4, update the cash book balance of $540 for Tahir's Sports Supplies.

7 Preparing a bank reconciliation statement

Referring to all of the information available for Natalie's Jewellery Store in questions 1, 3 and 5, prepare a bank reconciliation statement dated 1 June 2012.

8 Preparing a bank reconciliation statement

Referring to all of the information available for Tahir's Sports Supplies in questions 2, 4 and 6, prepare a bank reconciliation statement dated 1 August 2013.

9 The complete process

On 1 November 2012, the following bank statement covering October was received by the head of the accounts team at Vecki Wholesale Flowers.

MIDBAY BANK plc

Bank statement for Vecki wholesale flowers

Date		Details	Dr	Cr	Balance	
			$	$	$	
Oct	1	Balance			4 310	Cr
	3	447802 JKJ Imports	2 730		1 580	Cr
	11	Cash and cheques		1 640	3 220	Cr
	13	CHR	240		2 980	Cr
	18	447804	630		2 350	Cr
	21	DD Regional Telecoms plc	550		1 800	Cr
	23	Cash and cheques		1 890	3 690	Cr
	25	Credit transfer: M Deosaran		490	4 180	Cr
	26	447805 Gobin Traders	1 480		2 700	Cr
	27	SO Transcity Properties	820		1 880	Cr
	28	Interest		50	1 930	Cr

The business's cash book (bank columns) for the same month was as follows.

BOOKS OF VECKI WHOLESALE FLOWERS

Cash book (bank columns only)

Dr								Cr
Oct	1	Balance	4 310	Oct	1	JKJ Imports	(chq 447802)	2 730
	7	Sales	1 640		3	Electricity	(chq 447803)	490
	20	Sales	1 150		12	Admin expenses	(chq 447804)	630
	20	M Lall	740		23	Gobin Traders	(chq 447805)	1 480
	28	Sales	1 370		26	L Thomas	(chq 447806)	810
					27	Rent	(standing order)	820
					31	Balance	c/d	2 250
			9 210					9 210
Nov	1	Balance b/d	2 250					

a Compare the two records.

b Tick all items that appear in both documents.

c Update the cash book balance at 1 November 2012.

d Prepare a bank reconciliation statement dated 1 November 2012.

10 The complete process

On 1 June 2012, the following bank statement covering May was received by the accounts department of the business called Elite Publishing.

WESTOWN BANK plc

Bank statement for Elite publishing

Date		Details	Dr	Cr	Balance	
			$	$	$	
May	1	Balance			7328	Cr
	5	Cash and cheques		3395	10723	Cr
	6	110744 MLD Books	2242		8481	Cr
	8	110747 Abbey Stationery Ltd	1631		6850	Cr
	14	Credit transfer: investment interest		480	7330	Cr
	17	DD Hydro water	722		6608	Cr
	19	110746 Circle Wholesales	1039		5569	Cr
	20	Cash and cheques		4437	10006	Cr
	22	CHR	330		9676	Cr
	29	SO Publishers Society membership	350		9326	Cr
	30	Interest		90	9416	Cr

The business's cash book (bank columns) for the same month was as follows.

BOOKS OF ELITE PUBLISHING

CASH BOOK (Bank columns only)

Dr								Cr
May	1	Balance	7328	May	2	MLD Books	(chq 110744)	2242
	2	Sales	2595		3	Palmleaf Stores	(chq 110745)	1833
	2	Dass Books Ltd	800		3	Circle Wholesales	(chq 110746)	1039
	18	Sales	4437		5	Abbey Stationery Ltd	(chq 110747)	1631
	27	Sales	3375		18	General expenses	(chq 110748)	538
					31	Balance	c/d	11252
			18535					18535
June	1	Balance b/d	11252					

a Compare the two records.

b Tick all items that appear in both documents.

c Update the cash book balance at 1 June 2012.

d Prepare a bank reconciliation statement dated 1 June 2012.

11 The bank reconciliation process when there is an overdrawn bank balance

Mara Black, the owner of Best Value Carpets, has made the following records available for her business.

CITYCHOICE BANK plc

Bank statement for Best Value Carpets

Date		Details	Dr	Cr	Balance	
			$	$	$	
April	1	Balance			4 500	Dr
	5	800602 Mungroo Wholesale Ltd	2 300		6 800	Dr
	8	Cash and cheques		4 700	2 100	Dr
	14	DD Eastern Electricity Ltd	800		2 900	Dr
	18	800605 Taylor Textiles	1 400		4 300	Dr
	28	CHR	500		4 800	Dr

The business's cash book (bank columns) for the same month was as follows.

BOOKS OF BEST VALUE CARPETS

Cash book (bank columns only)

Dr								Cr
April	3	Sales	4 700	April	1	Balance		4 500
	28	Sales	4 200		2	Mungroo Wholesale Ltd	(chq 800602)	2 300
	30	Balance c/d	400		7	Drawings	(chq 800603)	400
					12	Rent	(chq 800604)	700
					13	Taylor Textiles	(chq 800605)	1 400
			9 300					9 300
				May	1	Balance	b/d	400

a Update the cash book balance at 1 May 2012.

b Prepare a bank reconciliation statement dated 1 May 2012.

12 The bank reconciliation process when there is an overdrawn bank balance

The bank statement and cash book (bank columns) for June 2012 have been made available by John Stevens, the owner of Cycle Stores.

SECURE BANK plc

Bank statement for Cycle Stores

Date		Details	Dr	Cr	Balance	
			$	$	$	
June	1	Balance			4 233	Dr
	6	Credit transfer: Cycle World Retail		1 220	3 013	Dr
	9	374112 Lakeford Ltd	1 885		4 898	Dr
	11	DD Regional Power Supplies plc	478		5 376	Dr
	16	CHR	612		5 988	Dr
	17	374116	675		6 663	Dr
	21	Cash and cheques		2 083	4 580	Dr
	26	374113	417		4 997	Dr
	28	SO Best Properties plc	840		5 837	Dr

The business's cash book (bank columns) for the same month was as follows.

BOOKS OF CYCLE STORES

Cash book (bank columns only)

Dr								**Cr**
June	17	Sales	2 083	June	1	Balance		4 233
	29	Sales	4 114		3	Lakeford Ltd	(chq 37412)	1 885
	30	Balance c/d	3 183		8	General expenses	(chq 37413)	417
					9	Water charges	(chq 37414)	630
					12	Castle Furnishings plc	(chq 37415)	592
					13	Drawings	(chq 37416)	675
					24	Lakeford Ltd	(chq 37417)	948
			9 380					9 380
				July	1	Balance	b/d	3 183

a Update the cash book balance at 1 July 2012.

b Prepare a bank reconciliation statement dated 1 July 2012.

c Explain why John Stevens' business benefits from the monthly preparation of bank reconciliation statements.

13 Working from a list of items – bank statement balance not stated

On 30 November 2012 the cashier at Eton Ltd discovered that the balance at bank as shown in the business's cash book did not agree with the balance shown on the bank statement. The balance shown in the cash book was $7432 (debit).

A comparison of the two records produced the following information:

- The bank had not yet recorded the total of cash and cheques, $1733, paid in on 29 November.
- A direct debit payment of $871 for electricity charges had been omitted from the cash book.

- Two cheques had not yet been presented for payment: T Pulchan $775 and KT Singh $903.
- No record had been made in the cash book of bank charges, $261, deducted from the Elton Ltd's account or interest of $50 which had been added to the account.

a Update Eton Ltd's cash book balance on 30 November 2012.

b Prepare a bank reconciliation statement dated 30 November 2012 that shows the original balance shown on the bank statement received on this date.

14 Working from a list of items – bank statement balance not stated

On 31 July 2012, Sophia Thomas received a bank statement for her business that showed a closing balance which differed from that recorded in her cash book. On this date the cash book balance was overdrawn by $885.

The following discrepancies between the two records were found:

- Bank charges of $96 had been omitted from the cash book.
- A cheque sent to a supplier, H Khan, for $947, did not appear on the bank statement.
- The bank statement showed a credit transfer of $1040 from a customer, Excel Products Ltd, which had not been recorded in the cash book.
- The bank had yet to record cash sales of $2108 paid in on 29 July 2012.
- A standing order payment of $481 for insurance premiums had not yet been recorded in the cash book.

a Update Sophia Thomas's cash book balance on 31 July 2012.

b Prepare a bank reconciliation statement dated 31 July 2012 that shows the original balance shown on the bank statement received on that date.

PREPARING FOR THE EXAMINATION

(The following questions cover Unit 23)

MULTIPLE-CHOICE QUESTIONS

15 For what reason is a bank reconciliation statement prepared?

A It allows the business's cashier to compare the business's cash book bank balance with the actual bank balance

B It allows the business's cashier to reconcile the petty cash balance with the bank balance

C It enables the bank to compare the business's receipts with the business's payments

D It enables the business's cashier to calculate the liquid capital

16 A business has just received a bank statement and the process of updating the cash book is underway. Which of the following items will increase the bank balance in the cash book?

A Bank charges

B Credit transfers received

C Direct debit payment

D Standing order payment

17 Raslinda was preparing her business's bank reconciliation statement and she was aware of the following details:

- Bank balance in the cash book, $6000 debit
- Unpresented cheques, $1500
- Amounts not yet credit by the bank, $900.

What is the balance shown on the bank statement?

A $1600

B $5600

C $6600

D $8400

18 The owner of a business has just updated his business's cash book on receipt of a bank statement. The owner will now prepare the bank reconciliation statement. Which of the following items should appear in this statement?

A Credit transfers received

B Direct debits

C Standing orders

D Unpresented cheques

19 The bank columns of a business's cash book showed a balance of $2000 credit. When the bank statement was received, the following additional entries were made in the bank columns of the cash book:

- Bank charges $600
- Interest received $400

What was the bank balance as shown by the updated cash book?

A $1000 credit

B $1800 credit

C $2200 credit

D $3000 credit

OTHER QUESTIONS

20 Samah has been comparing her cash book (bank columns) for May 2012 with her business's bank statement for this period. Her cash book shows a balance at bank of $840 on 31 May 2012.

She has noticed that a payment by cheque for $720 shown as a credit entry in her cash book appears correctly as a debit entry in the bank statement.

a Explain why items shown in the cash book are recorded differently in the bank statement.

Samah has identified the following items in her bank statement which have not yet been recorded in her cash book.

	$
Bank charges	90
Standing order payments	620
Bank interest received	50
Credit transfer from customer	880

b Prepare Samah's cash book at 31 May 2012 to find the updated balance.

Samah has noticed that the following items recorded in her cash book have not yet been recorded on the bank statement:

- A cheque in payment of a supplier, $550
- Cash sales paid into the bank on 30 May, $640

c Complete the following bank reconciliation statement at 31 May 2012.

	$
Balance as per updated cash book at 31 May 2012	
Unpresented cheque	
Amount not yet credited	
Balance as per bank statement at 31 May 2012	

d State two advantages of preparing bank reconciliation statements.

24 Control accounts

Introduction

The accounts of payables are kept in a purchases ledger and the accounts of receivables are kept in a sales ledger. In the books of account of some businesses, these ledgers can be very extensive, including possibly hundreds or even thousands of personal accounts. You can imagine how useful it would be if it was possible to check the accuracy of these two ledgers with simple processes that take only a few minutes to carry out. Fortunately, there are such processes. They are called 'control accounts' and they are explained in this unit.

LEARNING OUTCOMES

When you have reached the end of this unit you will be able to:

- describe why businesses use sales and purchases ledger control accounts
- identify the sources of information used for making control account entries
- prepare purchases ledger and sales ledger control accounts.

The sales ledger control account

A control account checks the arithmetical accuracy of part of the accounting system (in this case the sales ledger). It is made up of totals of all of the transactions that have been posted to that part of the accounting system (in this case transactions that affect credit customers).

KEY TERM

Sales ledger control account: a process for checking the arithmetical accuracy of the sales ledger.

Illustration 1 The idea behind a sales ledger control account

You are told the following:

- Total trade receivables at 1 January was $10 000.
- Total credit sales for the year were $100 000.
- Total amounts received from credit customers was $95 000.

It only takes a moment to work out that the total of all the trade receivables account balances at 31 December should be $15 000.

If you put this information in account form, it would look like this.

Dr		Cr	
	$		$
Opening balance	10 000	Receipts	95 000
Credit sales	100 000	Balance c/d	15 000
	110 000		110 000
Balance b/d	15 000		

This is a simple version of a **sales ledger control account**. You can see that the account is, in effect, a total trade receivables account.

The account shows that the total of the trade receivables accounts should be $15 000. You could then check with the sales ledger and see if all of the individual balances on the trade receivables accounts (and there could be many of them) total $15 000. If so, then it is assumed that the sales ledger has been prepared correctly.

24.1 Preparing sales and purchases ledger control accounts

Sales ledger control account

To check a sales ledger you need to make sure that the sales ledger control account contains the totals of all the transactions that have affected receivables. Here is a list of the most likely transactions. The list also shows where you would obtain the totals that you need to prepare the sales ledger control account.

Transactions	Source of information
Total credit sales	Sales journal
Total receipts	Cash book
Total discounts allowed	Cash book
Total sales	Sales returns journal
Sales journal	General journal

STUDY TIP

The sales ledger control account is only concerned with information about trade receivables. So, for example, do not enter cash sales in the control account.

Illustration 2 Preparing a sales ledger control account

At the end of March 2012, the owner of a business checked that the accuracy of the sales ledger. The following information was obtained relating to March 2012.

Transactions	Source of information	$
Total of trade receivables balances on 1 March	Control account for February	12 000
Total credit sales	Sales journal	83 000
Total receipts	Cash book	71 000
Total discounts allowed	Cash book	3 000
Total sales returns	Sales returns journal	4 000
Total bad debts	General journal	1 000

Here is the control account for March 2012.

Dr — Sales ledger control account — Cr

March	1	Opening balance b/d	12 000	March	31	Receipts	71 000
	31	Credit sales	83 000		31	Discounts allowed	3 000
					31	Sales returns	4 000
					31	Bad debts	1 000
					31	Balance c/d	16 000
			95 000				95 000
April	1	Balance b/d	16 000				

Notes:

1. A sales ledger control account always resembles a trade receivables account. However, the control account is not part of the double-entry accounting system.
2. The sales ledger control account tells you that the total of all trade receivables at 31 March should be $16 000. This should correspond to the total of all the balances in the sales ledger at that date.

You can now try question 1 on page 250.

Purchases ledger control account

The purchases ledger can also be checked using this system of taking totals from the books of original entry.

Here is a list of the most likely transactions to affect trade payables and the source of information for preparing the **purchases ledger control account**.

Transactions	Source of information
Total credit purchases	Purchases journal
Total payments	Cash book
Total discounts received	Cash book
Total purchases returned	Purchases returns journal

KEY TERM

Purchases ledger control account: a process for checking the arithmetical accuracy of the purchases ledger.

You can now try questions 2 to 4 on page 250.

Illustration 3 Preparing a purchases ledger control account

At the end of May 2012, the owner of a business checked the accuracy of the purchases ledger. The following information was obtained for May 2012.

Transactions	Source of information	$
Total of trade payables balances on 1 May	Control account for April	23 000
Total credit purchases	Purchases journal	61 000
Total payments	Cash book	57 000
Total discounts received	Cash book	2 000
Total purchases returns	Purchases returns journal	5 000

Here is the control account for May 2012.

Purchases ledger control account

Dr				Cr			
May	31	Payments	57 000	May	1	Opening balance b/d	23 000
	31	Discounts received	2 000		31	Purchases	61 000
	31	Purchases returns	5 000				
	31	Balance c/d	20 000				
			84 000				84 000
				June	1	Balance b/d	20 000

Notes:

1 A purchases ledger control account always resembles a trade payables account. However, the control account is not part of the double-entry accounting system.

2 The purchases ledger control account tells you that the total of all trade payables at 31 May should be $20 000. This should correspond to the total of all the balances in the purchases ledger at that date.

STUDY TIP

A purchases ledger account is only concerned with information about trade payables. So, far example, do not enter cash purchases in the control account.

Benefits of control accounts

Control accounts are very useful for the following reasons:

- They provide a quick **check on the arithmetical accuracy** of the sales and purchases ledgers.
- They provide **information about total trade receivables and total trade payables** for inclusion in a trial balance and end of year financial statements.
- They **help prevent fraud** because the work of the individuals who keep the sales and purchases ledger will be checked regularly by a more senior member of staff.

Limitations of control accounts

It is possible for the closing balance on a control account to match the total of the balances in the ledger, but for there still to be errors that have not been detected. For example there could be errors of commission in the sales ledger which would not have any effect on the total of sales ledger balances. There could also be errors of omission or original entry which would have the same impact on both records.

24.2 Other entries in control accounts

STUDY TIP

Always remember that a sales ledger control account resembles a total trade receivables account.

A purchases ledger control account resembles a trade payables account.

DID YOU KNOW?

Control accounts are sometimes called 'total accounts', for example 'sales ledger total account'.

There are some more unusual transactions that can affect the accounts of trade receivables and trade payables and that must, therefore, be taken into account when preparing control accounts.

Credit balances on sales ledger accounts

Occasionally a trade receivables account will have a credit balance. This may sound rather strange at first, but it can happen if a customer overpays their account.

Illustration 4 Trade receivables account with a credit balance

Jody Dass is a customer of Home Developments Ltd. The following transactions took place during June 2012.

June 12 Goods were sold to Jody, $850
June 29 Jody paid the amount due by cheque, $850

So on 29 June, Jody's account is cleared.

However, on 30 June Jody noticed that some of the goods sold to her on 12 June with a value of $120 were faulty. It would be necessary to make an entry for returns. When the account is balanced on 30 June it will appear as follows.

Jody Dass account

Dr							Cr
June	12	Sales	850	June	29	Bank	850
	30	Balance c/d	120		30	Sales returns	120
			95 000				95 000
				July	1	Balance b/d	120

In effect Jody has overpaid, and her account temporarily shows a credit balance. Home Developments Ltd may have to send Jody a cheque to refund the $120 that has been overpaid. If any sales ledger accounts have credit balances, this fact needs to be reflected when the sales ledger control account is prepared.

It is also possible that a trade payable account could show a debit balance. It follows that this will occur when a business overpays a supplier. Any debit balance on a trade payable account must be considered when preparing a purchases ledger control account.

Dishonoured (returned) cheques

A business can receive a cheque from a credit customer in payment of the amount due, only to find that the bank will not accept that cheque when it is paid into the business's bank account. This normally happens because the customer has insufficient funds in their own account to cover the amount of the cheque. In the business's books of accounts the entries for the receipt of the cheque are cancelled out as follows:

Debit	Trade receivables account
Credit	Bank column of cash book

As you know, any transaction that affects the account of a trade receivable must also be reflected in the sales ledger account. In the case of **dishonoured cheques** the information will be obtained from the cash book.

Contra entries

A business could find that one of its suppliers is also one of its customers. For example, a business that provides an office cleaning service could find that it purchases cleaning materials from one of its customers. Where this situation arises it is usual for only the net amount due to be paid off.

Illustration 5 Contra entries

During June, Webb's Cleaning Services purchased cleaning materials on credit from Deepclean Ltd, value $300. Webb's Cleaning Services also charged Deepclean Ltd $180 for cleaning the company's offices.

In this situation Webb's Cleaning Services can send a cheque to Deepclean Ltd for the net amount due, $120. This would happen after the balance in the sales ledger had been transferred to the purchases ledger. The accounts would then appear as follows:

PURCHASES LEDGER

Deepclean Ltd account

Dr							Cr
June	30	Deepclean Ltd (sales ledger)	180	June	12	Purchases	300
	30	Bank	120				
			300				300

SALES LEDGER

Deepclean Ltd account

Dr							Cr
June	17	Sales	180	June	30	Deepclean Ltd (purchases ledger)	180

Notes:

1. A journal entry should be used to record this transfer.
2. The effect of contra entries is to reduce the balance on each of the personal accounts involved.
3. Similar entries would be required if it was necessary to transfer the balance of the purchases ledger account to the sales ledger account.

Since a **contra entry** affects both the account of a receivable and of a payable, it will also need to be recorded in the sales ledger control account and purchases ledger control account.

Refunds

A **refund** occurs when money is returned to a trade receivable, perhaps because they have overpaid the amount due. Refunds to trade receivables are recorded as follows:

Debit	Trade receivable account
Credit	Bank account

It is also possible for a trade payable to pay a refund following an overpayment. Refunds from trade payables are recorded as follows:

Debit	Bank account
Credit	Trade payable

Where refunds occur entries need to be made in the control account and the information is obtained from the cash book.

STUDY TIP

Any contra entry must be recorded in both the sales ledger control account and the purchases ledger control account.

KEY TERM

Dishonoured cheque: a cheque that a bank will not accept for payment because the payee (individual making the payment) does not have enough funds in their account to cover the amount being paid.

Contra entry (control accounts): when a business deals with another business or organisation as both a customer and a supplier, the balances of the two accounts are set off against one another to find the net balance.

Refund: a repayment to a customer who has overpaid, or a repayment made by a supplier who has been overpaid.

More about preparing control accounts

Interest charged on overdue accounts

One way of trying to encourage credit customers to pay on time is to charge interest on overdue accounts. The double entry for any interest charged to the customer is:

Debit Trade receivables account
Credit Interest received account

Of course, a supplier may also encourage a business to settle their account more promptly by charging interest on overdue accounts.

Debit Interest charges account
Credit Trade payables account

A journal entry is required to initiate these entries. Interest received and interest charged will need to be shown in the relevant control account.

Sales ledger control account

Illustration 6 Preparing a more advanced sales ledger control account

Here are some details to be used in the preparation of a sales ledger control account.

Debit balances in the sales ledger on 1 November 2012	16 350
Credit balances in the sales ledger on1 November 2012	490
Credit sales	43 270
Sales returns	1 150
Receipts from trade receivables	37 240
Discounts allowed	680
Dishonoured cheques	300
Interest charged on overdue accounts	220
Refunds to trade receivables	70
Contra entries	480
Bad debts written off	510
Debit balances in the sales ledger on 30 November 2012	?
Credit balances in the sales ledger on 30 November 2012	130

Here is the sales ledger control account. The more unusual items are shown in bold.

Dr **Sales ledger control account** **Cr**

Nov	1	Opening balance	16 350	Nov	1	**Opening balance**	**490**
	30	Sales	43 270		30	Sales returns	1 150
	30	**Dishonoured cheques**	**300**		30	Bank	37 240
	30	**Interest charges**	**220**		30	Discounts allowed	680
	30	**Refunds**	**70**		30	Contras	480
	30	**Closing balance c/d**	**130**		30	Bad debts	510
					30	Closing balance c/d	19 790
			60 340				60 340
Dec	1	Balance b/d	19 790	Dec	1	**Balance b/d**	**130**

Purchases Ledger Control Account

Illustration 7 Preparing a more advanced purchases ledger control account

Here are some details to be used in the preparation of a purchase ledger control account.

Debit balances in the purchases ledger on 1 June 2012	520
Crebit balances in the purchases ledger on 1 June 2012	18 390
Credit purchases	26 880
Purchases returns	420
Payments to payables	19 750
Discounts received	770
Interest charged on overdue accounts	90
Refunds from trade payables	120
Contra entries	660
Debit balances in the purchases ledger on 30 June 2012	410
Credit balances in the purchases ledger on 30 June 2012	?

Here is the purchases ledger control account. The more unusual items are shown in bold.

Dr **Purchases ledger control account** **Cr**

June	1	**Opening balance**	**520**	June	1	Opening balance	18 390
	30	Purchases returns	420		30	Purchases	26 880
	30	Bank	19 750		30	**Interest charges**	**90**
	30	Discounts received	770		30	**Refunds**	**120**
	30	**Contras**	**660**		30	**Closing balance**	**410**
	30	Closing balance c/d	23 770				
			45 890				45 890
July	1	**Balance b/d**	**410**	July	1	Balance b/d	23 770

You can now answer questions 5–13 on pages 250–252.

When the control account balance and ledger account total do not agree

If the final balance of a sales ledger control account and the total of the balances in the sales ledger do not agree, this would indicate that there is an error (or errors) in the accounting system.

For example, an error could have made in a sales ledger account. Perhaps the sales ledger accounts clerk has misread a figure in the sales journal and entered this figure in a trade receivables account (e.g. in the sales journal the sale is recorded as $997, but it has been posted as $979).

Alternatively, perhaps the sales ledger control account is not correct. This could happen if there is an error in the total of one of the relevant books of prime entry because the entries have not been totalled correctly.

A similar set of explanations will apply if the purchases ledger control account balance does not agree with the total of the balances extracted from the purchases ledger.

Practice questions

DEVELOPING YOUR SKILLS

1 Preparing a sales ledger control account

Prepare a sales ledger control account for June 2012 from the following information.

Transactions	Source of information	$
Total of trade receivables balances on 1 June	Control account for May	9 000
Total credit sales	Sales journal	37 000
Total receipts	Cash book	31 000
Total discounts allowed	Cash book	3 000
Total sales returns	Sales returns journal	5 000
Total bad debts	General journal	1 000

2 Preparing a purchases ledger control account

Prepare a purchases ledger control account for the month ended 31 March 2012 from the following information.

Transactions	Source of information	$
Total of trade payables balances on 1 March	Control account for February	53 480
Total credit purchases	Purchases journal	185 920
Total payments	Cash book	161 310
Total discounts received	Cash book	4 370
Total purchases returns	Purchases returns journal	11 990

3 Preparing control accounts

The following information was extracted from a business's subsidiary books on 31 May 2012.

	$
Totals	
Sales journal	18 460
Purchases journal	11 270
Sales returns journal	980
Purchases returns journal	1 110
Cash book	
Receipts from trade receivables	16 440
Payments to trade payables	10 950
Discounts allowed	730
Discounts received	520
Journal	
Bad debts written off	400

On 1 May 2012 the following balances appeared in the control accounts:

- Purchases ledger control account $3 640
- Sales ledger control account $5 220

Prepare the business's control accounts for May 2012.

4 Preparing control accounts

The following information is to be entered in a business's control accounts for March 2012.

Transactions	$	Source of information
Bad debts written off	80	
Credit sales	63 490	
Credit purchases	42 110	
Discounts allowed	370	
Discounts received	260	
Payments to trade payables	39 650	
Purchases returns	580	
Receipts from trade receivables	59 120	
Sales returns	240	

On 1 March 2012 the following balances appeared in the control accounts:

- Purchases ledger control account $8 830
- Sales ledger control account $10 370

a Complete the column to show the source of each item of information required for the control accounts.

b Prepare the control accounts for March 2012.

5 Preparing a sales ledger account including other details

The following information is to be entered in a business's sales ledger control account for January 2012.

	$
Sales ledger balances at 1 January 2012	
Debit	7 400
Credit	230
Totals for the month:	
Credit sales	27 480
Sales returns	620
Receipts from trade receivables	21 930
Discounts allowed	330
Refunds to trade receivables	110
Bad debts	80
Interest charged on overdue accounts	70
Dishonoured (returned) cheques	190
Contras (sales ledger account balances transferred to the purchases ledger)	490
Sales ledger balances at 30 November 2012	
Debit	?
Credit	390

Prepare the sales ledger control account for January 2012.

The sales ledger clerk reported that the total of debit balances in the sales ledger on 31 January 2012 was $11 960. What conclusions should you draw from this information?

6 Preparing a purchases ledger account including other details

The following information is to be entered in a purchases ledger control account for October 2012.

	$
Purchases ledger balances at 1 October 2012	
Debit	830
Credit	31 620
Totals for the month	
Credit purchases	82 880
Purchases returns	5 370
Payments to trade payables	75 060
Discounts received	2 240
Refunds from trade payables	90
Interest charged on overdue accounts	250
Contras (purchases ledger balances transferred to the sales ledger)	270
Purchases ledger balances at 31 October 2012	
Debit	990
Credit	?

Prepare the purchases ledger control account for October 2012.

The purchases ledger clerk reported that the total of debit balances in the purchases ledger on 31 October 2012 was $31 760. What conclusions should you draw from this information?

PREPARING FOR THE EXAMINATION

(The following questions cover Unit 24)

MULTIPLE-CHOICE QUESTIONS

7 Which one of the following should be entered in a sales ledger control account?

A Cash sales
B Discounts allowed
C Discounts received
D Purchases

8 A sales ledger control account contained the following items at the end of the month

	$
Debit balance at beginning of the month	8 000
Credit sales for the month	12 500
Sales returns for the month	700
Cash received from receivables	9 600
Interest charged on overdue accounts for the month	150

How much was owed by credit customers at the end of the month?

A $10 050
B $10 350
C $11 450
D $11 750

9 Which one of the following should be entered in a purchases ledger control account?

A Cash purchases
B Discounts received
C Refunds to trade receivables
D Sales

10 What does the final balance on a correctly prepared purchases ledger control account represent?

A Profit on goods purchased and sold
B Total of cash purchases
C Total trade payables of the business
D Value of unsold purchases

OTHER QUESTIONS

11 The following entries were included in a business's sales ledger control account.

Which of the following shows a correct set of entries?

	Debit entries	Credit entries
A	Credit sales	Refunds to trade receivables Sales Discounts received
B	Credit sales Refunds to trade receivables	Discounts allowed Sales
C	Credit sales	Discounts received Sales Dishonoured cheques
D	Dishonoured cheques Cash sales	Receipts from trade receivables Discounts allowed

12 The owner of a business recently decided that it would be a good idea if control accounts were prepared at the end of each month.

a Identify and explain one benefit that would result from this decision.

Anthony is responsible for preparing purchases ledger and sales ledger control accounts for this business. On 30 April 2012 Anthony extracted the following information from the business's accounting records.

	$
Balances at 1 April 2012	
Sales ledger debit balance	14 790
Sales ledger credit balance	330
Purchases ledger debit balance	640
Purchases ledger credit balance	22 470
Sales	
Credit sales	51 830
Cash sales	22 450
Purchases	
Credit purchases	48 410
Cash purchases	8 350
Sales returns (from sales returns journal)	1 240
Purchases returns (from purchases returns journal)	930
Payments to trade payables	45 700
Receipts from trade receivables	52 600
Discounts allowed	440
Discounts received	760
Balances at 30 April 2012	
Sales ledger debit balance	?
Sales ledger credit balance	480
Purchases ledger debit balance	210
Purchases ledger credit balance	?

b Prepare a purchases ledger control account and sales ledger control account for April 2012. Select the relevant information from the details provided.

13 Cynthia has extracted the following details from her business's books of account on 31 January 2012.

	$
Balances at 1 January 2012	
Sales ledger debit balance	33 640
Sales ledger credit balance	730
Purchases ledger debit balance	440
Purchases ledger credit balance	29 780
Sales journal total for January 2012	95 460
Purchases journal total for January 2012	73 550
Sales returns journal total for January 2012	3 110
Purchases returns journal total for January 2012	4 830
General journal totals for January 2012	
Bad debts	970
Interest charged on customer's overdue accounts	80
Interest charged by supplier's on overdue accounts	140
Cash book totals for January 2012	
Receipts from trade receivables	85 370
Payments to trade payables	64 390
Cash sales	48 470
Cash purchases	3 260
Refunds to trade receivables who had overpaid their accounts	280
Dishonoured cheques received from trade receivables	730
Discounts allowed	1 140
Discounts received	2 080
Balances at 31 January 2012	
Sales ledger debit balance	?
Sales ledger credit balance	490
Purchases ledger debit balance	820
Purchases ledger credit balance	?

a Prepare a purchases ledger control account and sales ledger control account for January 2012. Select the relevant information from the information provided.

b Cynthia found that the debit balances on the sales ledger at 31 January 2012 did not agree with the balance of the sales ledger control account on that date. Identify and explain one reason why this may have happened.

25 Partnerships

Introduction

In this unit you will learn how to produce the accounting records required by partnerships.

What is a partnership?

A **partnership** is a form of business ownership in which there are at least two owners, called partners, who share the profits or losses made by the business.

Why form a partnership?

A partnership has several benefits that do not apply to a sole trader:

- There is the opportunity to raise more capital than would normally be possible if there was just one owner.
- The specialist skills and expertise of each partner can be brought together for the benefit of the business.
- With more than one owner, it may become easier to manage the business because the workload can be shared.

However, there are some disadvantages:

- Each partner will have **unlimited liability** for the debts of the business. This means that each partner is responsible for the debts of the partnership and could lose not just the capital contributed but also personal assets if the business fails. This is exactly the same disadvantage that is experienced by a sole trader.
- Decision making can be more difficult, or take longer, because the agreement of all the partners will be required to key aspects of running the business. Sometimes a good idea will not be implemented because one of the partners does not support it.
- All of the partners are jointly responsible for the debts of the partnership, even if an individual partner played no direct part in incurring the debt.
- A partnership business may be somewhat short-lived because it may have to close if one of the partners retires or dies.
- There has to be a high level of mutual trust between the partners. So for a partnership to be successful good relationships have to be maintained. This may not always be easy with the everyday stresses and strains of running a business.

LEARNING OUTCOMES

When you have reached the end of this unit you will be able to:

- explain the advantages and disadvantages of partnerships
- explain the importance of partnership agreements
- prepare appropriation accounts to show how profits or losses are shared among partners
- prepare ledger accounts to record partners' capitals
- prepare partners' current accounts to record drawings and shares of profits or losses
- record a partner's loan and loan interest
- prepare a partnership's income statement and balance sheet.

KEY TERM

Partnership: a form of business ownership where two or more individuals work together with the intention of making a profit.

Unlimited liability: in a partnership each partner is responsible for the debts of the partnership and could lose not just the capital contributed but also personal assets if the business fails. In the case of a sole trader, the owner could also lose not just the capital contributed but also personal assets if the business fails.

25.1 Sharing profits and losses

KEY TERM

Profit and loss sharing ratio: the ratio that is used to share any residual profit or loss of the partnership.

Normally partners make an agreement about how they intend to share the profits (or losses) made by the business and other key matters that could affect their relationship with each other. Once an agreement is made each partner must abide by its terms. It is usually considered wise for partners to have a formal written agreement because this can reduce the chance of disputes. However, this is not essential – the partners could just agree orally how they intend to share profit or losses.

Partners can make the profit/loss sharing arrangement very straightforward by simply agreeing to split profit or losses equally or in some other ratio, the **profit and loss sharing ratio**.

In addition partners will often agree:

- about the amount of capital to be invested in the business by each partner
- the responsibilities each partner will have in the management and running of the business
- a limit on each partner's drawings.

In many partnerships partners agree that the capital invested should be fixed, so that an individual partner cannot increase or decrease their capital contribution without the agreement of the other partners.

NUMERACY SKILLS

Reminder: how to work with ratios

It might be some time since you had to use ratios, so here is a reminder how to use ratios when working out answers in partnership accounts.

Step 1: Identify the ratio you are going to use (e.g. 5 : 3) and the profit/loss you are to divide in the ratio (e.g. $64 000).

Step 2: Add up each element in the ratio to give the number of 'parts' you are to use: 5 + 3 (i.e. 8 parts).

Step 3: Divide the profit (or loss) by the number of parts: $\frac{\$64\,000}{8}$. This would give $8000 per 'part'.

Step 4: Return to the ratio and take each element in turn to divide up the profit. So taking 5 parts first: the profit share would be 5 × $8000 = $40 000

Step 5: Take the other element(s) in the ratio. So taking 3 parts: the profit share would be 3 × $8 000 = $24 000.

Step 6: It is a good idea to do a double check to make sure the profit shares add up to the right figure. So: $40 000 + $24 000 = $64 000 – which is correct!

You can now answer questions 1 and 2 on page 262.

The formal written document drawn up by partners stating how they will work together and how they share profits and losses is called the **deed of partnership**.

It is quite common for partners to make more elaborate arrangements to ensure that partners are fairly rewarded for the various ways in which they have contributed to the business. There are a number of possibilities as follows:

- *Interest on capital*: each partner may be allocated a share of profits based on the relative size of their capital contributions. This is put into effect by giving each partner what is called **interest on capital** at some agreed rate per annum. As a result, the partner who has made the largest capital contribution receives a greater reward than the other partners who have contributed less.
- *Partnership salary*: a partner who has taken on a special role in the business and has, therefore, contributed more to the management and running of the partnership than the others, can be allocated an agreed amount of profit each year called a **partnership salary**.
- The partnership salary is a means of allocating some profit to a partner. This is not the same as an employee's salary, which would be charged as an expense in the income statement.

KEY TERM

Deed of partnership: the formal agreement between partners that states how profit and losses will be shared and the rules under which the partners will work together.

Interest on capital: a reward for each partner in the form of a share of profits that is based on the amount of capital contributed by each partner.

Partnership salary: a reward in the form of a share of profits for any partner who has particular responsibilities in running the business.

You can now answer questions 3 and 4 on page 262.

Illustration 1 Sharing profits and losses in a partnership

Rakesh and Stacy are in partnership sharing profits and losses in the ratio 2 : 1.

The partners' capital contributions are: Rakesh $100 000; Stacey $160 000.

The partners have agreed that there should be interest on capitals of 10 per cent per annum.

Stacy takes the most responsibility for managing the business. As a result the partners have agreed that Stacy should receive a partnership salary of $15 000 per annum.

During the year ended 31 October 2012 the partnership made a profit of $125 000.

Following the terms of their agreement, Rakesh and Stacy will share the profit of $124 000 as follows.

	Rakesh	Stacy
Profit to be shared $125 000	$	$
Interest on capitals (10% × capitals)	10 000	16 000
Salary		15 000
Residual profit ($125 000 less interest on capitals $26 000 and less salary $15 000) $84 000 shared in ratio 2 : 1	56 000	28 000
Total share of profits	66 000	59 000

Note: each reward given to a partner reduces the amount of profit left to be shared out.

KEY TERM

Residual profit: the profit of the partnership after all agreed rewards have been allocated to partners. (Residual *loss* is the loss of the partnership after all agreed rewards have been allocated.)

You can now try questions 5–8 on pages 262–263.

25.2 More about sharing profits and losses

KEY TERM

Interest on drawings: a penalty whereby a partner is charged interest on drawings. The interest takes account of the amount of the drawings.

- **Interest on drawings**: as well as rewarding partners for positive aspects of their contributions towards the success of the business, a partnership agreement can penalise partners for actions that could have had an adverse effect on the business's progress. Every time a partner takes cash drawings from the business, there is less money available to spend on running the business. As a result, some agreements contain a clause that charges each partner interest on drawings at a specified rate per annum. It should be noted that interest on drawings is *added* to the profit for the year. As 'rewards' for partners reduce the profit available for sharing, it follows that, as interest on drawings is a penalty (rather than a reward), the reverse should apply (i.e. it is added to profit).
- *Calculating interest on drawings*: often interest on drawings is calculated by multiplying a partner's total drawings for the year by the agreed interest percentage.

Illustration 2 Calculating interest on drawings

Ken and Jane are in partnership sharing profits and losses equally. However, they have agreed that interest of 5 per cent should be charged on drawings. During the year ended 31 December 2012, partners' drawings were:

	$
Ken	30 000
Jane	14 000

The partnership's profit for the year ended 31 December 2012 was $82 000.

Following the terms of their agreement, Ken and Jane will share the profit of $82 000 as follows.

	Ken	Jane
Profit to be shared $82 000	$	$
Interest on drawings(5% × drawings)	(1 500)	(700)
Residual profit ($82 000 **add** interest on drawings $2 200) $84 200 shared equally	42 100	42 100
Total share of profits	40 600	41 400

Notes:

1 Interest on drawings (as a penalty) increases the amount profit left to be shared out.

2 As a result of charging interest on drawings, Ken's total share of profits is less than Jane's. This reflects the fact that Ken deprived the business of more cash resources than Jane during the year.

LINKS...

See Illustration 3 for a further example of how interest on drawings is calculated and recorded in the books of a partnership.

What extra accounting records are required?

In most partnerships, the partners prefer to keep a separate record of their main capital contributions in a fixed capital account. Their drawings and shares of profits or losses are recorded in a separate current account. In addition, when preparing end-of-year financial statements, it is necessary to include a statement setting out how the profits and losses have been allocated.

The usual arrangement is as follows:

- *Drawings accounts*: recording each partner's drawings during the year. This account is closed at the year end and the total drawings are transferred to the partner's current account.
- *Capital accounts*: recording the main capital contribution of each partner and any additions or withdrawals of capital. Changes to a partner's fixed capital would be an unusual event and would normally have to be agreed by all of the partners.
- **Current accounts**: recording each partner's total drawings for the year and allocations of profits or losses at the year end. The balance of the current accounts can be:
  - credit (indicating that the partners are 'owed' money by the partnership because profit shares have exceeded drawings)
  - debit (indicating that the partners 'owe' money to the partnership because drawings have exceeded profit shares).
- **Appropriation account**: is prepared annually as part of the financial statements. The appropriation account records the profit or loss for the year (transferred from the income statement) and sets out the details of how the profit or loss is shared among the partners following the terms of the partnership agreement.

You can now answer questions 9 and 10 on pages 263–264.

KEY TERM

Current accounts: a record of each partner's annual drawings and shares of profits or loss.

Appropriation account: a part of the end-of-year income statements of a partnership recording how the profit or loss for the year is shared between the partners.

Fixed capitals: each partner's capital contribution remains unchanged unless all partners agree to an alteration.

Illustration 3 Preparing the partners' accounting records (part 1: information)

George and Huanna entered in partnership on 1 January 2012. The partners' **fixed capitals** are as follows:

	$
George	150 000
Huanna	180 000

The terms of the partnership agreement are:

- interest on total drawings is to be charged at 6 per cent per annum
- partners are entitled to interest on capitals at 10 per cent per annum
- Huanna should receive a salary of $16 000 per annum for taking a leading role in managing the business
- remaining profits or losses are to be shared in the ratio: George, Huanna – 3 : 2 respectively.

Partners' drawings totalled:

	$
George	32 000
Huanna	38 000

Interest on drawings will amount to the following.

		$
George	$32 000 × 6%	1 920
Huanna	$38 000 × 6%	2 280

During the year ended 31 December 2012 the partnership made a profit of $74 000. (Continued on page 258).

Preparing the accounting records

Note: you will see that in the example there is just one capital account, but with separate columns for each partner. This form of presenting partners' accounts has the advantage of saving time in making entries. It is recommended that this style of presentation is adopted rather than preparing individual accounts for each partner.

Illustration 3 (Continued) — Preparing the partners' accounts (part 2: the accounting records)

Step 1: Here are the capital accounts of the partners.

Capital accounts

Dr		George	Huanna				George	Huanna
		$	$				$	$ Cr
				Jan	1	Balances	150 000	180 000

Step 2: During the year each partner's drawings should be debited to the drawings account. At the year end the drawings account is closed off and the total drawings for the year are transferred to the current accounts.

Here are the drawings accounts of the partners.

Drawings accounts

Dr		George	Huanna				George	Huanna
		$	$				$	$ Cr
Jan–Dec	Bank	32 000	38 000	Dec	31	Current accounts	32 000	38 000

Step 3: At the end of the year the way profits and losses have been shared out between the partners is set out in detail as part of the end-of-year financial statements. It is important to follow strictly the terms of the partnership agreement.

Here is the appropriation account.

George and Huanna

Appropriation account for the year ended 31 December 2012

	$	$
Profit for the year		74 000
Add interest on drawings		
George	1 920	
Huanna	2 280	
		4 200
		78 200
Less interest on capitals		
George (10% × $150 000)	15 000	
Huanna (10% × $180 000)	18 000	
		(33 000)
		45 200

STUDY TIP

Do not forget to provide a full and correct title for all final accounting statements (e.g. 'Appropriation account for the year ended 31 December 2011'). Also, remember to bring down balances on current accounts as shown in the illustration.

George and Huanna

Appropriation account for the year ended 31 December 2012

	$	$
Less salary, Huanna		(16 000)
		29 200
Less shares of residual profit		
George (3/5ths)	17 520	
Huanna (2/5ths)	11 680	
		(29 200)

Note: it is usual to start by recording the interest on drawings first (as an addition) before dealing with the rewards (which are deducted). The account could be presented in a horizontal format. If this form of presentation is adopted, the profit for the year and interest on drawings will be credited, and the interest on capitals, salary and shares of residual profits will be debited.

Step 4: finally, prepare the current accounts of each partner, showing the profit shares allocated to each partner and also each partner's total drawings for the year.

Here are the partners' current accounts.

Dr — Current accounts — Cr

			George	Huanna				George	Huanna
			$	$				$	$
Dec	31	Drawings	32 000	38 000	Dec	31	Interest on capitals	15 000	18 000
	31	Interest on drawings	1 920	2 280		31	Salary		16 000
	31	Balance c/d		5 400		31	Residual profits	17 520	11 680
						31	Balance c/d	1 400	
			33 920	45 680				33 920	45 680
Jan	1	Balance b/d	1 400		Jan	1	Balance b/d		5 400

Notes:

1 Total drawings are transferred from the drawings account at the year end.

2 Interest on drawings is transferred from the appropriation account and is debited to the current accounts so that each partner is penalised.

3 Interest on capitals, partners' salaries and residual profit shares are credited to the current accounts so that each partner is rewarded.

4 Huanna has a credit balance on her current account because her drawings have been less than her total share of profits. Huanna is 'owed' $5 300 by the partnership.

5 George has a debit balance on his current account because his drawings has exceeded his profit share. George owes $1 400 to the partnership.

6 Once a partnership is established, each partner's current account will start with either a debit or credit balance brought forward from the previous year.

STUDY TIP

It is easy to forget that interest on drawings is an addition to the profit for the year in the appropriation account. It is a common mistake to deduct this item.

You can now answer questions 7 and 8 on page 263.

Partnership balance sheets

Partnership balance sheets

The balance sheet of a partnership will record assets and liabilities in exactly the same way as that of a sole trader. However, the capital section will need to reflect the fact that there are a number of owners and that each partner has a capital account and a current account.

Illustration 4 Preparing a partnership balance sheet

Here is the second part of the balance sheet based on the accounting records of George and Huanna in Illustration 3.

	$	$	$
Capital accounts	George	Huanna	
	150 000	180 000	330 000
Current accounts			
Interest on capitals	15 000	18 000	
Salary		16 000	
Residual profits	17 520	11 680	
	33 920	45 580	
Drawings	(32 000)	(38 000)	
Interest on drawings	(1 920)	(2 280)	
	(1 400)	5 400	4 000
			334 000

An alternative presentation of the balance sheet may be required, where only the final balances of the current accounts are shown. In this version, the second part of the balance sheet would appear as follows.

	$	$
Capital accounts		
George	150 000	
Huanna	180 000	
		330 000
Current accounts		
George	(1 400)	
Huanna	5 400	
		4 000
		334 000

Notes:

1. It is important to keep the capital accounts and the current accounts of the partners distinct in the second part of the balance sheet. So the capital account balances are shown with a subtotal line.
2. In the first version of the balance sheet the current accounts are shown in detail. Where this is required, provide each partner with a column and start the details with the opening balance (which could, of course, be negative). List all of the positive items first and then deduct negative items (such as drawings). The column should end with the current account balance at the balance sheet date. Use brackets to indicate negative figures.

KEY TERM

Partner's loan: amounts lent by a partner over and above, and quite separate from, the partner's capital contribution. Interest on the loan is charged to the income statement and credited to the partner's current account.

Partner's loans and the income statement

Sometimes a partner may make a loan to the partnership over and above any capital contribution. A **partner's loan** should be recorded as a non-current liability on the partnership balance sheet, assuming it is not due for repayment within the next financial year. The partner making the loan will expect to be rewarded with interest on the loan. The rate of interest will be agreed by all of the partners and will be recorded in the deed of partnership. From the accounting point of view it is important that the loan interest is recorded in the income statement just like all interest charges; it should not be recorded in the appropriation account. Interest on a partner's loan should be credited to the partner's current account because it increases the amount that the partnership owes the partner. In all other respects a partnership's income statement resembles that of a sole trader.

Here is a summary of how to treat a partner's loan.

	Double-entry records	
	Debit	**Credit**
When a partner makes a loan	Bank	Loan
When a partner's loan is repaid	Loan	Bank
When interest is given on a partner's loan	Income statement (expense)	Partner's current account

You can now answer questions 9–21 on pages 263–266.

Unit 25 Practice questions

DEVELOPING YOUR SKILLS

1 Calculating profit shares

Oliver, Penelope and Rajiv are planning to enter into partnership. They have not yet decided what profit/loss sharing ratio they should adopt. They have considered the following possibilities:

a Equal shares

b Oliver, Penelope, Rajiv – 5 : 3 : 2 respectively

c Oliver, Penelope, Rajiv – 4 : 2 : 1 respectively

They expect to make a profit of $63 000 during the first year.

Calculate each partner's share of this profit for each of the profit sharing arrangements a, b and c above.

2 Calculating profit shares

Jamal, Karen and Lewis are in planning to enter into partnership. They have not yet decided what profit/loss sharing ratio they should adopt. They have considered the following possibilities:

a equal shares

b Jamal, Karen and Lewis – 6 : 3 : 1 respectively

c Jamal, Karen and Lewis – 2 : 3 : 7 respectively

They expect to make a profit of $84 000 during the first year.

Calculate each partner's share of this profit for each of the profit sharing arrangements a, b and c above.

3 Calculating profit shares when there is interest on capitals and a partnership salary

Andy and Beverley are in partnership sharing profits and losses equally. They have agreed that each partner should be entitled to interest on capital at 10 per cent per annum and that Andy should be given a salary of $10 000 per annum for managing the business. The partners' capitals are:

	$
Andy	65 000
Beverley	72 000

Calculate each partner's share of the profit for the year ended 30 September 2012, when the partnership made a profit of $83 000.

4 Calculating profit shares when there is interest on capitals and a partnership salary

Robin, Sharla and Trevor are in partnership sharing profits and losses in the ratio 3 : 2 : 1. The partners have agreed that each partner should be entitled to interest on capital at 8 per cent per annum and that Shorla should be given a partnership salary of $9000 per annum. The partners' capitals are:

	$
Robin	200 000
Sharla	360 000
Trevor	240 000

Calculate each partner's share of the profit for the year ended 31 October 2012, when the partnership made a profit of $190 000.

5 Sharing profits and losses where there is interest on drawings

Keith and Louis are in partnership sharing profit and losses equally. However, the partners have agreed that interest should be charged on drawings at 12 per cent per annum.

During the year ended 31 December 2012 each partner's drawings was as follows:

	$
Keith	19 000
Louis	11 000

The partnership made a profit of $24 400 for the year ended 31 December 2012.

Calculate the following:

a Interest on Keith's drawings

b Interest on Louis's drawings

c Each partner's share of the profits for the year ended 31 December 2012

6 Sharing profits and losses where there is interest on drawings

Jackie and Keri are in partnership sharing profit and losses in the ratio 2 : 1 respectively. However, the partners have agreed that interest should be charged on drawings at 6 per cent per annum.

During the year ended 31 December 2012 each partner's drawings was as follows:

	$
Jackie	15 000
Keri	22 000

The partnership made a profit of $33 780 for the year ended 31 December 2012.

Calculate the following:

a Interest on Jackie's drawings

b Interest on Keri's drawings

c Each partner's share of the profits for the year ended 31 December 2012

7 Preparing partners' accounts

Donna and Elwin entered in to partnership on 1 January 2012. The partners agreed that:

a interest on total drawings should be charged at 7 per cent per annum

b each partner should receive interest on fixed capitals of 10 per cent per annum

c Elwin should receive an annual salary of $12000

d remaining profits or losses should be shared equally.

The following additional information is available.

	Fixed capitals	Drawings for the year ended 31 December 2012
	$	$
Donna	160 000	22 000
Elwin	140 000	24 000

The partnership made a profit of $58 000 during the year ended 31 December 2012.

Prepare the following:

a Partners' capital accounts

b Partners' drawings accounts

c Appropriation account for the year ended 31 December 2012

d Partners' current accounts

8 Preparing partners' accounts

Nicholas and Penelope entered into partnership on 1 April 2011. The partners agreed that:

- interest on total drawings should be charged at 12 per cent per annum
- interest should be allowed on fixed capitals at 10 per cent per annum
- Nicholas should receive a salary of $60 000 per annum
- remaining profits and losses should be shared in the ratio Nicholas, Penelope – 3 : 2 respectively.

The following additional information is available.

	Fixed capitals	Drawings for the year ended 31 March 2012
	$	$
Nicholas	360 000	75 000
Penelope	600 000	91 000

The partnership made a profit of $216 000 during the year ended 31 March 2012.

Prepare the following:

a Partners' capital accounts

b Partners' drawings accounts

c Appropriation account for the year ended 31 March 2012

d Partners' current accounts

9 Preparing end-of-year financial statements of a partnership including a partner's loan

Ishaka and Joshua are in partnership sharing profits and losses: Ishaka 60 per cent, Joshua 40 per cent.

At the end of the financial year, 30 September 2012, the following balances were extracted from the books of the partnership after calculation of the gross profit for the year.

Trial balance at 30 September 2012

	Dr	Cr
	$	$
Capital accounts		
Ishaka		240 000
Joshua		200 000
Cash at bank	31 000	

Current accounts		
Ishaka	4000	
Joshua		7000
Drawings		
Ishaka	47000	
Joshua	35000	
General expenses	68000	
Gross profit		237000
Inventory	63000	
Loan account (Ishaka)		40000
Non-current assets		
Cost	820000	
Provision for depreciation at 1 October 2011		340000
Trade payables		24000
Trade receivables	20000	
	1088000	1088000

Additional information:

- Non-current assets should be depreciated by 20 per cent per annum using the reducing balance method.
- General expenses due but unpaid at 30 September 2012 totalled $5000.
- The partners have decided that it is necessary to create a provision for doubtful debts amounting to 5 per cent of trade receivables at 30 September 2012.

The partnership agreement includes the following terms:

- Ishaka is entitled to interest of 10 per cent per annum on her loan.
- interest is charged on drawings. For the year under review interest on drawings amounts to: Ishaka, $4700; Joshua $3500.
- Joshua is to receive a partnership salary of $28000 per annum.

Prepare:

a An income statement for the year ended 30 September 2012

b An appropriation account for the year ended 30 September 2012

c Partners' current accounts

d A balance sheet at 30 September 2012. The balance sheet should show only the balances on the partners' current accounts at this date

10 End-of-financial-year statements of a partnership

Geeta and Henry are in partnership sharing profits and losses. The following trial balance was extracted from the business's books of account on 31 August 2012, the last day of the partnership's financial year.

Trial balance at 31 August 2012

	Dr	Cr
	$000	$000
Bank overdraft		7
Capital accounts		
Geeta		250
Henry		300
Current accounts		
Geeta	6	
Henry		8
Discounts	11	15
Drawings		
Geeta	40	
Henry	60	
Furniture and equipment		
Cost	220	
Provision for depreciation, 1 September 2011		66
General expenses	19	
Gross profit		291
Inventory, 31 August 2012	68	
Loan from Geeta		20
Premises at cost	660	
Provision for doubtful debts, 1 September 2011		6
Insurance	27	
Trade payables		18
Trade receivables	40	
Wages and salaries	139	
	1351	1351

Additional information (figures are shown in $000):

- Insurance $3 was prepaid at 31 August 2012.
- Wages and salaries due but unpaid totalled $12 at 31 August 2012.
- Depreciation should be provided on furniture and fittings at 20 per cent per annum using the straight-line method.
- The provision for doubtful debts should be maintained at 5 per cent of trade receivables.

The partnership agreement includes the following terms:

- Geeta is entitled to receive interest on her loan at 5 per cent per annum.
- Interest should be charged on total drawings at 10 per cent per annum.
- Geeta is entitled to receive a partnership salary of $28 per annum.
- Partners are entitled to receive interest on capital at the rate of 10 per cent.

Prepare:

a An income statement for the year ended 31 August 2012

b An appropriation account for the year ended 31 August 2012

c Partners' current accounts

d A balance sheet at 31 August 2012. The balance sheet should show only the balances on the partners' current accounts at this date

PREPARING FOR THE EXAMINATION

(The following questions cover Unit 25)

MULTIPLE-CHOICE QUESTIONS

11 A partnership appropriation account should include the following:

A Shares of residual loss, partnership salaries, drawings, interest on partners' loans

B Shares of residual loss, partnership salaries, interest on partners' loans, interest on partners' loans

C Shares of residual profit, partnership salaries, drawings, interest on capitals

D Shares of residual profit, partnership salaries, interest on drawings, interest on capitals

12 Fred and Garca are in partnership sharing profits and losses in the ratio 3 : 2 respectively. This year the partnership has made a loss of $90 000. Which entry should be made in Fred's current account?

A Credit $36 000

B Credit $54 000

C Debit $36 000

D Debit $54 000

13 Sara and Tarek are in partnership. They share profits and losses equally, but Tarek is entitled to receive a partnership salary of $18 000 per annum. The partnership made a profit of $72 000 this year. What is the total amount that should be credited to Tarek's current account?

A $27 000

B $36 000

C $45 000

D $54 000

14 Which of the following is debited to a partnership appropriation account?

A Interest on drawings

B Interest on a partner's loan

C Partner's salary

D Share of loss

15 Tina and Unitali are in partnership sharing profits and losses equally. Both partners are entitled to receive a partnership salary: Tina $15 000 and Unitali $5 000. This year the partnership made a small profit of $10 000.

What is Tina's net share of the partnership's profit for the year?

A $2 500

B $5 000

C $10 000

D $20 000

16 Martin and Nancy are in partnership with capitals of $240 000 and $120 000 respectively. The partners are entitled to interest on capital at 10 per cent per annum and remaining profits are shared equally. For the year ended 31 December 2012, the business made a profit of $144 000.

What is Martin's total share of profits from the business for the year ended 31 December 2012?

A $54 000

B $72 000

C $78 000

D $96 000

17 Yeung and Zara are partners in a business. The following current account of Yeung has been prepared by an inexperienced bookkeeper.

	$		$
Interest on capital	36 000	Balance b/d	1 500
Salary	45 000	Drawings	75 000
Balance c/d	85 500	Profit	90 000
	166 500		166 500

Assuming Yeung's opening balance is correctly recorded, what is the correct closing balance on his current account?

A $25 500

B $67 500

C $82 500

D $97 500

18 In the books of a partnership, which account should be debited with interest on drawings?

A Appropriation account

B Bank account

C Partners' current accounts

D Partners' drawings accounts

19 In the books of a partnership, the ledger entries for interest on drawings should be:

A Debit Appropriation account
Credit Partners' current accounts

B Debit Partners' current accounts
Credit Appropriation account

C Debit Partners' current accounts
Credit Partners' drawings accounts

D Debit Partners' drawings accounts
Credit Partners' current accounts

20 During the year ended 31 October 2012, the partnership of Electra and Farad made a profit of $85 000. Partners share profits equally after charging interest on drawings. For the year ended 31 October 2012, interest on drawings was: Electra $4 000 and Farad $7 000.

What was Farad's net share of the profits for the year?

A $30 000

B $41 000

C $44 000

D $55 000

OTHER QUESTIONS

21 Kirk and Linda recently agreed to form a partnership.

a State two possible problems that Kirk and Linda might experience by being in partnership.

Kirk and Linda prepared a deed of partnership which included an agreement to give each partner interest on capital, but to charge interest on drawings.

b Give one reason why the partners have agreed to give each partner interest on capital.

c Give one reason why the partners have agreed to charge interest on drawings.

The following appropriation account was prepared at the end of the partners' first financial year:

Kirk and Linda

Appropriation account
for the year ended 31 December 2012

	$	$
Profit for the year		65 000
Add interest on drawings		
Kirk (5% × $26 000)	1 300	
Linda (5% × $18 000)	900	
		2 200
		67 200
Less interest on capitals		
Kirk (10% × $80 000)	8 000	
Linda (10% × $60 000)	6 000	
		(14 000)
		53 200
Less shares of residual profit		
Linda	26 600	
Kirk	26 600	
		(53 200)

d Prepare the partners' current accounts for the year ended 31 December 2012.

Limited companies

Introduction

In this unit you are going to learn how to prepare the end-of-year financial statements of limited companies. You will learn about how a company is financed by issuing shares and by a special type of loan called a debenture, and about the special advantage of limited liability which is given to the owners of limited liability companies (i.e. the shareholders.)

'Limited company' is a convenient shortening of the more technically correct term **limited liability company**.

What is a limited company?

A limited company is a form of business organisation whose capital is divided into units called shares. Those who invest in a company own shares and are referred to as **shareholders**.

The most important feature of ownership of a limited company is that each shareholder's responsibility for the debts of the organisation is limited to the amount invested in the company. This means that should the organisation run into serious difficulties and face closure, shareholders cannot be asked to make any further contribution so that the company can pay its debts. This is in contrast to a sole trader or a partner who would have to use private funds if their business faced this situation. The correct term for this special privilege enjoyed by shareholders is **limited liability**, hence the term limited liability company. Individuals are far more likely to be inclined to invest in a company as a result of the benefit of limited liability because there is a clear limit to the risk they are taking. As a result, companies can be very large organisations with many shareholders, almost all of whom do not play any part in the day-to-day running of the organisation.

LEARNING OUTCOMES

When you have reached the end of this unit you will be able to:

- explain the meaning of the term 'limited liability'
- explain the terms 'authorised capital', 'issued capital', 'called-up share capital' and 'paid-up share capital'
- explain the differences between ordinary shares, preference shares and debentures
- calculate dividends
- prepare a company's appropriation account
- prepare a company's balance sheet.

KEY TERM

Limited liability company: an organisation owned by its shareholders whose liability for the debts of the company is limited to their shareholding.

Shareholders: the owners of the share capital of a limited company.

Limited liability: the liability of any shareholder for the debts of the company is limited to the amount of their shares.

26.1 Limited companies: the background

DID YOU KNOW?

Ltd and plc are used in the UK. However, different terminology may be found in some countries. For example, Pty Ltd or SA is used in some African countries, and Inc. is used in the US.

KEY TERM

Private limited company: a company whose shares are not available to the general public. The name of the company includes the abbreviation Ltd (limited).

Public limited company: a company whose shares are available to the general public. The name of the company includes the abbreviation plc (public limited company).

Authorised share capital: the maximum amount of share capital that a limited company may issue.

Issued share capital: the amount of share capital that has actually been issued by a limited company.

Directors: individuals who are appointed by shareholders to manage the company on their behalf.

Annual general meeting (AGM): a yearly meeting of shareholders where directors report on the performance of the company.

Ordinary shares: shares that receive a variable rate of dividend that is dependent on the profits available for distribution. These shares have voting rights.

Types of limited company

A **private limited company** is one where the ownership of shares is restricted to members of a family, their friends and possibly employees. They are generally small organisations with few shareholders. Members of the general public cannot invest in a private limited company. Shares in a private limited company are bought and sold privately and only with the consent of all the existing shareholders. A private limited could have just one shareholder. The abbreviation 'Ltd' appears in the title of a private limited company.

A **public limited company** is one in which the general public can invest. Shares in a public limited company are traded on stock exchanges. They are large organisations with hundreds or even thousands of shareholders. The abbreviation 'plc' appears in the title of a public limited company.

The capital of a limited company

When a limited company is formed a decision has to be made as to the maximum amount of capital that can be raised. This amount is known as the **authorised share capital**. It is not necessary to actually raise this amount immediately because initially the company will not require resources of that value. The capital actually raised is called the **issued share capital**.

The management of a limited company

Although shareholders are the owners of a limited company, most of them will not take part in the day-to-day running of the company. Instead, shareholders appoint **directors** to manage the company. Directors report to shareholders every year at an **annual general meeting (AGM)**. At this meeting shareholders take part in the election of directors.

Shares

Ordinary shares

All companies have **ordinary shares** which are also called *equity shares*.

- Ordinary shares have a face value or *nominal value*. Many ordinary shares have a nominal value of $1, but it is possible for shares to have a face value of, say, 50c, $2, etc.
- The owner of an ordinary share would expect to be rewarded for investing in the company by receiving an annual payment called a **dividend**. The amount of the annual dividend will depend partly on how much profit the company makes and partly on how the much the directors feel the company can afford to pay.

- Ordinary shares have voting rights that can be used at the AGM, for example in the election of directors.

Preference shares

Some companies also issue **preference shares**.

- Preference shares also have a nominal value (e.g. $1) and preference shareholders also expect to receive a dividend.
- However, the amount of dividend that can be paid to a preference shareholder is a fixed percentage of the amount invested. Preference shareholders are entitled to receive their fixed dividend as long as the company has made a profit.
- Preference shareholders are allocated their dividend before the allocation of a dividend to ordinary shareholders, and they would have their investment returned before ordinary shareholders should the company be wound up – hence the term 'preference' share.
- However, preference shareholders do not normally have any voting rights.

KEY TERM

Dividend: the reward paid to shareholders out of the profits of a limited company.

Preference shares: shares that are entitled to receive a fixed rate of dividend and that are ranked before ordinary shares for the payment of a dividend.

Called-up share capital: the part of the issued share capital of a company for which payment has been requested.

Paid-up share capital: the part of the called up share capital of a company for which payment has been received.

Issuing shares

When a company issues shares, the directors might decide that the full amount should be paid immediately. Alternatively, shareholders can be asked to pay for shares in instalments. The instalments that are due make up the **called-up share capital** of the company. The amounts actually received from shareholders make up the **paid-up share capital** of the company.

Illustration 1 Issuing shares

Albrex Ltd was formed on 1 January 2012 with a maximum capital of 100 000 6 per cent preference shares of $1 each and 800 000 ordinary shares of $1 each. On that date all of the preference shares and three-quarters of the ordinary shares were issued. Shareholders were required to pay in full for the preference shares on that date and to pay 50c per share for the ordinary shares. By 15 January 2012 all of the amounts due on the preference shares had been received and 90 per cent of the amount due on the ordinary shares had been received.

Here is a summary of Albrex's capital at 15 January 2012.

	Total $	Breakdown and calculations
Authorised capital	900 000	$800 000 in ordinary shares $100 000 in preference shares
Issued capital	700 000	$600 000 in ordinary shares (i.e. 75% × $800 00) $100000 in preference shares
Called-up share capital	400 000	$300 000 from ordinary shareholders (i.e. 50% × $600 000) $100 000 from the preference shareholder
Paid-up share capital	370 000	$270 000 from ordinary shareholders (i.e. 90% × $300 000) $100 000 from the preference shareholder

You can now answer questions 1 and 2 on page 279.

26.2 Limited company income statements and dividend calculations

KEY TERM

Debentures: long-term loans that carry a fixed rate of interest which must be paid each year and which is charged to the company's income statement.

Debentures

Debentures are a form of loan to a limited company. Debentures have a fixed rate of interest which is paid annually, usually in two six-monthly instalments. Debenture interest must be paid whether or not the company is making a profit. The interest is treated as an expense, just like any other interest payment, so it is charged to the company's income statement.

It is important to avoid confusing debentures, which are liabilities, with ordinary shares and preference shares, which are part of the capital of the company.

Debentures are repaid sometime in the future, but share capital is not repaid. So when debentures are issued, the date of repayment is normally clearly stated, so '8 per cent debentures 2020' refers to debentures with an 8 per cent interest rate which will be repaid in 2020. If a company should be wound up, debenture holders are repaid before preference shareholders and before ordinary shareholders.

The income statement

A limited company's income statement is very similar to that of a sole trader or a partnership. However, the following expenses will be included:

- Directors' fees and salaries: these are amounts paid to the directors for the work they do in running the company. They are also referred to as directors' remuneration
- Debenture interest

Illustration 2 Preparing a limited company's income statement

Riverflow Ltd's most recent financial year ended on 31 December 2012. On that date the following information was available.

	$
Business expenses	73 700
Cost of sales	104 800
Debenture interest	see note
Directors' salaries	62 400
Revenue	415 000

The company borrowed $80 000 in the form of 8 per cent debentures some years ago.

Here is the company's (summarised) income statement.

Riverflow Ltd

Income Statement for the year ended 31 December 2012

	$	$
Revenue		415 000
Less cost of sales		(104 800)
Gross profit		310 200
Less expenses		
Business expenses	73 700	
Debenture interest (8% × $80 000)	6 400	
Directors' salaries	62 400	
		(142 500)
Profit for year		167 700

You can now answer questions 3 and 4 on page 279.

Dividends

A company's directors must decide how any profits made by the company are to be used. If the company has profits, the directors must use some of the profits to finance the payment of the fixed preference share dividend. Any remaining profits can be used to finance an ordinary share dividend or they can be retained in the company. When directors announce dividends they have to bear in mind that will this will lead to a cash payment to shareholders. Directors have to consider not just whether the company has been profitable but also whether the company will have sufficient cash funds to pay the dividends. The directors may feel that some of the cash that would be spent on dividends could be better used for the benefit of the company. For example, the directors could be thinking of purchasing new non-current assets or replacing some existing non-current assets that are coming to the end of their life. It is possible that these decisions have already been made and the cash has already been spent.

Dividend calculations

You can now answer questions 5 and 6 on page 280.

Dividends are always based on the nominal value of the issued share capital of the company. Dividends can be expressed as a percentage of the issued share capital or as an amount per share.

KEY TERM

Retained earnings: profits that have not been used to finance the payment of dividends or have been transferred to a general reserve.

General reserve: part of the undistributed profits that have not been distributed as dividends and are set aside for some future use.

Illustration 3 Calculating preference share dividends

A company's authorised capital includes 150 000 8 per cent preference shares of $1 each. The company has issued 100 000 of these shares.

The annual dividend on preference shares is:

8% × issued capital ($100 000), i.e. $8000

Illustration 4 Calculating ordinary share dividends

A company's authorised capital includes 800 000 ordinary shares of $1 each. The company has issued half of these ordinary shares. The directors have announced an ordinary share dividend of 10 per cent.

The ordinary share dividend is:

10% × issued capital ($400 000), i.e. $40 000

Illustration 5 More dividend calculations

A company's authorised capital consists of 900 000 shares of $0.50 each. The company's issued capital is $400 000. The directors have announced a dividend of $0.05 per share.

Step 1: Calculate the number of issued shares.

Since the shares are$0.05 each, and the total issued capital is $400 000, the directors must have issued 800 000 shares.

Step 2: Calculate the ordinary share dividend.

800 000 × $0.05, i.e. $40 000

Undistributed profits

Any profits not distributed by the directors remains as a balance of undistributed profits called **retained earnings**. In future years these retained earnings can be used to finance dividends if the directors so desire. Directors can transfer some of the undistributed profits to what is called a **general reserve**. This would indicate to shareholders that the directors are not likely to use these profits for dividend purposes in the future and that they wish to strengthen the company's financial position.

26.3 The appropriation account and balance sheet of a limited company

The appropriation account

The directors' decisions about the distribution of profits are set in out in what is called an appropriation account, which is part of the company's end-of-year financial statements.

Illustration 6 | Preparing a company's appropriation account

Quendrill Ltd has an authorised capital consisting of 80 000 6 per cent preference shares of $1 each and 600 000 ordinary shares of $1 each. The directors have issued all of the preference shares and 400 000 of the ordinary shares.

During the year ended 31 December 2012 the company made a profit of $185 000. The directors have recommended the payment of the preference share dividend for the year and an ordinary share dividend of $0.20 per share. The directors have also decided to make a transfer of $70 000 to a general reserve.

On 31 December 2011 the company had retained earnings of $80 000.

Here is the company's appropriation account.

Quendrill Ltd

Appropriation account for the year ended 31 December 2012

	$	$
Profit for the year		185 000
Less:		
Proposed preference share dividend (6% × $80 000)	4 800	
Proposed ordinary share dividend (400 000 × $0.20)	80 000	
Transfer to general reserve	70 000	
		154 800
Retained earnings for the year ended 31 December 2012		30 200
Add: retained earnings from previous year		80 000
Retained earnings to carry forward		110 200

Notes:

1 Directors' recommendations about dividends have to be formally agreed by shareholders at the AGM, so until that happens dividends are 'proposed'.

2 The vertical form of presentation is preferred, but the account could be presented in horizontal format. Where this layout is preferred:

- debit entries are made for: the proposed dividends, the general reserve and the retained earnings to carry forward
- credit entries are made for: the profit for the year, the retained earnings brought forward from the previous years.

You can now answer questions 7 and 8 on pags 280–281.

The balance sheet

The balance sheet of a limited company resembles that of a sole trader or partnership. However, there are some important differences:

- Current liabilities should include any proposed dividends.
- Non-current liabilities include debentures.
- The capital section will show details of issued capital and undistributed profits (the general reserve and retained earnings).
- A note is provided of the authorised capital.

Illustration 7 Preparing a company balance sheet

Sentrex Ltd has an authorised capital of 100 000 7 per cent preference shares of $1 each and 900 000 ordinary shares of $0.50 each. On 31 December 2012 the following information was available.

	$
10% debentures 2024	120 000
Accruals	600
Cash at bank	16 700
General reserve	60 000
Inventories	30 000
Issued capital	
100 000 7% preference shares of $1 each fully paid	100 000
700 000 ordinary shares of $0.50 each fully paid	350 000
Non-current assets	
Cost	800 000
Provision for depreciation	130 000
Prepayments	300
Proposed dividends	
Preference share dividend	7 000
Ordinary share dividend	35 000
Retained earnings	47 200
Trade payables	7 000
Trade receivables	9 800

Here is the company's balance sheet.

Sentrex Ltd
Balance Sheet at 31 December 2012

	$	$	$
		Accumulated depreciation	Net book value
NON-CURRENT ASSETS	Cost		
	800 000	130 000	670 000
CURRENT ASSETS			
Inventory	30 000		
Trade receivables	9 800		
Prepayments	300		
Cash at bank	16 700		
		56 800	
CURRENT LIABILITIES			
Trade payables	7 000		
Accrual: debenture interest payable	600		
Proposed dividends: ordinary shares	35 000		
Proposed dividends: preference shares	7 000		
		(49 600)	
Net current assets			7 200
			677 200
NON-CURRENT LIABILITIES			
10% debentures 2024			(120 000)
Net assets			557 200
SHARES AND RESERVES			
Authorised share capital			
900 000 ordinary shares of $0.50 each			450 000
100 000 7% preference shares of $0.50 each			100 000
Issued share capital			
700 000 ordinary shares of $0.50 each fully paid			350 000
100 000 7% preference shares of $1 each fully paid			100 000
General reserve			60 000
Retained earnings			47 200
Total equity			557 200

Notes:

1. The authorised capital appears as a note on the balance sheet, so the figures are not included in the balance sheet total.
2. Ordinary shares should precede preference shares.
3. The vertical form of presentation is preferred. The balance sheet could be produced in horizontal form. If this layout is used the subheadings will appear as follows:
   - Left-hand side: non-current assets and current assets
   - Right-hand side: authorised capital (as a note), shares and reserves, non-current liabilities and current liabilities.

You can now answer questions 9–10 on page 281.

26.4 International standards and company financial statements

Note: this section covers material that is *not* currently examined by the syllabus. The information is provided for interest and because at some future date it may be directly relevant to those preparing for examinations.

Some changes to company financial statements

The International Accounting Standards (IASs) have made some changes to the way in which the financial statements of limited companies are presented. The important points to note are that:

- the income statement shows a figure for **operating profit** (this is profit before deducting interest charges), as well as the profit (or loss) for the year
- proposed dividends are *not* shown in the financial statements
- only dividends paid during the accounting year are shown in the financial statements
- transfers to reserves are no longer recorded
- the appropriation account is no longer prepared
- companies are required to prepare a **statement of changes in equity**
- the capital and reserves section of the balance sheet is headed '**Equity**'.

KEY TERM

Operating profit: profit before the deduction of interest charges.

Statement of changes in equity: a record of changes to retained earnings during a year.

Equity: the heading used for the capital and reserves section of a limited company's balance sheet.

Statement of changes in equity

Statements of changes in equity have replaced the appropriation account. The statement shows how retained profits have changed during a financial year. The statement records dividends actually paid during the year. Proposed dividends are no longer shown in financial statements. The main elements in the equity statement are, therefore:

- retained earnings at the beginning of the year
- profit or loss for the year
- dividends paid during the year
- retained earnings at the end of the year.

Illustration 8 Preparing a statement of changes in equity

Cortexic Ltd's financial year ended on 31 December 2012. The following information is available:

- At 1 January 2012 the company had retained earnings of \$275 000.
- During the year ended on 31 December 2012 the company made a profit of \$112 000.

- The directors paid an ordinary share dividend of $0.05 per share. The issued share capital of the company consists of 600 000 ordinary shares of $1 each.

Here is the statement of changes in equity.

Cortexic Ltd
Statement of changes in equity for the year ended 31 December 2012

	Retained Earnings
	$
Retained earnings, 1 January 2012	275 000
Add profit for the year	112 000
Less ordinary share dividend paid	(90 000)
Retained earnings, 31 December 2012	297 000

DID YOU KNOW?

A full statement of changes in equity would have columns to show changes (if any) in ordinary share issued capital, preference share issued capital, and changes in any other reserves. However, the illustration covers matters arising from the current syllabus.

You can now answer questions 11 and 12 on pages 281–282.

Income statements and balance sheets

The following illustration shows the other important changes in a company's financial statements arising from the IASs.

Illustration 9 Extracts from a company's end-of-year financials statements

The following extracts have been taken from the financial statements of Exquise Ltd.

Exquise Ltd
Income statement for the year ended 31 December 2012

	$	$
Revenue		960 000
Cost of sales		(468 700)
Gross profit		491 300
Less expenses		
Administration expenses	37 300	
Depreciation of non-current assets	53 800	
Wages and salaries	114 900	
		(206 000)
Operating profit		**285 300**
Finance costs		**(29 500)**
Profit for the year		**255 800**

Note: the bold section shows the important changes to note: operating profit, the deduction of 'finance costs' (such as debenture interest and also preference share dividends paid) before the figure for profit for the year.

Note: The bold items illustrate the important changes:

- Current liabilities no longer includes any reference to proposed dividends.
- 'Equity' is used as the heading of the capital and reserves section; total equity is used to describe the total of that section.

You can now answer questions 13–20 on pages 282–284.

Statement of changes in equity for the year ended 31 December 2012

	Retained earnings
	$
Retained earnings, 1 January 2012	280 000
Add profit for the year	260 000
Less ordinary share dividend paid	(200 000)
Retained earnings, 31 December 2012	340 000

Balance sheet at 31 December 2012 (summarised)

	$	$	$
NON-CURRENT ASSETS at net book value			833 000
CURRENT ASSETS		175 800	
Less current liabilities			
Trade payables	**83 700**		
Accruals	**5 100**		
		(88 800)	
NET CURRENT ASSETS			87 000
			920 000
Less non-current liabilities			(220 000)
			700 000
EQUITY			
Authorised share capital			
1 million ordinary shares of $1 each			1 000,000
Issued share capital			
360 000 ordinary shares of $1 each			360 000
Retained earnings			340 000
Total equity			700 000

Unit 26 Practice questions

DEVELOPING YOUR SKILLS

1 Identifying capital

Steve and Anna decided to form a private limited company on 1 July 2012 with an authorised capital of $500 000 consisting of 400 000 $1 ordinary shares and 100 000 8 per cent $1 preference shares. On that date Steve agreed to purchase all of the preference shares and 180 000 ordinary shares; Anna agreed to purchase 120 000 ordinary shares.

a State the value of the authorised share capital.

b State the value of the issued share capital.

Steve and Anna agreed that the shares should be paid for as follows:

- Preference shares in full.
- Ordinary shares: $0.50 immediately; $0.50 on 1 July 2012.

c State the value of the called-up share capital on 1 July 2012.

By 31 July 2012, Steve had paid in full for the preference shares and had paid $75 000 towards the ordinary shares; Anna had paid $55 000 towards the ordinary shares.

d State the value of the paid-up share capital on 31 July 2012.

2 Identifying capital

Nimesh decided to form a private limited company on 1 April 2012 with an authorised capital of $1 200,000 consisting of 2 000,000 $0.50 ordinary shares and 200 000 7 per cent $1 preference shares. On that date Nimesh agreed to purchase all of the preference shares and 600 000 ordinary shares. Nimesh's friend Rajinder agreed to purchase 100 000 ordinary shares, and another friend, Serena, agreed to purchase 80 000 ordinary shares.

a State the value of the authorised share capital.

b State the value of the issued share capital.

Nimesh, Rajinder and Serena agreed that the shares should be paid for as follows:

- Preference shares in full.
- Ordinary shares: $0.30 immediately; $0.20 on 1 January 2012.

c State the value of called-up share capital on 1 April 2012.

By 31 July 2012, Nimesh had paid in full for the preference shares and had paid $150 000 towards the ordinary shares; Rajinder had paid $22 000 towards the ordinary shares; Serena had paid in full for her ordinary shares.

d State the value of paid-up share capital on 31 July 2012.

3 Preparing a company's income statement

The following information has been taken from the books of Hayford Ltd at the end of its financial year, 31 August 2012.

	$
Business expenses	78 400
Debenture interest	see note 3
Directors' salaries	52 900
Inventories	
1 September 2011	33 800
31 August 2012	44 900
Non-current assets	
Cost	460 000
Provision for depreciation at 1 September 2011	80 000
Purchases	250 000
Revenue	640 000

Notes:

- Business expenses prepaid at 31 August 2012 were $1800.
- Depreciation should be provided on non-current assets at 25 per cent per annum using the reducing balance method.
- The company borrowed $140 000 in the form of 10 per cent debentures some years ago.

Prepare an income statement for the year ended 31 August 2012.

4 Preparing a company's income statement

The following information has been taken from the books of Sahera Ltd at the end of its financial year, 31 May 2012.

	$
Business expenses	34 700
Debenture interest	See note 4
Directors' salaries	32 400
Inventories	
1 June 2011	17 100
31 May 2012	14 200
Non-current assets	
Cost	85 000
Provision for depreciation at 1 June 2011	34 000
Provision for doubtful debts at 1 June 2011	1 100
Purchases	182 800
Revenue	395 000

Notes:

- Business expenses accrued at 31 May 2012 were $1800.
- Depreciation should be provided on non-current assets at 20 per cent per annum using the straight-line method.
- The provision for doubtful debts should be increased by $600.
- The company borrowed $50 000 in the form of 8 per cent debentures some years ago.

Prepare an income statement for the year ended 31 May 2012.

5 Calculating dividends

Part 1

Helixa Ltd has an authorised capital of 80 000 6 per cent preference shares of $1 each and 500 000 ordinary shares of $1 each. At 31 December 2012 all of the preference shares had been issued and were fully paid up, and half of the ordinary shares had been issued and were fully paid up.

On 31 December 2012 the directors agreed to recommend the payment of the preference share dividend for the year and an ordinary share dividend of 12 per cent.

Calculate:

- The preference share dividend
- The ordinary share dividend

Part 2

Iberon Ltd has an issued share capital consisting of 850 000 ordinary shares of $0.50 each.

On 31 December 2012 the directors agreed to recommend the payment of an ordinary share dividend of $0.10 per share.

Calculate the ordinary share dividend.

6 Calculating dividends

Part 1

Torsa Ltd has an authorised capital of 120 000 8 per cent preference shares of $1 each and 1 000,000 ordinary shares of $1 each. At 31 August 2012 all of the preference shares had been issued and were fully paid up, and three-quarters of the ordinary shares had been issued and were fully paid up.

On 31 December 2012 the directors agreed to recommend the payment of the preference share dividend for the year and an ordinary share dividend of 15 per cent.

Calculate:

- The preference share dividend
- The ordinary share dividend

Part 2

Uveron Ltd has an issued share capital consisting of 740 000 fully paid ordinary shares of $0.50 each.

On 31 December 2012 the directors agreed to recommend the payment of an ordinary share dividend of $0.08 per share.

Calculate the ordinary share dividend.

7 Preparing appropriation accounts

Spianato Ltd has an authorised share capital of 50 000 7 per cent preference shares of $1 each and 900 000 ordinary shares of $1 each. All of the preference shares have been issued and are fully paid, and 600 000 ordinary shares have been issued and are fully paid.

On 31 December 2012 the company's income statement showed that a profit of $272 000 had been made for the year ended on that date. The directors decided to:

- recommend the payment of the preference share dividend for the year

- recommend the payment of an ordinary share dividend of $0.30 per share
- transfer $50 000 to a general reserve.

At 1 January 2012 the company's retained earnings totalled $84 000.

Prepare an appropriation account for the year ended 31 December 2012.

8 Preparing appropriation accounts

Harnaise Ltd has an authorised share capital of 200 000 8 per cent preference shares of $1 each and 1 500,000 ordinary shares of $0.50 each. Half of the preference shares have been issued and are fully paid, and 1 000,000 ordinary shares have been issued and are fully paid.

On 30 September 2012 the company's income statement showed that a profit of $243 000 had been made for the year ended on that date. The directors decided to:

- recommend the payment of the preference share dividend for the year
- recommend the payment of a 20 per cent ordinary share dividend
- transfer $75 000 to a general reserve.

At 1 October 2011 the company's retained earnings totalled $117 000.

Prepare an appropriation account for the year ended 30 September 2012.

9 Preparing company balance sheets

Wenfod Ltd has an authorised capital of 40 000 8 per cent preference shares of $1 each and 800 000 ordinary shares of $1 each. On 31 December 2012 the following information was available.

7% debentures 2018	50 000
Accruals	500
Cash at bank	38 800
General reserve	72 400
Inventories	17 100
Issued capital	
40 000 8% preference shares of $1 each fully paid	40 000
600 000 ordinary shares of $1 each fully paid	600 000
Non-current assets	
Cost	960 000
Provision for depreciation	162 000
Prepayments	700
Proposed dividends	
Preference share dividend	3 200
Ordinary share dividend	60 000
Retained earnings	36 600
Trade payables	11 400
Trade receivables	19 500

Prepare a balance sheet at 31 December 2012.

10 Preparing company balance sheets

Emprix Ltd has an authorised capital of 140 000 7 per cent preference shares of $1 each and 1 400,000 ordinary shares of $0.50 each. All of the preference shares and half of the ordinary shares are issued and are fully paid.

On 31 July 2012 the following additional information was available.

9% debentures 2020	30 000
Bank overdraft	8 400
General reserve	40 400
Inventories	34 800
Non-current assets	
Cost	765 000
Provision for depreciation	183 200
Prepayments	400
Proposed dividends	
Preference share dividend	9 800
Ordinary share dividend	17 500
Provision for doubtful debts	400
Retained earnings	17 300
Trade payables	11 700
Trade receivables	8 100

Prepare a balance sheet at 31 July 2012.

11 Preparing a statement of changes in equity

Avalon Ltd's financial year ended on 30 September 2012. The following information is available:

- At 1 October 2011 the company's retained earnings were $143 000.
- During the year ended 30 September 2012 the company made a profit of $165 000.
- During the year ended 30 September 2012 the

directors paid an ordinary share dividend of $120 000.

Prepare a statement of changes in equity for the year ended 30 September 2012.

12 Preparing a statement of changes in equity

Zedtrex Ltd has an issued share capital of 1.5 million ordinary shares of $1 each. The following information is available about the financial year ended on 31 August 2012:

- At 1 September 2011 the company's retained earnings were $372 000.
- During the year ended 31 August 2012 the company made a profit of $641 000.
- During the year ended 31 August 2012 the directors paid an ordinary share dividend of $0.40 per share.

Prepare a statement of changes in equity for the year ended 31 August 2012.

13 Preparing end-of-year financial statements of a limited company based on IAS requirements

Jimplex Ltd's most recent financial year ended on 31 December 2012. On that date the following information was available.

	$	$
10% debentures		120 000
Administration and selling expenses	68 000	
Cash at bank	15 000	
Debenture interest	12 000	
Dividends paid	50 000	
Inventories at 1 January 2012	25 000	
Issued capital: 500 000 $1 ordinary shares		500 000
Non-current assets at net book value	900 000	
Purchases	384 000	
Retained earnings at 1 January 2012		115 000
Revenue		704 000
Trade payables		28 000
Trade receivables	13 000	
	1 467,000	1 467,000

Additional information at 31 December 2012:

- Inventories were valued at $32 000.
- Administration and selling expenses prepaid totalled $4000.
- Non-current assets should be depreciated by 20 per cent per annum using the reducing balance method.
- The company's authorised capital consists of 800 000 ordinary shares of $1 each.

Prepare the following:

a An income statement for the year ended 31 December 2012

b A statement of changes in equity for the year ended 31 December 2012

c A balance sheet at 31 December 2012

14 Preparing end-of-year financial statements of a limited company based on IAS requirements

Ortogon Ltd's most recent financial year ended on 30 June 2012. On that date the following information was available.

	$000	$000
8% debentures		30
Administration and selling expenses	148	
Bank overdraft		18
Cost of sales	543	
Debenture interest	24	
Inventories at 30 June 2012	31	
Authorised and issued share capital:		
1m ordinary shares of $1 each		1 000
6% preference shares of $1 each		400
Non-current assets at net book value	1 960	
Ordinary share dividends paid	150	
Preference share dividends paid	24	
Retained earnings at 1 January 2012		271
Revenue		1167
Trade payables		31
Trade receivables	37	
	2 917	2 917

Additional information at 30 June 2012 (all figures in $000):

- Administration and selling expenses were accrued $9.
- Non-current assets should be depreciated by 10 per cent per annum using the reducing balance method.

Prepare the following:

a An income statement for the year ended 30 June 2012

b A statement of changes in equity for the year ended 30 June 2012

c A balance sheet at 30 June 2012

PREPARING FOR THE EXAMINATION

(The following questions cover Unit 26)

MULTIPLE-CHOICE QUESTIONS

15 What does the abbreviation 'Ltd' mean at the end of the name of a business?

A The number of shareholders has a fixed limit

B There is a limit to the amount of sales revenue this business can achieve

C There is a limit to the number of debentures that can be issued

D The shareholders' liability for the debts of the business is limited

16 Which of the following is shown in the income statement of a limited liability company?

A Debenture interest

B Dividends proposed

C General reserve

D Retained earnings

17 A limited company has an authorised capital of 200 000 ordinary shares of $1 each. Half of the ordinary shares have been issued. The directors have required the payment of $0.50 per share. So far $0.40 per share has been received from shareholders.

What is the company's called up share capital?

A $40 000

B $50 000

C $100 000

D $200 000

18 A limited company has an authorised capital of 500 000 ordinary shares of $1 each. Eighty per cent of the ordinary shares have been issued. The directors have required the payment of $0.50 per share. So far $0.40 per share has been received from shareholders.

What is the company's paid up share capital?

A $160 000

B $200 000

C $400 000

D $500 000

19 Which of the following is a current liability in the balance sheet of a limited liability company?

A Debentures (2022)

B General reserve

C Preference share capital

D Proposed dividends

OTHER QUESTIONS

20 Treble Clef Ltd has a maximum capital of 200 000 7 per cent preference shares of $1 each and 1 800,000 ordinary shares of $1 each.

On 31 December 2012 the company had issued half of the preference shares and three-quarters of the ordinary shares. These shares were fully paid.

a State the total value of the company's authorised share capital.

b State the total value of the company's issued share capital.

c Explain what is meant by the term 'paid-up share capital'.

On 31 December 2012 the directors announced that the company had made a profit of $427 000 for the year ended on that date. The directors have decided to:

- recommend the payment of the preference share dividend for the year
- recommend an ordinary share dividend of $0.25 per share
- transfer $47 000 to the general reserve.

The retained profits brought forward from the previous year amounted to $88 000.

- **d** Calculate the amount of the proposed preference share dividend.
- **e** Calculate the amount of the proposed ordinary share dividend.
- **f** Prepare the company's appropriation account for the year ended 31 December 2012.

On 31 December 2012 the following additional information was available.

	$
Cash at bank	49 600
Debentures (6%) (2024)	80 000
General reserve at 1 January 2012	130 000
Inventories	47 900
Non-current assets	
Cost	2 600,000
Provision for depreciation at 31 December 2012	529 000
Trade payables	32 500
Trade receivables	29 000

- **g** Explain why debentures are described as 6 per cent and 2024.
- **h** Prepare a balance sheet at 31 December 2012.

27 Clubs and societies

Introduction

Clubs and societies exist for the benefit of their members and their main objective is to provide facilities for their members to use and enjoy. Unlike businesses, they are not formed with the aim of making a profit for the owner(s), so they are referred to as non-profit making organisations.

In this unit you will learn about the accounting records that are prepared for small clubs and societies. Accounting records are more limited than those of a business because the provision of activities is more important than financial affairs. Members appoint a **treasurer** who reports to the annual general meeting at the year end on:

- the cash position, because, just like a business, a club or society must be able to pay its debts on time
- whether the club has sufficient income to cover its running costs and have sufficient finances to maintain or improve its existing resources
- the overall picture of the club's financial position.

In larger clubs and societies a full double-entry system could be maintained, but for smaller organisations the treasurer is likely to prepare:

- a cash book, which is summarised in the form of a **receipts and payments account** for presentation to the club committee and members at the annual meeting
- an **income and expenditure account**, which is similar to an income statement but is designed to show whether running costs have been covered by income and whether there is a surplus or deficit for the year
- a balance sheet to show members an overall picture of the financial position.

LEARNING OUTCOMES

When you have reached the end of this unit you will be able to:

- prepare a receipts and payments account
- prepare an income and expenditure account
- prepare accounting records for subscriptions
- prepare accounting records for other fund-raising activities
- make adjustments to income and expenses
- calculate the accumulated fund
- prepare the balance sheet of a club or society.

KEY TERM

Treasurer: the individual appointed by the members of a club or society to manage its financial affairs.

Receipts and payments account: an annual summary of the club or society's cash book.

Income and expenditure account: an annual summary that shows whether the club made a surplus or a deficit.

27.1 Preparing a receipts and payments account

Note: for convenience throughout the following units reference is made only to clubs. However, all of the points made could apply equally well to a society.

Recording money transactions

Clubs may receive money from a variety of sources. Here are some typical examples:

- Members: it is usual for members to pay an annual subscription which enables them to use the club's facilities. Sometimes members pay a one-off membership fee when they first join the club.
- Money-raising activities: although clubs do not set out to make a profit, they may raise funds to help run the club or make improvements. For example, a club might sell refreshments, sell tickets for social evenings and competitions, etc.
- Loans: a club might be able to arrange a loan.
- Donations: individuals or organisations might be prepared to make a donation to a club.

The club treasurer, with the approval of a committee of members, will be responsible for making the following payments:

- Running costs: including expenses such as electricity, telephone, wages of anyone employed by the club, repairs to the club's assets, rent or hire of land and buildings used by the club.
- Expenses of money-raising activities: for example the cost of refreshments, prizes for competitions, etc.
- Purchase of non-current assets: from time to time existing assets will need to be replaced and new and better facilities may be purchased.
- Repayment of loans.

The receipts and payments account

During the course of a year a club's treasurer will keep a detailed record of every receipt and payment of money in a cash book. At the end of the year a summary will be prepared of these items to present to the club committee and, possibly, all of the club's members. The summary is called a receipts and payments account. The receipts and payments account will inform members of the reasons behind any increase or decrease in the club's cash funds.

Illustration 1 | A club's receipts and payments account

The treasurer of the Emden Community Film Club presented the following summary of the club's cash book. Here is the club's receipts and payments account.

EMDEN COMMUNITY FILM CLUB

Receipts and payments account
for the year ended 31 December 2012

RECEIPTS	$	PAYMENTS	$
Opening balance of cash in hand and cash at bank	854	Hire of community hall	740
Members' subscriptions	2 840	Refreshment costs	182
Sales of refreshments	337	Hire of films	885
Donation from local business	200	Interest on loan from member	24
Loan from member	300	Purchase of projecting equipment	2 200
		Club secretary's expenses	108
		Closing balances of cash in hand and cash at bank	392
	4 531		4 531

Notes:

1 The account is set out using a very simple format so that members who do not have any special knowledge of accounting can easily understand the contents.

2 Some treasurers may prefer to use a vertical style of presentation.

3 The opening and closing balances shown in a receipts and payments account are the balances of cash in hand and at bank as recorded in the treasurer's cash book for the period.

4 Members will find this account helpful in understanding why the club's cash funds have reduced by $462 during the year.

You can now answer questions 1 and 2 on page 295.

27.2 Preparing an income and expenditure account

The income and expenditure account

If a club is to survive it must make sure that its income is sufficient to cover its running costs. In order to provide members with a detailed answer to this key point, the treasurer will prepare an income and expenditure account.

This account is similar in many ways to a business's income statement and it should be drawn up following the same principles, including the accruals principle. As a result, adjustments will have to be made to expenses for accruals and prepayments, and depreciation of non-current assets will have to be taken into account.

It is likely that the amount received from members for their subscriptions will also need to be adjusted to take account of the fact that some members will have failed to pay their annual subscription on time, or that some other members may have paid their subscriptions for next year.

Illustration 2 Preparing a simple income and expenditure account

Here is the film club's income and expenditure account based on the information in Illustration 1 and the following additional information:

- The amount paid for the hire of the community hall includes charges of $60 which are for the next financial year.
- The club's secretary has not yet paid an amount due for expenses of $40.
- Some members have not yet paid their subscription for 2012 and a total of $320 is owed.
- In addition to the new projecting equipment, the club has non-current assets that cost $4 800. All non-current assets should be depreciated by 20 per cent per annum on cost.

EMDEN COMMUNITY FILM CLUB

Income and expenditure account for the year ended 31 December 2012

INCOME	$	$
Subscriptions (received $2 840 + due $320)	3 160	
Refreshment sales	337	
Donation	200	
		3 697
EXPENDITURE		
Hire of community hall	680	
Cost of refreshments (paid $740 – prepaid $60)	182	
Hire of films	885	
Loan interest	24	
Secretary's expenses (paid $107 + due $40)	148	
Depreciation of non-current assets (20% × ($4 700 + new $2 200))	1 400	
		(3 319)
Surplus of income over expenditure		378

Notes:

1 The account records only income and expenses, so assets such as the cash balances and the purchase of the film projector are not included, and liabilities such as the loan from a member are not included.

2 Donations and gifts are usually regarded as part of the club's income unless told otherwise.

3 The vertical form of presentation is preferred, but the account could be set out in a horizontal format. In this layout the expenditure would be shown on the debit side and the income would be shown on the credit side.

4 The account shows that income has been greater than expenditure. Instead of the word 'profit' the term 'surplus' is used. If expenditure exceeds income, then the term 'deficit' is used rather than the word 'loss'.

5 The club members will be able to use this account to understand how the club made enough income to more than cover its running costs.

Adjustments to expenditure

It may be necessary to consider opening as well as closing adjustments when calculating the correct amount of an expense to charge to a club's income and expenditure account. Here is an example of how to approach this situation.

You can now answer questions 3 and 4 on page 295.

Illustration 3 Preparing an expense account with opening and closing adjustments

The Topgear Cycle Club rents its clubhouse. For the year ended 31 December 2012 the treasurer is able to provide the following information:

- 1 January 2012: rent due was $180
- January–December 2012: payments for rent totalled $3850
- 31 December 2012: rent prepaid for 2013 was $250

It is possible to make an arithmetical calculation or prepare a ledger account to calculate the correct amount to charge to the income and expenditure account.

By arithmetical calculation:

	$
Rent paid during the year	3 850
Less amount due on 1 January for 2011	(180)
Less amount prepaid on 31 December for 2013	(250)
Income from subscriptions for 2011	3 420

Using an expense account:

Dr		Rent account	Cr
Bank (payments)	3 850	Opening balance (due)	180
		Income and expenditure account	**3 420**
		Closing balance (prepaid) c/d	250
	3 850		3 850
Balance b/d	250		

DID YOU KNOW?

When dealing with adjustments to income or expense items, always use the accruals principle. This means that: information that is to do with the current year should be included, information that relates to any other year should be excluded. You may find it easier to remember this idea with the simple statement: this year IN, any other year OUT.

27.3 Subscriptions and fund-raising activities

Preparing subscription accounts

Calculating the correct amount of subscription income for a year is done using the accruals principle. It is possible to work out the correct figure to use by making a calculation or by using a subscriptions account.

Illustration 4 Calculations of subscription income

The Double-Fault Tennis Club charges its members a subscription of $40 per annum. During the year ended 31 December 2011, the club received $880 for subscriptions. This sum included $120 received from members for their subscriptions for 2012. Four members failed to pay their subscriptions for 2011 on time.

Here are two ways of calculating the subscription income.

By arithmetical calculation:

	$
Subscriptions received during the year	880
Less subscriptions received for 2012	(120)
Add subscriptions due but not yet received (4 × $40)	160
Income from subscriptions for 2011	920

Using a subscriptions account:

Dr		Subscriptions account	Cr
Income and expenditure account	920	Bank (amounts received)	880
Closing balance (received in advance) c/d	120	Closing balance (due) c/d	160
	1 040		1 040
Balance b/d	160	Balance b/d	120

Notes:

1 The amount of cash received is credited to the subscriptions account. This entry would be matched by a debit entry in the club's bank account.

2 The income for the year is debited to the subscriptions account. The matching credit entry would be on the credit side of the income and expenditure account.

3 Subscriptions due is a debit balance brought down, so it is a current asset to the club.

4 Subscriptions received in advance is a credit balance brought down, so it is a current liability to the club.

In Illustration 5 the calculation of subscription income becomes more complicated because there are adjustments to be made at the *beginning* of the year as well as at the end of the year.

Illustration 5 More calculations of subscription income

During the year ended 31 December 2012 the Double-Fault Tennis Club continued to charge its members an annual subscription of $40 per member. During the year ended on that date a total of $1200 was received from members; this included the $160 due from the previous year. At 31 December 2012, six members had paid their subscription for 2013 in advance, but nine members had yet to pay their subscription for 2012.

Arithmetical calculation:

	$
Subscriptions received during the year	1 200
Less subscriptions due from 2011	(160)
Add subscriptions received for the current year received in 2011	120
Add subscriptions due for 2012 (9 × $40)	360
Less subscriptions received for 2013 (6 × $40)	(240)
Income from subscriptions for 2012	1 280

Using a subscriptions account:

Dr	Subscriptions account		Cr
Balance b/d		Balance b/d	
(due from 2011)	160	(received in advance in 2011)	120
Income and expenditure account	**1 280**	Bank (amounts received)	1 200
Balance c/d (received in advance)	240	Balance c/d (due)	360
	1 680		1 680
Balance b/d	360	Balance b/d	240

You can now answer questions 5 to 8 on page 296.

Fund-raising activities

When a club tries to raise extra funds from specific activities and events, members should be provided with information about their success or otherwise.

Illustration 6 How to show a profit (or loss) from fund-raising

In the case of the Emden Community Film Club (see Illustrations 1 and 2) you may remember the income and expenditure account showed separate details about refreshments: income $337 and expenditure $182. Members may have found it helpful if the account had made it clear that this activity made a profit for the club of $155. Here is how this could be done.

EMDEN COMMUNITY FILM CLUB (Extract)

Income and expenditure account for the year ended 31 December 2012

	$	$	$
INCOME			
Subscriptions		xxx	
Refreshment sales	**337**		
Less cost of refreshments	**(182)**		
Profit on refreshments		**155**	
Donation		xxx	
			xx
EXPENDITURE			
Hire of community hall		xxx	
etc.		xxx	

Where the information about an activity or event is more complicated, it is recommended that a separate account is prepared first to calculate the profit or loss on the activity.

Illustration 7 Preparing a separate account to calculate profit or loss

The Appendix Book Club raises funds by selling second-hand books in the local village. The following information is available about the year ended 30 September 2012.

	$
Sales of second-hand books	3 870
Purchases of second-hand books	2 140
Inventory of second-hand books:	
1 October 2011	480
30 September 2012	710

The treasurer prepared the following account to show the profit made on this activity:

Second-hand books account for the year ended 30 September 2012

	$	$
Revenue from book sales		3 870
Less:		
Opening inventory	480	
Add purchases	2 140	
	2 620	
Less closing inventory	(710)	
		(1 910)
Profit on second-hand book sales		1 960

The profit of $1960 should be entered in the income section of the annual income and expenditure account.

STUDY TIP

If you prepare a separate account to calculate the profit or loss made on an event or activity, do not forget to enter the profit or loss in the income and expenditure account.

Club balance sheets

The accumulated fund

In a business the owners invest their private funds, which is referred to as the capital of the business, and during a financial year owners can withdraw funds in the form of drawings.

However, in the case of club, members are not required to make a similar investment and so are not allowed to make any withdrawals of funds. Over a period of time, if a club makes an annual surplus (see 27.2 above) this will gradually accumulate, and this figure is referred to as the club's **accumulated fund**. The accumulated fund can be calculated by subtracting the total amount of liabilities from the total value of assets.

KEY TERM

Accumulated fund: the total of a club's surpluses over a period of years. It is the equivalent of a business's capital.

Illustration 8 Calculating a club's accumulated fund

The Hereton Social Club had the following assets and liabilities at 1 January 2012.

	$
Amounts due to suppliers of refreshments	240
Cash in hand and at bank	450
Clubhouse	180 000
Furniture and equipment	8 200
Inventory (refreshments)	720
Loans from members	3 200
Subscriptions due from members	360

The club accumulated fund at 1 January 2012 is as follows.

	$	$
Totals assets		
Cash in hand and at bank	450	
Clubhouse	180 000	
Furniture and equipment	8 200	
Inventory (refreshments)	720	
Subscriptions due from members	360	
		189 730
Less total liabilities		
Refreshments suppliers	240	
Loans from members	3 200	
		(3 440)
Accumulated fund		186 290

Preparing a club's balance sheet

Club balance sheets resemble those of businesses. They can be set out with a horizontal or vertical layout, and they will show members the details of the club's assets and liabilities at a particular date. However, the capital section of the balance sheet will be replaced by the accumulated fund. This section will show details of the balance of the accumulated fund brought forward from the previous year with the surplus for the year added or deficit for the year subtracted.

DID YOU KNOW?

Many small clubs do not prepare balance sheets or income and expenditure accounts because their affairs are very straightforward. For example, these clubs may not possess any non-current assets or have accruals or prepayments. In these situations, the club treasurer may report to members by just preparing a receipts and payments account.

Illustration 9 Preparing a club's balance sheet

The treasurer of the MegaWave Surf Club reported that the club had made a surplus of $6300 for the year ended 31 October 2012. The treasurer also provided the following information.

	$
Accrual: secretary's fee	160
Accumulated fund, 1 November 2011	19 180
Bank overdraft	1 870
Prepaid administration expenses	220
Subscription due	480
Subscriptions received in advance	990
Surfboards and equipment at valuation	27 800

Here is the club's balance sheet for 31 October 2012.

MEGAWAVE SURF CLUB: Balance sheet at 31 October 2012

NON-CURRENT ASSETS	$	$	$
Surfing equipment at valuation			27 800
CURRENT ASSETS			
Other receivable (prepaid administration expenses)	220		
Other receivable (subscriptions due)	480		
		700	
Less CURRENT LIABILITIES			
Other payable (subscriptions received in advance)	990		
Other payable (accrual: secretary's fees)	160		
Bank overdraft	1 870		
		(3 020)	
Net current liabilities			(2 320)
			25 480
ACCUMULATED FUND			
Balance at 1 November 2011		19 180	
Add surplus for year		6 300	
			25 480

STUDY TIP

It is easy to make a mistake when entering information about subscriptions on a balance sheet. Subscriptions due should be recorded as a current asset – this item represents money due to the club. Subscriptions received in advance should be recorded as a current liability, as the amount is, in effect, owed back to the members at the date of the balance sheet.

Where a club's accumulated fund is less than the value of non-current assets it will have net current liabilities. It is often the case that these clubs need an overdraft facility to pay their running costs (as in Illustration 9) or they will have to raise loans from members.

You can now answer questions 9–18 on pages 296–300.

Unit 27 Practice questions

DEVELOPING YOUR SKILLS

1 Preparing a receipts and payments account

The treasurer of the Newtown Sports Club records all of the club's money transactions in a cash book. At the end of the club financial year, 31 December, the treasurer summarises all of the details in the cash book to prepare a receipts and payments account. The treasurer has supplied the following information about the year ended 31 December 2012.

On 1 January the club had total cash balances (cash in hand and cash at bank) of $720.

The club received money from the following sources:

- Members' subscriptions totalled $3850
- Entrance fees for sports competition raised $620
- A local businessman donated $500 to the club
- A member lent the club $800 to help pay for some new sports equipment

The treasurer made the following payments:

- Rent of sports grounds, $1200
- Purchase of new sports equipment, $2700
- Competition prizes, $450
- Loan interest, $40
- Coach hire for away matches, $900
- Administration expenses, $170

Prepare the club's receipts and payments account for the year ended 31 December 2012.

2 Preparing a receipts and payments account

Students at the Kingstown High School have formed a Music Society. One of the students has been acting as the society's treasurer. The treasurer has provided the following information about the year ended 31 July 2012.

At 1 August 2011 the society had total cash funds of $840.

Receipts during the year were from the following:

- Members' subscriptions: each member pays an annual subscription of $25. Subscriptions were received from 230 members.
- Ticket sales for performances raised $930.
- A loan from the school of $1000 helped with the purchase of musical instruments.
- Parents of some of the students made gifts of money totalling $450.

Payments during the year were for the following:

- Tuition fees for music lessons, $2500
- Hire of school facilities for performances, $480
- Purchase of musical instruments, $3800
- Cost of refreshments for performances, $280
- Loan interest, $50
- Administration costs, $140

Prepare the club's receipts and payments account for the year ended 31 July 2012.

3 Preparing an income and expenditure account

Using the information in question 1 and taking account of the following additional information, prepare the club's income and expenditure account for the year ended 31 December 2012.

Additional information:

- Some members have not paid their subscription for 2012 and owe the club $420.
- Some other members have paid their 2013 subscription during the year ended 31 December 2012, $80.
- Rent of sports ground was prepaid, $240, at 31 December 2012.
- Administration expenses, $30, were due at 31 December 2012.
- At 1 January 2012 the club's sports equipment was valued at cost $11 300 – all sports equipment should be depreciated by 20 per cent on cost for the year.

4 Preparing an income and expenditure account

Using the information in question 2 and taking account of the following additional information, prepare the club's income and expenditure account for the year ended 31 July 2012.

Additional information:

- Five members had not paid their subscription for the year under review, but eight other members had paid their subscription for the current year and for the year ending 31 July 2013.

- Tuition fees, $320, were due but unpaid at 31 July 2012.
- Administration costs, $80, were prepaid at 31 July 2012.
- The society owned musical instruments with a value of $18400 at 1 August 2011 – all musical instruments should be depreciated by 10 per cent on cost for the year.

5 Calculating subscription income and using subscription accounts

The Pageturner Book Club charges its members an annual subscription of $30 each. During the year ended 31 December 2011 the club's treasurer received $810 in subscriptions. This sum included $150 received from members for subscriptions for 2012. At 31 December 2011 three members had failed to pay their 2011 subscription.

a Calculate the club's subscription income for 2011.

b Prepare a subscriptions accounts for 2011.

6 Calculating subscription income and using subscription accounts

The GoforGold Athletics Club charges it members an annual subscription of $70 each. During the year ended 31 December 2011, $2310 was received from members for their annual subscriptions. This sum included subscriptions from eight members for 2012. At 31 December 2011, five members had failed to pay their 2011 subscription.

a Calculate the club's subscription income for 2011.

b Prepare a subscriptions accounts for 2011.

7 Calculating subscription income and using subscription accounts

The following information is available for the Pageturner Book Club for the year ended 31 December 2012 (see also question 5).

As well as the opening balances on the subscription account on 1 January 2012 (see question 5) the following additional information is available.

The club has maintained the annual subscription rate at $30 per member. The sum of $1110 was received from members for annual subscriptions during the year ended 31 December 2012. This included the subscriptions due at the beginning of the year and $120 received from members for their 2013 subscription. By 31 December 2012, six members had failed to pay their subscription for 2012.

a Calculate the club's subscription income for 2012.

b Prepare a subscriptions accounts for 2012.

8 Calculating subscription income and using subscription accounts

The following information is available for the GoforGold Athletics Club for the year ended 31 December 2012 (see also question 6).

As well as the opening balances on the subscription account on 1 January 2012 (see question 6) the following additional information is available.

The club has maintained the annual subscription rate at $70 per member. The sum of $2870 was received from members for annual subscriptions during the year ended 31 December 2012. This included the subscriptions due at the beginning of the year and $350 received from members for their 2013 subscription. By 31 December 2012, two members had failed to pay their subscription for 2012.

a Calculate the club's subscription income for 2012.

b Prepare a subscriptions accounts for 2012.

9 Preparing a club's balance sheet

The Merlin Sailing Club's most recent financial year ended on 30 April 2012. On that date the club's treasurer reported a surplus for the year of $3390 and provided the following additional information.

	$
Accumulated fund at 1 May 2011	45 750
Other receivable (boathouse rent prepaid)	440
Cash at bank and in hand	1 130
Loans from members (repayable 2018)	4 000
Sailing equipment at valuation	52 300
Other payable (secretary's expenses due)	110
Other receivable (subscriptions due)	770
Other payable (subscriptions received in advance)	1 390

Prepare the club's balance sheet at 30 April 2012.

10 Preparing a club's balance sheet

The Matchpoint Badminton Club's treasurer has reported a deficit of $2850 for the year on 31 August 2012. At this date the following additional information is available.

	$
Accumulated fund at 1 September 2011	2 960
Badminton equipment at valuation	2 180
Bank overdraft	1 780
Cash in hand	130
Other receivable (general expenses prepaid)	80
Other payable (hire of badminton court: charges due)	330
Inventory (refreshments)	450
Loans from members	800
Other receivable (subscriptions due)	410
Other payable (subscriptions received in advance)	230

Note: the loans from members are due for repayment in October 2012.

Prepare the club's balance sheet at 31 August 2012.

11 Preparing end-of-year financial statements

The Curtain-up Drama Club was formed several years ago. The club's treasurer is able to supply the following information about the year ended 31 December 2012.

At 1 January the club had the following assets and liabilities.

	$
Costumes and stage sets at valuation	11 900
Prepaid hire of community centre	270
Subscriptions due from members	90
Cash at bank	3 150
Administration expenses due	140
Subscriptions received in advance	320

Receipts and payments account for the year ended 31 December 2012

RECEIPTS	$	PAYMENTS	$
Balance at bank 1 January 2012	3 150	Hire of community centre	1 740
Members' subscriptions	3 200	Purchase of new costumes and stage sets	5 800
Gifts from members	350	Administration expenses	490
Ticket sales for productions	4 480	Competition prizes	380
Competition receipts	630	Balance at bank 31 December 2012	3 400
	11 810		11 810

On 31 December:

- members' subscriptions due were $220
- members' subscriptions received in advance were $110
- $180 was owing for hire of the community centre
- some administration expenses were prepaid, $50
- costumes and stage sets were revalued at $13 500.

Prepare the following:

a A calculation of the club's accumulated fund at 1 January 2012

b A subscriptions account for the year ended 31 December 2012

c An income and expenditure account for the year ended 31 December 2012

d A balance sheet at 31 December 2012

12 Preparing end-of-year financial statements

The treasurer of the Glades Social Club is able to provide the following information about the club's most recent financial year which ended on 30 June 2012.

Assets and liabilities at 1 July 2011 were as follows.

	$
Cash at bank	3 840
Club buildings cost	
Cost	280 000
Provision for depreciation	21 000
Club furniture and equipment at valuation	17 500
Inventory: refreshments	870
Subscriptions due	650
Subscriptions received in advance	210
General expenses due	380

Receipts and payments account for the year ended 30 June 2012

RECEIPTS	$	PAYMENTS	$
Balance at bank 1 July 2011	3 840	Purchase of refreshments	1 750
Members' subscriptions	6 750	General expenses	4 440
Loans from members	600	Purchase of furniture and equipment	6 750
Sales of refreshments	2 470	Balance at bank 30 June 2012	720
	13 660		13 660

Additional information:

- The loans from members are interest free, but are to be repaid in January 2013.
- Suppliers of refreshments were owed $310 on 30 June 2012.
- General expenses were prepaid, $60, on 30 June 2012.
- There was a refreshments inventory valued at $380 on 30 June 2012.
- Members' subscriptions, $480, were due on 30 June 2014.
- Members' subscriptions, $710, had been received in advance for the year ended ending 30 June 2013.
- The club buildings should be depreciated by 2.5 per cent on cost.
- The treasurer revalued the furniture and equipment at $20 500 on 30 June 2012.

Prepare the following:

a A calculation of the club's accumulated fund at 1 July 2011

b A subscriptions account for the year ended 30 June 2012

c A refreshments account for the year ended 30 June 2012

d An income and expenditure account for the year ended 30 June 2012

e A balance sheet at 30 June 2012

(The following questions cover Unit 27)

MULTIPLE-CHOICE QUESTIONS

13 Which one of the following statements concerning the purpose of a receipts and payments account of a social club is correct?

A It does not include any capital expenditure

B It shows how much club members owe for subscriptions

C It shows the surplus or deficit for the year

D It summarises the details shown in the cash book

14 The treasurer of a social club was preparing the income and expenditure account for the year ended 31 December 2012. The following information was available about the cost of hiring the community centre in 2012:

- On 1 January the club owed $320 in hire charges.
- During the year ended 31 December 2012 $1740 was paid in hire charges.
- On 31 December the club owed $410 in hire charges.

What was the correct amount to be charged to the income and expenditure account?

A $1010

B $1650

C $1830

D $2450

15 The Jubilee Sports Club raises funds by providing refreshments at all sporting events. The following information is available about the year ended 31 August 2012.

	$
Inventory	
1 September 2011	3200
31 August 2012	3800
Purchases	8200
Revenue	12100

How much profit will this activity have made for the club?

A $3100

B $3900

C $4500

D $7100

16 The Sparta Athletics Club charges its members an annual subscription of $60 each. During the year ended 31 May 2012, $960 was received in subscriptions. However, this included subscriptions from six members who had paid their subscription for the year ended 31 May 2013 in advance. At 31 May 2012, eight members had failed to pay their subscription for the year ended on that date.

What was the club's subscription income for the year ended 31 May 2012?

A $600

B $840

C $960

D $1080

17 The Singalong Choral Society received $8400 in subscriptions from members during the year ended 31 December 2012. At 1 January 2012 the club had received $370 in advance for subscriptions for 2012. At 31 December 2012, $420 was owing from members for subscriptions for 2012.

What was the club's subscription income for the year ended 31 May 2012?

A $8350

B $8400

C $8450

D $9190

OTHER QUESTIONS

18 Rackets Tennis Club's financial year ended on 30 September 2012 when the treasurer was able to provide the following information.

At 1 October 2011 the club's balance sheet included the following.

	$
Accumulated fund	7230
General expenses prepaid	30
Subscriptions due from members	240
Subscriptions received from members in advance	80
Tennis equipment at net book value	6300

Receipts and payments account for the year ended 30 September 2012

	$		$
Balance at bank 1 October 2011	740	Transfer of funds to a savings account	1800
Members' subscriptions	2990	General expenses	490
Tennis competition receipts	680	Tennis competition expenses	520
Interest received on savings account	110	Purchase of tennis equipment	1500
		Balance at bank 31 December 2012	210
	4520		4520

At 30 September 2012:

- subscriptions due but unpaid totalled $320
- general expenses prepaid were $90
- competition expenses due were $40.

The treasurer depreciates all tennis equipment by 10 per cent per annum based on the value of equipment at the end of the financial year.

a Prepare a subscriptions account to show the club's income from subscriptions for the year ended 30 September 2012.

b Prepare an income and expenditure account for the year ended 30 September 2012.

c Select two items that appear in the receipts and payments account that should not be included in the income and expenditure account and explain why they should not appear.

d Select one item that appears in the income and expenditure account that was not shown in the receipts and payments account and explain why it does not appear.

28 Manufacturing accounts

LEARNING OUTCOMES

When you have reached the end of this unit you will be able to:

- distinguish between direct material, direct labour, prime cost and overhead costs
- understand and make adjustments for work in progress
- calculate the factory cost of production
- prepare manufacturing financial statements: income statements and balance sheets
- make adjustments to financial statements.

Introduction

Previous units have covered the accounts of businesses that trade in goods and services. Trading businesses buy goods from suppliers and sell them on to other businesses or private individuals. In this unit it will be possible to look at the accounts of manufacturing organisations that produce goods rather than purchasing them.

A manufacturer's accounting system will be similar to those already considered. For example, end-of-year financial statements will include an income statement and balance sheet prepared from the detailed double-entry records. In the case of a manufacturing partnership or company, there will be also be an appropriation account to show how profits have been distributed.

The main difference is that it is necessary to work out just how much was spent on producing goods rather than purchasing them from elsewhere. This additional information is recorded in a manufacturing account which is prepared before an income statement.

How to work out the cost of making a product

Whatever product you think of, there are almost certain to be some particular costs that are bound to arise in making that product. For example, perhaps at the moment you are sitting at a desk. Here are some of the costs that are likely to be involved in making a desk:

- Raw materials (probably wood, perhaps some metal)
- Labour costs (i.e. payments to those who made the desk, perhaps using tools or machinery to do so)
- Cost of operating a workshop, or production area, or maybe a factory building, which would include:
  - electricity (to provide light and power for the machinery and equipment)
  - insurance (e.g. of the machinery)
  - depreciation of the machinery and equipment
  - rent of the production area (assuming it is not owned by the business)

When all of these costs are added together it is possible to calculate the cost of producing the desks rather than buying them.

28.1 Preparing a manufacturing account

A manufacturing account is used to show the total cost of producing goods during a financial year. The account lists the costs that can be associated with the production area, which could be anything from a small workshop to a large factory. In a simple **manufacturing account** the costs are organised in two groups:

- **Direct costs**: these are the manufacturing costs that can be associated with an individual product (raw materials and wages paid to those who actually make the goods). These two direct costs are the first to be shown in the manufacturing account and are subtotalled to show a figure called the **prime cost**. The term 'direct' is used because it is known exactly how much should be spent on raw materials and wage cost involved in making one unit of production. The direct cost of materials is based on purchases of raw materials, with an adjustment made for opening and closing inventories of raw materials, to give a figure called the **cost of raw materials consumed**.
- **Indirect costs**: these are the other costs that can be linked to the manufacturing process; they are the costs of operating a separate area for the production of goods (the workshop or factory). Indirect costs are independent of the quantity of goods being prepared. These would include all of the costs arising from having machinery and equipment, as well as electricity, insurance, rent, and so on. Also included in this category would be wages or salaries (*indirect labour*) paid to employees who work in the production area, but who do not actually produce goods, e.g (supervisors and factory managers). The term 'indirect' is used because it would not be possible to know exactly how much of any of these costs could be linked to the production of one unit. Indirect costs are shown as the second section in a manufacturing account, and the costs are subtotalled to give a figure for total **factory overheads**.

Work in progress

It is very unlikely that all products will be completely finished at the moment when the end-of-year financial statements are prepared. On the production line there will be some items that are nearly finished, whereas other items will be in the early stages of being turned into the finished article. The cost of unfinished goods is called **work in progress**. An opening inventory of work in progress should be added to the cost of production, as these items will have been completed during the year under review. The closing inventory of work in progress is deducted from the cost of production for the year, ensuring that the cost of production represents only amounts spent on goods actually finished during that year.

KEY TERM

Manufacturing account: the first part of the end-of-year financial statements of a manufacturing organisation that shows the total cost of producing goods.

Direct costs: manufacturing costs that are attributable to a single product, particularly direct materials and direct labour.

Prime cost: the total of direct costs.

Cost of raw materials consumed: the direct cost of raw materials used during a financial year.

Indirect costs: manufacturing costs that cannot be attributed to one product.

Factory overheads: the total of indirect costs.

STUDY TIP

Indirect costs should only include costs that are to do with manufacturing. It is important that the costs of administration, distributing goods, selling goods and any financial charges are not included in this category. Non-manufacturing costs should continue to appear in the income statement.

Illustration 1	Preparing a manufacturing account

Arbour Ltd manufacture sports equipment. The following information was taken from the company's books of account for the year ended 30 September 2012.

	$
Depreciation of factory machinery	40 000
Direct wages	165 000
Factory electricity	17 000
Factory insurance	3 000
Indirect factory wages and salaries	47 800
Inventories: raw materials	
1 October 2011	19 500
30 September 2012	23 200
Purchases of raw materials	132 100
Rent of factory	22 000
Repairs to factory machinery	1 800

Here is the company's manufacturing account.

ARBOUR LTD

Manufacturing account for the year ended 30 September 2012

	$	$
Raw materials		
Opening inventory	19 500	
Add purchases	132 100	
	151 600	
Less closing inventory	(23 200)	
Cost of raw materials consumed		128 400
Direct wages		165 000
Prime cost		293 400
Factory overheads		
Depreciation of machinery	40 000	
Electricity	17 000	
Insurance	3 000	
Indirect wages and salaries	47 800	
Rent	22 000	
Repairs to machinery	1 800	
		131 600
Cost of production		425 000

Notes:

1 Direct costs are shown first and subtotalled; the subtotal is labelled prime cost.

2 Factory overheads are shown in a second section with a heading and are subtotalled.

3 The total of all the manufacturing costs is labelled 'cost of production'. This figure represents the cost of producing finished goods, which is then transferred to the income statement and replaces the item 'purchases'.

KEY TERM

Work in progress: partly finished goods.

STUDY TIP

Do not forget to show the labels 'Cost of raw materials consumed', 'Prime cost' and 'Cost of production' when preparing a manufacturing account. This is an important part of the proper presentation of this account.

You can now answer questions 1 and 2 on page 307.

28.2 Manufacturer's end-of-year financial statements

Adjustments and the end-of-year financial statements

It will be necessary to make adjustments for prepayment, accruals, and so on, when preparing a manufacturer's end-of-year financial statements. It will also be necessary to share certain costs between the different sections of the business. For example, a manufacturer could pay rent for all of the premises occupied by the business. It would then be necessary to charge part of the total rent to the factory and part to the offices of the business. As a result an appropriate amount of rent would be charged to the manufacturing account and the remainder to the income statement.

Illustration 2 Making adjustments and recording work in progress

Quills Ltd manufacture writing equipment. On 30 June 2012, the following information was available.

	$
Cost of raw materials consumed	240 000
Depreciation of machinery	50 000
Direct wages	180 000
Indirect wages	44 000
Insurance of factory	8 500
Rent	12 000
Work in progress	
1 July 2011	2 800
30 June 2012	3 400

Additional information at 30 June 2012:

1 Direct wages due but unpaid totalled $6 300.

2 Rent is to be shared: three-fifths to the factory, two-fifths to administration.

3 Insurance $1 700 was prepaid.

Here is the manufacturing account based on this information.

QUILLS LTD

Manufacturing account for the year ended 30 June 2012

	$	$
Cost of raw materials consumed		240 000
Direct wages ($180 000 + $6 300 due)		186 300
Prime cost		426 300
Factory overheads		
Depreciation of machinery	50 000	
Indirect wages and salaries	44 000	
Insurance ($8 500 − $1 700 prepaid)	6 800	
Rent ($\frac{3}{5}$ of $12 000)	7 200	
		108 000
		534 300
Add opening work in progress		2 800
		537 100
Less closing work in progress		(3 400)
Cost of production		533 700

You can now answer questions 3 and 4 on page 307.

A manufacturer's income statement

Just like any other business, a manufacturer's income statement is designed to show the gross profit on selling goods (i.e. finished goods) and the profit or loss for the year. The first part of the income statement will include the cost of production and this will replace the item 'purchases'. All of the information in this section of the income statement will be about finished goods.

The second part of a manufacturer's income statement will show the deduction of non-factory costs from the gross profit.

Illustration 3 Preparing a manufacturer's income statement

Here is an income statement for Quills Ltd (see also Illustration 2).

QUILLS LTD

Income statement for the year ended 30 June 2012

	$	$
Revenue		885 000
Less opening inventory of finished goods	32 300	
Add cost of production	533 700	
	566 000	
Less closing inventory of finished goods	(29 000)	
Cost of sales of finished goods		(537 000)
Gross profit		348 000
Less expenses		
Depreciation of office equipment	5 500	
Financial charges	3 200	
Insurance ($\frac{2}{5}$ of $12 000)	4 800	
Selling expenses	11 400	
		(24 900)
Profit for the year		323 100

Manufacturers' balance sheets

The balance sheet of a manufacturer is the same as the balance sheets for other types of business. There is just one important point of difference: a manufacturer's balance sheet will show three figures for inventories: raw materials, work in progress and finished goods.

DID YOU KNOW?

Sometimes a manufacturer might have to buy in finished goods from another supplier. This can happen if there are problems running the factory that cause a loss of normal production – perhaps a machine has broken down or there has been an industrial dispute. It could be that the manufacturer has a contract to supply goods to a customer and that the only way this order can be completed is by buying in goods.

Purchases of finished goods should be included as an extra cost in the first section of the income statement.

Illustration 4 Preparing the balance sheet of a manufacturer

The following summarised information is available about Kontex, a manufacturing business, at the end of its financial year, 30 November 2012.

	$
Capital	174 600
Cash at bank	4 800
Drawings	32 100
Inventories	
raw materials	17 400
work in progress	2 300
finished goods	14 900
Non-current assets at net book value	149 800
Profit for year	45 300
Trade payables	12 500
Trade receivables	11 100

Kontex

Balance sheet at 30 November 2012

	$	$	$	$
NON-CURRENT ASSETS at net book value				149 800
CURRENT ASSETS				
Inventories				
Raw materials	**17 400**			
Work in progress	**2 300**			
Finished goods	**14 900**			
		34 600		
Trade receivables		11 100		
Cash at bank		4 800		
			50 500	
Less current liabilities				
Trade payables			(12 500)	
Net current assets				38 000
				187 800
CAPITAL				
Opening balance			174 600	
Add profit for year			45 300	
			219 900	
Less drawings			(32 100)	
				187 800

You can now answer questions 5–14 on pages 308–312

Practice questions

DEVELOPING YOUR SKILLS

1 Preparing a manufacturing account

Zenuf & Co. manufacture bicycle alarm systems. The following information is available about the business's most recently completed financial year ended 31 March 2012.

	$
Depreciation of factory machinery	36500
Direct wages	184800
Factory insurance	4700
Factory maintenance and repairs	2200
Factory power	15300
Factory supervisor's wages	44900
Inventories: raw materials	
1 April 2011	28100
31 March 2012	25600
Purchases of raw materials	164900

Prepare a manufacturing account for the year ended 31 March 2012. Show clearly the cost of raw materials, prime cost, total factory overheads, cost of production.

2 Preparing a manufacturing account

Argo & Sons are boatbuilders. The following information is available about the business's most recently completed financial year ended 31 August 2012.

	$
Direct wages	345000
Factory insurance	18700
Factory fuel charges	32300
General factory expenses	7100
Indirect factory wages and salaries	64200
Inventories: raw materials	
1 September 2011	54200
31 August 2012	61700
Machinery maintenance charges	4400
Purchases of raw materials	406000
Rent of factory premises	64800

Note: the annual charge for the depreciation of machinery is based on taking 20 per cent of the cost of all machinery held at the year end. On 31 August 2012 the business owned machinery that cost $480000.

Prepare a manufacturing account for the year ended 31 August 2012. Show clearly the cost of raw materials, prime cost, total factory overheads, cost of production.

3 Making adjustments and recording work in progress

Marco Enterprises manufacture children's toys. On 31 October 2012 the following information was available about the business's financial year which ended on that date.

	$
Direct wages	157340
Electricity charges	6640
Factory insurance	4380
Factory manager's salary	38430
Inventories: raw materials	
1 November 2011	17830
31 October 2012	16590
Inventories: work in progress	
1 November 2011	3830
31 October 2012	2750
Machinery repairs	3550
Purchases of raw materials	148600

Additional information at 31 October 2012:

- Factory machinery should be depreciated by $23000.
- Factory manager's salary due but unpaid, $560.
- Factory insurance $480 was prepaid.
- Electricity charges should be shared: $\frac{5}{8}$ factory; $\frac{3}{8}$ office.

Prepare a manufacturing account for the year ended 31 October 2012.

4 Making adjustments and recording work in progress

Crossgrain Ltd are furniture manufacturers. On 31 March 2012 the information on the following page was available about the business's financial year which ended on that date.

	$
Direct wages	188 750
Factory electricity charges	4 450
Indirect wages	32 360
Inventories: raw materials	
1 April 2011	27 490
31 March 2012	26 120
Inventories: work in progress	
1 April 2011	4 450
31 March 2012	4 990
Rent of factory buildings	15 440
Purchases of raw materials	211 360
Water charges	4 640

Additional information at 31 March 2012:

- Factory machinery should be depreciated by 25 per cent per annum using the reducing balance method. On 1 April 2011 the net book value of machinery was $88 000.
- Factory electricity charges, $390, were due but unpaid.
- Rent of factory buildings, $1080, was prepaid.
- Water charges should be shared: factory $\frac{3}{4}$; office $\frac{1}{4}$.

Prepare a manufacturing account for the year ended 31 March 2012.

5 Preparing income statements and balance sheets

The Belford Manufacturing Company's financial year ended on 31 December 2012. On this date the following information was available after the preparation of the business's manufacturing account.

	$
Capital	69 900
Cash at bank	3 400
Drawings	27 000
Inventory at 1 January 2012: finished goods	13 600
Inventories at 31 December 2012	
Raw materials	15 700
Work in progress	4 800
Finished goods	12 500
Machinery at net book value on 31 December 2012	66 000
Office equipment at net book value on 1 January 2012	14 000
Office wages	23 200
Revenue	332 000
Selling expenses	11 000
Trade payables	7 200
Trade receivables	6 400

Notes:

1. The manufacturing account showed that the cost of production for 2012 was $224 000.
2. The inventory of finished goods was valued at $12 500 on 31 December 2012.
3. Office wages due on 31 December 2012 totalled $400.
4. The office equipment should be depreciated by $1800.

   Prepare the following:

   a An income statement for the year ended 31 December 2012

   b A balance sheet at 31 December 2012

6 Preparing income statements and balance sheets

Hashmi owns a manufacturing business. The following information was available after the preparation of his business's manufacturing account for the year ended 31 October 2012.

	$
Administration expenses	14 300
Bank overdraft	2 900
Capital	434 600
Cost of production	385 000
Drawings	41 600
Factory non-current assets at net book value on 31 October 2012	440 000
Interest charges	1 100
Inventories at 1 November 2011	
Finished goods	38 600
Inventories at 31 October 2012	
Raw materials	45 300
Work in progress	5 700
Office non-current assets at net book value on 1 November 2011	16 400
Revenue	563 000
Selling expenses	8 400
Trade payables	17 900
Trade receivables	22 000

Notes:

1 The manufacturing account showed that the cost of production for 2012 was $424 600.

2 The inventory of finished goods was valued at $42 300 on 31 October 2012.

3 Selling expenses $300 were prepaid on 31 October 2012.

4 The office non-current assets should be depreciated by $2200.

Prepare the following:

a An income statement for the year ended 31 October 2012

b A balance sheet at 31October 2012.

7 Preparing end-of-year financial statements for a manufacturer

Paula Osborne owns a manufacturing business. On 31 July 2012 she prepared the following trial balance to show information about the business's financial year which ended on that date.

Trial balance at 31 July 2012

	Dr	Cr
	$	$
Administration expenses	8 200	
Cash at bank	4 400	
Capital		113 200
Direct wages	147 350	
Drawings	28 240	
General expenses	72 500	
Indirect wages and salaries	31 550	
Inventories at 1 August 2011		
Raw materials	12 490	
Work in progress	2 780	
Finished goods	9 380	
Machinery at net book value	64 000	
Office equipment at net book value	12 400	
Office salaries	23 880	
Purchases of raw materials	181 220	
Revenue		488 230
Trade payables		5 170
Trade receivables	8 210	
	606 600	606 600

Additional information:

1 Inventories at 31 July 2012 were valued as follows: raw materials $11 120; work in progress $3280; finished goods $7420.

2 Direct wages due but unpaid at 31 July 2012 totalled $1370.

3 General expenses should be shared: factory $\frac{9}{10}$; office $\frac{1}{10}$.

4 Depreciation should be provided as follows: machinery $12 800; office equipment $1240.

Prepare the following:

a A manufacturing account for the year ended 31 July 2012

b An income statement for the year ended 31 July 2012

c A balance sheet at 31 July 2012

8 Preparing end-of-year financial statements for a manufacturer

Suman's Enterprises manufactures car accessories. The following trial balance was extracted from the business's books of account on 31 May 2012.

Trial balance at 31 May 2012

	Dr $	Cr $
Bank overdraft		2 490
Capital		125 500
Direct wages	229 400	
Drawings	34 500	
Factory plant and machinery		
Cost	330 000	
Provision for depreciation at 1 June 2011		132 000
Financial charges	1 800	
Inventories at 1 June 2011		
Raw materials	36 000	
Work in progress	4 500	
Finished goods	12 650	
Office equipment at net book value	18 400	
Office running costs	17 300	
Other factory expenses	22 400	
Purchases of raw materials	182 370	
Rent	28 700	
Revenue		662 100
Selling expenses	7 120	
Trade payables		14 340
Trade receivables	11 290	
	936 430	936 430

Additional information:

1 Inventories at 31 May 2012 were valued as follows: raw materials $27 800; work in progress $3800; finished goods $14 810.

2 Other factory expenses due at 31 May 2012 totalled $540.

3 Office running costs prepaid at 31 May 2012 totalled $390.

4 Rent should be shared: factory $\frac{6}{7}$; office $\frac{1}{7}$.

5 Provide for depreciation of non-current assets as follows: factory plant and machinery at 20 per cent per annum on cost; office equipment $2 760.

Prepare the following:

a A manufacturing account for the year ended 31 May 2012

b An income statement for the year ended 31 May 2012

c A balance sheet at 31 May 2012

PREPARING FOR THE EXAMINATION

(The following questions cover Unit 28)

MULTIPLE-CHOICE QUESTIONS

9 Which one of the following factory costs is a direct cost?

A Insurance

B Production workers' wages

C Rent

D Supervisor's salary

10 Which one of the following is required when calculating prime cost?

A Depreciation of machinery

B Direct wages

C Factory overheads

D Office expenses

11 Ignoring work in progress, which of the following statements correctly defines cost of production?

A Prime costs less direct costs

B Prime costs less factory overheads

C Prime costs plus direct costs

D Prime costs plus factory overheads

12 The following details appeared in a manufacturer's trial balance.

	$
Direct wages	80 000
Factory rent	40 000
Indirect wages	30 000
Machinery depreciation	20 000
Raw materials	100 000

Which of the following figures represented the manufacturer's prime cost?

A $130 000

B $180 000

C $240 000

D $270 000

13 The following information has been provided from which it is possible to calculate a manufacturer's cost of production.

	$
Prime cost	100 000
Factory overheads	30 000
Work in progress	
Opening inventory	20 000
Closing inventory	10 000

The cost of production is:

A $60 000

B $80 000

C $120 000

D $140 000

OTHER QUESTIONS

14 Whizzo Products is an organisation that manufactures sports equipment. The business's most recent financial year ended on 31 August 2012. The owner of the business is Rakesh Somaya who has provided the following information.

Inventories:

	At 1 September 2011	**At 31 August 2012**
	$	**$**
Raw materials	37 800	42 900
Work in progress	5 250	4 790
Finished goods	39 600	32 700

For the year ended 31 August 2012:

	$
Direct factory wages	75 600
Factory running costs	27 300
Factory supervisor's salary	32 400
Purchases of raw materials	92 500
Revenue	440 000

Additional information:

- Direct factory wages $2400 was due but unpaid at 31 August 2012.
- Depreciation should be provided on factory plant and machinery at 20 per cent per annum using the straight-line method. The cost of factory plant and machinery was $270 000.

a Explain to Rakesh Somaya the reason for preparing a manufacturing account.

b Prepare a manufacturing account for the year ended 31 August 2012.

c Calculate the business's gross profit for the year ended 31 August 2012. Show the details of your calculation.

29 Incomplete records

Introduction

The owners of some small businesses do not keep a full set of accounting records. This may be because they feel they do not have the time to keep proper records. Also, small businesses do not need to keep full accounting records due to the low volume of business they do. Owners may be satisfied with the information they can obtain from more basic recordkeeping.

If only basic records are kept, the owner or manager of the business will not enjoy all of the benefits of having a full accounting system and they are less likely to understand how well, or otherwise, the business is performing. It will mean, for example, that comprehensive financial information about the business will not be available. Detailed accounting records are an important aid to decision making, so it is likely that the effective management of a business could be impaired where there are incomplete records. A lack of detailed accounting records is also likely to incur an extra expense for the business because it may be necessary to pay an accountant to prepare the most important financial statements.

In this unit you will learn about two methods that can be used to discover important aspects of a business's performance despite the fact that there are limited accounting records.

1 The first method enables the profit or loss to be calculated where a business has the minimum information available.
2 The second method enables the preparation of more detailed end-of-year financial statements for a business that can supply more than the minimum information used in method 1 above.

LEARNING OUTCOMES

When you have reached the end of this unit you will be able to:

- prepare opening and closing statements of affairs
- calculate profits or losses from changes in capital over time
- calculate sales, purchases and other information so that an income statement can be prepared
- use accounting ratios to arrive at missing figures.

Calculating profits and losses from minimal information

Preparing statements of affairs

If the value of a business's assets and liabilities at the beginning and end of a financial period is known, it is possible to calculate a figure for capital at each of these dates. This is the first stage is calculating the profit (or loss) made by a business where there is very limited financial information. The details about assets and liabilities are set out in a **statement of affairs**. A statement of affairs closely resembles a balance sheet. However, the term 'balance sheet' is not used because the business does not have a ledger from which balances can be extracted.

KEY TERM

Statement of affairs: a summary of a business's assets, liabilities and capital at a given date.

Illustration 1 Preparing statements of affairs

Suzi owns a retail business. She has kept very limited financial records. However, she has been able to provide the following information about her business's assets and liabilities at the beginning and end of the trading year that ended on 30 September 2012.

	1 October 2011 $	30 September 2012 $
Cash at bank	3 600	5 200
Delivery vehicle	18 000	16 000
Inventory	14 400	15 300
Shop furniture and equipment	11 900	13 800
Trade payables	1 700	1 100

Here are the statements of affairs for each of these dates.

Statement of affairs at 1 October 2011

	$	$
NON-CURRENT ASSETS		
Delivery vehicle	18 000	
Shop furniture and equipment	11 900	
		29 900
CURRENT ASSETS		
Inventory	14 400	
Cash at bank	3 600	
	18 000	
Less current liabilities		
Trade payables	1 700	
		(16 300)
Net current assets		46 200
CAPITAL		46 200

Statement of affairs at 30 September 2012

	$	$
NON-CURRENT ASSETS		
Delivery vehicle	16 000	
Shop furniture and equipment	13 800	
		29 800
CURRENT ASSETS		
Inventory	15 300	
Cash at bank	5 200	
	20 500	
Less current liabilities		
Trade payables	1 100	
Net current assets		(19 400)
		49 200
CAPITAL		49 200

Calculating profit or loss for a financial year

By comparing the capital figures shown in the statements of affairs it is possible to see that the net value of the business has increased during the year. This begins to give a picture of whether the business has made a profit or loss during the period, but it is not the full story. It is also necessary to consider whether the change in the figure for capital has also been affected by drawings and/or by further investment in the business by the owner.

Illustration 2 How to calculate the profit or loss for a financial year

Returning to the story of Suzi's business (see Illustration 1), Suzi withdrew cash during the year totalling $18 300 for private use. Suzi has also said that she won $1800 in a competition on 1 May 2012 which she invested in the business.

Here is an arithmetical calculation of the profit or loss for the year.

	$
Capital at 30 September 2012	49 200
Less capital at 1 October 2011	46 200
Increase in capital during year	3 000
Add back drawings	18 300
	21 300
Less additional capital	1 800
Profit for the year	19 500

The following steps should be taken in order to calculate the profit for the year:

Step 1: Calculate whether capital has increased or decreased during the year by deducting the opening capital from the closing capital.

Step 2: Add back drawings. Drawings are added back to show the change in capital that would have occurred if there had been no drawings.

Step 3: Deduct any additional capital. Additions to capital are deducted to show what the change in capital would have been had the additions not taken place.

Step 4: The final figure, if positive, is profit for the year; a negative figure would indicate a loss for the year.

Here is an alternative approach that uses the capital section format for a balance sheet as a template for the calculation.

CAPITAL		
Opening balance	46 200	
Add profit	?	
	?	
Add additional capital	1 800	
Less drawings	(18 300)	
		49 200

The missing figure can then be inserted by working backwards through the information to show:

CAPITAL		
Opening balance	46 200	
Add profit	**19 500**	
	65 700	
Add additional capital	1 800	
Less drawings	(18 300)	
		49 200

You can now answer questions 1 and 2 on page 324.

29.2 Preparing end-of-year financial statements from basic records

Preparing an income statement

It is possible to prepare end-of-year financial statements for a business with limited accounting records. This is possible where the owner is able to provide:

- details of assets and liabilities at the beginning and end of the year, and
- details of money transactions (perhaps in the form of a simple cash book or perhaps from summarising the details shown in the business's bank statements).

Calculating sales and purchases figures

In order to start preparing an income statement it will be necessary to have information about sales and purchases. Where a business has only cash sales and cash purchases, these figures can be taken directly from the summarised cash book. Where a business has credit sales and purchases, it will be necessary to prepare calculations using:

- opening balances of trade receivables and trade payables
- receipts from credit customers and payments to credit suppliers
- discounts allowed to credit customers and discounts received from credit suppliers
- closing balances of trade receivables and trade payables.

LINKS...
The technique used to calculate credit sales and credit purchases is to prepare total trade receivables and total trade payables accounts along exactly the same lines as described in Unit 24.

Illustration 3 Calculating credit sales

Saleem can only provide limited accounting records for his business. For the year ended 30 June 2012 he is able to inform you of the following.

	At 1 July 2011	At 30 June 2012
	$	$
Trade receivables	8 700	9 100

Cash book (extract)

	$		$
Total receipts from credit customers	56 100		

Credit sales can be calculated as follows.

Step 1: Prepare a total receivables account and record the information given above.

Total trade receivables account

	$		$
Opening balance	6 700	Bank	56 100
		Closing balance c/d	9 100

Step 2: Close the total receivables account, inserting the missing figure for credit sales as the balancing item.

Total trade receivables account

	$		$
Opening balance	6 700	Bank	56 100
Credit sales	**58 500**	Closing balance c/d	9 100
	65 200		65 200
Balance b/d	9 100		

Alternatively, the same result can be obtained as the result of an arithmetical calculation.

	$
Total receipts	56 100
Less opening balance of trade receivables	6 700
	49 400
Add closing balance of trade receivables	9 100
Credit sales	**58 500**

In the arithmetical method, the accruals principle is applied by deducting the opening balance of trade receivables because it relates to sales for the previous year. The closing balance of receivables is added because it relates to sales for the current year.

Illustration 4 Calculating credit purchases

Returning to Saleem's business, he is able to provide the following additional information.

	At 1 July 2011 $	At 30 June 2012 $
Trade payables	4 300	3 700

Cash book (extract)

$		Discounts Received $	Bank $
	Total payments to credit suppliers	900	27 200

Following similar procedures, credit purchases can be calculated as follows.

Step 1: Record the available information.

Total trade payables account

	$		$
Bank	27 200	Opening balance	4 300
Discounts received	900		
Closing balance c/d	3 700		

Step 2: Close the account and enter the missing figure for credit purchases as the balancing item.

Total trade payables account

	$		$
Bank	27 200	Opening balance	4 300
Discounts received	900	**Credit purchases**	**27 500**
Closing balance c/d	3 700		
	31 800		31 800
		Balance b/d	3 700

Using the alternative, arithmetical approach.

	$
Total payments	27 200
Add discounts received	900
Total amount settled	28 100
Less opening balance of trade payables	4 300
	23 800
Add closing balance of trade payables	3 700
Credit purchases	**27 500**

In the arithmetical method, the accruals principle is applied by deducting the opening balance of trade payables as this relates to the previous year's credit purchases. The closing balance of trade payables is added because it relates to the current year's credit purchases.

Expenses and the income statement

You can now answer questions 3–6 on pages 324–325.

The summarised cash book will provide the main source of information for expenses to be included in the income statement. However, it will be necessary to make adjustments to the amounts paid during the financial year for accruals and prepayments. It will also be necessary to include an appropriate depreciation charge on non-current assets.

STUDY TIP

If a business has allowed and/or received cash discounts, remember to include them in the total trade receivables and trade payables account when calculating credit sales and credit purchases. It is also important to remember to include the discounts in the business's income statement.

LINKS...

The techniques used to calculate the correct expense charge for a year using the accruals principle where there are opening and closing adjustments was demonstrated in Unit 27 on page 289.

It is possible that some expenses will need to be adjusted for accruals and prepayments at the beginning of the year as well as at the end of the year.

DID YOU KNOW?

The technique of using a total trade receivables account could, for example, also be used to find the closing balances of trade receivables if this was not known. In this situation, the owner of the business would need to provide information about the opening balance, total receipts from receivables and credit sales for the year in question.

A similar process could be used to find the closing balance of trade payables.

29.3 Using ratios to find missing figures

Where the owner of a business is able to provide information about any or all of the following ratios, it is possible to develop techniques for finding the missing figures required in the income statement:

- Gross profit margin
- Rate of inventory turnover
- Mark up

Illustration 5 Using mark up to find revenue

Zi Ting has not been able to provide full information about her business's financial affairs to the year ended 30 June 2012. She wants to know her business's total sales for the year ended on that date. She is able to provide the following details:

- The cost of sales for the year ended 30 June 2012 was $140 000.
- The business always applies a mark up of 50 per cent when pricing goods for sale.

Revenue can be calculated as follows.

Step 1: Prepare the first section of the income statement.

Income statement (extract) for the year ended 30 June 2012

	$
Revenue	?
Cost of sales	(140 000)
Gross profit	?

Step 2: Use the information about mark up to calculate the gross profit, i.e. 50 per cent of cost of sales = $70 000.

Income statement (extract) for the year ended 30 June 2012

	$
Revenue	?
Cost of sales	(140 000)
Gross profit	70 000

Step 3: Complete the outline section from the income statement to show the missing revenue figure, which must be $210 000.

Income statement (extract) for the year ended 30 June 2012

	$
Revenue	**210 000**
Cost of sales	(140 000)
Gross profit	70 000

NUMERACY SKILLS

Using ratios

The first two ratios were covered in Unit 20. Here is a reminder of how they are calculated:

Gross profit margin is:

$$\frac{\text{Gross profit margin} \times 100}{\text{Revenue}}$$

Rate of inventory turnover is:

$$\frac{\text{Cost of sale}}{\text{Average inventory}}$$

The new ratio, mark up, is calculated as follows:

$$\frac{\text{Gross profit} \times 100}{\text{Cost of sales}}$$

DID YOU KNOW?

Mark up is a measure of how much profit is made on each product sold compared to its cost. Many trading businesses operate with a mark-up policy that is applied to every product that they sell.

Illustration 6 Using gross profit margin to calculate purchases

Josh has not kept full accounting records. He wishes to know his business's total purchases for the year ended 31 December 2012. He is able to supply the following information.

	$
Inventory	
1 January 2012	7 200
31 December 2012	8 900
Total revenue for 2012	84 000

Josh has maintained a strict pricing policy in force throughout 2012 so that his gross profit margin has always been 25 per cent.

Purchases can be calculated as follows.

Step 1: Prepare the first section of the income statement and insert the three available figures.

Step 2: Use the gross profit margin of 25 per cent to find the missing gross profit figure, i.e. 25 per cent of $84 000 is $21 000.

Income statement (extract) for the year ended 31 December 2012

	$	$
Revenue		84 000
Less opening inventory	7 200	
Add purchases	?	
	?	
Less closing inventory	8 900	
Cost of sales		?
Gross profit		21 000

Step 3: Work backwards through the missing items to find the missing purchases figure.

- First of all the cost of sales must be $63 000 (sales less gross profit).
- Then the subtotal before the closing inventory must be $71 900 (cost of sales plus the closing inventory).
- Finally the purchases must be $64 700 (previous figure of $71 900 less the opening inventory).

Here is the final version of the extract from the income statement:

Income statement (extract) for the year ended 31 December 2012

	$	$
Revenue		84 000
Less opening inventory	7 200	
Add purchases	**64 700**	
	71 900	
Less closing inventory	(8 900)	
Cost of sales		(63 000)
Gross profit		21 000

Illustration 7 Using rate of inventory turnover to find purchases

Tony is not able to provide full details about his business's financial position at the end of the accounting year, 31 March 2012. However, he has been able to provide the following information:

	$
Inventory	
1 April 2011	8000
31 March 2012	10000
Total revenue for the year ended 31 March 2012	150000

The business achieves a rate of inventory turnover 12 times a year.

Purchases can be calculated as follows.

Step 1: Prepare the first section of the income statement in outline, recording any known figures.

Income statement (extract) for the year ended 31 December 2012

	$	$
Revenue		150000
Less opening inventory	8000	
Add purchases	?	
	?	
Less closing inventory	(10000)	
Cost of sales		?
Gross profit		?

Step 2: The rate of inventory turnover can be used to find the cost of sales. Here is the formula:

$\frac{\text{Cost of sales}}{\text{Average inventory}}$ i.e. $\frac{\text{Cost of sales}}{9000}$ so cost of sales is \$108000 (i.e. \$9000 × 12)

Step 3: The purchases figure can now be calculated as follows:

- Cost of sales add closing inventory gives \$108000 + \$10000 = \$118000
- Deduct opening inventory (\$118000 – \$8000 = \$110000

Step 4: The gross profit is revenue \$150000 less cost of sales \$108000 = \$42000

Here is completed extract.

Income statement (extract) for the year ended 31 December 2012

	$	$
Revenue		150000
Less cost of sales		
Opening inventory	8000	
Add purchases	**110000**	
	118000	
Less closing inventory	(10000)	
		(108000)
Gross profit		42000

You can now answer questions 7 and 8 on pages 325–326.

29.4

Preparing end-of-year financial statements: an illustration

Illustration 8 Preparing financial statements from incomplete records

Rajiv owns a small wholesale business. He has not kept a full accounting system but is able to provide the following information about the financial year ended on 31 October 2012.

All purchases and sales were on credit.

The business's assets and liabilities were as follows:

	1 November 2011	31 October 2012
	$	$
Cash at bank	1 180	2 650
Fittings and equipment at net book value	67 500	63 400
Inventories	13 860	14 920
Rent prepaid	740	–
Trade receivables	11 920	10 820
Trade payables	8 450	?
Wages due	560	690

A summary of the business's bank statements is as follows.

Summarised bank account

	$		$
Opening balance b/d	1 180	Trade payables	78 400
Trade receivables	165 500	Drawings	25 400
		Rent	9 800
		Wages	50 430
		Closing balance c/d	2 650
	166 680		166 680

Rajiv's policy is to achieve a gross profit margin of 50 per cent.

Preparing the answer

Start by finding as many of the missing figures as possible.

Step 1: Calculate the opening capital.

Statement of affairs at 1 November 2011

	$	$	$
NON-CURRENT ASSETS			
Fittings and equipment			67 500
CURRENT ASSETS			
Inventory	13 860		
Trade receivables	11 920		
Other receivable (rent prepaid)	740		
Cash at bank	1 180		
		27 700	
Less current liabilities			
Trade payables	8 450		
Other payable (wages due)	560		
		(9 010)	
Net current assets			18 690
			86 190
CAPITAL			**86 190**

Step 2: Calculate credit sales.

Total trade receivables account

	$		$
Opening balance	11 920	Bank	165 500
Credit sales	**164 400**	Closing balance c/d	10 820
	176 320		176 320
Balance b/d	10 820		

Step 3: Calculate other costs to be entered in the income statement.

Rent	$
Amount paid	9800
Add opening balance prepaid	740
	10540

Wages	$
Amount paid	50430
Less opening balance due	560
	49870
Add closing balance due	690
	50560

Depreciation of fittings and equipment	$
Net book value at 1 November 2011	67500
Less net book value at 31 October 2012	63400
	4100

Step 4: Prepare the income statement (which will also show the missing figure for purchases). The cost of sales has first been derived using the information about gross profit margin (which is 50 per cent of revenue). The purchases figure could then be derived from adding back the closing inventory and deducting the opening inventory.

Rajiv

Income statement for the year ended 31 October 2012

	$	$
Revenue		164400
Less opening inventory	13860	
Add purchases	**83260**	
	97120	
Less closing inventory	14920	
Cost of sales		82200
Gross profit		82200
Less:	10540	
Rent		
Wages	50560	
Depreciation of fittings and equipment	4100	
		65200
Profit for the year		17000

Step 5: Now the purchases figure is known, it is possible to calculate the trade payables at 31 October 2012.

Total trade payables account

	$		$
Bank	78400	Opening balance	8450
Closing balance c/d	**13310**	Credit purchases	83260
	91710		91710
		Balance b/d	13310

Step 6: Prepare the balance sheet at 31 October 2012.

Balance sheet at 31 October 2012

	$	$	$
NON-CURRENT ASSETS			
Fittings and equipment			63400
CURRENT ASSETS			
Inventory	14920		
Trade receivables	10820		
Cash at bank	2650		
		28390	
Less current liabilities			
Trade payables	13310		
Other payable (wages due)	690		
		(14000)	
Net current assets			14390
			77790
CAPITAL			
Opening balance		86190	
Add profit for the year		17000	
		103190	
Less drawings		(25400)	
			77790

You can now answer questions 9–18 on pages 327–330.

Practice questions

DEVELOPING YOUR SKILLS

1 Preparing statements of affairs and comparing capitals

Sherelle recently set up in business. She has little experience of keeping accounting records, but she needs to let the tax authorities know how much profit or loss she made during her first year of trading. She is able to supply the following information.

	1 January 2012	31 December 2012
	$	$
Bank loan	–	25 000
Cash at bank	80 000	3 600
Delivery van	14 000	12 000
Fixtures and fittings	–	8 500
Inventories	7 400	11 200
Shop premises	–	95 000
Trade payables	6 300	8 900

Sherelle withdrew $21 700 from the business bank account during the year for private use. On 1 July 2012 she received a cheque for $4000 from her parents as a gift to help her run the business. The cheque was paid into the business bank account.

a Prepare statements of affairs at 1 January 2012 and 31 December 2012.

b Set out a calculation of the business's profit or loss for 2012.

2 Preparing statements of affairs and comparing capitals

Zak owns a retail unit. He has not found it possible to keep detailed accounting records and prefers to pay an accountant to calculate his business's annual profit or loss.

The following information is available about the year ended 31 May 2012.

	1 June 2011	31 May 2012
	$	$
Bank overdraft	–	5 180
Cash at bank	6 290	
Furniture and equipment	17 300	14 900
Inventories	11 200	13 340
Loan from JL Finance Ltd		8 000
Prepaid rent	740	
Trade payables	4 710	5 580
Trade receivables	3 760	3 130
Wages due		530

Zak's drawings for the year ended 31 May 2012 totalled $23 520. On 1 February 2012 Zak won $25 000 in a lottery competition. He paid half of this prize into the business's bank account.

a Prepare statements of affairs at 1 June 2011 and 31 May 2012.

b Set out a calculation of the business's profit or loss for the year ended 31 May 2012.

3 Calculating credit sales and credit purchases

Hooper does not have a full set of accounting records for his business. However, he is able to supply the following information relating to the year ended 30 April 2012.

Concerning trade receivables:

- Balance of $8700: amount due from trade receivables 1 May 2011.
- Receipts of $53600 from trade receivables during the year ended 30 April 2012.
- Balance of $7200: amount due from trade receivables 30 April 2012.

Concerning trade payables:

- Balance of $4900: amount owing to trade payables 1 May 2011.
- Payments of $37 300 to trade payables during the year ended 30 April 2012.

- Balance of $5200: amount owing to trade payables 30 April 2012.

Calculate the following for the year ended 30 April 2012:

a Total credit sales

b Total credit purchases

4 Calculating credit sales and credit purchases

The following information has been extracted from the limited accounting records kept by Jasmine for her business. The information relates to the year ended 31 August 2012.

	At 1 September 2011	At 31 August 2012
	$	$
Trade receivables	19 150	22 860
Trade payables	14 320	11 970

Cash book (extract)

	$		$
Total receipts from trade receivables	103 820	Total payments to trade payables	85 400

Calculate the following for the year ended 31 August 2012:

a Total credit sales

b Total credit purchases

5 More calculations of credit sales and credit purchases

Anisa has not had time to keep full accounting records for her business. However, the following information is available concerning the year ended 31 May 2012.

	At 1 June 2011	At 31 May 2012
	$	$
Trade receivables	9420	11 130
Trade payables	6280	5910

Calculate the following for the year ended 31 May 2012:

a Total credit sales

b Total credit purchases

6 More calculations of credit sales and credit purchases

Vikesh has not been able to keep a full double-entry system to record his business's financial affairs. However, he is able to provide the following information about trade receivables and trade payables.

At 1 January 2012:

- trade receivables owed $21 390.
- trade payables were owed $15 990.

During the year ended 31 December 2012:

- trade receivables paid $112 300
- trade payables were paid $66 530
- discounts received totalled $1340
- a bad debt, $140, was written off.

At 31 December 2012:

- trade receivables owed $20 720
- trade payables were owed $17 010.

Calculate the following for the year ended 31 December 2012:

a Total credit sales

b Total credit purchases

7 Preparing end-of-year financial statements from incomplete records

Tarek, the owner of Bestprice Furniture Stores, has not maintained a full set of accounts during the year ended 30 June 2012. However, he is able to provide the following information about his business.

Cash book (extract)

	Discounts allowed	Bank		Discounts received	Bank
	$	$		$	$
Trade receivables	880	48 760	Trade payables	490	31 570

Assets and liabilities as follows:

	1 July 2011	30 June 2012
	$	$
Cash at bank	8420	1570
Shop fittings and equipment at net book value	22400	19900
Inventories	14180	12380
Prepaid rent	850	720
Trade payables	8240	9780
Trade receivables	11550	12690
Wages accrued	420	710

Cash book (extract)

	$		$
Balance, 1 July 2011 b/d	8420	Rent	11470
		General expenses	15220
Total receipts from trade receivables	116510	Drawings	8000
		Wages	31460
		Total payments to trade payables	57210
		Balance 30 June 2012 c/d	1570
	124930		124930

a Calculate the business's capital at 1 July 2011.

b Calculate the following missing figures for the year ended 30 June 2012:

i Credit sales

ii Credit purchases

iii Rent

iv Wages

v Depreciation of shop fittings and equipment

c Prepare the income statement for the year ended 30 June 2012 and a balance sheet at that date.

8 Preparing end-of-year financial statements from incomplete records

Alex has never kept full accounting records. However, at 30 April 2012, the end of his business's financial year, he is able to provide the following information.

At 1 May 2011 the business's statement of affairs contained the following details.

	$
Cash at bank	2300
Delivery vehicle at net book value	22400
Electricity charges accrued	350
General expenses prepaid	480
Inventory	16600
Trade payables	4300
Trade receivables	6140
Capital	43270

Cash book (extract)

	$		$
Balance, 1 July 2011 b/d	2300	Rent	6820
		General expenses	11240
Total receipts from trade receivables	82980	Electricity charges	4110
		Loan repayments	2000
Bank loan	10000	Drawings	24900
		Total payments to trade payables	45120
		Balance 30 June 2012 c/d	1090
	95280		95280

At 30 April 2012 the following additional information was available:

- Inventory was valued at $19300.
- General expenses were prepaid $270.
- Electricity charges accrued, $440.
- The delivery vehicle was revalued at $19700.
- Trade receivables totalled $7480.
- Trade payables totalled $3950.

a Calculate the following missing figures for the year ended 30 April 2012:

i Credit sales

ii Credit purchases

iii General expenses

iv Electricity charges

v Depreciation of the delivery vehicle

b Prepare the income statement for the year ended 30 April 2012 and a balance sheet at that date.

9 Using ratios to find missing figures

Using markup to find revenue

a A business had cost of sales of $85 000 for the year ended 31 December 2012. The business's policy is to use a mark up of 20 per cent to calculate selling prices.

Prepare a summarised extract from an income statement for the year ended 31 December 2012 to show revenue.

Using gross profit margin to find purchases

b A business had total revenue for the year ended 29 February 2012 of $380 000. The business always achieves a gross profit margin of 25 per cent. At 1 March 2011 inventories were valued at $18 900; on 29 February 2012 inventories were valued at $16 500.

Prepare an extract from an income statement for the year ended 29 February 2012 to show purchases.

Using rate of inventory turnover to find purchases

c A business normally achieves a rate of inventory turnover of 20 times a year. On 1 September 2011 the business had inventories valued at $16 000; on 31 August 2012 inventories were valued at $14 000.

i Calculate the business's cost of sales for the year ended 31 August 2012.

During the year ended 31 August 2012 the business's total revenue was $420 000.

ii Prepare an extract from the business's income statement for the year ended 31 August 2012 to show the gross profit for the year.

10 Using ratios to find missing figures

Using mark-up to find revenue

a A business had cost of sales of $240 000 for the year ended 31 March 2012. The business's policy is to use a mark up of 25 per cent to calculate selling prices.

Prepare a summarised extract from an income statement for the year ended 31 March 2012 to show revenue.

Using gross profit margin to find purchases

b A business had total revenue for the year ended 30 November 2012 of $880 000. The business always achieves a gross profit margin of 15 per cent. At 1 December 2011 inventories were valued at $42 100; on 30 November 2012 inventories were valued at $33 700.

Prepare an extract from an income statement for the year ended 30 November 2012 to show purchases.

Using rate of inventory turnover to find purchases

c A business normally achieves a rate of inventory turnover of 15 times a year. On 1 July 2011 the business had inventories valued at $23 500; on 30 June 2012 inventories were valued at $26 500.

i Calculate the business's cost of sales for the year ended 30 June 2012.

During the year ended 30 June 2012 the business's total revenue was $505 000.

ii Prepare an extract from the business's income statement for the year ended 30 June 2012 to show the gross profit for the year.

11 Preparing financial statements from incomplete records using ratios

Alice has not been able to maintain a full set of accounting records for her wholesale business, Alice Catering Supplies. However, she has been able to provide the following information about the year ended 30 September 2012.

Assets and liabilities were as follows.

	At 1 October 2011	At 30 September 2012
	$	$
Non-current assets at net book value	590 000	560 000
Inventories	72 400	?
Trade receivables	33 100	33 700
Trade payables	19 400	22 100
Insurance prepaid	800	–
Wages accrued	–	1 100
Cash at bank	11 200	25 100

Summarised bank account for the year ended 30 September 2012 was as follows overleaf.

Bank Account

	$		$
Balance, 1 October 2011 b/d	11 200	Drawings	53 700
Amounts received from trade receivables	449 400	Total payments to trade payables	219 800
		Insurance	16 200
		General expenses	51 500
		Wages	94 300
		Balance 30 September 2012 c/d	25 100
	460 600		460 600

Alice always achieves a gross profit margin of 50 per cent.

On 30 September 2012 she was unable to check the value of inventories.

a Calculate the following missing figures:
   i Capital at 1 October 2011
   ii Revenue and purchases for the year ended 30 September 2012
   iii Expenses to be charged to the income statement for the year ended 30 September 2012

b Prepare an income statement for the year ended 30 September 2012. Use the gross profit margin to calculate the gross profit, the cost of sales and the closing inventory.

c Prepare a statement of affairs at 30 September 2012.

12 Preparing financial statements from incomplete records using ratios

John can only provide limited information about his business's financial year which ended on 30 June 2012.

Assets and liabilities at 1 July 2011 were as follows.

	$
Non-current assets at net book value	285 000
Inventories	17 480
Trade receivables	6 580
Trade payables	8 190
General expenses prepaid	460
Rent accrued	290
Cash at bank	4 140

Summarised bank account for the year ended 30 June 2012 was as follows.

Bank Account

	$		$
Balance, 1 July 2011 b/d	4 140	General expenses	14 440
Amounts received from trade receivables	94 880	Total payments to trade payables	43 800
		Rent	8 180
		Drawings	17 220
		Non-current assets	15 000
		Balance 30 June 2012 c/d	380
	99 020		99 020

Additional information at 30 June 2012:

- Inventories are valued at $18 520.
- The amount due from trade receivables is $8 340.
- John has revalued the non-current assets at $291 000.
- Rent prepaid is $440.
- General expenses due are $310.

The business has a rate of inventory turnover of three times a year.

a Calculate the following:
   i Revenue for the year ended 30 June 2012
   ii Expenses to be charged to the income statement

b Prepare an income statement for the year ended 30 June 2012 using the rate of inventory turnover to calculate the cost of sales and missing purchases figure.

Note: a statement of affairs at 30 June 2012 is not required.

(The following questions cover Unit 29)

MULTIPLE-CHOICE QUESTIONS

13 Which of the following does not appear in a statement of affairs?

A Non-current assets

B Prepayments

C Purchases

D Trade payables

14 The following information is available about a business for the year ended 31 December 2012:

	$
Capital 1 January 2012	49 000
Capital 31 December 2012	58 000
Drawings for the year ended 31 December 2012	12 000
Additional capital introduced during 2012	4 000

What is the business's profit for the year ended 31 December 2012?

A $1 000

B $13 000

C $17 000

D $21 000

15 The owner of a business is able to supply the following information about the year ended 31 March 2012.

	At 1 April 2011	At 31 March 2012
	$	$
Total assets	85 000	96 000
Total liabilities	11 000	9 000

There were no owner's drawings during the year ended 31 March 2012, but the owner did make an additional investment in the business of $6 000.

What is the business's profit for the year ended 31 March 2012?

A $3 000

B $7 000

C $17 000

D $19 000

16 The following information is available about a business that does not have a full set of accounting records.

	$
Trade receivables 1 October 2011	12 500
Trade receivables 30 September 2012	10 000
Receipts from trade receivables for the year ended 30 September 2012	228 500

What is the business's revenue for the year ended 30 September 2012?

A $226 000

B $228 500

C $231 000

D $251 000

17 Michael has not kept a full set of accounting records for his business. However, he is able to provide the following information.

Inventories at 1 January 2012	$16 000
Inventories at 31 December 2012	$18 000
Rate of inventory turnover for the year ended 31 December 2012	10 times

What is the business's purchases for the year ended 31 December 2012?

A $160 000

B $168 000

C $172 000

D $180 000

OTHER QUESTIONS

18 Jane Pulchan has not kept a full set of accounting records for her business for the year ended 31 July 2012. All of her business's purchases and sales are on credit. She is able to provide the following information.

At 1 August 2011:

	$
Amounts owed by trade receivables	14 480
Amounts owed to trade payables	11 140

For the year ended 31 July 2012:

	$
Amounts received from trade receivables	85 750
Amounts paid to trade payables	58 400
Discounts allowed	1 320
Discounts received	860

At 31 July 2012:

	$
Amounts owed by trade receivables	12 690
Amounts owed to trade payables	9 480

a Calculate Jane Pulchan's credit sales and credit purchases for the year ended 31 July 2012.

Jane's gross profit margin for the year ended 31 July 2012 was 25 per cent. Her inventory on 1 August 2011 was $7 450. Unfortunately she was not been able to value her inventory on 31 July 2012.

b Explain what is meant by gross profit margin.

c Prepare an extract from the business's income statement for the year ended 31 July 2012 showing the gross profit for the year and the closing inventory.

A

Accounting the selecting, classifying and summarizing of financial data in a way that provides the owners of businesses (and others) with useful information in order to help them assess performance and plan future activities.

Accounting equation this links the three elements that are a feature of all businesses, i.e. assets, liabilities and capital. The equation is: Assets = Capital + Liabilities.

Accounting policies the rules and procedures that are adopted by a business when producing its financial statements.

Accounting principles the basic rules that are to be applied by all those who prepare accounting records; these are also called accounting concepts.

Accruals principle in order to calculate a true and fair profit, income for a financial year is matched exactly with expenses that relate to that accounting year whether paid or not. This principle is also called the matching principle.

Accumulated fund the total of a club's surpluses over a period of years. It is the equivalent of a business's capital.

Ageing schedule of trade receivables a list of all amounts due from credit customers shown in a sequence based on how long the debt has been outstanding.

Amounts not yet credited amounts paid into a business's bank statement but which have not yet been recorded on the bank statement as credit entries.

Analysis column in a petty cash book this is a means of classifying each payment to provide totals to be posted to general ledger accounts.

Annual general meeting (AGM) a yearly meeting of shareholders where directors report on the performance of the company.

Appropriation account a part of the end-of-year income statements of a partnership recording how the profit or loss for the year is shared between the partners.

Assets resources with a monetary value that are owned by a business.

Authorised share capital the maximum amount of share capital that a limited company may issue.

B

Bad debt a trade receivable that will not be paid.

Bad debt recovered when a debt that has previously been written off is settled by the customer.

Balance sheet a statement that shows an organisation's assets, liabilities and capital at a particular date which is prepared at the end of a financial period.

Balancing accounts the process of calculating the net amount left in an account and clearly stating this as a debit or credit balance at the beginning of the next accounting period.

Bank charges payments deducted automatically from a current account at regular intervals as a reward to the bank for operating the account.

Bank reconciliation statement a document prepared by businesses at regular intervals (say monthly) to check that their bank records agree with those provided by the bank.

Bank statement a copy of a customer's bank account, sent to the customer at regular intervals.

Bookkeeping the recording of financial information, particularly transactions, in a systematic way.

Books of prime entry this is where transactions are listed prior to being posted to the double-entry records. Sometimes referred to as subsidiary books.

Business entity principle a business's transactions and the owner's private transactions are recorded separately in a business's accounting system.

C

Called-up share capital the part of the issued share capital of a company for which payment has been requested.

Capital the investment made by the owner(s) of a business.

Capital employed the total of capital and non-current liabilities, which is a key element in the analysis of how well a business has performed. Alternatively, the same figure can be found by adding non-current assets and working capital.

Capital expenditure money spent on non-current assets that is intended to be of benefit in future financial years.

Carriage inwards the cost of transporting goods, paid by a business on its own purchases. This expense is added to purchases in the first section of the income statement.

Carriage outwards the cost of transporting goods, paid by a business on its sales to customers. This expense is recorded in the second part of the income statement.

Cash book a book of prime entry in which all cash and bank transactions are recorded.

Cash discount a reduction in the amount paid by credit customers, or to credit suppliers, when accounts are settled within an agreed time limit.

Cash transactions financial activities involving the immediate use of money.

Closing accounts the process of completing an account that does not have a balance.

Closing inventory goods unsold at the end of a trading year.

Compensating error where two or more errors of the same amount cancel each other out.

Consistency principle accounting policies should be carried out in the same way year on year.

Contra entry (cash book) the transfer of cash to the bank, or the withdrawal of cash from the bank. These transactions result in both the debit entry and credit entry for the transaction being recorded in the cash book columns.

Contra entry (control accounts) when a business deals with another business or organisation as both a customer and a supplier, the balance of the two accounts are set off against one another to find the net balance.

Cost of raw materials consumed the direct cost of raw materials used during a financial year.

Cost of sales the value at cost price of goods sold during a trading year. It is found as follows: Opening inventory + Purchases − Closing inventory. It is sometimes called the cost of goods sold.

Credit the right-hand side of an account.

Credit note the source document that records the amount to be deducted from (or allowed against) a previous invoice to avoid a business being overcharged. Usually the business has returned goods to the supplier.

Credit transactions financial activities when the payment or receipt of money is delayed.

Credit transfer the automatic transfer of funds into a business's bank account by one of the business's customers.

Glossary

Current accounts a record of each partner's annual drawings and shares of profits or loss.

Current assets assets that are quickly turned into cash and are of benefit to the business for a short time (less than one year).

Current liabilities liabilities that will be settled in the near future (in less than one year).

Current ratio current assets in relation to current liabilities. The ratio is sometimes called the working capital ratio. It is always expressed in the form xx : 1, e.g. 1.8 : 1.

D

Debentures long-term loans that carry a fixed rate of interest which must be paid each year and which is charged to the company's income statement.

Debit the left-hand side of an account.

Debit note a source document used by a purchaser to notify the seller that goods are being returned and the amount that should be deducted from the amount due. Alternatively, a debit note is occasionally issued by the seller of goods to notify the purchaser of an undercharge.

Deed of partnership the formal agreement between partners that states how profit and losses will be shared and the rules under which the partners will work together.

Depreciation the loss in value of a non-current asset over its useful life.

Direct costs manufacturing costs that are attributable to a single product, particularly direct materials and direct labour.

Direct debit authority is given to a bank by one of its customers to make payments on its behalf to another organisation. The amount paid will be the sum requested by that organisation up to a specified limit.

Directors individuals who are appointed by shareholders to manage the company on their behalf.

Dishonoured cheque a cheque that a bank will not accept for payment because the payee (individual making the payment) does not have enough funds in their account to cover the amount being paid.

Dividend the reward paid to shareholders out of the profits of a limited company.

Double entry the process of making two entries for every transaction.

Drawings the withdrawal of money by the owner of a business for private use.

Duality principle every transaction has two aspects leading to the making of two entries for each transaction in the accounting system.

E

Equity the heading used for the capital and reserves section of a limited company's balance sheet.

Error of commission where a debit or credit entry is made in the wrong account.

Error of complete reversal when the account that should have been debited is credited in error, and the account that should have been credited is debited in error.

Error of omission where a transaction is overlooked so that no debit and credit entry is made in the accounts.

Error of original entry when a mistake is made transferring an amount from a source document to a book of prime entry so both the debit entries and credit entries are incorrect.

Error of principle where a debit or credit entry is made for the correct amount but in the wrong class of account.

Expense accrual an amount owing for expenses at the end of a financial period.

Expenses payments made to purchase goods or services to run the business on a day-to-day basis.

F

Factory overheads the total of indirect costs.

Fixed capitals each partner's capital contribution remains unchanged unless all partners agree to an alteration.

G

General ledger a part of the double-entry system that is used to keep all of the accounts, other than those for trade payables (kept in the purchases ledger) and trade receivables (kept in the sales ledger).

General reserve part of the undistributed profits that have not been distributed as dividends and are set aside for some future use.

Going concern principle while a business continues to trade, assets are valued at cost less depreciation. When a business ceases to trade, assets are valued at their realisable value.

Goods for own use a transaction where the owner of a business keeps goods for private use which would otherwise have been available for sale. This transaction is sometimes referred to as inventory drawings.

Goodwill the additional value of an established and successful business, above the value of its tangible assets. Goodwill is an intangible asset.

Gross profit the difference between the income from sales and the expenditure on goods sold.

I

Imprest a system for maintaining a petty cash book which gives the petty cashier responsibility for a fixed petty cash float.

Income and expenditure account an annual summary that shows whether the club made a surplus or a deficit.

Income statement an end-of-financial-period statement that shows a business's gross profit and profit for that period (usually a year). (At one time this was known as the trading and profit and loss account.)

Indirect costs manufacturing costs that cannot be attributed to one product.

Intangible assets assets which have a monetary value but which do not have a physical presence

Interest on capital a reward for each partner in the form of a share of profits that is based on the amount of capital contributed by each partner.

Interest on drawings a penalty whereby a partner is charged interest on drawings. The interest takes account of the amount of the drawings.

Interested parties individuals and organisations who are affected by or concerned about how a business performs.

Inter-firm comparison analysing the performance of similar businesses and using the results to indicate success or under-achievement.

International Accounting Standards a set of rules and guidelines that businesses in many countries must follow in producing financial statements.

Inventory goods owned by a business that have not yet been sold.

Issued share capital the amount of share capital that has actually been issued by a limited company.

J

Journal a book of prime entry used to make the first record of transactions that it would not be appropriate to record in the other books of prime entry (cash books and other journals).

L

Ledger the book in which all financial accounts are kept.

Liabilities amounts owed by a business to other businesses, organisations or individuals.

Limited liability the liability of any shareholder for the debts of the company is limited to the amount of their shares.

Limited liability company an organisation owned by its shareholders whose liability for the debts of the company is limited to their shareholding.

Liquidity a business's ability to have available sufficient cash to pay its short-term debts.

Lower of cost or net realisable value the rule that must be applied to the valuation of inventories.

M

Manufacturing account the first part of the end-of-year financial statements of a manufacturing organisation that shows the total cost of producing goods.

Miscast incorrectly totalled. Undercast would mean that a total is too small; overcast would mean that a total is too large.

Money measurement principle in accounting, only transactions that have a definite monetary value are recorded.

N

Net book value the value of a non-current asset which takes account of its cost less the total depreciation to date.

Net current assets a term often used instead of working capital and calculated in the same way: i.e. current assets less current liabilities. When the figure is negative the term should be 'net current liabilities.

Net realisable value sale value less any costs to be incurred before a sale can take place.

Non-current assets assets that should be of benefit to the business for a long time (more than one year).

Non-current liabilities liabilities that will be settled in the longer term (longer than one year).

O

Opening inventory goods unsold at the beginning of a trading year. The amount will be the same as the closing inventory from the previous year.

Operating profit profit before the deduction of interest charges.

Order of permanence the sequence used to list items on a balance sheet. It begins with items that are likely to be longest lasting and ends with items that are likely to be shortest lasting.

Ordinary shares shares that receive a variable rate of dividend that is dependent on the profits available for distribution. These shares have voting rights.

Other receivables term used on a balance sheet to include prepaid expenses and income accrued.

Other payables term used on a balance sheet to include accrued expenses and income prepaid.

P

Paid-up share capital the part of the called up share capital of a company for which payment has been received.

Partner's loan amounts lent by a partner over and above, and quite separate from, the partner's capital contribution. Interest on the loan is charged to the income statement and credited to the partner's current account.

Partnership a form of business ownership where two or more individuals work together with the intention of making a profit.

Partnership salary a reward in the form of a share of profits for any partner who has particular responsibilities in running the business.

Percentage of gross profit to revenue (gross profit margin) gross profit in relation to revenue (measured as a percentage).

Percentage of profit to revenue (profit margin) profit in relation to revenue (measured as a percentage).

Petty cash small cash payments.

Petty cash book the book of prime entry used to make the first record of petty cash payments.

Petty cash voucher the source document for each petty cash payment.

Preference shares shares that are entitled to receive a fixed rate of dividend and that are ranked before ordinary shares for the payment of a dividend.

Prepaid expense the payment of an expense in advance of the accounting year to which it relates.

Prime cost the total of direct costs.

Private limited company a company whose shares are not available to the general public. The name of the company includes the abbreviation Ltd (limited).

Profit and loss sharing ratio the ratio that is used to share any residual profit or loss of the partnership.

Profit the difference between a business's income (sales) and expenditure (purchases and expenses). At one time this final profit figure was called 'net profit'.

Profitability a measure of performance highlighting profit in relation to the resources used in the business.

Provision for doubtful debts an amount set aside from profits to take account of the likelihood that some trade receivables will not pay the amount due and so will reduce the value of this asset on a balance sheet. Sometimes the alternative name 'provision for bad debts' is used.

Prudence an accounting principle that requires that where there is doubt, asset and profit values are understated rather than overstated, and, conversely, that losses and liabilities are overstated rather than understated.

Prudence principle where there is uncertainty, profits should be under- rather than overstated; losses and liabilities should be over- rather than understated.

Public limited company (plc) a company whose shares are available to the general public. The name of the company includes the abbreviation plc.

Purchase invoice the source document that provides information about goods purchased on credit and the amount due.

Purchases journal the book of prime entry used to record purchases of goods on credit. The information required to prepare this journal is taken from purchase invoices.

Purchases ledger a part of the double-entry system that is used to keep the personal accounts of trade payables.

Glossary

Purchases ledger control account a technique for checking the arithmetical accuracy of the purchases ledger

Purchases returns journal the book of prime entry used to list in date order details shown on credit notes relating to goods returned to suppliers.

Purchases returns goods sent back by a business to the supplier.

Q

Quick ratio liquid assets in relation to current liabilities. Liquid assets are all of a business's current assets excluding inventories. This ratio is often referred to as the 'acid test ratio' and is also expressed in the form xx : 1.

R

Rate of inventory turnover cost of sales divided by average inventory (expressed as 'so many times' in a particular financial year, e.g. '12 times').

Realisable value sale value.

Realisation principle a sale occurs when the customer pays or when an invoice is issued for the goods or services.

Receipts and payments account annual summary of a club or society's cash book.

Reducing balance method where the annual depreciation charge is based on the value of the non-current asset at the beginning of the year under review. This method is also referred to as the diminishing balance method.

Refund a repayment to a customer who has overpaid, or a repayment made by a supplier who has been overpaid.

Residual profit the profit of the partnership after all agreed rewards have been allocated to partners. (Residual loss is the loss of the partnership after all agreed rewards have been allocated.)

Residual value the value of a non-current asset at the end of its useful life – sometimes referred to as the scrap value.

Retained earnings profits that have not been used to finance the payment of dividends or have been transferred to a general reserve.

Return on capital employed (ROCE) the profit made by the business in relation to the funds invested in the business (i.e. owner's capital and non-current liabilities). The ratio is expressed as a percentage.

Revaluation method where the annual depreciation charge is based on comparing the estimated value of a group of non-current assets at the end of a financial year with the value at the beginning of the financial year.

Revenue expenditure money spent on running costs that benefits only the current financial year.

S

Sales invoice the source document that provides information about goods sold on credit and the amount due.

Sales journal the book of prime entry used to record sales of goods on credit. The information required to prepare this book of prime entry is taken from sales invoices.

Sales ledger a part of the double-entry system that is used to keep the personal accounts of trade receivables.

Sales ledger control account a technique for checking the arithmetical accuracy of the sales ledger.

Sales returns goods sent back to a business by a customer.

Sales returns journal the book of prime entry used to list in date order details shown on copies of credit notes relating to goods returned by customers.

Shareholders the owners of the share capital of a limited company.

Source documents written documents that provide information from which accounting records can be prepared. They provide evidence that particular transactions took place.

Standing order a bank's customer gives instructions for the automatic payment to another organisation of a fixed amount at regular intervals.

Statement of account a summary of transactions that have taken place between a supplier and a credit customer. The statement provides a means of checking the accuracy of accounts and of reminding customers how much they owe.

Statement of affairs a summary of a business's assets, liabilities and capital at a given date.

Statement of changes in equity a record of changes to retained earnings during a year.

Straight-line method where the annual depreciation charge is based on the cost of the non-current asset and is the same amount each year. This method is also called the equal instalment method.

Suspense account a temporary account used to make the totals of a trial balance agree.

T

T account a two-sided form used to record transactions affecting a particular aspect of a business's financial activities.

Trade discount a reduction in price given as a reward for buying in large quantities.

Trade payables are amounts owed by a business to suppliers.

Trade payables payment period trade payables in relation to credit purchases. The ratio is usually expressed in days.

Trade receivables are amounts owed to the business by customers.

Trade receivables collection period trade receivables in relation to credit sales. The ratio is usually expressed in days.

Transaction a financial activity or financial event.

Treasurer the individual appointed by the members of a club or society to manage its financial affairs.

Trial balance a summary of all the accounts in a business's books of account which provides a check on the accuracy of the double entry.

True and fair the principle that accounting records should be factually accurate and present a reasonable estimate of, or judgement about, the financial position.

U

Unlimited liability in a partnership each partner is responsible for the debts of the partnership and could lose not just the capital contributed but also personal assets if the business fails. In the case of a sole trader, the owner could also lose not just the capital contributed but also personal assets if the business fails.

Unpresented cheques cheques that have not been cleared by the bank and have not yet been recorded on a business's bank statement.

W

Work in progress partly finished goods.

Working capital the difference between total current assets and current liabilities. The figure (which can be positive or negative) gives some idea of the funds available to run the business on a day to day basis.

Index

Note: Key terms (glossary terms) are in **bold** type.

Index